Shenandoah County Virginia

*Abstract of Wills
1772-1850*

Amelia C. Gilreath

HERITAGE BOOKS
2007

HERITAGE BOOKS
AN IMPRINT OF HERITAGE BOOKS, INC.

Books, CDs, and more—Worldwide

For our listing of thousands of titles see our website
at
www.HeritageBooks.com

Published 2007 by
HERITAGE BOOKS, INC.
Publishing Division
65 East Main Street
Westminster, Maryland 21157-5026

Copyright © 1980 Amelia C. Gilreath

All rights reserved. No part of this book may be reproduced or transmitted in any form or by any means, electronic or mechanical, including photocopying, recording or by any information storage and retrieval system without written permission from the author, except for the inclusion of brief quotations in a review.

International Standard Book Number: 978-1-58549-684-6

Will Book A - page 6

JOSEPH ABELL, Parish of Beckford, County of Frederick, Colony of Virginia, Planter. Wife: Jane Abell. Her three children: John; George; Margaret. Mentions: John Abell, son of John Abell, Sen. My son: Joseph Abell. Grandsons: Jeremiah Abell and Ezekiel Abell. Mentions: Part of land to be sold to Peter Cop and Charles Reagan - shall be titled by Lord Fairfax or the Grantees.
Exors: Tergas Crons and wife, Jane Abell
Wit: John Sevesque, Charles Reagan and Benjamin Barclay
Dated: 25 Nov. 1772   Proved: 26 May 1773

Will Book B - page 320

HENRY ACHER, Shenandoah County. Wife: Catharine. Sons: Michael; Jacob; George. Seven young children: (only 3 sons named). Mentions: twenty-five acres of land purchased from Daniel Griffen.
Exors: Philip Snapp and wife, Catharine
Wit: Daniel Shearer and George Dull
Dated: 9 Feb. 1787   Proved: 23 Feb. 1787

Will Book X - page 478

AARON ALLEN, Shenandoah County. Wife: Elizabeth Allen - the field containing 19 3/4 acres and woodland containing 7 acres. Sons: Reuben; George; Thomas.
Exor: Raphael Conn
Wit: Jno. Smith and E. R. Jordan
Dated: 26 Oct. 1839   Proved: 11 Aug. 1845

Will Book L - page 278

BETTY ALLEN, Shenandoah County. Son: Davis Allen - one dollar. Other children: Reuben Allen; Israel Allen; Mary Smith; Lydia Bond; Bathisheba Supton; Betty Haires; Sisly Schooly; Deborah Walton.
Exors: Son, Israel Allen and son-in-law, Isaac Smith
Wit: William Steenberger, Samuel Hawkins and Aaron Hawkins
Dated: 11 June 1818   Proved: 12 Feb. 1821

Will Book R - page 93

ISRAEL ALLEN, Shenandoah County. Wife: Sarah Allen.
Son: John J. Allen - all the tract of land I purchased from Michael Weaver that lies on the west side of the main Stage road; also, part of the tract I purchased of Reuben Allen, also, 1/6 of my mountain tract and 20 acres adjoining the Weaver tract. Son: George W. Allen - entire tract of land lying on both sides of the North Branch of the Shenandoah River, the same left to me by my father, Jackson Allen, dec'd. Dau: Polly Miller. Mentions: Erasmus Pitman, son of my late dau. Catharine who has departed this life. Five youngest children: Israel Allen; James Monroe Allen; Reuben Allen; Joseph Allen; Homer Allen (youngest son).
Exor: Son, John J. Allen
Wit: Samuel Windle, John Foltz and Isaac Samuels
Dated: 9 Sept. 1830

CODICIL to Will of ISRAEL ALLEN - Mentions: bequeath to my son, John J. Allen the further sum of $100.00 annually until my youngest son arrives of age.
Wit: William Steenberger, Joseph H. Samuels and Benjamin Hawkins.
Dated: 30 Oct. 1831   Proved: 12 Dec. 1831

Will Book B - page 262

JACKSON ALLEN, Shenandoah County. Wife: Betty. Youngest son: Israel Allen - all that plantation lying on the south side of the Shenandoah River adjoining lands of Joseph Allen. Eldest son: Reuben Allen - all the plantation lying on the north side of the Shenandoah River joining lands of Reuben Allen, dec'd. (140 acres). Other children: Davis; Betty; Cislia; Deborah; Mary; Barbara; Lydia.
Exors: Son, Reuben Allen and wife, Betty Allen
Wit: Joseph Allen, Edward Bond, Ruben Moore and John Oneal
Dated: 26 Feb. 1785   Proved: 28 Sept. 1786

Will Book F - page 371

JOSEPH ALLEN, Shenandoah County. Wife: Eunice Allen. Sons: Benjamin Allen; Jackson Allen; Thomas Allen; Wesley Allen. Son: Joseph Allen - 118 acres of land. Son: William Allen - 1/4 part of tract of land called the Pine Survey, together with 23 acres of bottom land adjoining William Moore. Son: Rhesa Allen - remainder of land whereon I now live. Daus: Sarah Ozburn; Susanna Bond; Mary Allen and Anna Allen.
Exors: Son, Jackson Allen and John Walton
Wit: Moses Walton, Benjamin Allen, Bernard Getz and Samuel Walton.
Dated: 28 May 1805   Proved: 10 Sept. 1805

Will Book A - page 240

REUBEN ALLEN, SENIOR, County of Shanando. Wife: Lydia Allen. Son: Thomas Allen - 1/3 part of all my land. Son: Aaron Allen - 1/3 part of all my land. Son: John Allen - 1/3 part of all my land. Dau: Hannah Allen - one thousand pounds. Dau: Mary Allen - one thousand pounds. Mentions: Mary Brinker, dau. of Conrad Brinker - one hundred pounds.
Exors: John Reuben, Joseph Moore, Jackson Jofeph, Reuben Allen, Junior.
Wit: Joseph Mathany, Tav^r Beale, John Bond and Reuben Moore
Dated: 1 Sept. 1779   Proved: 25 Nov. 1779

Will Book H - page 216

ROBERT ALLEN, late of the State of Pennsylvania but now of the County of Shenandoah. Wife: Mary. Daus: Jany Templeton, wife of John Templeton; Agnefs (otherwise called Nancy), wife of John Day. Sons: James Allen; John Allen (dec'd.). Grandson: Ralph Allen (son of my dau. Agnefs, otherwise called Nancy), 12 years old. Grandson: John James Allen, son of my son, James Allen.
Exor: Son, James Allen
Wit: George Hoffman, Adam Heishell and Alexander Pollock
Dated: 5 Dec. 1801   Proved: 10 Oct. 1803

Will Book Y - page 456

SARAH ALLEN, Shenandoah County. Grandchildren: Erasmus Pitman (son of my dec'd. dau. Catharine Pitman); Sarah Miller; Ira Miller; Benjamin Miller; Catharine Miller; Israel Miller; Richard Miller (children of my dec'd. dau. Mary Miller).
Exor: Son, John Allen
Wit: Samuel Windle and Jacob Ruby
Dated: 2 July 1842   Proved: 12 March 1849

Will Book M - page 88

THOMAS ALLEN, Shenandoah County. Wife: Abegail Allen - all the plantation on which I now live; lease I purchased of John Miller; house and lot in Front Royal I purchased of William Reynolds; negroes Davy and his wife, Polley; Bank stock I purchased on the Bank at Richmond and two banks in Winchester. Mentions: the two children of my dec'd. son, William Allen - land I purchased of George Harding and land I purchased of John Harding; land I purchased of John Smith; together with the Water Grist Mill purchased of George Harding; land I purchased of William Rufsell, Esq; together with the land my dec'd. son purchased of different persons. Grandson: Thomas M. Allen. Dau: Deborah Rufsell. Three grandsons: Thomas, William and Robert Rufsell. Son: Thomas Allen - tract of land purchased of Daniel Hackney; tract of land purchased of William Jennings; tract of land I purchased of Henry Harding; tract I purchased of William C. Williams and William Jennings, Jr.; 1/2 tract I purchased of the Grantees which Zachariah McKay formerly owned; 1/2 tract I purchased of Thomas Johnston; 1/2 tract purchased of Jacob Miller; negro man named Samuel and his wife Caty; negro girl, Beck; also, my sword. Son: Robert Allen - the remaining halfs of the three last mentioned tracts of land; also, the plantation after my wife's decease; another tract of land I purchased of Cunningham, lying on the top of Blue Ridge; negro man named George. Son: David Allen - plantation I purchased of William Keller; land I purchased of Thomas C. Martin; lot in Front Royal purchased of John Wall; money arising from sale of land in Hampshire Co.; rent due on farm I purchased of Cornelius Free; negro man named Somerset; my share of the Front Royal Libarian Society. Three grandsons: Algernon S. Allen; Thomas G. Allen; William T. Allen. Deceased dau: Rebecca Williamson. Grandson: Philip D. Williamson - tract of land I purchased of George Harding; land includes in the Deed made me by Simon Carson, up Cave Run; Lot I purchased of George Pierce; negro woman named Fanny.
Exors: Sons, Thomas and David Allen, nephew, Isaac Miller.
Wit: William Uroe, Samuel Hopewell, P. Sensoney, William Carson and Mordecai Cloud.
Dated: 27 Sept. 1815

CODICIL to Will of THOMAS ALLEN - Mentions: in consequence of death of my son, Robert M. Allen, my dau.-in-law, Rebecca Allen, widow of dec'd. son, Robert M. Allen to have and possess 1/3 part of all property and Estate which I have devised and bequeathed in last Will and Testament to my dec'd. son, Robert M. Allen.
Wit: David H. Allen, Thomas Allen, Jr. and M. Cloud
Dated: 13 Sept. 1819   Proved: 9 Sept. 1822

Will Book K - page 436

FREDERICK ALTDOERFFER, Shenandoah County. Wife: Christina.
Sons: John Altdoerffer (oldest); George Altdoerffer.
Exor: Henry Hockman, Jr.
Wit: Samuel R. Bader and John Boehm
Dated: 5 Nov. 1816   Proved: 11 May 1818

Will Book B - page 237

ERNEST AMMON, Shenandoah County. Wife: Margaretha - all
my moveable Estate and the whole of my inheritance.
Exors: Wife, Margaretha and Henry Koch
Wit: Daniel Brubaker, Frederick Comer and Phillip Comer
Dated: 27 April 1786   Proved: 13 Jan. 1787

Will Book N - page 404

FREDERICK ANDERICK, Shenandoah County. Wife: Elizabeth.
Dau: Barbara, wife of Philip Six - 20 acres of land adjoining land of Peter Helsley and Isaac Six on southeast side of Timber Ridge. Son: John Anderick - remaining part of lands and plantation. Dau: Sarah.
Exors: Son, John Anderick and Abraham Rinker
Wit: Joseph Anderick, Philip Helsley and Nicholas Helsley
Dated: 18 Feb. 1826   Proved: 11 April 1826

Will Book Z - page 120

ELIZABETH ANDERSON, Shenandoah County. Daus: Elizabeth
and Margarett.
Exor: Dr. William Magruder
Wit: Jacob Ott, Jr. and Emanuel Hines
Dated: 3 June 1849   Proved: 7 Jan. 1850

Will Book W - page 112

MARY ANDERSON, Shenandoah County. Dau: Catharine Anderson -
the whole of my property, both real and personal.
No Exor. named
Wit: David Crawford and Samuel Bare
Dated: 22 Nov. 1824   Proved: 11 April 1842

Will Book Y - page 482

SAMUEL ANDERSON, Shenandoah County. Wife: Maria Anderson - my negro man, Henry; my negro girl, Mary; also, all the lands in Town of Woodstock formerly belonging to John Anderson and Elizabeth Anderson (children of John Anderson, dec'd.); also, the claim I hold against George Rye. Sisters: Catharine Anderson; Mary Ott; Elizabeth McGahey. Step-dau: Emily Sauck. My nieces: Elizabeth Anderson; Margaret Anderson; Mary Hill. Nephews: Washington Anderson; Samuel Anderson; James Anderson.
Exors: Jacob Ott, Jr. and wife, Maria Anderson
Wit: George Rye and Joseph Irwin
Dated: 10 April 1845

CODICIL to Will of SAMUEL ANDERSON - Mentions: Revoke the said legacies given to James Anderson. Give my wife, Maria, land I purchased of James Anderson. Give my sister, Catharine Anderson $500.00 addition.
Wit: George Rye, Joseph Irwin and William Ott
Dated: 2 July 1848   Proved: 9 April 1849

Will Book W - page 492

ELIZABETH ANDRICK, Shenandoah County, widow and relic of Frederick Andrick, dec'd. Daus: Barbary Six; Sarah Six, wife of Peter Six. Four grandchildren: Eliza Ann Six (dau. of Barbary Six); Sally Six; Mary Six; Elizabeth Six.
No Exor. named
Wit: George Shrum and Joseph Andrick
Dated: 15 March 1842   Proved: 13 May 1844

Will Book A - page 25

FREDERICK ANDRICK, Dunmore County, Colony of Virginia. Wife: Anna Andrick. Sons: Frederick Andrick; George Andrick; Jacob Andrick.
Exors: John Keller and Jacob Rinker, Jr.
Wit: _____(Ger.); Christian Dellinger and Jacob Rinker Sen.
Dated: 8 Sept. 1772   Proved: 24 Nov. 1772

Will Book T - page 252

SARAH ANSPACK, Woodstock, Shenandoah County. Sister:
Eve. Ten nieces: Mary Trout; Elizabeth Trout; Rebecca
Trout (daus. of Philip Trout, dec'd.); Rebecca Hickman,
wife of Thomas Hickman of Hampshire Co.; Mary Myres,
wife of Samuel Myres now of Front Royal; Elizabeth Trout
(daus. of Henry Trout, dec'd.); Mary Scantling, wife of
James Scantling of Hardy Co. and Wardensville; Sarah
Yager; Rebecca Yager; Elizabeth Yager (daus. of Simeon
Yager of town of Woodstock.
Exor: Isaac Trout (of Philip Trout)
Wit: Isaac Trout and Enoch G. Yager
Dated: 23 Oct. 1830   Proved: 7 March 1836

Will Book F - page 146

PETER ARTERBURN, Shenandoah County. Wife: Sarah Arterburn.
My sons and daughters: (not named).
Exor: Wife, Sarah
Wit: Bradford Taylor, John Hawley and Nancy Hawley
Dated: 23 May 1796   Proved: 11 July 1803

Will Book L - page 66

CHRISTINA ARTZ, Shenandoah County. Children: John Artz;
Elizabeth; Christian; Mary Artz; Rebecca.
Exor: Son, John Artz
Wit: Joseph Hockman and Jacob Hockman
Dated: 22 Feb. 1819   Proved: 13 May 1819

Will Book K - page 391

HENRY ARTZ, Shenandoah County. Wife: Christina. Daus:
Elizabeth Artz; Mary Artz; Sally Burner, wife of Jonas
Burner. Sons: Henry Artz; Benjamin Artz; Jacob Artz;
John Artz.
Exors: Sons, Henry Artz and John Artz
Wit: Michael Haas, Abram Lambert and Simeon Yager
Dated: 12 Oct. 1817   Proved: 9 Feb. 1818

Will Book K - page 171

JOHN ARTZ, Shenandoah County. Wife: (not named). Sons:
John; Jacob Artz. Daus: Anna Elizabeth Capp and Mary.
Exors: Sons, John Artz and Jacob Artz
Wit: Benjamin Bowman, Sen. and Henry Hockman
Dated: 24 June 1816   Proved: 8 Oct. 1816

Translation from the German language to the English
language by oath of Samuel R. Bader.

Will Book K - page 131

JOHN ATWOOD, Shenandoah County. Wife: Elizabeth. Son-in-Law: John George - to have the plantation. Daus:
Nancy; Jane; Elizabeth; Susanna. Sons: Thompson (youngest);
John; Edwin; William; James.
Exors: Son, Edwin and John George
Wit: John Holmes and Edmond Holmes
Dated: 21 June 1816   Proved: 12 Aug. 1816

Will Book F - page 64

GEORGE AUMILLER, Parish of Beckford, Shenandoah County.
Wife: Mary Aumiller. Son: Henry Aumiller. Daus: Mary
Aumiller; Eave Catharena Aumiller.
Exor: Wife, Mary
Wit: Conrad Lickliter, John Smith and Adam Lickliter
Dated: 15 March 1802   Proved: 10 Jan. 1803

Will Book K - page 229

CATHERINE BACHMAN, Shenandoah County. Daus: Barbara,
wife of George Hepner; Anna, wife of Peter Oberholser.
Son: Henry Bachman. My brother: Abraham Neff (dec'd.)
Exors: Peter Oberholser and George Hepner
Wit: David Neff and Abraham Neff
Dated: 2 Nov. 1813   Proved: 10 March 1817

Will Book F - page 31

JOHN BACHMAN, Shenandoah County. Wife: Ann. Children:
Abraham; Daniel; Jacob; Christian; David; John; Ann; Mary.
Exors: John Cagy and John Click (the younger)
Wit: Jacob Hershberger, Balzer Hup, Mary Coffman and
Jacob Stiegel
Dated: 6 June 1802   Proved: 13 Sept. 1802

Will Book E - page 494

PHILIP PETER BACKER, SENIOR, Shenandoah County. Son:
Philip Peter Backer - all my plantation whereon I now
live containing 340 acres. Son: Anthony Backer - one
thousand dollars current money. Daus: Margarite;
Resina and Barbara. Mentions: sons of Anthony (grandsons):
Philip; John; Joseph; Jacob. Grandson: Daniel Eberly
(Jeremiah Eberly is father of grandson).
Exors: Philip Peter Backer, Jeremiah Eberly and Henry
Sweetzer
Wit: Alexander Hite, Anthony Rosenberger and Philip
Pittman.
Dated: 11 Jan. 1802   Proved: 8 March 1802

Will Book G - page 276

HEIRONIMUS BAKER, Shenandoah County. Wife: Mary Gertrout.
Sons: George and Henry Baker - all my Estate about 400
acres. Daus: Barbara, wife of Jacob Lambert; Margaret,
wife of Christopher Dosh; Abalon, wife of Philip Countz;
Elizabeth, wife of William Frye.
Exors: Two sons-in-law, Christopher Dosh and Philip
Countz
Wit: Alexander Hite, James Stephenson and Thomas Newell
Dated: 8 Jan. 1795   Proved: 9 March 1807

Will Book U - page 37

PHILIP BAKER, Shenandoah County. Wife: Dorothy. Son: Isaac Baker - two parcels of land, one containing 148 1/4 acres, other containing 50 acres. Son: Joseph Baker - two parcels of land, one containing 142 1/2 acres, the other containing 42 acres. Son: Henry Baker - two parcels of land, one containing 124 1/2 acres, the other containing 42 acres. Son: Philip Baker - two parcels of land, one containing 80 acres, the other containing 35 acres. Sons: Samuel Baker and Lewis Baker - two parcels of land, one containing 267 acres, the other 67 acres. Daus: Rebecca Ramy, relick of John Ramy, dec'd.; Catharine Wendel, wife of Benjamin Wendel; Christina, wife of John Hoover. Mentions: my proportion of Rosina Muck's Estate; Bond on Jacob Breekbill; Bond on Lewis Dunham.
Exors: Sons, Isaac Baker and William Baker
Wit: Phineas Orndorff, George Hottel and Peter Hamman
Dated: 5 Feb. 1834   Proved: 12 June 1837

Wills and Accts. (1809-1863) - page 1

LEONHARD BALTHIS, SENIOR, Shenandoah County. Two sons: Leonhard Balthis and William Balthis - the house I live in. Sons: John Balthis; George Balthis; Valentine Balthis. Three daus: Mary Hoffman, wife of Christian Hoffman; Regina Copenhefer, wife of George Copenhefer; Elizabeth Reagan, wife of Jacob Reagan. Mentions: My land in Kentucky (1,000 acres) - to be sold.
Exor: Son, John Balthis
Wit: George Cooper, Philip Spengler, John Machir and Jacob Cook
Dated: 11 Nov. 1808   Proved: 15 May 1809

Will Book R - page 309

ADAM BARB, Shenandoah County. Wife: Anna. My children: David; Adam; Jacob; Elizabeth, wife of Peter Baker; Anna, wife of Adam Sayger; Catharine, wife of George Lomas; Magdalene.
Exors: Sons, Adam and Jacob Barb
Wit: Jacob Miller, John Poke, Henry Barb and _____ (Ger.)
Dated: 28 March 1821   Proved: 13 Aug. 1832

Will Book S - page 344

ADAM BARB, Shenandoah County.　Wife: Ruth Barb.　My children: (not named).
Exor: Stephen Strotherman
Wit: George Shrum and Henry Bower, Jr.
Dated: 22 May 1834　　　　　Proved: 10 Nov. 1834

Will Book L - page 117

HENRY BARB, Shenandoah County.　Wife: Catharine.　Son: Henry Barb - my plantation and land containing 142 acres. Grandson: Gideon Barb (son of my son, Henry).　Son: William Barb.　Daus: Elizabeth, wife of Henry Wocker; Caty, wife of Jacob Haltiman; Peggy, wife of Adam Fout; Susanna, wife of Christian Goodnight; Lydia, wife of John Lutz; Rachael, wife of Daniel Haltiman.
Exors: Son, Henry Barb and George Weaver
Wit: William Good, Benjamin Coffman and Philip Sayger
Dated: 14 July 1819　　　　　Proved: 13 Sept. 1819

Will Book W - page 252

SAMUEL BARE, Town of Woodstock, Shenandoah County. Wife: Christina.　Dau: Rebecca.　Son: Joseph.　My surviving children: (not named).
Exor: Son, Naason
Wit: David Rodeffer, M. S. Bair and Joseph Irwin
Dated: 17 Dec. 1842　　　　　Proved: 9 Jan. 1843

Will Book B - page 447

MICHAEL BARNETT, County of Shanando.　Wife: Catharine. Sons: William Barnett and Michael Barnett.　Dau: Margaret Shaver, wife of John Shaver.　Mentions: George Borden; Mary Parkely (dau. of Jacob Parkely).
Exors: George Mavis and Edward Tomlinson
Wit: Samuel Mills, John Bauman and John Mesins
Dated: 2 Feb. 1788　　　　　Proved: 24 April 1788

Will Book E - page 57

ANN BARRINGTON, County of Shenandoah. Son: William.
Son: Andrew - to be bound out to learn a trade. Daus:
Betsy, wife of Jeremiah Cooper; Mary; Martha; Peggy.
Exor: Neighbor, Jacob Stiegel
Wit: William Branham, Betty Branham, Godfrey Grandel and
Davis Allen
Dated: 28 Oct. 1796   Proved: 13 Dec. 1796

Will Book F - page 463

JOSEPH BARUKER, Shenandoah County. Brother: Adam - all the
land which I have in possession.
No Exor. named
Wit: Joshua Summers, _____(Ger.), _____(Ger.)
Dated: 25 Aug. 1805   Proved: 8 Sept. 1808

Will Book P - page 106

MARGARET BATTICE, Shenandoah County. Dau: Regina Battice -
all of my Estate. Mentions: Mary Kerns; Jacob Battice;
William Battice and John Battice.
Exor: Abraham Hockman
Wit: Samuel Huddle and Henry Hockman
Dated: 17 April 1829   Proved: 11 May 1829

Will Book S - page 490

WILLIAM BAUSERMAN, SENIOR, Shenandoah County. Daus:
Magdalene (now deceased) and her husband, John Bushong;
Mary, wife of Jacob Golladay; Susannah, her husband, George
Bowman; Elizabeth, her husband, Henry Hockman (dec'd.).
Sons: Jacob Bauserman; William Bauserman; Isaac Bauserman.
Sons: Abraham and Reuben Bauserman - land and plantation
whereon I now live, also, adjoining tract I purchased from
George BQWman. Grandchildren: Reuben Hockman and Katherine
Hockman.
Exors: Son, Abraham Bauserman and son-in-law, George Bowman
Wit: Benjamin Kronk and Henry Bauserman
Dated: 27 Sept. 1832   Proved: 10 March 1835

Will Book L - page 48

MICHAEL BAUZERMAN, Shenandoah County. Mentions: Catharine Bauzerman, dau. of Frederick Bauzerman, now Catharine Somanstine.
Exor: George F. Hupp
Wit: Martin Hupp, David Crabell and John Rootz
Dated: 19 Dec. 1818   Proved: 8 March 1819

Will Book W - page 29

LEWIS BEARSH, Shenandoah County. Wife: Catharine Bearsh. Children of my wife, Catharine Bearsh (formerly Catharine Miller): Lydia; Abraham; Maria; George; Rosana.
Exor: Wife, Catharine Bearsh
Wit: William Moreland, Henry Marshall and George Sheets (Of Jacob).

At Court held in County of Shenandoah, 8 Nov. 1841, the last Will and Testament of Lewis Bearsh, dec'd. was contested by George Bearsh. The Court being of the opinion that it be admitted to probate as the true last Will and Testament of said Lewis Bearsh, dec'd. and recorded.
Dated: 28 Oct. 1841   Proved: 8 Nov. 1841

Will Book P - page 225

CHARLES BEAZLEY, Shenandoah County. Wife: Sarah Beazley - the plantation I purchased of John Shelton containing 139 acres adjoining land of Moses Lehew, Eli Chadduck and others, also, three negroes. Two sons: Mark Beazley and Isaac Beazley - the plantation I purchased of Lewis Pence containing 167 1/2 acres adjoining lands of Benjamin Blackford and Martin Kibler and Eli Chadduck. Three oldest daus: Nancy Redmond; Phebe Rodeheffer; Elizabeth Richard. Youngest dau: Rebecca Beazley - negro boy named Henry (son of Esther). Other daus: Mary Griffith; Esabella Broy; Mariam Beazley. Three grandchildren: Mary Peterson; Charles Peterson; Sarah Ann Peterson (heirs of my late dau., Sarah Peterson, dec'd.).
Exors: Sons, Mark Beazley and Isaac Beazley
Wit: Whorton Jones, James Fristoe and Eli Chadduck
Dated: 5 May 1829

CODICIL to Will of CHARLES BEAZLEY - Mentions: My Exors. keep my estate together and no sale until 25 Dec. 1830.
Dated: 4 June 1829   Proved: 12 Oct. 1829

Will Book K - page 163

ROSINA BECK, Shenandoah County, widow and relick of John
Beck, dec'd. Daus: Rosina, wife of David Munch; Magdalene,
wife of John Lonas. Sons: George Stigler and David
Stigler. Grandchildren: John Fry; Elizabeth Fry; Peter
Fry; Lidia Fry (children of my dec'd. dau., Frainey).
Exor: Grandson, John Fry
Wit: Jacob Noel, George Dellinger and Jacob Rinker
Dated: 1 July 1811   Proved: 7 Oct. 1816

Will Book E - page 434

PETER BECKER, County of Shenandoah. Wife: Maria. Sons:
John; Adam; Peter. Three daus: (not named). Mentions:
land which I hold by Deed from George Bernherd containing
330 acres.
Exors: Wife, Maria and son-in-law, Jacob Funkhouser
Wit: Jacob Hardein and Wendel Melcher
Dated: 9 March 1796   Proved: 8 June 1801

Written in the German language and the translation
thereof by David Jordan and ordered to be recorded.

Will Book F - page 464

TOBIAS BECKTEL, Shenandoah County. Wife: Catharine Becktel.
Son-in-Law: Lawrence Zink. Eight children: John Becktel;
Henry Becktel; Mary; Elizabeth; Barbara; Magdalene; Eve;
Dorotha.
Exors: Henry Hottel and George Jacob Helsly
Wit: Lawrence Zink and Charles Helsel
Dated: 29 March 1805   Proved: 8 Sept. 1806

Will Book F - page 26

MATHIAS BENDER (PAINTER), Shenandoah County. Wife: Christina. Son: John Bender - plantation whereon he now dwells containing 226 acres. Son: George Bender - upper part of the old tract of land containing 200 acres and the big stone house. Son: Philip Bender - the under tract of land whereon he now dwells containing 156 acres. Son: Adam Bender - middle part of the aforesaid plantation, the small stone house and the two barns (144 acres). Son: Mathias Bender - a certain tract of land lying on the Big Road containing 185 acres. Sons: Peter Bender and David Bender - tract lying on Stoney Creek which I bought of John Lesher with the Mills containing 376 acres. Dau: Christina - small negro girl named Sally. Daus: Catharine, wife of Jacob Emswiller and Mary, wife of Isaac Barret.
Exors: Jacob Lantz and Peter Snider
Wit: Jacob Rinker, Joseph Bowman and Conrad Smith
Dated: 27 July 1802   Proved: 13 Sept. 1802

Will Book V - page 492

PHILIP BENDER (PAINTER), Shenandoah County. Wife: Christina Bender. Son: John Bender - all the lands upon which he now resides, also, 8 acres next to said, George Bender. Son: Samuel Bender - tract of land whereon he now lives purchased of George Riddle. Son: Jacob Bender (dec'd.). Dau: Catharine Maphis. Grandson: Jacob Lantz. Granddaughter: Elizabeth Maphis (late Elizabeth Lantz). Oldest child of Catharine Maphis: Regina Bender, wife of Isaac Bender.
Exors: Sons, Samuel Bender and John Bender
Wit: John Emswiller, Frederick Hoffman, Samuel Mohler and R. M. Conn
Dated: 2 Sept. 1840   Proved: 9 Aug. 1841

Will Book G - page 446

ABRAHAM BEYDLER, Shenandoah County. Wife: Barbara Beydler. Son: Jacob Beydler - plantation and tract of land whereon I now live. Sons: Abraham Beydler; Ulrick Beydler. Daus: Susanna Beydler; Elizabeth, wife of David Craybill; Barbara, wife of George Fisher; Catharine, wife of Henry Hockman; Mary, wife of Daniel Huddle. Mentions: children's grandfather, Ulrick Hockman (dec'd.) of State of Pennsylvania.
Exors: Jacob Coffman and Daniel Huddle (son of George Huddle)
Wit: Samuel R. Bader, Michael Roth and John Roth
Dated: 17 April 1807   Proved: 9 April 1810

Will Book Y - page 501

ABRAHAM BEYDLER, Shenandoah County. Wife: Dorothy Beydler - my plantation. Daus: Catharine Hoffman, wife of John Hoffman; Mary Shaver, wife of George Shaver; Rebecca Beydler, wife of Abraham Beydler, Junior; Rachel Byrd, wife of Mounce Byrd; Barbara Funkhouser, wife of Jacob Funkhouser; Anna Schmucker, wife of Joseph Schmucker; Sarah Wisman, wife of Isaac Wisman. Mentions: the Farm called River Farm containing 184 acres to be sold. My stock in Valley Turnpike.
Exors: Abraham Beydler, Jr. and Isaac Wisman
Wit: Joseph Wattson, James Ruddell and Nimrod Hoffman
Dated: 12 April 1848

CODICIL to Will of ABRAHAM BEYDLER - Mentions: 20 acres of land adjoining land of Allen Kibler - to be sold.
Dated: 12 April 1848   Proved: 11 June 1849

Will Book B - page 460

JACOB BEYER, Shanando County. Wife: Magdalena. Sons: Adam; Leonhard; Jacob; John. Daus: Moly; Lifs; Peggy.
Exor: Brother-in-law, John Knisfly
Wit: _____(Ger.); Antony A. Knisfly, David Jordan
Dated: 2 May 1788   Proved: 31 July 1788

Will Book N - page 495

GEORGE BILLER, Shenandoah County. Wife: Catharine.
Exor: Son, Christian Biller
Wit: None
Dated: 10 May 1826   Proved: 13 Nov. 1826

Proved that the said handwriting with the signature thereto is handwriting of said, George Biller, dec'd. by oath of George Biller, Junior and Rebecca Biller.

Will Book P - page 315

ABRAHAM BIRD, Shenandoah County. Wife: Rachel - my mallatto woman, Sall and her two children, Hannah and Nathan. Son: Abraham - all the lands and plantation whereon I now live, also, my mallatto boy, Isaac. Son: Mark - 400 acres of land taken out of tract of 1,954 acres lying on the North Fork of Kentucky River, also, my mallatto boy, Rofs. Son: George - negro boy, Billy. Five daus: Magdalene; Elizabeth; Mary; Catharine; Margaret.
Exors: Son, Abraham Bird and William S. Rufsell
Wit: Joseph Jay, William Manuel and David Coffman
Dated: 11 Aug. 1808   Proved: in Commonwealth of Kentucky - 8 May 1829
Proved: Shenandoah Co. 11 Jan. 1830

Will Book S - page 127

HANNAH BIRD, Shenandoah County. Son: Mark - my negro man, Edmund. Son: Reuben A. Bird. Dau: Lydia Bird.
Exor: Son, Reuben A. Bird
Wit: Henry Tutt and Reuben Jordan
Dated: 7 Nov. 1833   Proved: 13 Jan. 1834

Will Book O - page 168

MICHAEL BIXLER, Shenandoah County. Wife: Anna. Mentions: Son, John and dau. Nancy Bixler - all the property after death of my wife, their mother. Sons: Peter Bixler and Michael Bixler. Dau: Molly Winders, wife of Clem Winders - piece of land whereon John Strickler now lives. Dau: Lufsa Ailshire, wife of Daniel Ailshire.
Exor: Son, John Bixler
Wit: Joseph Evans, Thomas Blackford and George Young
Dated: 1826   Proved: 8 Oct. 1827

Will Book C - page 157

JACOB BLESSING, County of Shenandoah, yeoman. Wife: Elizabeth. Sons: Jacob; Lewis; Christian; John; Henry; Abraham. Daus: Elizabeth; Barbara; Magdalene; Catharine; Christina.
Exors: Sons, Jacob and Lewis
Wit: Sebation Stigeler, George Weaver, Sen. and John Stigeler
Dated: 25 Feb. 1790   Proved: 5 April 1790

Will Book P - page 456

LEWIS BLESSING, Green County, State of Ohio. Wife:
Elizabeth. Son: John Blessing - 150 acres being part of
490 acres that I purchased of Jonathan Paul. Son: Abraham.
Dau: Mary (single) - 150 acres of land. Dau: Elizabeth
(single) - 190 acres of land.
Exor: Son, John Blessing
Wit: John E. Beatty, Samuel C. Finley and Jonah Tullis
Dated: 15 Aug. 1825   Proved: State of Ohio
                            10 Sept. 1825
                            Shenandoah Co. 11 May 1830

Will Book R - page 18

MICHAEL BLIND, Shenandoah County. Son: David Blind -
five hundred dollars in consequence of his inability
to labour (as he is a cripple). Sons: William Blind;
Jacob Blind; Michael Blind; Isaac Blind; Abraham Blind.
Daus: Catharine Blind; Elizabeth, wife of David Funkhouser;
Rebecca, wife of Jacob Doll; Mary, wife of William Wiseman;
Sarah, wife of Abraham Wiseman; Flora, wife of Samuel
Funkhouser; Rachael, wife of David Weaver. Mentions:
grandchildren, the children of Peter Blind, dec'd.
Exors: Samuel Funkhouser and son, David Blind
Wit: Phineas Orndorff, Henry R. Browning and _____ (Ger.)
Dated: 11 April 1831   Proved: 9 Aug. 1831

Will Book Q - page 57

PETER BLIND, Shenandoah County. Wife: Hannah Blind - all
my Estate, real and personal. Sons: Soloman Blind; Jacob
Blind; Isaac Blind. Daus: Mary Ann Blind; Barbara
Strickley; Elizabeth Blind; Catharine Blind; Sophia Blind.
Exor: Wife, Hannah Blind
Wit: Joseph Wattson and George Swartz
Dated: 15 June 1830   Proved: 13 Sept. 1830

Will Book T - page 48

PHILIP BLY, Shenandoah County. Nephew: Jonathan Bly -
all of everything that is coming to me - money that I have
at Mrs. E. Supinger's.
Exor: Nephew, Jonathan Bly
Wit: Samuel Boehm and John Swayne
Dated: 6 June 1835   Proved: 13 July 1835

Will Book B - page 283

PHILLIP BLY, Shenandoah County. Wife: Mary Magdelon.
Children: Jacob Bly; George Bly; John Bly; Phillip Bly;
Barbara Coons; Elizabeth Bly. Mentions: Sons-in-Law,
Phillip Coons and John Pope.
Exors: Sons, Jacob Bly and George Bly
Wit: Phillip Pear, Peter Hurbough and George Snapp
Dated: 19 May 1786   Proved: 19 June 1786

Will Book Z - page 178

GEORGE BODELL, SENIOR, New Market, Shenandoah County.
Wife: Mary. Dau: Malinda - the house and lot so long
as she may live and remain single. Other children:
Mary Long; Kathern Douglas; Jonas; William; Adam;
Michael Bodell; George Bodell; David Bodell, Elizabeth
Kipps.
No Exor. named
Wit: Charles Spitzer, John Maloney and William Shomo
Dated: 19 May 1849   Proved: 11 March 1850

Will Book E - page 201

JACOB BOEHM, County of Shenandoah. Wife: Mary Boehm.
Son: Samuel Boehm - plantation whereon I live. Son:
Daniel. Daus: Regenia; Barbara; Franey; Catharine; Mary;
Elizabeth; Dorothy.
Exors: Reuben Boehm and Daniel Boehm
Wit: George Lind, Thomas Newell and Christian Niglswonger
Dated: 17 July 1798   Proved: 11 Sept. 1798

Will Book E - page 99

SAMUEL BOEHM, County of Shenandoah. Wife: Elizabeth.
Son: Daniel Boehm - plantation or tract of land about 200
acres, the same I now live. Sons: Jacob Boehm; Rubin
Boehm. Daus: Barbara and Regina Boehm - 25 pounds each for
their trouble had and taken toward their helpless mother
my said wife. Daus: Magdalene; Heustant; Elizabeth
Funkhouser; Mary Lockmiller.
Exors: My two sons, Jacob and Reuben Boehm
Wit: Thomas Newell, John Supinger and Alexander Hite
Dated: 8 June 1795   Proved: 12 June 1797

Will Book F - page 322   NUNCUPATIVE WILL

JOHN PHILIP BOOKER, Shenandoah County. Wife: Nancy.
Three children: Son, William and dau., Salley - to go
to their grandfather, meaning Edward Lawrence. Third
child (not named).
Wit: Charles Sexton and Daniel Cloud
Dated: 8 April 1804   Proved: 13 April 1804

Will Book M - page 387

AUGUSTINE BORDEN, Shenandoah County. Eldest son: Joseph
Borden - 40 acres conveyed to me by my father; 50 acres
I purchased of John Tipton; slave, Thomas. Youngest son:
Augustine Borden - 110 acres conveyed to me by my father,
Reincard Borden; slave, Alfred. Dau: Ellen, wife of
Phineas Orndorff - slave, Abigail. Dau: Katharine, wife
of George Lentz - infant slave, Rebecca. Youngest dau:
Hannah Borden - female slave, Rosina. Daus: Rachael, wife
of Philip Keil; Rosina, relick of Philip Painter; Sarah,
wife of William Miller.
Exors: Sons, Joseph Borden and Augustine Borden
Wit: Joseph Swartz and John Swartz
Dated: 13 March 1824   Proved: 12 July 1824

Will Book D - page 341

MICHAEL BORGER, Shenandoah County. Wife: Ann Mary.
Youngest son: George Borger - my plantation whereon I
now live. Other two sons: Henry and Michael Borger.
Exor: George Henry Lindemood
Wit: Charles Smith, Michael Lindemood and William Rider
Dated: 25 May 1794   Proved: 8 July 1794

Will Book N - page 220

FREDERICK BOSSERMAN, Shenandoah County. Wife: Judith
Bosserman. Son: Frederick Bosserman - plantation and
tract of land whereon I now live. Sons: Henry Bosserman
and Samuel Bosserman. Daus: Christina, wife of Thomas
Baker; Mary, wife of Adam Bly; Catharine, wife of Joseph
Sommerton; Elizabeth, wife of David Roth; Sarah Bosserman.
Exors: Son, Henry Bosserman and son-in-law, David Roth
Wit: Jacob Huddle, Jun. and Samuel R. Bader
Dated: 6 Dec. 1815   Proved: 9 May 1825

Will Book A - page 223

HENRY BOUGHMAN, SENIOR, Dunmore County, Colony of Virginia.
Wife: Barbary. Sons: Henry; John and Jacob Boughman.
Mentions: Jacob Holeman's land.
Exors: Jacob Boughman and wife, Barbara
Wit: None
Dated: 15 July 1777   Proved: 25 Nov. 1779
Duplicate Will - Will Book B - page 148

Will Book K - page 112

CHRISTIAN BOWER, Shenandoah County. Wife: Elizabeth.
Children: Elizabeth, wife of John Rubfreit; Catharine,
wife of Adam Zerkel; Margaret, wife of Nathaniel Zeveher;
Mary Barbara, wife of Peter Fernler. Mentions: children
of my dau. Ann Mary Scrwind(dec'd.), late wife of Peter
Scrwind.
Exor: Jacob Rinker
Wit: John Conn, George Feltz, Jr. and Jacob Noel
Dated: 11 Aug. 1810   Proved: 9 April 1816

Will Book F - page 528

HENRY BOWER, Shenandoah County. Wife: Elizabeth. Son:
Lawrence Bower. Dau: Elizabeth, wife of Adam Deel of the
State of Pennsylvania. Mentions: grandchildren (children
of my son, Lawrence Bower).
Exor: Son, Lawrence Bower
Wit: Jacob Rinker, George Rinker and Henry Rinker
Dated: 13 April 1794   Proved: 9 June 1806

Will Book W - page 28

HENRY BOWER, Shenandoah County. Wife: Magdalen Bower -
retain my house and tenements including the Saw Mill.
Children: Christena Bower; Mary, wife of George Sine;
Clarisey Bower; Ann Bower; Henry Bower, Jr. Mentions:
George Bower, child of my dau., Christena Bower.
Exor: Peter Craik (Craig)
Wit: George Shrum and Daniel Brumback
Dated: 29 April 1841   Proved: 13 Dec. 1841

Will Book O - page 279

DANIEL BOWMAN, Beckford Parish, Shenandoah County.
Wife: Anna Marie. Son: Daniel Bowman - the farm whereon
I now live containing 358 acres. Son: John Bowman - land
whereon he now lives containing 84 1/2 acres purchased from
Daniel Wendle. Son: Benjamin Bowman - all my claim in the
land whereon he now lives. All the rest of my children:
(not named).
Exor: Son, Henry Bowman
Wit: George Bowman, Henry Wakeman and John Wakeman
Dated: 18 Dec. 1824   Proved: 7 April 1828

Will Book W - page 67

EVE BOWMAN, Shenandoah County. Son: David. Daus:
Elizabeth; Rebecca; Mary.
No Exor. named.
Wit: John Snyder, James Ruddell and Philip Stover
Dated: 17 March 1835

CODICIL to Will of EVE BOWMAN - Mentions: an increase to
son, David Bowman.
Wit: same as above
Dated: 11 March 1841   Proved: 7 Feb. 1842

Will Book E - page 144

GEORGE ADAM BOWMAN, County of Shenandoah. Wife: Mary.
Son: Henry Bowman - half of land in town of Woodstock
which joins Abraham Lambert and John Helmick. Son:
Peter Bowman - other half of my Lott in town of Woodstock.
Sons: Adam Bowman; George Bowman; John Bowman. Daus:
Susannah Flora; Mary Sibert; Betsy Sibert. Mentions:
granddaughter, Betsy Sibert.
Exors: Sons, Henry Bowman and Peter Bowman
Wit: John Gaw, Robert Gaw and Daniel Smith
Dated: 8 Oct. 1796   Proved: 12 Dec. 1797

Will Book N - page 521

ISAAC BOWMAN, Shenandoah County. Wife: Mary - whole of the several tracts of land on which I now reside in County of Shenandoah. Sons: Philip (eldest); Abraham; Joseph and John - valuable land in State of Indiana. Dau: Susannah, wife of William H. Richardson, now resident in the State of Ohio - 500 acres being lot #202, Illinois Military Grant in the State of Indiana. Dau: Eliza B., wife of Joseph M. Faunteroy in County of Frederick - 500 acres in the said Illinois Grant in State of Indiana. Younger children: Isaac; George; Robert; Washington; Mary; Rebecca. Nephew: George Brinker. Mentions: children of my first wife (not named). Mentions: Lots in town of Jeffersonville in State of Indiana; my ferry across the Ohio River; tract of land in Indiana Grant containing 156 acres; tract of land on waters of Green River and Delaware Creek in State of Kentucky containing 1,400 acres; my brick dwelling house; my stone house; my Merchant Mill; my tract called the Island tract; slaves.
Exors: Wife, Mary, nephew, George Brinker and four sons, Isaac, George, Robert and Washington.
Wit: Samuel Kercheval, Richard M. Sigdnor and Will M. Bayley
Dated: 20 June 1824

CODICIL to Will of ISAAC BOWMAN - Mentions: I was appointed Guardian of my four elder children, to wit: Philip; Abraham; Catharine and Susannah in order to receive their portions of the Legacy due their mother who was one of the daus. of Philip Gatewood, dec'd.
Wit: same as above
Dated: 20 June 1824   Proved: 13 Nov. 1826

Will Book Y - page 411

JOHN BOWMAN (son of David), Shenandoah County. Wife: Mary. Son: David - Use and possession of plantation known as Frank's Place, bequeathed unto my wife by her father, Jacob Lantz, Senior. Son: Jacob - certain lands which he now occupies. Unmarried son: Samuel. Unmarried daus: Lydia and Ann.
Exor: Son, Samuel Bowman
Wit: J. P. Rinker, Samuel Tisinger and Jackson Wetzell
Dated: 9 Nov. 1847   Proved: 12 Feb. 1849

Will Book V - page 506

SARAH BOWMAN, Shenandoah County. Mentions: George Maphis, son of John Maphis, dec'd. - all my Estate.
No Exor. named
Wit: John M. Maphis and Joseph Layman
Dated: 15 April 1840   Proved: 9 Aug. 1841

Will Book Y - page 304

SUSAN BOWMAN, Town of Woodstock, Shenandoah County. Dau: Amelia, wife of Robert Davis. Sons: Samuel Bowman and Robert Bowman.
Exor: William W. Magruder
Wit: James Fravel and Ephraim Grabill
Dated: 22 Dec. 1846   Proved: 8 May 1848

Will Book S - page 85

JOHN BOYD, Shenandoah County. Wife: Frances Boyd. All my children: William Boyd; Caroline Boyd; Virginia Boyd; John F. Boyd; Rachael Amanda Boyd; Stephen Decatur Boyd; James Wilson Boyd; Henry Prater Boyd.
Exor: Brother-in-Law, William Woodward
Wit: Mordecai Cloud, Richard Fish and Benjamin Hockman
Dated: 31 July 1833

CODICIL To Will of JOHN BOYD - Mentions: old friend Mary Talbert (widow). Additional provisions to wife and children.
Wit: same as above
Dated: 4 Aug. 1833   Proved: 11 Nov. 1833

Will Book X - page 239

PETER BOYER, Shenandoah County. Wife: Elizabeth Boyer. Son: George K. Boyer - sold him 60 acres of land called Jackson Place - I give him the balance of my land. Sons: Jacob Boyer and William Boyer. Daus: Sarah Stover; Margaret Shearman; Catharine Ritenour. Son-in-Law: Jacob Shearman.
Exor: Son, George K. Boyer
Wit: Robert Fergerson and Joseph Wattson
Dated: 6 Dec. 1838   Proved: 8 June 1845

Will Book W - page 444

REBECCA BOYERS, Shenandoah County. Mentions: Harriet Hoshour and her children, viz: Rebecca; Samuel and Catharine - all my Estate both real and personal.
Exor: Peter Hoshour
Wit: W. W. Magruder, John Clinedinst and John Keffer
Dated: 31 July 1843   Proved: 12 Feb. 1844

Will Book U - page 448

DANIEL BRANNAMAN, Shenandoah County. Wife: Mary.
Mentions: friend, Martha Barrington. Nephew: Henry Kagey (son of Jacob Kagey, dec'd.).
Exor: Nephew, Henry Kagey
Wit: Moses Walton, Martin Roof and Reuben Walton
Dated: 3 June 1820

CODICIL to Will of DANIEL BRANNAMAN - Mentions: if wife to die her share should be given to Martha Barrington for her long and faithful service.
Wit: Joel Pennybacker and _____(Ger.)
Dated: 11 June 1831   Proved: 10 Dec. 1838

Will Book A - page 205

ADAM BROADBACK, County of Shanando, Colony of Virginia, yeoman. Oldest son: name not mentioned. Sons: Adam; John; Jacob; Phillip. Daus: Anna Y. and Barbary. Mentions: George Hoan and son-in-law, Abraham Funkhouser.
Exors: Son, Adam Broadback and son-in-law, Abraham Funkhouser
Wit: None
Dated: 20 Dec. 1772   Proved: 25 March 1779

Will Book L - page 404

JOHN BROBECK, Shenandoah County. Wife: Mary Brobeck,
Dau: Margaret Brobeck. Father: John Brobeck.
Exor: Isaac Beas
Wit: William Baker, Daniel Baker, Joseph Brobeck and Adam Snapp
Dated: 4 Dec. 1821   Proved: 7 Jan. 1822

Will Book E - page 356

HENRY BROCK, County of Shenandoah. Wife: Mary. Son: Michael - 118 acres of land, part of the plantation whereon I now live adjoining lands of Michael Neas, Rudolph Brock and Christian Moyer. Son: Jacob - 104 acres of land. Sons: Rudolph; Henry; Abraham; George. Daus: Magdalena; Christina; Juliana; Susannah; Barbara; Lea; Mary; Catharine; Sarah.
Exors: Adam Neas and Jacob Siegle
Wit: Philip Pence, John Nease, Isaac Brownlow and Jacob Siegle
Dated: 21 May 1795   Proved: 11 March 1800

Will Book U - page 25

HENRY BROWNING, Shenandoah County. Wife: (not named). Three children: Mildred, wife of Lewis Hottle; Jane; John Henry. Mentions: send my son, John Henry, to William F. Broadus if he is still teaching. Mentions: 20 dollars towards putting a stone or brick wall around the graveyard on John Copp's farm.
Exor: William McCord
Wit: Abraham Stoner, Jacob Funkhouser and John Hockman
Dated: 19 May 1837   Proved: 12 June 1837

Will Book F - page 265

ABRAHAM BRUBAKER, SENIOR, Shenandoah County, farmer. Wife: Barbara. Son: Abraham - the plantation where he now lives adjoining the town of Woodstock. Son: John - home plantation where I now live. Son-in-Law: Abraham Stickler - 4 acres of meadow. Son: Peter - that plantation adjoining my old place which I purchased of Samuel Stover. Mentions: Dau. Barbara's heirs - the Mill and plantation below the Town of Woodstock. Dau: Elizabeth - several tracts of land lying in County of Rockingham. Daus: Susana; Catharina; Christina; Anna Maria. Mentions: land on top of Blue Ridge in County of Culpeper - to be sold.
Exors: Son-in-law, Isaac Strickler and John Roads
Wit: Levi Keenan and Samuel Strickler
Dated: 20 Nov. 1804   Proved: 10 Dec. 1804

Will Book M - page 225

CHARLES BUCK, Shenandoah County. Wife: (not named) - dwelling house and barn; 185 acres; one negro named David; one negro named Susan (dau. of Judah); negro girl named Eveline. Dau: Letty Catlett - land lying in the fork of the Shenandoah River and Passage Creek which stands both the Grist Mill and Saw Mill. Son: Samuel - 200 acres. Son: Thomas - 180 acres. Son: John - 240 acres. Son: Charles - 252 acres. Son: William - 308 acres. Dau: Polly Bayly - 210 acres.
Exors: Five sons, Thomas, Samuel, John, Charles and William.
No Witnessess
Dated: 26 May 1819   Proved: 5 Sept. 1823

Will Book W - page 305

WILLIAM BULER (BEELER), Shenandoah County. My mother: Catharine Buler - my farm adjoining Rudy Rosenbarger, Henry Rosenbarger, George Dellinger and others.
Exor: My father, John Buler
Wit: Wattson Peery and Philip Swartz
Dated: 19 Oct. 1843   Proved: 8 Jan. 1844

Will Book E - page 231

SIMON BURKHEAD, County of Shenandoah. Wife: Mary Eva. Sons: Simon and George. Daus: Barbara and Elizabeth.
Exor: Wife, Mary Eva
Wit: Jacob Stiegle, Peter Bird and George Shaver
Dated: 26 Nov. 1792   Proved: 12 March 1799

Will Book O - page 234

CATHARINE BURNER, Shenandoah County. Mentions: friend, Amy Arrington. Mentions: Dau. Sarah Burner (alias Sarah Harrow) and son, John Cooley - my house in town of Woodstock that I purchased of George Grandstaff
Exor: Son, Stephen Odell
Wit: Michael Ott, Jno. Ott and Simeon Yager
Dated: 1 Oct. 1827

CODICIL to Will of CATHARINE BURNER - Mentions: my father, Jacob Burner of Powells Fort.
Wit: Michael Ott and Simeon Yager
Dated: 22 Dec. 1827   Proved: 11 Feb. 1828

Will Book C - page 236

JACOB BURNER, County of Shenandoah. Sons: Michael; Jacob; John; Joseph; Samuel. Daus: Mary Beam; Elizabeth Rufner; Matlener Himer; Barbary Stover; Christiner Burner; Esther Burner; Katharine Burner; Franky Burner. Mentions: Children of dau. Ann Ruffner, dec'd.
Exors: Jacob Heastant, Mark Grove and Peter Heastant
Wit: _____(Ger.), Nathaniel Stewart, Peter Lionbarger, Jacob Burner and Charles Gordon.
Dated: 5 April 1785

CODICIL to Will of JACOB BURNER, Parish of Beckford, farmer. Mentions: Dau. Esther Burner further sum more than her share, the sum of 12 pounds.
Wit: Edisin Young, _____(Ger.), William Harris, John Burner and Leithia Burner
Dated: 19 July 1790   Proved: 30 Dec. 1790

Will Book A - page 375

JACOB BURNER, JUNIOR, Parish of Beckford, County of Shanando. Wife: Anny Burner - tract of land on North River of Shanando containing 270 acres. Sons: Abraham Burner and Isaac Burner. Daus: Catharine Burner and Barbary Burner.
Exors: Brother, Michael Burner, Benj. Rufner, wife, Anny Burner
Wit: S. Foley, John Haastent, Michael Judd and Benj. Rufner.
Dated: 28 Feb. 1782   Proved: 28 March 1782

Will Book F - page 385

JONATHAN BUSWELL, Shenandoah County, farmer. Wife: Anna
Buswell. Son: George Buswell - part cut off my old plantation
whereon I now live. Son: John Buswell - remainder of old
place whereon I live (25 acres). Three daus: Elizabeth
Coffman; Susanna Spitler; Barbara Strickler.
Exors: Son, George Buswell and son-in-law, David Coffman
Wit: Christian Alshite, Christian Hershberger and _____(Ger.)
Dated: 10 Nov. 1805   Proved: 9 Dec. 1805

Will Book K - page 257

ANDREW BYRD, Shenandoah County. Wife: Solina. Brothers:
John; Jacob; Henry and Peter Bird.
Exor: John Pentz
Wit: George Mourey, J. Peter Smucher and _____(Ger.)
Dated: 13 March 1815   Proved: June 1817

Will Book M - page 127

CLARA BYRD, Shenandoah County. Two sons: William and Mounce -
all personal property which I obtained from my late husband's
Estate (Mounce Byrd, dec'd.).
Exor: Son, William
Wit: George M. Pennybacker and D. Pennypacker
Dated: 30 Jan. 1822   Proved: 9 Dec. 1822

Will Book P - page 319

JOHN BYRD, Shenandoah County. Wife: Catherian.
Dau: Catharine, wife of George Will - my plantation.
Grandson: William Will - the balance of my plantation.
Exors: William Will and George Moury
Wit: John Moore, John Pence and _____(Ger.)
Dated: 9 Sept. 1825   Proved: 8 Feb. 1830

Will Book U - page 421

WILLIAM BYRD, SENIOR, Shenandoah County. Mentions: children of my brother, Mounce Byrd, now deceased, to wit: Clara, wife of Benjamin Miller; William Byrd; Polly Byrd; Catharine, wife of Edward Walton; Mounce Byrd; Derick Byrd; Abraham Byrd; Sally Byrd.
Exor: Joseph H. Samuels
Wit: George Pennybacker, G. B. Samuels and Joel Pennybacker
Dated: 17 Sept. 1827   Proved: 12 Nov. 1838

Will Book B - page 216

JOHN CALFEE, County of Shanando. Wife: (not named). Sons: Charles; William; James; Benjamin; Henry; John. Daus: Bettey and Sarah.
Exors: Wife and son, Charles
Wit: Duskin Tibbs, William Crum and John Hoy
Dated: 15 April 1785   Proved: 30 March 1786

Will Book B - page 205

ALEXANDER CAMPBELL, Shenandoah County. Wife: Lettice Campbell. Sons: Alexander Campbell and Ellick. Daus: Letty Campbell and Catharine Campbell. Grandchild: Samuel.
Exors: Wife, Lettice Campbell and John Wilson
Wit: Joseph Colvill Vance, Brigit Wilson and Lettice Campbell.
Dated: 27 Dec. 1783   Proved: 26 Jan. 1786

Will Book F - page 424

CHARLES CAMPBELL, Shenandoah County. Wife: Agnefs Campbell. Two sons: Andrew Campbell and John Hamilton Campbell. Eldest dau: Elizabeth Campbell, wife of John Campbell. Daus: Janet; Agnefs; Margaret.
Exors: Sons, Andrew Campbell and John Hamilton Campbell
Wit: Walter Newman, James Lokay and David Strickler
Dated: 27 Oct. 1798   Proved: 8 April 1800

Will Book A - page 419

RICHARD CAMPBELL, Woodstock, County of Shanando. Wife:
Rebekah. Children: (not named).
Exors: George Harrison and Tav⁻. Beale, Gent.
Wit: William McKay, Jos. Carnagey and John Anderson
Dated: 22 Sept. 1778   Proved: 28 March 1782

Will Book E - page 418

ANDREW CAPP, County of Shenandoah. Wife: Mary Elizabeth.
Sons: John; Jacob; George; Michael. Daus: Elizabeth; Eve;
Mary.
Exors: John Nicholas Dull and son, George
Wit: Daniel Hottle and Jacob Hottle, Jr.
Dated: 21 Oct. 1800   Proved: 9 March 1801

Will Book A - page 400

JAMES CARNAGIE, Town of Woodstock, County of Shenandoah,
Scotch descent. Mentions: brother, Andrew Carnagie - eight
thousand pounds. Mentions: John Machir, Jr. - my house.
Mentions: children of my cousin, Alexander Machir.
Exors: Alexander Machir and Col. Tav⁻ Beale
Wit: Rebecca Campbell, John Huffman and Peter Wolfenberger
Dated: 11 Aug. 1780   Proved: Aug. 1780

Will Book O - page 465

SOLOMON CARRIER, Beckford Parish, Shenandoah County.
Mentions: Jacob Klanahan and Jacob Coverstone (son of
Barbara Burner) - all my Estate divided equally between
them.
No Exor. named
Wit: George Sibert, Jacob Burner and George McInturf
Dated: 22 Oct. 1828   Proved: 10 Nov. 1828

Will Book M - page 369

CHARLES CATLETT, Shenandoah County. Wife: Catharine (now dec'd.). Dau: Susannah Mitchell - tract of land whereon I now live containing 180 acres, also, tract of land called Stoney Branch tract containing 133 acres, also, two negroes. Dau: Sally Buck - tract of land whereon my son-in-law, John Buck and her now live containing 200 acres, also, two negroes Mentions: Children of my said dau. Susannah (not named). Mentions: grandchildren, viz: Philip Allensworth; Eliza Allensworth; Harrison Allensworth (children of my dau. Eliza, dec'd.) - three slaves named Nanny, Philip and James. Mentions: father of dec'd wife, Philip Gatewood, dec'd. Mentions: husband of my dec'd. dau. Eliza, James Allensworth. Exors: Philip Williams, John Buck, Samuel Richardson and John Catlett.
Wit: None
Dated: 14 May 1822   Proved: 7 June 1824

John Gatewood made oath that the signature of Charles Catlett be the same in the handwriting of said Charles Catlett, dec'd

* First Will of Charles Catlett dated 23 Sept. 1819 before his wife Catharine's decease. Will Book M - page 406.

Will Book S - page 34

ADAULPH (ADOLPH) CAUFFMAN, SENIOR, Shenandoah County. Mentions: Elizabeth Cauffman, wife of John Cauffman (son of Daniel) - 50 acres of land. George Cauffman (brother of Andrew, of Andrew) - 50 acres of land. Adolph Cauffman, Junior - 50 acres of land. George Cauffman's dau: Christina, wife of John Philips - 25 acres of land. Rosannah Cauffman, widow of my brother, Andrew Cauffman, dec'd. - 50 acres of land. Andrew Cauffman, dec'd. (?) - 50 acres of land. Andrew Cauffman (son of Jacob Cauffman) - 25 acres of land. Andrew Cauffman (son of Andrew Cauffman, dec'd.) - the balance of my land. Mentions: sister of Elizabeth Cauffman (wife of John), Christina Hottel. Magdalene Rinker, wife of George Rinker of Indiana. My brother: George Cauffman.
Exor: Andrew Cauffman (of Andrew, dec'd.)
Wit: George Shrum and William Philips
Dated: 13 July 1833   Proved: 12 Aug. 1833

Will Book P - page 411

ANDREW CAUFFMAN, SENIOR, Shenandoah County. Wife: Rosannah Cauffman. Son: Andrew Cauffman - plantation whereon I now live. Son: George Cauffman - the plantation whereon he now lives. Daus: Magdalene, wife of George Rinker (of Indiana); Christina, wife of George Hottel; Elizabeth, wife of John Coffman.
Exors: William Philips and son, George Cauffman, Jr.
Wit: George Shrum and Adolph Cauffman
Dated: 13 Dec. 1825

CODICIL to Will of ANDREW CAUFFMAN, SENIOR - Mentions: Reconsidered some of the points therein and made alterations.
Wit: same as above
Dated: 22 July 1829   Proved: 12 April 1830

Will Book S - page 166

GEORGE CAUFFMAN, SENIOR, Shenandoah County. Wife: Christina Cauffman. Dau: Mary Bird, wife of John Bird (dec'd.). Granddaughter: Catharine Dinges, dau. of my dau. Rachel (dec'd.). Dau: Rebecca Cauffman - 40 acres of land.
Exor: Son, John Cauffman
Wit: George Shrum and Jacob Dellinger
Dated: 20 July 1833   Proved: 10 March 1834

Will Book W - page 348

MARY CATHARINE CAUFMAN, Shenandoah County, widow of Augustine Caufman of Stoney Creek. Daus: Christina Wetsel; Mary Riffey; Barbary Holler; Marelean Fadely. Sons: Adam Coffman; Mathias Coffman; John Coffman. Grandson: Henry Siver
Exor: Dau., Elizabeth Fadeley
Wit: John Ewing, Margaret Ewing and David Fadely
Dated: 5 Nov. 1840   Proved: 7 Aug. 1843

Will Book L - page 45

JOHN CAULDWELL, Shenandoah County. Wife: Elizabeth.
Children: David; Mark; Sally; Elizabeth; Mary Catherina.
Mentions: negro man, Jerry.
Exor: John Kagey, Senior
Wit: George Pennybacker and Daniel Pennybacker
Dated: 7 Jan. 1818   Proved: 13 April 1818

Will Book B - page 396

JOHN CIRCUS, Hampshire County in Virginia. Mentions:
My friend, Elizabeth Miller, wife to William Miller of
Shenandoah County - all my Estate both real and personal
consisting of Bonds on certain people in the State of
Pennsylvania; also, a chest in possession of the Widow
Barbary Graff living in Strawsburg, Township in Lancaster
County.
Exor: Elizabeth Miller
Wit: William Reynolds, Elizabeth Reynolds and Rebekah
Miller
Dated: 29 Sept. 1787   Proved: 25 Oct. 1787

Will Book N - page 439

THOMAS CLAIG, SENIOR, Shenandoah County. Wife: Elizabeth
Claig. My children: (not named).
Exor: Wife, Elizabeth Claig
Wit: Samuel Gardner, Samuel Hopewell and Jacob Cline
Dated: 30 Jan. 1826   Proved: 7 Aug. 1826

Will Book Q - page 282

LUCINDA CLAYTON, Shenandoah County. Sisters: Mary Grove;
Nancy.
No Exor. named
Wit: Thomas A. Irwin and George Fisher
No date   Proved: 9 May 1831

Will Book M - page 95

WILLIAM CLAYTON, Town of Strasburg, Shenandoah County.
My ten children: Eliza; Lucinda; Nancy; Susannah; Polly;
Hannah; Marinda; Harriet; Julian; Amila.
Exors: Anthony Spengler and David Stickley
Wit: Joseph Spengler, Martin Zea and Philip Spengler, Jr.
Dated: 8 Sept. 1822   Proved: 7 Oct. 1822

Will Book O - page 466

DAVID CLEINDENDST, Shenandoah County. Wife: Polly
Cleindendst - all my real and personal Estate.
Exor: Andrew Hoffman
Wit: Joseph Irwin, Samuel Johnston and Henry Allison
Dated: 16 Oct. 1828   Proved: 10 Nov. 1828

Will Book O - page 71

MICHAEL CLEM, Shenandoah County. Wife: Rebecca Clem.
Son: Jacob Clem - 250 acres of land in agreement between
my son and myself on 11 May 1824 in hands of Joseph
Strickler. Son: John Clem - tract of land in Powell's
Fort containing 160 acres. Son: Daniel Clem - parcel of
land in Powell's Fort (100 acres). Son: Joseph Clem -
one half tract of land which was conveyed by Henry
Sibert to Adam Hoak and from Hoak to me containing 200
acres. Son: Henry Clem. Dau: Elizabeth Nickoles - the
remaining half of above mentioned land. Dau: Catharine
Strickler - 200 acres of land in Powell's Fort and my
negro woman named Fans.
Exor: Son-in-law, David Strickler
Wit: Joseph Strickler, Michael Clem and Jonas Alleshire
Dated: 11 Feb. 1827   Proved: 12 March 1827

Will Book O - page 313

REBECCA CLEM, Shenandoah County, widow and relick of Michael
Clem. Mentions: Elizabeth Clem, wife of my son, Jacob Clem
and Julia Clem, wife of my son, John Clem. Sons: Daniel
Clem and Henry Clem.
Exor: Son, John Clem
Wit: William Almond, William Harris and _____(Ger.)
Dated: 29 Oct. 1827   Proved: 13 May 1828

Will Book A - page 478

JOSEPH CLEVINGER, Shenandoah County. Wife: Mary.
Children: (not named).
Exors: Wife, Mary and brother, Asa Clevinger
Wit: Hugh Kenndy and John Smith
Dated: 28 Jan. 1783　　　　　　Proved: 27 March 1783

Will Book F - page 110

MICHAEL CLIPPLE, SENIOR, Shenandoah County. Dau: Barbare, present husband, Jacob Supinger - tract of land containing 230 acres and another 430 acres. Son: Philip Klippel, if yet living (I do order and direct the due proclamation shall be made in several of the Newspapers of the United States of America for the information whether the said Philip Klippel is yet living). Mentions: grandsons, Michael Supinger and Peter Supinger. Mentions: granddaus., Christina Supinger and Elizabeth Supinger.
Exors: Jonas Crable and John Hahn, Sen.
Wit: Alexander Hite, Jacob Hite and _____(Ger.)
Dated: 24 Dec. 1801

CODICIL To Will of MICHAEL CLIPPLE, SENIOR - Mentions: Grandchildren, Michael Supinger and Elizabeth Supinger. Mentions: Son-in-Law, Jacob Supinger.
Wit: _____(Ger.), John Smith and John Wiscarver
Dated: 12 Oct. 1802　　　　　　Proved: 12 April 1803

Will Book N - page 392

MATHIAS CLIZER, Shenandoah County. Wife: Barbara. Three sons: David; Martin; John Clizer. Dau: (not named).
Exors: Sons, Martin and John Clizer
Wit: Raphael Conn, Reuben Miller and Joseph Evans
Dated: 27 Aug. 1824　　　　　　Proved: 13 March 1826

Will Book I - page 208

DANIEL CLOUD, Shenandoah County. Wife: Elizabeth Cloud.
Sons: Mordecai and Daniel - 1,300 acres I hold by patent
in State of Ohio. Son: Isaac - tract whereon I now live
including what I purchased of my brother, William Cloud
and John Lehew. Dau: Sally - one quarter of Section of
land purchased in State of Ohio of Gardner. Dau: Rebekah
Hall. Granddaughter: Mary Booker (her mother Nancy Hendren).
Mentions: William Ramey, son of Aaron Ramey.
Exors: Wife, Elizabeth Cloud, Samuel Richardson, Thomas
Buck, Sen. and Thomas Buck, Jr.
Wit: Reuben Moore, Spencer Lehew and Isaac Miller
Dated: 17 Feb. 1813   Proved: 10 April 1815

Will Book B - page 471

HENRY CLOUD, Shenandoah County. Sons: Mordecai Cloud;
Daniel Cloud; William Cloud. Daus: Letice; Elizabeth;
Hanah; Nancy; Mary; Margaret; Winefret.
Exors: Sons, William Cloud and Daniel Cloud
Wit: Spencer Lehew, John Lehew and James Cloud
Dated: 6 Aug. 1787   Proved: 25 Sept. 1788

Will Book Y - page 407

GEORGE CLOWER, Shenandoah County. Brother: Henry Clower -
all my real and personal property.
No Exor. named
Wit: David Rodeffer and John Keffer
Dated: 27 Sept. 1848   Proved: 8 Jan. 1849

Will Book Z - page 157

JOHN CLOWER, Shenandoah County. Wife: Frances Clower.
My children: Isabella Anderson, wife of Alexander Anderson;
Jacob B. Clower; Joseph H. Clower; Elizabeth Ott, wife of
George Ott; John G. Clower; Catharine Clower; George B.
Clower; Frances Clower; Susan Bowman, wife of Robert Bowman.
Exors: Sons, Jacob B. Clower and Joseph H. Clower
Wit: W. W. Magruder and John H. Rau
Dated: 21 Jan. 1850   Proved: 12 Feb. 1850

Will Book U - page 360

ABRAHAM COCHENOUR, Shenandoah County. Wife: (not named).
My children: (not named).
Exor: Michael Neff
Wit: Joseph Gochenour and Abraham Kagey
Dated: 26 Aug. 1838   Proved: 10 Sept. 1828

Will Book H - page 258

CATHARINE COFFELT, late of Rockbridge County, Virginia, now
of Shenandoah County. Son-in-Law: Abraham Rust, husband of
my dau. Elizabeth - one dollar. Son-in-Law: Mathias Rust,
husband of my dau. Annamaria - 25 cents. Daus: Magdalena,
wife of Henry Nickolas; Catharina, wife of George Brightlaw.
Sons: Jacob; Henry; Augustine.
Exors: Son, Jacob and George Shoemaker
Wit: George Feather, Christopher Hickle and _____(Ger.)
Dated: 19 Feb. 1811   Proved: 12 Aug. 1812

Will Book A - page 177

ELIAS COFFELT, Dunmore County in Virginia. Wife: Mary Barbara
Son: Daniel Coffelt. Eldest dau: Elizabeth. Other children:
(not named).
Exors: Brother, George Coffelt and wife, Mary Barbara
Wit: Jacob Rinker, Jr., Richard Hudson and Isaac Funkhouser
Dated: 10 March 1778   Proved: 20 Aug. 1778

Will Book Y - page 112

ANDREW COFFMAN, Shenandoah County. Wife: Catharine Coffman.
Sons: John Coffman; Joseph Coffman; Samuel Coffman. Daus:
Lucy (Susy) Rodes; Elizabeth Groves; Polly Stoll; Rachael
Wasfield; Catharine Williams; Hannah Fadeley.
Exor: Son, John Coffman
Wit: George Shrum and Aaron Fravel
Dated: May 1845   Proved: 8 June 1847

Will Book F - page 324

MARTIN COFFMAN, Shenandoah County, Farmer. Wife: Maria.
Son: Joseph Coffman - parcel of land commonly called John Taylor's place containing 258 acres. Sons: Isaac and Benjamin Coffman - parcel of land commonly called Beveridge's place containing 222 acres. Son: John Coffman - parcel of land commonly called the white house place. Son: David Coffman - parcel of land commonly called the Hocksbill place. Sons: Martin and Peter Coffman - have received their full portion of Legacy heretofore. Son: Jacob Coffman. Daus: Barbara; Maria; Magdalene; Anna; Christina.
Exor: John Roads
Wit: David Beaver and Abraham Strickler
Dated: 5 Feb. 1805   Proved: 9 April 1805

Will Book C - page 15

MICHAEL COFFMAN, SENIOR, now of Rockingham County, State of Virginia. Seven children, three sons and four daughters of which three daughters now dead (not named)
Exors: Son, David Kauffman and Abraham Brannaman
Wit: three witnesses - signed in German
Dated: 12 Dec. 1788   Proved: 30 April 1789

Will Book H - page 296

MICHAEL COFFMAN, Shenandoah County. Wife: Mary Coffman.
Children: Nancy Coffman; Michael Coffman; John Coffman; Samuel Coffman.
Exors: John Neff and Mary Coffman
Wit: Joseph Evans and Joseph Little
Dated: 16 Oct. 1812   Proved: 9 Nov. 1812

Will Book U - page 495

ROSANAH COFFMAN, Shenandoah County, relick of Andrew Coffman, dec'd. Son: Andrew Coffman. Granddaughters: Catharine Coffman (dau. of my son, Andrew); Rosanah Coffman.
Exor: Son, Andrew Coffman
Wit: George Shrum and Frederick Shrum
Dated: 24 July 1837   Proved: 11 Feb. 1839

Will Book E - page 345

JOHN COILE, County of Shenandoah. Wife: Betty Coile. Sons: John Coile; Jacob Coile; Henry Coile; Peter Coile; Abraham Coile. Daus: Catharine Coile; Elizabeth, wife of Michael Burger; Susannah Coile; Dorothy Coile; Rosina Coile.
Exors: George Dellinger and Peter Overholtzer
Wit: Jacob Rinker, John Godfrey and Jacob Rinker, Jr.
Dated: 19 Dec. 1798   Proved: 14 Jan. 1800

Will Book G - page 382

SAMUEL COLVILLE, Shenandoah County. Wife: Agnes Colville. Sons: James and John Colville - my land containing 350 acres. Mentions: three sons of my late dau. Mary Vance, viz: James; William and John Vance.
Exors: Two sons, James and John Colville
Wit: George Lind, Thomas Newell, James Stephenson
Dated: 28 March 1803   Proved: 11 Dec. 1809

Will Book F - page 54

ADAM COMER, Shenandoah County. Son: Frederick - 50 acres. Son: Philip - land whereon I live. Son: Adam of the State of North Carolina. Daus: (not named).
No Exor. named
Wit: Jacob Blosser, George Gander and D. Laid
Dated: 14 March 1801   Proved: 13 Dec. 1802

Will Book F - page 268

JOHN COMER, SENIOR, Shenandoah County. Wife: Mary Ann. Son: Daniel - 30 acres. Son: Jonas - 30 acres. Son: John - 30 acres. Daus: Catharine Richards; Elizabeth Nail; Mary Wimer; Sarah
Exor: Wife, Mary Ann
Wit: Martin Comer, Henry Comer and Dabny Ford
Dated: 6 Oct. 1804   Proved: 10 Dec. 1804

Will Book N - page 343

JONAS COMER, Shenandoah County. Wife: Sally. Brother: John Comer. Mentions: my mother (not named).
Exor: Daniel Blofer
Wit: Isaac Wright and Samuel Comer
Dated: 8 Nov. 1825   Proved: 12 Dec. 1825

Will Book F - page 15

MICHAEL COMER, Shenandoah County. Son: Michael - plantation whereon I live which I value at three hundred pounds. Sons: Philip; Christopher; John; Augustine; Daniel; Samuel. Daus: Elizabeth; Catharine; Julian.
Exors: Son, Michael and friend, Christian Forrer
Wit: John Mundell, Samuel Forrer and William Marye
Dated: 25 Sept. 1799   Proved: 7 June 1802

Will Book L - page 107

MICHAEL COMER, SENIOR, Shenandoah County. Wife: Elizabeth. Son: Isaac Comer - plantation whereon I now live. Heirs: John Comer; Michael; Jacob; Samuel; Isaac; Susannah; Elizabeth; Magdalin; Catharin; Mary; Barbara; Anna.
Exors: Son, Samuel Comer and friend, Joseph Evans, Esq.
Wit: Thomas Blackford, John N. Kemp and George Jones
Dated: 8 Dec. 1818   Proved: 9 Aug. 1819

Will Book Q - page 56

RUTH CONN, County of Shenandoah, late of Frederick County. Brothers: Raphael Conn and James Conn. Sister: Sarah Duvall. Nephews: James Conn, Jr. and Raphael Conn, Jr. Niece: Mary Conn. Mentions: I liberate my three slaves, John or Jack; Sylva and Esau after the decease of my brother, James Conn.
Exor: Brother, James Conn
Wit: Thomas Brittan and Henry Forrer
Dated: 25 Feb. 1830   Proved: 9 Aug. 1830

Will Book V - page 491

WILLIAM CONNER, Shenandoah County. Granddaughter: Leah Lockmiller. Daus: Polly Brill; Nancy Willis; Betsy Rosebrough; Ruth Hurbaugh; Martha Lockmiller; Levina Boehm. Sons: James Conner; Severn Conner; William Conner; John Conner, Samuel Conner.
Exor: Mounce Byrd
Wit: John Swayne and Samuel Shell
Dated: 12 March 1840   Proved: 12 July 1841

Will Book L - page 1

ZADOCK CONNER, Shanadoa County. Wife: Rosanna.
Exor: Wife, Rosanna
Wit: Moses Allen, John Lockhart and William Lawrance
Dated: 16 June 1797   Proved: 13 Oct. 1817

Will Book R - page 508

JOHN COOK, SENIOR, Shenandoah County. Wife: Barbary Cook. Son: John Cook - lower part of my land including the Sawmill. Dau: Mary Cook - next part including the mansion house and 25 acres. Son: Jacob Cook - upper part of tract adjoining Gabriel Sager. Dau: Magdalin, wife of John Gibler.
Exor: Son, Jacob Cook
Wit: George Shrum and George Wisman, Jr.
Dated: 8 Sept. 1829   Proved: 12 Oct. 1829

Will Book I - page 192

GEORGE WASHINGTON COONS, Shenandoah County. Two sisters: Abigail and Nancy, living in State of Ohio (Highland Co., Liberty Township) - my two lots in town of Hilsborough, Ohio; also, Due Bill in the hands of Mr. Oliver Harris. Brother: Isaac - eighty dollars in gold and silver; one silver watch at the house of Mr. David Kauffman, Shenandoah Co., Virginia; Book on Life of Washington, in hands of Mrs. Elizabeth Windle. Brother: Michael.
Exors: Brother, William R. Coons, David Kauffman and Abrose C. Booton
Wit: Elizabeth Windle, John B. Kauffman, Elizabeth French
Dated: 28 Feb. 1815   Proved: 13 March 1815

Will Book Y - page 508

ELIZABETH COOPER, Shenandoah County. My two children:
William S. and Mary Elizabeth. Mentions: I appoint my
brother, Samuel G. Stephenson, guardian for my son,
William S. and my friend F. Milton Ervine guardian for
my dau. Mary Elizabeth.
Exor: Samuel G. Stephenson
Wit: W. Gatewood, William Stephenson and Nimrod Clayton
Not dated   Proved: 12 June 1849

Will Book M - page 61

GEORGE COOPER, Town of Strasburg, Shenandoah County. Son:
Samuel - house I now live in with two Lotts attached. Son:
Joseph - the house Samuel now lives in purchased at public
sale which Philip Grim formerly owned. Son: Henry - my
house and Lot on the back street which I purchased of Joseph
Stover. Sons: Isaac and John. Dau: Rebecca - two Lotts
which I bought of Christley Stover's Estate. Dau: Mary -
my Lot adjoining property of Jacob Cook, dec'd. Mentions:
son, George's three children (not named).
Exor: Son, Samuel
Wit: William Balthiz, Jacob Reagen and Will M. Bayly
Dated: Jan. 1821   Proved: 13 March 1822

Will Book T - page 528

GEORGE COOPER, Shenandoah County. Dau: Elizabeth C. - all
my real Estate which has been procured with the property
of my wife, the mother of Elizabeth C.
Exor: Jacob Ott
Wit: John F. Haynes and P. Williams, Jr.
Dated: 1 March 1837   Proved: 13 March 1837

Will Book Z - page 26

MARY MAGDALENE COOPER, Shenandoah County. Dau: Elizabeth
Miley, wife of Isaac Miley - all my personal property.
Exor: Isaac Miley
Wit: William Moreland and William Ott
Dated: 6 Oct. 1848   Proved: 10 Sept. 1849

Will Book A - page 431

JACOB COPENHAFER, County of Shanando, town of Strafburg. Being called to the field in the cause of American Liberty to be defended... not knowing what may befall me... that I may never see my dear wife and children anymore ... that I shall never forsake them ... Wife: Susanna. Oldest son: John. Son: George. Young children: (not named).
Exor: Wife, Susanna
Wit: Simon ____ (Ger.), Alex. Michir and Philip Hoffman
Dated: 7 Nov. 1780   Proved: 29 Aug. 1782

Will Book V - page 38

GEORGE COPP, Shenandoah County. Wife: Susannah - my negro woman slave, Rosina. Son: Samuel Copp - the plantation whereon he now lives consisting of three tracts of land; also, about 2 acres now in the occupancy of John Good; also, negro slave, Elias. Son: William Copp - tract of land whereon I now live containing 202 acres; also, negro boy slave, Amos. Other children: Jacob Copp; Andrew Copp; John Copp; Mary Spigle, wife of Michael Spigle.
Exors: Son, Jacob Copp and son-in-law, Michael Spigle
Wit: William Spigle, Samuel Williams and John Hahn, Sen.
Dated: 29 April 1839   Proved: 12 Aug. 1839

Will Book Z - page 235

CATHARINE COVERSTONE, Shenandoah County. Sister: Elizabeth Clem - house and lot I own in Town of Edinburg.
No Exor. named
Wit: George McInturf and Henry Cullers
Dated: 25 Jan. 1850   Proved: 11 Feb. 1850

Will Book R - page 381

JACOB COVERSTONE, Shenandoah County. Wife: Elizabeth Coverstone. Mentions: Wife to rent out for profit the Grist Mill and Sawmill. Dau: Catharine. Rest of my children: (not named).
Exors: Son, Daniel Coverstone and son-in-law, David McInturf
Wit: George Bowman, William Moreland and Polly Clem
Dated: 7 Feb. 1831   Proved: 12 Nov. 1832

Will Book M - page 173

ABRAHAM CRABILL, Shenandoah County. Sister: Rachael Crabill.
Mentions: Six nephews, Emanuel Pitman; David Pitman; Jonathan
Pitman; Abraham Pitman (children of my sister Susannah Pitman,
now dec'd.); Levi Crabill; Obed Crabill (sons of my brother
Jonas Crabill). Mentions: 460 acres of land to be sold.
Exor: Nephew, Abraham Pitman
Wit: P. Williams and Anthony Spengler

CODICIL to Will of ABRAHAM CRABILL - Mentions: Jacob Eberly
and Jeremiah Eberly.
Wit: same as above
Dated: 21 May 1821   Proved: 12 May 1823

Will Book P - page 99

CHRISTIAN CRABILL, Shenandoah County. Wife: Barbara Crabill.
Sons: William Crabill and David Crabill - plantation whereon
I now live. Son: John Crabill. Daus: Rebecca Strickler,
widow of Daniel Strickler; Catharine, wife of Daniel Eberly;
Susannah, wife of Samuel Kerns. Mentions: Joseph and Noah
Roads, children of my dau. Mary (dec'd.).
Exors: Sons, David Crabill, William Crabill and John Crabill
Wit: Christian Hockman and George Hockman
Dated: 20 Feb. 1829   Proved: 11 May 1829

Will Book R - page 378

DAVID CRABILL, SENIOR, Shenandoah County. Wife: Elizabeth -
my slave named Nancy. Son: Abraham Crabill - tract of land
I purchased of Lewis Dougherty, also, tract I purchased of
William Elzey and a small tract of about 6 acres I hold by
patent. Dau: Mary, wife of Jacob Kagey - the plantation
whereon I now live after the death of my said wife. Children
of my dau., Catharine Lambert, now deceased, viz: William
Lambert; Joseph Lambert; Elizabeth Lambert; Mary Catharine
Lambert. Mentions: Isaac Lambert, husband of my dec'd dau.
Catharine.
Exor: Son, Abraham
Wit: Robert Turner, Samuel Williams and P. Williams
Dated: 8 June 1831   Proved: 12 Nov. 1832

Will Book C - page 86

JOHN CRABILL, Shenandoah County. Son: Christian - my plantation whereon I now live. Sons: Abraham; John; Benjamin; David. Dau: Madalene.
Exors: Abraham Hockman and Philip Windle
Wit: John Williams, David Golladay and John Mauk
Dated: 30 Dec. 1788   Proved: 31 Dec. 1789

Will Book O - page 174

JONAS CRABILL, Shenandoah County. Wife: Mary. Son: Obed - land on south side of North River Shenandoah on which my manor house stands (total 255 acres). Son: Levi - the land I purchased of Peter and Joseph Bowman (125 acres), also, 45 acres I purchased of Jacob Sommer, also, 92 acres off of several tracts, also, 7 acres Patented land and 11 acres purchased of Isaac Hoffman, also, part of land purchased of Jonathan Pittman and Jacob Supinger. Mentions: grandson, Jonas S. (son of my son, Lewis).
Exors: Sons, Levi Crabill and Obed Crabill
Wit: D. Stickley, George Hupp and Joseph Spengler
Dated: 12 Aug. 1825   Proved: 12 Nov. 1827

Will Book V - page 469

MARY CRABILL, Shenandoah County. Grandson: Jonas Crabill. Two sons: Levi and Obed.
Exor: Son, Levi Crabill
Wit: Joseph Spengler, John Spengler and Philip Stickly
Dated: 21 Nov. 1835   Proved: 7 June 1841

Will Book T - page 336

RACHAEL CRABILL, Shenandoah County. Six nephews: David Pitman; Emanuel Pitman; Jonathan Pitman; Abraham Pitman (children of my sister, Susannah Pitman, now dec'd.); Levi Crabill and Obed Crabill, sons of my brother, Jonas Crabill.
Exor: Nephew, Levi Crabill
Wit: Anthony Spengler and Jacob Eberly
Dated: 7 Oct. 1826   Proved: 13 June 1836

Will Book X - page 477

DAVID CRAWFORD, Shenandoah County. My children: (not named). Mentions: Executors to control and manage my Estate for a term of 10 years.
Exors: Mark Bird and son, William Crawford
Wit: W. W. Magruder and William Ott
Dated: 19 Oct. 1845   Proved: 9 Nov. 1846

Will Book G - page 330

ELIZABETH CRISSER, Shenandoah County. Dau: Barbara Hockman, wife of Abraham Hockman, present husband, Jacob Funk. Grandchildren: Catharine Hockman; Elizabeth Hockman; Rebecca Hockman; Sarah Hockman; Lidia Hockman. Son: John Sharrer - one dollar and no more. Mentions: Grandfather of son, Ulrick Longnecker.
Exor: Son-in-law, (not named)
Wit: Alexander Hite and Jacob Stover
Dated: 8 June 1809   Proved: 11 Sept. 1809

Will Book G - page 103

MICHAEL CROUSE, SENIOR, Shenandoah County. Wife: Catharine. Sons: Jacob; Michael; Daniel. Daus: Elizabeth, wife of Christian Click; Susannah, wife of Adam Winegardner. Mentions: I was guardian to Benjamin, Mary and Ann Kauffman. Mentions: Heirs of Joseph Smith. Mentions: 150 acres in Rochingham County for use and benefit of our Church and Church members which is known by the name of Dunkers, to be left in the hands of Martin Carver and John Click, Jr. and Benjamin Bowman. Mentions: 84 acres in Shenandoah County owned jointly with Henry Lindamood.
Exors: Jacob Lantz and John Kagy
Wit: Henry Fry, George Henry Lindamuth and Jacob Fry
Dated: 18 June 1807   Proved: 7 Sept. 1807

Will Book A - page 80

ANN CRUM, Parish of Beckford, County of Dunmore, Colony of Virginia. Son: John Crum. Mentions: Benjamin Strickler.
Wit: Conrad Painter and Frederick Covner
Dated: 12 May 1775   Proved: 23 May 1775

Will Book E - page 58

JOHN CULLERS, County of Shenandoah. Wife: Mary. Children: (not named). Mentions: my father (not named) who at present is living with me.
Exors: Wife, Mary Cullers and son-in-law, Henry Burner
Wit: Peter Peters, Daniel Golladay, Adam Reddenour and Jeremiah McKay
Dated: 16 Sept. 1796   Proved: 13 Dec. 1796

Will Book N - page 264

RUTH CUNNINGHAM, Shenandoah County. Son: John Cunningham - one dollar. Son: William Cunningham - one dollar. Son: Jonathan Cunningham - one dollar. Dau: Mary, wife of Jonathan Hall - all my clothes. Dau: Sarah, wife of John Ruble - one dollar. Dau: Hannah Cunningham - all my Estate. Mentions: Leah Holler, dau. of Augustine Holler.
Exor: Augustine Holler
Wit: George Coffelt and Absalom Rinker
Dated: 15 May 1819   Proved: 9 Aug. 1825

Will Book I - page 469

JOHN DAKE, SENIOR, Shenandoah County. Wife: Catharine. Son: John Dake. Daus: Elizabeth Dake; Magdalena, wife of Peter Haller; Barbara Dake; Eve Dake.
Exor: George Lantz
Wit: Absalom Rinker and Jacob Coffeld
Dated: 2 Jan. 1815   Proved: 12 Sept. 1815

Will Book A - page 98

ADAM DARTING, Beckford Parish, County of Dunmore, Colony of Virginia. Sons: Philip Gerrard Darting; John Philip Darting; Adam Darting. Dau: Ann Apple Mavis.
Exors: Henry Fravill and son, Adam Darting
Wit: Jacob Rapeholtz, Lawrence Wolfe and William Webb
Dated: 16 May 1776   Proved: 22 May 1776

Will Book A - page 96

PHILIP GARRET DARTING, Parish of Beckford, County of Dunmore. Colony of Virginia. Wife: Barbra. Six children: Adam; Caty; Hannah; Philip; Mary; Petter. Mentions: brother, Adam Darting; brother-in-law, George Grinsler; brother, John Philip Darting. Mentions: My Will and Order that my sons be learned to read and write and my daus. to read. Mentions: my brother John Philip Darting to take my son, Adam, and learn him a trade.
Exors: Brother, Adam Darting and George Mavis
Wit: Joseph Pugh; Jacob Holeman and Adam Darting
Dated: 25 Oct. 1773   Proved: 27 May 1776

Will Book E - page 101

HENRY DAVID, County of Shenandoah, yeoman. Wife: Magdalena. Son: Jacob - all my land and plantation. Sons: Henry; Michael; William. Daus: Mary; Maglina; Margareta; Susanna.
Exors: Wife, Magdalena and son, Jacob
Wit: Samuel Smith, Philip Schirtzer and D. Downey
Dated: 23 Feb. 1790   Proved: 9 April 1794

Will Book F - page 339

STEPHEN DEDEWICK, Shenandoah County. My three daus: Becky; Sarah; Rachael. Son: Jacob Dedewick - all my real Estate containing 240 acres.
Exors: Jacob Dedewick and son-in-law, Henry Snarr
Wit: Alexander Hite, P. Baker and _____(Ger.).
Dated: 16 Nov. 1804   Proved: 10 June 1805

Will Book V - page 8

HENRY DELINGER, Shenandoah County. Wife: Elizabeth Delinger.
Exor: Alexander Anderson
Wit: Elijah Shaver and Daniel Burner
Dated: 4 April 1839   Proved: 13 May 1839

Will Book A - page 403

CHRISTIAN DELLINGER, County of Shenandoah. Wife: Magdalene.
Sons: Christian; George Dellinger; Emanuel. Daus: Magdalene;
Sybilla; Rosina; Dorothy.
Exors: Wife, Magdalene and son, George Dellinger
Wit: Frederick Dellinger, Jacob Rinker, Sen. and Jacob
Rinker, Jr.
Dated: 1 July 1780   Proved: Aug. 1780

Will Book I - page 216

FREDERICK DELLINGER, Shenandoah County. Wife: Margareta.
Mentions: four children of my brother, John Dellinger, dec'd.
viz: Henry Dellinger; Frederick Dellinger; John Dellinger;
Rebecca Dellinger. Mentions: two children bound out to me,
which I have raised, Isaac McCord and Mary McCord (now the
wife of my brother-in-law, Jonathan Fravel). Mentions:
Nephew, Henry Dellinger - that plantation whereon I now
dwell (67 acres).
Exors: Brother-in-law, Jonathan Fravel and nephew, Henry
Dellinger.
Wit: David Jordan, Martin Moily, _____(Ger.) and
Joseph Irwin
Dated: 6 Dec. 1814   Proved: 11 April 1815

Will Book U - page 1

GEORGE DELLINGER, Shenandoah County. Son: George
Dellinger - all my real Estate. Son: Benjamin. Daus:
Magdalen; Margaret; Elizabeth; Catharine. Mentions:
children of my dau. Doratha. Grandsons: George Pennewit
and Christian Dellinger (of my son, George).
Exor: Son, George Dellinger
Wit: Moses Walton and Reuben Walton
Dated: 28 July 1828   Proved: 10 April 1835

Will Book N - page 489

MARGARET DELLINGER, Shenandoah County. Nephew: Frederick Dellinger - my negro boy, Levi. My father: Henry Fravel (dec'd). Mentions: Henry Dellinger; Rebecca Dellinger; John Dellinger. Mentions: Polly Fravel, wife of my brother, Jonathan Fravel.
Exors: Brother, Jonathan Fravel and nephew, Henry Dellinger
Wit: P. Williams and James C. Williams
Dated: 18 Nov. 1823   Proved: 9 Oct. 1826

Will Book X - page 175

MARTIN DELLINGER, Shenandoah County. Wife: (not named) - the land I now live on. Daus: Elizabeth; Leah, wife of Isaac Fadely. Sons: Absalom Dellinger and Joshua Dellinger. Mentions: land I own in Hardy Co. and the piece of land I bought from Jacob and John Lantz - to be sold.
Exor: Jacob Lantz
Wit: John Lantz, Jacob Fravel and Philip Fry
Dated: 16 Dec. 1844   Proved: 12 May 1845

Will Book A - page 65

ABRAHAM DENTON, SENIOR, County of Dunmore, Colony of Virginia. Wife: Mary Denton. Son: Abraham Denton. Daus: Phebe Plumly and Martha Moore.
Exors: Wife, Mary Denton and William Reno
Wit: Mary Little, Dorothy Clock, Elizabeth Smith and Mary Careason
Dated: 12 Aug. 1774   Proved: 27 Sept. 1774

Will Book B - page 332

JOHN DENTON, Shenandoah County. Wife: Margaret Denton. Sons: George; Jacob; Benjamin. Daus: Phebe; Christina; Mary; Martha; Margaret; Secvilla.
Exor: Elijah Odell
Wit: Targus Cron, Thomas Smelling and Tane Cron
Dated: 13 Sept. 1777

CODICIL to Will of JOHN DENTON - Mentions: Son, Isaac.
Dated: 9 Sept. 1780   Proved: 26 April 1787

Will Book B - page 310

SIMON DERK, Shenandoah County. Wife: Catharine. Sons: John Derk (eldest); Jacob Derk, George Derk. Dau: Mary Elizabeth now living in Pennsylvania and being blind. Mentions: two grandsons, sons of Jacob Derk, viz: Simon Derk and Tobino Derk.
Exors: John Felmoyers and Jacob Roush
Wit: Jacob Rinker, Jr., Simon Berger and John Coile
Dated: 11 April 1785   Proved: 22 Feb. 1787

Will Book D - page 229

GEORGE DEW, Shenandoah County. Mentions: George Gautzer - everything what I have at present. Mentions: Widow Stickler - that bag with all things therein now in possession of her own house; her son, Jacob Stickler - that bag with everything therein which is in possession of Daniel Grant at Stover Town and such property as I have at the house of John Haas.
No Exor. named
Wit: Philip Sonner and Andrew Hoffman
Dated: 26 Dec. 1792   Proved: 11 June 1783

Translated from the German original to English by David Jordan.

Will Book F - page 86

ADAM DICKER, Shenandoah County. My six children: Jacob Dicker; David Dicker; John Dicker; Adam Dicker (only 4 named).
Exors: Christian Alshite and John Dicker
Wit: _____(Ger.); Abraham Spittler and Abraham Spittler,
Dated: 7 March 1803   Proved: 12 April 1803

Will Book B - page 107

JOHN DODSON, of Shenandoah in Commonwealth of Virginia. Wife: Elizabeth. Son: Peter Dodson - all my land and plantation whereon I now live containing 400 acres. Son: Charles Dodson. Daus: Elizabeth, married to John Coile; Ann, married to Michael Callender.
Exor: Son, Peter Dodson
Wit: Jacob Rinker, Jr., George Rinker and Henry Rinker
Dated: 16 Nov. 1779   Proved: 26 Aug. 1784

Will Book E - page 393

PETER DODSON, County of Shenandoah. Wife: Mary. Sons:
Joseph; Jacob; William (dec'd.). Daus: Ruth; Dorcas; Martha;
Caster, which is married to Henry Kile. Mentions: land
which is in dispute with me and David Fately.
Exors: Thomas Ryan and Christly Dellinger
Wit: Jacob Rinker, Jr. and Joseph Fultz
Dated: 4 Sept. 1800   Proved: 13 Oct. 1800

Will Book N - page 439

ELIZABETH DOLL, Shenandoah County. Brothers and Sisters:
Nicholas Doll (dec'd.); Frederick Doll; Catharine Cibler,
wife of William Cibler; Mary Roots, wife of Michael Roots;
Barbara Hottel, wife of Joseph Hottel (dec'd.). Mentions:
Children of Jacob Copp and Eve his wife, viz: Reuben Copp;
Ann Copp; Susan Copp; Eve Copp; Elizabeth Copp; Jacob Copp.
Exor: My friend, Jacob Copp
Wit: Phineas Orndorff, George Fetzer and George Keller
Dated: 4 April 1825   Proved: 7 Aug. 1826

Will Book A - page 173

CHRISTOPHER DOSH, SENIOR, Strasburg, Dunmore County and
Colony of Virginia. Wife: Elizabeth. Son: Christopher.
Daus: Regina; Elizabeth; Barbara; Mary; Catharine; Magdalene.
Exor: Son-in-law, George Cooper
Wit: Hieronomus Baker, Alexander Hite and Jonas Foltz
Dated: 11 Dec. 1775   Proved: 28 Aug. 1778

Will Book G - page 209

CHRISTOPHER DOSH, Town of Strasburg, Shenandoah County.
Wife: Margaret Dosh. Sons: John; George; William, Wife's
father: Hieronomus Baker (dec'd.).
Exors: Son, John Dosh and friend, Henry Hawn
Wit: George Lind, George Smith and Peter Hoffman
Dated: 13 May 1808   Proved: 13 June 1808

Will Book H - page 508

GERVAS DOUGHERTY, Shenandoah County. Children: William Dougherty; Sarah Duskins; Phebe Peral; John Dougherty; Elijah Dougherty; Abraham Dougherty; Mary Dougherty; Elizabeth Anderson.
Exors: David Wintorf and Frederick Wintorf
Wit: Elizabeth Yager, Abraham Lambert, Sarah Lambert and Simeon Yager
Dated: 11 July 1812   Proved: 7 March 1814

Will Book R - page 382

DARBY DOWNEY, Shenandoah County. Wife: Lythia. Son: Eleazer Downey - the whole of the plantation whereon I now live. Sons: John Downey; Darby Downey; William Downey. Daus: Elizabeth McClune; Susannah Miller. Mentions: Children of my dau. Sarah Painter and children of my dau. Mary McIlree.
Exor: Son, Eleazer Downey
Wit: Charles Lovell, Philip Huffman and P. Williams
Dated: 12 Feb. 1820   Proved: 12 Nov. 1832

Will Book A - page 292

WILLIAM DOWNEY, County of Shannando. Sister: Mary James. Brothers: John Downey and Darby Downey.
Exor: Brother, Darby Downey
Wit: Mitchel Reed, Daniel Mathany and John Dundor
Dated: 13 Sept. 1780   Proved: 30 Nov. 1780

Will Book P - page 226

NICHOLAS DRUCK (TRUCK), Shenandoah County. Wife: Susanna. Eight children: George Druck; John Druck; Henry Druck; Mary, wife of Jacob Bauckman; Philip Druck; Nicholas Druck; Rebecca, wife of Samuel Schmucker; Catharine, wife of Henry Tisinger. Mentions: Agreement with son, George Druck over certain lands sold to him, agreement in hands of James Sterrett.
Exor: Absalom Rinker
Wit: James A. Arthur, Thomas White and William Henson
Dated: 19 Sept. 1829   Proved: 12 Oct. 1829

Will Book G - page 278

WILLIAM HEDGEMAN DULANEY, Town of Woodstock, Shenandoah
County. Wife: Elizabeth P. Dulaney. Son: Fortunatus F.
Dulaney - all my medicines, my medical, surgical and school-
books, my surgical instruments and apparatus belonging to
my shop. Son: William - to be taught the anatomy of the
human frame, materia, medica, surgery, midwifery sufficently
to make him qualified to commence the practice of Physic.
Son: Elkanah - be educated as a lawyer, my law books. Son:
Charles - to be taught the laws of this State, to obtain a
Licence to practice law. Dau: Peggy - all my books of
novels and Romance, her mother's rings and jewels. Mentions:
Father-in-Law, William Shackelford. Mentions: tract of
land I bought of David Golladay commonly called Roddy's
Place; tract of land at Powell's Fort - to be sold.
Exor: Nephew, William Abbott
Wit: H. F. Greenwood, John Effinger and J. E. Hinger
Dated: 30 Nov. 1808   Proved: 9 Jan. 1809

Will Book V - page 292

ABRAHAM DULL, Shenandoah County. Mentions: Charles C.
Maurer hereby appointed trustee for my brother, Philip
Dull's family.
Exor: Charles C. Maurer
Wit: James Fetzer and George Shaver
Dated: 25 Aug. 1840   Proved: 12 Oct. 1840

Will Book Y - page 67

ISAAC DUNIVAN, Shenandoah County. Mentions: John Sager.
Son: Thomas Dunivan. Granddaughter: Mary Ann Dunivan
(dau. of my son, Thomas). Daus: Mary Ann and Elizabeth
Dunivan.
Exor: John Sager
Wit: Elias Fisher, William Gochenour and Joseph Rhodes
Dated: 26 March 1847   Proved: 12 April 1847

Will Book A - page 131

ISAAC DURST, Dunmore County and Colony of Virginia.
Brothers: Samuel; Benjamin; Joseph; Paul; Abram. Sister:
Mary. Mentions: Mother (not named) and Charles Taylor.
Exors: Mounce Bird and Jacob Holeman
Wit: Leonard Tutweiler, Daniel Branaman and Paulser Hoop
Dated: 16 March 1776   Proved: 26 Aug. 1777

Will Book A - page 111   NUNCUPATIVE WILL

MARY DURST, County of Dunmore, widow of Abraham Durst.
Son: Samuel Durst - being of the age of 21. Son: Abraham
Durst. Dau: Mary Durst.
Exor: Mary Durst.

This was a deathbed Will given by Samuel Durst, Leonard
Tutweiler and Henry Grock - sworn before John North.
Wit: Mary Durst, Henry Kagy and Edwin Young
Dated: 25 March 1777   Proved: 25 March 1777

Will Book Y - page 304

JAMES DYSERT, Shenandoah County. Wife: Mary. Son:
Abraham Able. Daus: Leah, wife of Philip Fry; Catharine.
Exors: Son, Abraham Able Dysert and Jacob Lantz
Wit: Catharine Grandstaff and William Kribs
Dated: 13 April 1848   Proved: 8 May 1848

Will Book T - page 370

DANIEL EBERLY, Town of Strasburg, Shenandoah County. Wife:
(not named). Son: Joseph - the brick house and other
buildings on lot 46 in Strasburg. Dau: Susan - house and
lots lying in Strasburg that I inherited from my Aunt,
Elizabeth Eberly. Sons: Isaac and Jacob - lots in town of
Strasburg. Dau: Mary - part of the mine bank adjoining
lands of George Eberly and George Hupp, also, land of
Peter Hoffman, dec'd. that I inherited from my father.
Youngest child: Sarah - lot of land containing 7 acres
purchased from John Shull and Maria, his wife.
Exor: William Baker
Wit: John Hamilton, George Eberly and Jacob Eberly
Dated: 1 May 1836   Proved: 8 Aug. 1836

Will Book E - page 303

JEREMIAH EBERLY, County of Shenandoah. Wife: (not named).
Son: John Jacob - to have two lots behind Alexander Hite
with the little house on it. Son: Jeremiah. Daus:
Elizabeth and Christina.
Exors: Henry Piper and George Cooper (shoe-maker)
Wit: Simon Harr and George Miller
Dated: 26 Jan. 1786

CODICIL to Will of JEREMIAH EBERLY - Mentions: wife and
dau., Elizabeth.
Wit: John Snider, Christopher Dosh and Henry Hawn
Dated: 28 Sept. 1792   Proved: 10 Sept. 1799

A true copy proven per me, Alexander Hite, a translation
from the original German.

Will Book M - page 430

JEREMIAH EBERLY, Town of Strasburg, Shenandoah County.
Wife: Catharine. Sons: Daniel; George; Jacob. Daus:
Catharine; Christina; Elizabeth. Mentions: deceased
brother (not named) who resided in Kentucky.
Exors: Son, Daniel Eberly and Anthony Spengler
Wit: Will M. Bayley, Samuel Kern, Sen., Joseph Spengler
and Jonathan Pitman
Dated: 23 Aug. 1824   Proved: 13 Sept. 1824

Will Book T - page 89

MARY ELIZABETH EBERLY, of Strasburg, Shenandoah County.
Mentions: Daniel Eberly - lots in Town of Strasburg where
I now live, adjoining Rosina Muck and John Dosh. Mentions:
George Eberly (brother of Daniel Eberly). Mentions:
Jacob Eberly - half of out lot adjoining Adam Keister.
Exors: Daniel Eberly and Jacob Eberly
Wit: Joseph Wattson and Joseph Zea
Dated: 4 Jan. 1833   Proved: 12 Oct. 1835

Will Book I - page 170

SARAH EDMONDS, Shenandoah County. Dau: Nancy Halley.
Grandson: Elias Edmonds.
Exor: John Halley
Wit: William Wroe, Robert H. Foster, Maximillian Robertson,
and Joseph Brown.
Dated: 4 Feb. 1814   Proved: 9 Jan. 1815

Will and Accts. (1809-1863) - page 192

JOHN IGNATIOUS EFFINGER, SENIOR, Shenandoah County.
Wife: Barbara. Sons: Michael; William; John; Peter.
Daus: Catharine, wife of Jacob Jacobs; Lucy, wife of
John Windle; Elizabeth Thompson; Rebecca Fletcher, wife
of John Fletcher; Mary, wife of Samuel Bender; Barbara,
wife of Michael Bare. Mentions: grandchildren, the heirs
of my son, Samuel Effinger (now dec'd.). Mentions:
slave, Bob.
Exor: Son, Michael Effinger
Wit: P. Williams, Christian Miller and Charles Fisher
Dated: 23 March 1837   Proved: 4 Sept. 1839

Will Book A - page 409

RACHAEL EGAN, Parish of Beckford, County of Shanndoah and
Colony of Virginia. Mentions: Ruth Whitson - my kinswoman;
Joseph Barnes; Charles Barnes. Ruth Whitson's children:
Catharine Whitson and Rachael Whitson. Mentions: Rachael
Whitson to have my Negro woman, Susy, for 10 years, after
experation of term the said negro woman to be set free.
Mentions: my slave, Negro Duk, to be set free. Mentions:
John Barnes - 400 acres of land lying on the Caterbar River
in South Carolina.
Exors: Henry Nelson, Jr. and Charles Barnes
Wit: John Hall, Moun Moody and John Longeare
Dated: 18 Nov. 1780   Proved: 30 Nov. 1780

Will Book R - page 229

JACOB EMSWILLER, Shenandoah County. Wife: Catharine.
Son: Henry - all my farm whereon I now live. Son: John -
all my lands in the County of Rockingham, the farm whereon
he now lives, with two other small tracts. Son: George -
the farm whereon he now lives on Stony Creek. Son: Jacob -
all that farm whereon he now lives. Dau: Christnah, wife
of John Evey - the farm whereon she now lives. Daus:
Elizabeth, wife of John Rinehart; Magdaline, wife of
Martin Foltz; Susanna, wife of Michael Tusinger; Mary
Foland, wife of Henry Foland; Catharine, wife of Philip
Painter; Barbara, wife of Christian Heatwald; Eve, wife
of Abraham Lantz. Grandsons: Philip Emswiller (son of
my son, John) and John Foland. Mentions: Children of my
dau: Magdaline, wife of Martin Foltz; children of my dau.
Susanna, wife of Michael Tusinger (except Isaac and
Magdalien - children of her first husband).
Exor: Son, Henry
Wit: Moses Walton and Jacob Lantz
Dated: 5 Nov. 1831

CODICIL to Will of JACOB EMSWILLER - Mentions: Revoke the
clause for dau. Magdalene, wife of Martin Foltz; rovoke
clause for dau. Barbara, wife of Christian Heatwald; change
amount of legacies to be paid.
Wit: P. Williams and Joseph Ludwig
Dated: 14 Jan. 1832   Proved: 7 May 1832

Will Book F - page 69

ELIZABETH ERISMAN, Shenandoah County, widow and relick of
Jacob Erisman, dec'd. Sons: Samuel and Christian Fover.
Mentions: three children of my son, Henry, viz: Samuel;
Mary and Elizabeth. Mentions: children of my son, Daniel.
Exors: Sons, Christian Fover and Samuel Fover
Wit: William Marye, William Abbott and _____ (Ger.)
Dated: 18 Oct. 1802   Proved: 7 March 1803

Will Book W - page 117

GEORGE ERWIN, Shenandoah County. Son-in-Law: Samuel
Frye - all my lands. Sons: Philip; George; John; Joseph.
Daus: Christina; Elizabeth; Barbara; Eve; Magdaline.
Mentions: Elizabeth Frye (dau. of Samuel Frye) and grandson: George Krouce (son of Joseph Krouce).
Exors: Jacob Rinker and Jonathan Miller
Wit: Jacob Noel and Jacob Noel, Jr.
Dated: 9 June 1841   Proved: 9 May 1842

Will Book K - page 64

PETER ESHELMAN, Shenandoah County. Wife: Katharine Eshelman.
Sons: Adam Eshelman (eldest); Tobias (youngest); Samuel.
Eight daus: Elizabeth Eshelman; Mary Bond; Katharine Eshelman
Sarah Eshelman; Barbara Eshelman; Magdalene Eshelman; Rebecca
Eshelman and Anna Eshelman. Mentions: 67 acres of land that
I bought of John Smith.
Exors: John Hamman and son, Adam Eshelman
Wit: _____(Ger.), Anthony Funkhouser and Joseph Walton
Dated: 8 Dec. 1815   Proved: 9 April 1816

Will Book E - page 283

ELIJAH EVANS, Powell's Fort, County of Shenandoah. Wife:
Susanna. Sons: David; James; Samuel. Daus: Susanna; Mary;
Margot. Dau: Cloeve - one dollar for her disobedience.
No Exor. named
Wit: Hezekiah Evans, Andrew Cabey and John Dederick
Dated: 25 Feb. 1799   Proved: 11 June 1799

Will Book K - page 25

JEREMIAH EVANS, Shenandoah County. Wife: Mary Ann Evans.
Sons: Elijah Evans and Jesse Evans - land whereon I now
live to be equally divided between them. Sons: Jeremiah
Evans; Hezekiah; William. Daus: Mary Ann; Betsy.
Exor: David Gore
Wit: J. Gatewood, Michael Klem and Thomas Dickeman
Dated: 27 Feb. 1816   Proved: 11 March 1816

Will Book V - page 172

DAVID FADELY, Shenandoah County. Wife: Elizabeth Fadely - all the part of land on which I live to include my dwelling house to Jacob Hollar's land. Son: Augustine - the above land after my wife's decease. Son: Kenas Fadely - the Saw Mill and part of land adjoining it. Two sons: William Henry and Lorenzo - the balance of the home tract. Son: David - my house and one acre of land lying on Stony Creek. Son: Jackson Fadely - all my tract of land lying on other side of Stony Creek adjoining John Coffman. Son: Eli Fadely - tract of pine land adjoining Jacob Lantz and James Disert. Three daus: Elizabeth Ann; Hetty; Mary Ann.
Exors: Son, Jackson Fadely and Jacob Lantz
Wit: John E. Erwin and George Coffelt
Dated: 11 Dec. 1839   Proved: 9 March 1840

Will Book F - page 255

FREDERICK FANSLER, Shenandoah County. Wife: Barbara Fansler - whole of my plantation. Children: (not named).
Exor: John Shoemaker
Wit: Henry Hetzele, Jacob Ruby and Jacob Lantz
Dated: 14 Sept. 1804   Proved: 8 Oct. 1804

MARGARET FANSLER, Shenandoah County, widow. Son: Peter Fansler - all of my Estate both real and personal. Mentions: other four sons and four daus. (not named).
Exor: Son, Peter Fansler
Wit: William Kirlin, David Kirlin and Philip Bower
Dated: March 1819   Proved: 13 Sept. 1824

Will Book S - page 322

NICHOLAS FARTICK, Shenandoah County. Son: Andrew Fartick - all my plantation and lands whereon I now live. Son: Jacob Fartick. Daus: Christenah, wife of Jacob Waggonner; Elizabeth wife of Peter Bushong. Mentions: Nanna Minick (dau of Mathias Minick).
Exor: Son, Andrew Fartick
Wit: George Moore and Reuben Moore
Dated: 9 Oct. 1829   Proved: 13 Oct. 1834

Will Book U - page 281

JACOB FAUBER, Shenandoah County. Mentions: my son, Peter Fauber and dau. Elizabeth Fauber - my real Estate consisting of 104 acres of land, but if either should marry, land to be sold. If both should marry, land to be sold. Sons: Jacob Fauber; John Fauber; Christian Fauber; Joseph Fauber. Dau: Mary Good, widow of Samuel Good, dec'd. Three grandchildren: Jacob Reedy; John Reedy and Abraham Reedy, children of my dec'd. dau., Magdalene Reedy.
Exor: Son, Christian Fauber
Wit: Benjamin Kronk and Peter Hockman
Dated: 28 Aug. 1830

CODICIL to Will of JACOB FAUBER - Mentions: Son, Joseph Fauber, son-in-law, John Reedy (dec'd) and grandchildren.
Wit: Peter Hockman and Jacob Hahn
Dated: 16 March 1835   Proved: 12 March 1838

Will Book V - page 238

PETER FAUBER, Shenandoah County. Sister: Elizabeth Fauber. Mentions: Abraham Fauber (son of Christian).
No Exor. named
Wit: Abraham Rosenberger and John G. Schmitt
Dated: 21 Jan. 1840   Proved: 8 June 1840

Will Book G - page 412

GEORGE FECKLEY, SENIOR, Shenandoah County. Wife: Anna
Feckley. Son: George Feckley, Jun. - plantation I now
live on (100 acres). Daus: Anna, wife of Mark Miller;
Barbara, wife of Mathias Smootz; Frainey, wife of George
Keller.
Exor: Jacob Rinker, Sr.
Wit: Samuel R. Bader, Frederick Boferman and _____(Ger.)
Dated: 8 April 1809   Proved: 9 Jan. 1810

Will Book E - page 111

JOHN FELLSMIRE (FELSMOYER), Shenandoah County. Wife:
Susannah. Five sons: John Fellsmire and Abraham Fellsmire
(three not named). Daus: Elizabeth; Susannah Lutz;
Rosina Rynhart; Modelena; Catharina. Mentions: three surveys
of land lying in the County of Rockingham
Exors: Michael Sigler, Adam Holker and Adam Werterberger
Dated: 20 June 1797

CODICIL to Will of JOHN FELLSMIRE -
Wit: Michael Sigler and Abraham Ruth
Dated: 28 June 1797   Proved: 12 Sept. 1797

Will Book G - page 233

DIDRICK FERNSLER, Shenandoah County. Wife: Elisa Margaret.
My children: Henry Fernsler (oldest son); Frans and Catharine
Gour; Elizabeth Werdenberger; John and Christina Peters;
Peter Fernsler; Barbara Roush; Frederick and William Fernsler.
Exors: Son, Peter Fernsler and Michael Crous
Wit: Jacob Hamman, George Nees and Jacob Hamman, Jun.
Dated: 11 March 1806   Proved: 12 Sept. 1808

Will Book F - page 202

SABASTIAN FESELL, Shenandoah County. Nephew: John Fesell
Exor: Nephew, John Fesell
Wit: _____(Ger.) and John Hammon
Dated: 9 March 1802   Proved: 13 Feb. 1804

Will Book X - page 339

GEORGE FETZER, Shenandoah County. Wife: Magdalene.
Sons: David; George; John; William; Samuel. Son: David -
my real Estate possessed by him on the Smootz farm. Daus:
Eliza; Mary; Lydia; Susannah; Catharine. Mentions: debt
to John Haun secured by Deed of trust to be paid by sale
of 30 acres of woodland of the tract I purchased from
Abraham Smootz.
Exor: Samuel C. Williams
Wit: Joseph Irwin, Henry Gochenour and Samuel Windle
Dated: 14 Oct. 1845   Proved: 10 Feb. 1846

Will Book W - page 311

SAMUEL FETZER, Shenandoah County. Wife: Mary Ann Fetzer -
the house and lot now occupied by me. Mentions: lot in
town of Woodstock which is my shop and the house now
occupied by Peter Zimmerman - to be sold.
Exor: George Rye
Wit: Joseph Fravel and Henry Renner
Dated: 27 May 1843   Proved: 12 June 1843

Will Book P - page 105

JAMES FINLEY, SENIOR, Shenandoah County. My nephew:
Jacob Orndorff.
Exor: Nephew, Jacob Orndorff
Wit: Thomas Sanders, Henry Ricard and James Conner
Dated: 25 Nov. 1828   Proved: 11 May 1829

Will Book I - page 64

GEORGE FISHER, SENIOR, Shenandoah County. Wife: Barbara
Fisher. Sons: George Fisher; Adam Fisher; David Fisher;
Jacob Fisher; John Fisher; William Fisher; Martin Fisher;
Samuel Fisher. Daus: Rebecca, wife of John White; Sarah
Fisher; Elizabeth, wife of John Kohenour; Catharine, wife
of Mathias Stover; Susannah, wife of John Johnson; Rachael
Fisher; Anna Fisher; Christina Fisher. Mentions: Estate
I purchased of John Mauck and Christina, his wife (late
Christina Painter) - shall be sold.
Exors: Son, Jacob Fisher and son-in-law, John Kohenour
Wit: Joseph Arthur, William P. Leeper and Adam Rodhaver
Dated: 13 April 1814   Proved: 9 May 1814

Will Book U - page 113

JACOB FISHER, SENIOR, Shenandoah County. Wife: Anna Fisher.
Granddaughter: Anna Maria Fisher (who lives with me). Grandson: Jacob Fisher (who lives with me).
Exor: Jabob Crabill
Wit: John Thornberry, John Rhode, Ferdinand Schmucker and Jacob Cook.
Dated: 25 May 1837   Proved: 10 July 1837

Will Book T - page 273

REUBEN FITZER, Shenandoah County. Wife: Mary. Dau: Elizabeth Payton - the whole of my Estate. Brother: Samuel Fetzer.
Exors: Brother, Samuel Fetzer and brother-in-law, George Rye
Dated: 19 Feb. 1836   Proved: 11 April 1836

Will Book F - page 50

JACOB FOGELSONG, Shenandoah County. Wife: Catharine.
Mentions: Lot in town of Stephenburg that I had from my father's Estate. Mentions: Brothers and sisters (not named).
Exor: Philip Windle
Wit: Jacob Bushong, Casper Hemp and David Windle
Dated: 1 Aug. 1802   Proved: 11 Oct. 1802

Will Book Y - page 335

GEORGE FOLTZ, Shenandoah County. Son: Daniel Foltz - 124 acres of land conveyed to me by Joseph Foltz. Son: John Foltz - 440 acres of land, being the home plantation. Dau: Louise, wife of Philip Lindamude - 318 acres of land being same my son-in-law now resides. Son: Bolthis Foltz - 320 acres of land in Fairfield County, Ohio. Son: George Foltz. Daus: Leah, wife of Peter Houser; Elizabeth, wife of George Coffelt.
Exor: Son, John Foltz
Wit: A. Rinker, Jonathan Miller and John Miller
Dated: 20 April 1839   Proved: 7 Aug. 1848

Will Book A - page 345

JOHN MARTIN FOLTZ, County of Shanando and State of Virginia. Wife: Margarett. Son: Daniel Foltz - 120 acres of land, part of tract of land I now live on, along Peter Haller's line. Son: John Martin Foltz - 120 acres, part of tract joining Nicholas Albert's land. Eldest son: John Foltz - remainder of my tract of land being 144 acres. Son: Fred. Foltz. Daus: Catharine; Rosianna; Elizabeth; Margarett; Christinna; Maryann; Magdalene.
Exors: Wife, Margarett and son-in-law, Christian Hyse
Wit: Jacob Rinker, Jr., Peter Foltz, and _____(Ger.)
Dated: 19 Jan. 1782   Proved: 28 Feb. 1782

Will Book G - page 307

GEORGE FORSTER, Shenandoah County. Wife: Barbara Forster. Children: Catharine Forster; Elizabeth Forster; John Forster.
Exors: Michael Roth and Jacob Gochenour, Sen.
Wit: Samuel R. Bader, M. Hupp and _____(Ger.)
Dated: 17 April 1809   Proved: 8 May 1809

Will Book D - page 6

CATHERINA FOUSH, Shenandoah County. Mentions: My father (not named) - one cow and calf and house and furniture and all my Estate.
Exor: Adam Daker
Wit: Peter Lionberger, John Metz, Paul Dust and Andrew Seiber
Dated: 4 April 1789   Proved: 28 April 1791

Will Book G - page 158

PHILIP FOUST, Shenandoah County. Wife: Margrate. Son: Ludwig Foust - part of my plantation whereon he now lives joining Philip Bender's line and John Bender's line. Mentions: Philip Foust and Jacob Foust (sons of Ludwig Foust).
Exor: Wife, Margrate
Wit: Jacob Lantz, Philip Painter and _____(Ger.)
Dated: 1 Dec. 1807   Proved: 11 Jan. 1808

Will Book V - page 64

ELIZABETH FRAVEL, Shenandoah County.   Son: Joseph Fravel -
all my Estate.
No Exor. named
Wit: Henry Fravel the 4th, Samuel Fetzer and Andrew Bushong
Dated: 12 Sept. 1836   Proved: 9 Sept. 1839

Will Book N - page 330

GEORGE FRAVEL, Shenandoah County.   Wife: Alice Fravel.
My brother: (not named).
Exor: Wife, Alice
Wit: Joseph Irwin, James Allen and Henry Fravel
Dated: 3 Oct. 1825   Proved: 7 Nov. 1825

Will Book O - page 335

JACOB FRAVEL, Shenandoah County.   Four eldest children:
Samuel; Eli; Mary; Elsy.   Younger children: Jacob; William;
Rebecca; Anna.
Exor: Brother, Jonathan Fravel
Wit: John Painter, Isaac Dannor and William Rinehart
Dated: 14 Jan. 1828   Proved: 7 July 1828

Will Book U - page 150

JONATHAN FRAVEL, Shenandoah County.   Son-in-Law: Joseph
Hockman.   Sister: Mary.
Exor: Son-in-law, Joseph Hockman
Wit: Samuel Rinker, Joseph Fravel, Frederick Dellinger
and John Rinker
Dated: 21 Sept. 1837   Proved: 13 Nov. 1837

Will Book V - page 96

MARY FRAVEL, Shenandoah County.   Brother: Jonathan Fravel -
all my Estate.
Wit: Jonathan Fravel
Wit: P. Williams, Robert Turner and John G. Schmitt
Dated: 29 May 1824   Proved: 7 Oct. 1839

Will Book L - page 214

HENRY FRAVELE, SENIOR, Shenandoah County. Son: Jonathan Fravele - the plantation and tract of land whereon I now live (200 acres). Son: George Fravele - a certain plantation and tract of land containing 152 acres. Son: Benjamin Fravele - all lands and Mills I purchased from the widow and heirs of Mathias Wilkin (230 acres). Sons: Henry Fravele and Jacob Fravele. Daus: Elizabeth, wife of John Hoover; Anna Dellinger, widow of John Dellinger (dec'd.); Margaret Dellinger, widow of Frederick Dellinger (dec'd.); Mary Fravele; Rebecca, wife of Jacob Bowman. Mentions: Children of my son, Joseph Frevele (dec'd.); children of my deceased dau. Barbara Wilkin, late the wife of George Wilkin. Mentions grandson, Henry Wilkin (son of dau. Barbara) and granddau., Anna Wilkin. Mentions: granddau., Barbara, wife of John Jordan.
Exors: Sons, Jacob Fravele and Jonathan Fravele
Wit: Jacob Rinker, Jacob Noel, Robert Gaw and Simeon Yager
Dated: 18 Jan. 1819   Proved: 8 May 1820

Will Book M - page 261

HENRY FRY, Shenandoah County. Wife: Christina Fry. Son: John Fry. Mentions: Note on George Lindamood (son of Henry) for the sum of 300 dollars and note on Jacob Fry for the sum of 105 dollars.
Exors: Andrew Lindamood and Jacob Noel
Wit: Jacob Noel, Benjamin Hudson and Samuel Stickley
Dated: 11 Nov. 1822   Proved: 8 Dec. 1823

Will Book S - page 455

JOHN FRY (son of Henry), Shenandoah County. Wife: Philbena - the mansion house, springhouse and barn. Sons: Moses and George - plantation I now live on equally divided. Mentions: 300 acres on Strait Branch to be sold. Other children: Lydia; Dianna; Rebecca; John and Hanson
Exors: Jacob Lutz and son, Moses
Wit: William Fry, Philip Lindamood and John Foltz
Dated: 18 Aug. 1834   Proved: 9 March 1835

Will Book M - page 172

BENJAMIN FRYE, Shenandoah County. Wife: Magdalena.
Dau: Rachael Bond, wife of George Bond - one negro girl
named Betsey. Three sons: Joseph; Benjamin; John. Daus:
Leah and Anna. Mentions: My slaves to be sold.
Exors: Sons, Joseph Frye, Benjamin Frye and John Frye
Wit: Joseph Watson, Joseph Frye, Sen. and Jacob Frye
Dated: 15 March 1823   Proved: 12 May 1823

Will Book X - page 174

JACOB FRYE, Shenandoah County. Dau: Phelpina Frye -
my small house now occupied by Isaac Lindamood. Sons:
John Frye; Henry Frye; Michael Frye; William Frye; Samuel
Frye; Jacob Frye. Daus: Christina, wife of Absalom Frye;
Molly, wife of John Good; Lydia, wife of Samuel Swartz;
Rebecca, wife of Isaac Lindamood.
Exor: John Foltz (of Joshua)
Wit: John Swartz and Reuben Bauserman
Dated: 4 Aug. 1840   Proved: 7 April 1845

Will Book G - page 283

JOHN FRYE, Shenandoah County. Wife: Anna Frye. Son-in-
Law: Jonathan Orndorf, his wife Priscilla Orndorf - 200
acres lying in Frederick and Shenandoah Counties bequeathed
to me by my father, Joseph Frye and another tract of 173
acres bequeathed to me aforesaid. Also, another tract
conveyed to me by Josiah Watson containing 172 acres. Son:
Joseph Frye.
Exors: Moses Russell, Henry Richards and son-in-law,
Jonathan Orndorf
Wit: Robert Brent, Joseph Whyson, Henry Hambleton
Dated: 7 Feb. 1809   Proved: 13 March 1809

Will Book V - page 261

JOHN FRYE, Shenandoah County. Wife: Mary Frye. Sons:
Absalom Frye; Elijah Frye; Samuel Frye; Philip Frye;
Henry Frye; George Frye; John Frye. Dau: Polly Moyer.
Exor: Jacob Noel
Wit: Samuel Stickley, Jacob Noel and Abraham Funkhouser
Dated: 12 Nov. 1825   Proved: 10 Aug. 1840

Will Book Z - page 131

JOHN FRYE, Shenandoah County. Son: John A. Frye - a portion of my real estate and following slaves - Zack, Robert, Polly and her children. Dau: Elizabeth Booten and her children (those by her former and present husband) - the balance of my real estate and the following slaves - Aaron, Abraham, Isaac and Jacob.
Exors: George Grandstaff and son, John A. Frye
Wit: Nathaniel Humston, Christian Comer and Samuel Williams
Dated: 22 April 1848   Proved: 11 Feb. 1850

Will Book A - page 341

JOSEPH FRYE, Shanando County, farmer. Wife: Ann Frye. Son: John Frye - the plantation he now lives upon. Son: Benjamin Frye - home plantation. Sons: Will Frye; Abraham Frye; Jacob Frye. Daus: Mary Cockley; Elizabeth; Rebecca; Ann; Catharine. Mentions: My Will my young sons and daughters shall have schooling, the girls to learn to read and my son, Jacob, to read and cypher.
Exors: Wife, Ann and sons, John and Benjamin Frye
Wit: Robert Jameson, Henry Richards and John Snapp
Dated: 19 Aug. 1781   Proved: 27 Sept. 1781

Will Book L - page 263

JOSEPH FRYE, Shenandoah County. Wife: Sarah - one negro woman named Patty and her child, Charles.
Exor: Henry Kerns, Sen.
Wit: Henry Richards, Lewis Emett and _____(Ger.)
Dated: 25 Oct. 1820

CODICIL to Will of JOSEPH FRYE - Mentions: My Exor. at liberty to sell my plantation for the benefit of my family.
Dated: 10 Nov. 1820   Proved: 15 Nov. 1820

Will Book K - page 423

JOHN FULTZ, Shenandoah County. Brother-in-Law: William Philips - my plantation where on my brother-in-law now lives. Brothers: Martin Fultz; Frederick Fultz; Daniel Fultz. Sisters: Catharine Shireman, wife of Barney Shireman; Mary Kronk, wife of William Kronk; Margaret Naiswander, wife of Jacob Naiswander; Molly Hammon, wife of John Hammon; Rosannah Haisey, wife of Christian Haisey; Elizabeth Rorer, wife of Henry Rorer; Christina Philips, wife of William Philips.
Mentions: John Philips.
Exor: Jacob Sheetz
Wit: George Shrum, William Coffman and Andrew Coffman
Dated: 14 Feb. 1818   Proved: 9 March 1818

Will Book A - page 149

ADAM FUNK, Shanandoah County, Colony of Virginia. Wife: Magdalene Funk. Children: John Funk (eldest son); Adam Funk; Abraham Funk; Barbara; Catharine; Mary; Dorothy; Elizabeth.
Exors: Henry Fravel and William Kelp
Wit: Jacob Funk, John Cook and Henry Hockman
Dated: 10 March 1778   Proved: 30 April 1778

Translated for the German language per ... Jacob Rinker, Jr.

Will Book C - page 115

HENRY FUNK, Shenandoah County, yeoman. Sons: Jacob and Harvey. Daus: Elizabeth; Caty; Barbary. Mentions: Child belonging to my deceased dau. Mary, namely Caty Supinger. Mentions: Jacob's dau., Elizabeth, wife of Frederick Fetzer. Mentions: 1,155 acres of land whoupon I now dwell; tract adjoining the same containing 170 acres purchased of John Johnson; tract of 294 acres near Strawsburg; 5 acres of meadow on out town lot; tract on the Big Spring; tract of 500 acres about two miles and a half from Big Spring. tract of 500 acres on the waters of Olin in Sufrings Valley.
Exor: Son, Jacob
Wit: William Jennings, Jacob Smith, Christopher Hawn, Tomy Miller and John Smith
Dated: 20 Oct. 1789   Proved: 25 Feb. 1790

Will Book U - page 361

ISAAC FUNK, of Strasburg, Shenandoah County. Four children: Judith Funk; Noah Funk; Obed Funk; Flora Funk.
Exors: Daniel Stickley and son, Noah Funk
Wit: Andrew Hoffman, Abner Long, Joseph Wattson and D. Stickley
Dated: 22 Feb. 1838   Proved: 10 Sept. 1838

Will Book E - page 21

ABRAHAM FUNKHOUSER, (son of John, Senior, dec'd.), Shenandoah County. Wife: Magdalene. Sons: Daniel (youngest); Samuel; Abraham. Daus: Barbara; Ann; Magdalene; Mary; Regina.
Exors: Son, Daniel Funkhouser and brother, David Funkhouser
Wit: Jacob Seiver, Jacob Funkhouser and John Brobeck
Dated: 11 April 1796   Proved: 14 June 1796

Will Book E - page 430

BARBARA FUNKHOUSER, widow of Christian Funkhouser, dec'd.,
County of Shenandoah. Three sons: John Six; Isaac Six;
Daniel Funkhouser. Daus: Barbara Funkhouser (youngest);
Elizabeth Six, wife of Adam Poke and Catharine Six, wife
of William Stoner.
Exors: Isaac Six and son-in-law, Adam Poke
Wit: _____(Ger.), George Keller and John Conn
Dated: 22 July 1797   Proved: 8 June 1801

Will Book K - page 406

CHRISTIAN FUNKHOUSER, Shenandoah County. Wife: Catharine
Funkhouser. My ten children: John; Christian; Rachael;
Maria Funkhouser (only 4 named).
Exor: Son, Christian
Wit: Abraham Funkhouser and David Funkhouser
Dated: 20 May 1817   Proved: 9 March 1818

Translation thereof in the English language was proved by
the oath of Samuel R. Bader.

Will Book X - page 363

DANIEL FUNKHOUSER, Shenandoah County. Wife: Catharine
Funkhouser. Two youngest sons: Absalom Funkhouser and
Levi Funkhouser - the plantation whereon I now live in-
cluding the small piece of land which I bought of Adam
Eshelman - to be equally divided between them, also, land
I bought of Thomas Hall. Son: Solomon Funkhouser - land
which I bought of Stephen Hickle in Hampshire Co. Son:
Martin Funkhouser - the tanyard and land I bought of William
Snydor. Sons: Anthony Funkhouser and Abraham Funkhouser.
Son-in-Law: Joseph Switzer and my dau. Anna, his wife -
the plantation whereon they now live (100 acres) which I
bought of Nathaniel Humston. Mentions: my colored woman,
Susan, shall not be sold but have her choise to live with
any of my children.
Exor: Joseph Watson
Wit: John Mourey, Frederick Mourey and Valentine Roads
Dated: 1 Jan. 1834

CODICIL to Will of DANIEL FUNKHOUSER - Mentions: sons,
Absalom and Levi.
Wit: Adam Eshelman and Tobias Eshelman
Dated: 16 Feb. 1836   Proved: 9 March 1846

Will Book V - page 97

DANIEL FUNKHOUSER, Shenandoah County. Chrandchildren: William D. Funkhouser and Mary Funkhouser (children of my son, Jacob Funkhouser, dec'd.) - 165 acres of land I obtained by virtue of a warrent from the land office. Granddau: Eliza Baker, wife of Samuel Baker - 6 acres of said farm on which my son Jacob lived. Son: Isaac Funkhouser - the plantation on which I live (225 acres). Sons-in-Law: Daniel Shambough and Philip Borden.
Exors: Son, Isaac Funkhouser and sons-in-law, Daniel Shambough and Philip Borden
Wit: Joseph Wattson, Martin Boehm and Peter Stickley
Dated: 29 March 1839   Proved: 13 May 1839

Will Book H - page 150

DAVID FUNKHOUSER, Shenandoah County. Wife: Elizabeth. My sisters: Barbara, wife of Godfrey Miller; Mary, wife of John Link. Mentions: brothers and sisters of my said wife, Elizabeth (not named). Mentions: children of my brother, Daniel Funkhouser, dec'd.
Exor: Jacob Rinker
Wit: Andrew Bergman, Jacob Rider and Peter Chrack
Dated: 12 Jan. 1812   Proved: 11 Feb. 1812

Will Book I - page 181

GEORGE FUNKHOUSER, Shenandoah County. Wife: Barbary. Sons: Andrew; Abraham; George; Jacob. Dau: Peggy
Exor: Brother, Abraham Funkhouser
Wit: Moses Walton, Daniel Tufsing and Daniel Funkhouser
Dated: 18 Jan. 1815   Proved: 13 Feb. 1815

Will Book E - page 110

ISAAC FUNKHOUSER, Shenandoah County. Wife: Anna. Sons: Isaac; Daniel; David. Daus: Barbara and Anna.
Exors: Sons, Daniel and David
Wit: Philip Miller, John Kann and Isaac Funkhouser
Dated: 25 May 1797   Proved: 12 Sept. 1797

A true translation by Jacob Rinker

Will Book E - page 482

JACOB FUNKHOUSER, County of Shenandoah. Wife: Dorotha.
Sons: George (oldest); David; Jacob; Abraham; Joel; Daniel;
John. Daus: Mary (eldest) and Dorotha. Mentions: land in
Rockingham County.
Exors: Son, George and Michael Crowes, Sen.
Wit: Francis Neff, James Rinehart and Herbert Winegardner
Dated: 26 Sept. 1801   Proved: 11 Jan. 1802

Will Book F - page 224

JACOB FUNKHOUSER, SENIOR, Shenandoah County. Wife: Franey.
Daus: Elizabeth Funkhouser and Mary Blind, wife of Michael
Blind. Son: Jacob - my plantation whereon I now live containing 316 acres. Son: Daniel Funkhouser.
Exors: Henry Keller and son, Jacob Funkhouser
Wit: Daniel Funkhouser, _____(Ger.) and Christian
Funkhouser
Dated: 13 Jan. 1804   Proved: 11 June 1804

Will Book X - page 428

JACOB FUNKHOUSER, Shenandoah County. Son: John Funkhouser - land whereon he now lives (135 acres). Son: Christian Funkhouser. Son: Abraham - the plantation and land I now live on (300 acres). Dau: Elizabeth.
Exor: Son, Abraham Funkhouser
Wit: Peter Baker, Sen., Christian Baker and Abraham Stover
Dated: 22 May 1846   Proved: 12 Oct. 1846

Will Book G - page 76

JOHN FUNKHOUSER, Shenandoah County. Wife: Barbara. Son:
John Funkhouser - 165 acres. Son: David Funkhouser - 145
acres. Daus: Mary; Elizabeth, wife of David Weaver; Susannah;
Barbara; Christina.
Exor: Son-in-law, David Weaver
Wit: Jacob Rinker, Jacob Seiver and Abraham Funkhouser
Dated: 3 Sept. 1802   Proved: 8 June 1807

Will Book O - page 70

JOHN FUNKHOUSER, (son of John Funkhouser, dec'd.), Shenandoah County. Wife: Dorothe Funkhouser. Son: Henry Funkhouser - my land and plantation, devised to me by my father, John Funkhouser, dec'd., when he comes to be 21 years of age.
Dau: Katharina Funkhouser.
Exors: Henry Hockman, Sen. (son-in-law of Abraham Beydler, dec'd.), William Stoner and my brother, David Funkhouser
Wit: Samuel R. Bader and William Seiver
Dated: 2 Dec. 1825   Proved: 10 July 1826

Will Book M - page 511

KATHARINE FUNKHOUSER, Shenandoah County. Daus: Rachael Boehm; Katharine Dunavan; Anna Boehm; Sarah Funkhouser. Sons: John Boehm; David Boehm. Mentions: children of Benjamin Boehm, dec'd. Mentions: Isaac Dunavan and Abraham Crabill.
Exor: Joseph Walton
Wit: David Piper, Jr. and Joseph Piper
Dated: 17 Dec. 1824   Proved: 10 Jan. 1825

Will Book Y - page 219

MARGARET FUNKHOUSER, widow of Jacob Funkhouser, Shenandoah County. Son: Isaac. Daus: Isabella Hisey; Eliza Funkhouser; Mary A. Sensony (dec'd.). Grandchildren: Martha Funkhouser and Milton Funkhouser (heirs of my son, Jacob Funkhouser, dec'd.). Son-in-Law: William Funkhouser.
Exor: William Baker
Wit: Abraham Stover and Jacob G. Feller
Dated: 19 Jan. 1847   Proved: 10 Jan. 1848

Will Book L - page 418

PETER GABLE, Shenandoah County. Wife: Elizabeth Gable - land whereon I now live containing 223 acres adjoining Adam Rudolph and W. M. Cloud. Sons: Daniel Gable; Henry; Abraham. Daus: Sarah; Rachael; Polly; Elizabeth Shireman; Catharine Peer; Peggy Wilt; Christina Garrett.
Exor: Benjamin Williams, Sen.
Wit: Elijah Richards, Adam Rudolph and Isaac Hurbough
Dated: 26 May 1821   Proved: 11 Feb. 1822

Will Book L - page 228

GEORGE GANDER, Shenandoah County. Wife: Anne. Sons: Henry Gander (eldest) and John Gander. Daus: Barbara Boraker, wife of Michael Boraker; Eliza Strickler, wife of Henry Strickler; Franey Judd, wife of John Judd. Mentions: Grandson, John Judd - only son and heir of my dau. Ann Judd, dec'd.
Exors: John Strickler and Anne Gander
Wit: Abram Strickler, John Strickler and George Roadcap
Dated: 4 Oct. 1819   Proved: 7 Aug. 1820

Will Book B - page 409

JOHN GARBER, SENIOR, Shenandoah County. Wife: Barbara. Children: John; Samuel; Martin; Anna; Abraham; Jacob; Daniel; Catharine; Joseph; Magdalene. Son-in-Law: Daniel Miller.
Exors: Sons, Samuel and Martin
Wit: Michael Wine, John Click, Jun. and Jacob Neff
Dated: 4 Sept. 1787   Proved: 27 Dec. 1787

Will Book I - page 202

MARTIN GARBER, Shenandoah County. Wife: Rebecca. Son: Jacob - plantation whereon I now reside (284 acres) and land in Rockingham County which I bought of John Cook (19 1/2 acres). Daus: Rebecca; Elizabeth (eldest); Catharine. Mentions: land in Hardy County I purchased of Christian Euman. Mentions: Solome Huber, wife of my son, Jacob.
Exors: Son-in-law, John Wine, son, Jacob Garber and son-in-law, Samuel Bauman
Wit: Peter Foltz, Ludwig Rinehart, Michael Kuns, Jacob Rinker and George Dellinger
Dated: 21 Jan. 1815   Proved: 14 March 1815

Will Book R - page 136

CHARLES GATEWOOD, Shenandoah County. Mentions: Chaney Gatewood and Wright Gatewood to act as Guardians of my children.
Exors: Chaney Gatewood and Wright Gatewood
Wit: Isaac Overall, James Holmes, Gibson Roy and William Holmes
Dated: 29 Oct. 1831   Proved: 13 Feb. 1832

Will Book E - page 150

PHILIP GATEWOOD, Shenandoah County. Wife: Susanna Gatewood - land whereon I now live called Reeds Place, also, five of her choise of the negroes. Dau: Catherine Catlett - two negroes named Milley and Izbell, also, tract of land called Stonybranch. Son: John Gatewood - two negroes named Pat and Frederick, also, land my said son lives on called Beards Place. Dau: Elizabeth Bowman - two negroes named Rachael and Mareah.
Exors: Wife, Susanna Gatewood, son, John Gatewood, Charles Catlett and Isaac Bowman
Wit: John Buck, Charles Buck and Thomas Buck
Dated: 9 Aug. 1786   Proved: 11 June 1793

Will Book O - page 20

JOHN GAW, Howard County, State of Missouri. Wife: (not named). My children (including those by my first and second marriages): (not named). Dau: Catharine Kingan.
Exors: Son-in-law, William Payne and Patrick McMannus
Wit: Henry Bingham, George Tompkins and George Bellas
Dated: 11 Sept. 1822   Proved: 8 Jan. 1827
                               (Shenandoah County)

An authenticated copy of the last Will and Testament of John Gaw, dec'd., late of the State of Missouri.

Will Book P - page 223

ROBERT GAW, town of Woodstock, Shenandoah County. Wife: Barbara Gaw. Mentions: son, Jacob R. Gaw and Isaac Trout - all the goods, wares and merchandize now in my store and the power to carry on the Mercantile business at my present storehouse. Son: Robert Gaw, Jun. - to be educated at the deaf and dumb asylum in Philadelphia, Penna. Sons: Joseph Gaw and John Gaw. Daus: Mary Hoffman; Elizabeth Crawford, wife of David Crawford. Son: Jacob Gaw - the house and lot on which I now live in town of Woodstock and 10 acres out lot adjoining Dr. Irwin and Abraham Fravel. Dau: Rebecca Gaw - house and two lots which I purchased of my brother, John Gaw, in Woodstock, also, five acres adjoining Christian Miller, Sen. and Capt. Jacob Rinker. Mentions: Catharine Smith (a girl whom I raised) - the house and lot which formerly belonged to Isaac Gibbons and now in possession of Charles Fisher. Mentions: son-in-law, David Crawford, to be Guardian of my son, Robert Gaw.
Exors: Son, Jacob Gaw and son-in-law, David Crawford
Wit: Joseph Samuels, Alfred Irwin and George Schmucker
Dated: 29 Aug. 1829   Proved: 7 Sept. 1829

Will Book A - page 163

ULRICH GEFFELER (FELLER), Shanando County. Wife: Catharina.
Son: Johannes Feller - 100 acres of land. Son: Christian -
3 year old mare and 100 acres of land. Son: Ulry (Ulrich) -
100 acres. Son: Joseph. Daus: Eva; Magdalena; Barbara.
Exors: Wife, Catharina, Michael Burner and Jesse Shoe
Wit: Ulry Hefsler, George Westenberger and Frederick Alldenfer
Dated: 21 April 1778   Proved: 29 May 1778

Will Book P - page 261

JOHN GEYER, Shenandoah County. Wife: Madalene. My brother:
David Geyer, Nephew: John Geyer (son of my brother, Jacob).
Mentions: children of my brothers, Jacob, George, Henry and
Andrew. My sisters: Elizabeth; Catharine; Gertrout.
Exors: Philip Williams, Jr. and Abraham Geyer (son of John
Geyer)
Wit: Samuel Ott and P. Williams
Dated: 17 July 1829   Proved: 7 Sept. 1829

Will Book S - page 319

MAGDALENA GIBLER, widow of Philip Gibler, dec'd., Shenandoah
County. Daus: Susan Miller, of Joseph Miller, dec'd.;
Elizabeth Horn, of Benjamin Horn, dec'd. Son: William Gibler.
Mentions: money due me from Thomas McCord and money due me
by Stephen Bowman.
Exor: George Grandstaff (of Philip)
Wit: John Grandstaff, John Leggett and Joseph Fetzer
Dated: 27 Aug. 1834   Proved: 13 Oct. 1834

Will Book F - page 288

PHILIP GIBLER, Shenandoah County. Wife: Magdalena. Son:
John Gibler - that plantation whereon I now dwell. Other
children: Catharine, wife of Peter Ligget; Maria; Elizabeth;
Sally; William; Susanna; Joseph.
Exors: Wife, Magdalena, son, John Gibler and Nicholas Wisman
Wit: David Jordan, _____ (Ger.) and Christian Miller
Dated: 9 Nov. 1804   Proved: 11 March 1805

Will Book A - page 509

JOHN GILLOCK, County of Shanando, Commonwealth of Virginia.
Wife: Hannah. Children: (not named).
Exors: Wife, Hannah and brother-in-law, Peter Wolfinburg
Wit: Joseph Pugh, Samuel Wells and _____(Ger.)
Dated: 28 Feb. 1782   Proved: 28 May 1783

Will Book A - page 142

CHRISTOPHER GISTERT, Dunmore County, Colony of Virginia,
yeoman. Wife: Rosina. Son: Christopher. Dau: Eva Rosina.
Exors: Wife, Rosina and son, Christopher
Wit: Henry Simund, Jacob Yost and Leonard Balthas
Dated: 27 May 1777   Proved: 30 April 1778

Will Book O - page 147

JOHN GLENN, Shenandoah County. Wife: (not named).
Son: George D. Glenn - my lot of ground in town of Luray.
Daus: Julia Ann Miller; Sarah Holmes; Catharine Woods,
wife of Charles Woods. Young children living at home
with me: (not named).
Exor: Benjamin Blackford
Wit: William Harris, Frederick Holtzman and William Leeper
Dated: 31 Jan. 1825   Proved: 12 Sept. 1825

Will Book C - page 266

HENRY GOAR, Shenandoah County, planter. Wife: Catharine
Goar. Eldest son: John Goar - 100 acres of that plantation
whereon I now live joining the County line. Son: Isaac
Goar - 150 acres of land joining John Goar and Jacob Rambo's
line and Henry Goar's line on the south side of the River,
also, one lott of half acre in New Market. Youngest son:
Robert - 150 acres or the remainder. Daus: Lydia Elizabeth;
Sarrah; Eleanor; Margaret; Ann.
Exors: Wife, Catharine Goar and John Oneal
Wit: John Oneal and Jacob Rambo
Dated: 23 April 1785   Proved: 28 April 1791

Will Book H - page 152

ABRAHAM GOCHENOUR, Shenandoah County. Sons: Henry Gochenour; Samuel Gochenour; Abraham Gochenour. Daus: Elizabeth; Cathari Mary.
Exor: Jacob Hottel, Jun.
Wit: P. Williams, _____(Ger.) and Jacob Ott
Dated: 18 Feb. 1812   Proved: 9 March 1812

Will Book U - page 360

ABRAHAM GOCHENOUR, Shenandoah County. Wife: (not named). Children: (not named).
Exor: Michael Neff
Wit: Joseph Gochenour and Abraham Kagey
Dated: 26 Aug. 1838   Proved: 10 Sept. 1838

Will Book K - page 230

EMANUEL GOCHENOUR, Shenandoah County. Wife: Magdalene. Dau: Christina.
Exors: Wife, Magdalene and John Mirly
Wit: Joseph Mirly and Philip Wiscarver
Dated: 27 Jan. 1817   Proved: 10 March 1817

Will Book G - page 379

JACOB GOCHENOUR, SENIOR, Shenandoah County. Wife: Elizabeth Gochenour. Sons: Daniel Gochenour; John Gochenour; Jacob Gochenour; Joseph Gochenour; Shem Gochenour. Daus: Elizabeth, wife of George Howbert; Barbara, wife of Philip Bare; Ann, wife of Jacob Fisher; Ester, wife of David Stover; Catherine, wife of John Craybill; Magdalene, wife of John Stover; Rebecca wife of Henry Jordan, Mentions: my granddaughter, Mary Fisher that I raised and Rebecca Fisher (children of my dau. Mary (dec'd.), late wife of George Fisher.
Exors: Son, John Gochenour and Jacob Crabill, Sen.
Wit: Martin Hupp, Michael Roth and Samuel R. Bader
Dated: 13 Oct. 1809   Proved: 13 Nov. 1809

Will Book X - page 106

JOHN GOCHENOUR, SENIOR, Shenandoah County. Wife: Elizabeth.
Step-dau: Ann Blazer. Mentions: Son, Henry Gochenour and
grandson, John Gochenour (son of my son, Christian) - shall
have my farm or plantation which I now live on. Sons:
Daniel Gochenour; Abraham Gochenour; John Gochenour; Jonathan
Gochenour. Daus: Christina, widow of Christian Hoffman;
Barbara Gochenour. Grandchildren: Jacob, Christian, Joseph
and Elizabeth Gochenour.
Exor: Son, Henry Gochenour
Wit: Benjamin Harman and Abraham Smootz
Dated: 26 Sept. 1844   Proved: 10 March 1845

Will Book W - page 28

JOSEPH GOCHENOUR, Shenandoah County. Wife: Elizabeth.
Youngest child: Anna. Son: Henry. Other children: (not
named).
Exor: Brother-in-law, Henry Neff
Wit: Michael Neff, John Dingledine and Jno. Rice
Dated: 4 Nov. 1841   Proved: 13 Dec. 1841

Will Book W - page 482

JOSEPH GOCHENOUR, Shenandoah County. Daus: Mary Gochenour;
Eliza; Rachael; Sarah. Son: Levy Gochenour.
Exor: Abraham Schmutz
Wit: Jacob Gochenour and George Shrum
Dated: 20 Nov. 1843   Proved: 8 April 1844

Will Book D - page 400

JACOB GOLLADAY, SENIOR, County of Shanando. Wife: Mary
Golladay. Sons: John Golladay; Joseph; David; Jacob;
Daniel. Daus: Ann Golladay (youngest); Susannah; Elizabeth;
Christina; Magdaline. Mentions: 109 acrse in Powell's
Fort and my Lot in town of Woodstock.
Exors: Son, David Golladay and William Bauzerman
Wit: Job Combs, Rebecca Golladay and John Golladay
Dated: 28 Feb. 1795   Proved: 10 March 1795

Will Book N - page 329

JACOB GOOD, Shenandoah County. Wife: Elizabeth. Sons: Samuel; William; Jacob; John. Daus: Susannah Miller; Elizabeth, wife of William Andy; Mary, wife of Christian Sourwine.
Exors: Son, Samuel and son-in-law, Christian Sourwine
Wit: Reuben Moore, John A. Nice and Mary Walton
Dated: 8 Oct. 1825   Proved: 7 Nov. 1825

Will and Accts. (1809-1863) - page 176

JACOB GOOD, Shenandoah County. Wife: Mary Good. My children: (not named).
Exor: Green B. Samuel
Wit: Jacob Yager and John G. Schmitt
Dated: 21 Feb. 1833   Proved: 11 April 1833

Will Book M - page 94

MARY GOOD, Shenandoah County. My children: Jacob Good; William Good; Abraham Good; Ester Sherfey; Elizabeth Good; Mary Good; Susanna Coffman. Mentions: Michael Basler (son of my dau. Mary Good).
Exor: George Weaver
Wit: Henry Barb, John Good and Philip Deterick
Dated: 24 May 1821   Proved: 7 Oct. 1822

Will Book N - page 225

SAMUEL GOOD, Shenandoah County. Wife: Mary Good. Dau: Frances.
Exor: Peter Hockman
Wit: Phineas Orndorff and Jacob Hottel
Dated: 1 May 1825   Proved: 13 June 1825

Will Book G - page 211

WILLIAM GOOD, Shenandoah County. Wife: Mary. Eldest son: Jacob Good - tract of land containing 200 acres in Bedford County, Virginia. Son: William Good - 126 acres of land. Son: Abraham - 126 1/2 acres of land along John Click's line. Son: Benjamin. Daus: Elizabeth; Mary; Susanna. Dau: Barbara - has sold her legacy to David Coffman. Dau: Esther - 108 acres of land. Mentions: grandson, William Good and son-in-law, David Coffman.
Exors: Jacob Miller and Michael Wine
Wit: Abraham Sherfig and George Weaver
Dated: 19 Dec. 1806   Proved: 13 June 1808

Will Book Q - page 195

WILLIAM GORDEN, Shenandoah County. Wife: Jane - all that I possess on earth.
No Exor. named
Wit: John Lansberry, John Blackwood and William Watkins
Dated: 12 April 1830   Proved: 7 March 1831

Will Book F - page 398

CHRISTIAN GRABIL, Shenandoah County. Wife: Francey. Son: Abraham Grabil - part of my tract of land whereon I now live granted to me by Deed from Thomas Lord Fairfax bearing date 20 Sept. 1768. Son: Daniel Grabil - remainder of my land (175 acres). Other children: Jacob Grabil; Barbara Grabil; Mary Grabil; Henry Grabil; Christina Grabil; Christian Grabil. Mentions: 20 pounds due me by Henry Burner.
Exors: Henry Burner and Jacob Gochenour (son of Joseph)
Wit: Jacob Rinker, John Haas and Joseph Gochenour
Dated: 13 Sept. 1805   Proved: 13 Jan. 1806

Will Book M - page 91

JACOB GRABILL, Shenandoah County. Wife: Margaret. Adopted son: Abraham Neff - my plantation and Mill (120 acres). Daus: Anna Grabill; Elizabeth Miley, wife of Martin Miley. Son: John Grabill (now in the State of Ohio).
Exor: Henry Kern
Wit: Samuel R. Bader, Jacob Niswander and Henry Wilkins
Dated: 13 Oct. 1820   Proved: 7 Oct. 1822

Will Book M - page 195

GEORGE GRANDSTAFF, SENIOR, Shenandoah County. Son: Philip Grandstaff - notes on Peter Miller to the amount of two hundred and fifty pounds due at different times - a gift to Philip. Children of my son, George Grandstaff (dec'd) - 200 acres purchased from heirs of George Ziegler (dec'd.). Mentions: Barbara Grandstaff (widow of my son, George). Mentions: Magdalene, the wife of John Helsy.
Exors: Grandson, George Grandstaff (of my son Philip)
Wit: John A. Frye, William Philips and Edward Currin
Dated: 25 Sept. 1822   Proved: 9 June 1823

Will Book L - page 233

JOHN GRIFFITH, SENIOR, Shenandoah County. Wife: Catharine. Son: David - tract of land containing 336 acres I purchased from Jacob Miller. Dau: Mary - the house I now occupy and 6 acres of land around it. Son: John. Daus: Sally; Rachael; Elizabeth; Nancy; Elanor and Catharine (dec'd.). Children of my deceased son, William, viz: Samuel; John; Daniel; Ester; Elizabeth - the land I purchased from Pearson Judd containing 136 acres.
Exor: Son, David Griffith
Wit: William S. Marye, James T. Marye and John Nunn
Dated: 28 Aug. 1816   Proved: 11 Sept. 1820

Will Book E - page 199

BENJAMIN GRIMES, Shenandoah County. Wife: Betty. Mentions: What may be coming to me of Charles Buck on acc't. of my crop after settlement with him - the whole of the above shall go toward satisfying Samuel Richardson on acc't. of my son Samuel ..... Samuel do serve him till the whole be satisfied. Mentions: My daughter Rose I leave to Samuel Richardson. Daus: Minca and Nancy I desire to be bound to William Night and William Kerford. My wife I leave to chuse her master that will pay her five pounds per year.
Exors: William Helms and Charles Buck
Wit: William Richardson and Samuel Richardson
Dated: 23 March 1797   Proved: 12 Dec. 1797

Will Book I - page 102

SUSANNAH GROVE, Shenandoah County. Son: Daniel Grove - 50 acres of land which I purchased from Daniel Beaver in the State of Ohio. Other children: Joseph Grove and Frainey Grove. Mentions: the above three children are my younger children (others not named).
No Exor. named
Wit: Jonathan Moore, Jacob Brumbach, _____ (Ger.) and John Roads
Dated: 10 Nov. 1813   Proved: 12 Sept. 1814

Will Book B - page 291

CHRISTIAN GROVES, County of Shanando. Wife: Ester. Sons: Samuel; David; John; Christian. Daus: Machdelene; Barbary; Anne; Mary Elizabeth; Ester; Susanna; Catey and a child not yet born. Mentions: Children of my first wife is to have no share of the Estate in Pennsylvania.
Exors: Emanuel Rufner and John Musselman
Wit: Peter Lionburger, Martin Coffman and _____ (Ger.)
Dated: 9 June 1786   Proved: 27 July 1786

Will Book L - page 25

GEORGE GRUBS, Shenandoah County. Wife: (not named). Mentions: the two orphan children of Daniel Stover (dec'd.), viz: Mary Stover and Alexander Stover. Mentions: Enoch Yager, son of Simeon Yager. Dau: Eve, now the property of Philip Williams.
Exor: John Alsep
Wit: Abraham Lambert, Jr. and Mathias Zehring

CODICIL to Will of GEORGE GRUBS - Mentions: Catharine Burner; Joseph Robertson; Joseph Alsep (son of John Alsep).
Dated: 3 Jan. 1819   Proved: 11 Jan. 1819

Will Book A - page 129

JACOB GUYGER, Dunmore County. Wife: Mary Guyger. Son-in-Law: Jacob Moul. My children: (not named).
No Exor. named
Wit: James Cunningham and Michael Rorh
Dated: 2 Jan. 1773   Proved: 22 July 1777

Will Book L - page 65

JACOB HAAS (HOUSE), Shenandoah County. Wife: Christina.
Son: John Haas - rights, title, interest and claim of the
landed Estate as divised to me by the last Will of Adam Kelp
(late the Commonwealth of Pennsylvania), dec'd. Son: Jacob
Haas - two small tracts of land containing together 100 acres
in Shenandoah County. Son: Philip Haas - tract of land containing 35 1/2 acres on the Narrow Passage Creek which I
purchased from Christian Creabill; also, parcel containing
32 acres conveyed to me by my father, John Haas. Son: Isaac
House - tract of land containing 77 acres I purchased from
Adam Kelp and Jonathan Kelp. Sons: George House and Jonathan
House - remainder of my land and plantation whereon I now
live containing 138 acres. Four daus: Elizabeth Creabill,
widow; Rebecca House; Catharine, wife of John Attdoerffer;
Polly House.
Exors: Son, John House and friend, George Grandstaff (son
of Philip)
Wit: Peter Miller, Jr., Jacob Rinker, Peter Miller, Sen.
Dated: 3 March 1817   Proved: 13 April 1819

Will Book E - page 443

JOHN HAAS, SENIOR, Shenandoah County. Wife: Catharina.
Sons: John and Jacob. Daus: Anna Maria, wife of John Heise;
Christena, wife to Abraham Gochenour; Elizabeth, wife to
Philip Crousdorf; Maria, wife to Henry Geeding.
Exors: Wife, Catharina and son, John Haas
Wit: David Jordan, George Grandstaff and Jacob Creabill
Dated: 15 April 1793   Proved: 13 July 1801

Will Book F - page 465

GEORGE HAHN, Shenandoah County, yeoman. Wife: Maria Catharine
Daus: Maria Catharine Miller; Anna Susanna Copp; Sophia Borden
Mary Elizabeth Elsheid. Sons: Jacob; John; Henry.
Exors: Son, Jacob and son-in-law, George Copp
Wit: Frederick Bofserman, _____(Ger.) and Samuel R. Bader
Dated: 21 Feb. 1801   Proved: 8 Sept. 1806

Will Book K - page 246

HENRY CHRISTOPHER HAHN, Shenandoah County. Wife: Maria Magdalene Hahn. Mentions: Barbara Cooper, wife of George Cooper, Sen.; Marie Lutz; John Dosh and his son, Henry Dosh; George Dosh; William Dosh; Maria Ann Dosh; Rebeckah Cooper and Patsy Cooper (both being daus. of George Cooper).
Exors: Friends, John Dosh and George Dosh
Wit: William Bayley, Samuel Gardner and George Cooper
Dated: 4 Oct (no year)   Proved: 13 May 1817

Translation thereof in the English language by the oath of Samuel R. Bader

Will Book T - page 527

MARY MAGDALENE HAHN, Town of Strasburg, Shenandoah County. Mentions: Ann Dosh, widow and relick of my nephew, William Dosh, dec'd. - my house and two lotts in town of Strasburg. Four children of my dec'd. nephew, William Dosh: John H.C. Dosh; Mary Catharine Dosh; Samuel H. Dosh; Thomas W. L. Dosh. Nephews: George Dosh and John Dosh. Nieces: Rebecca Lapopp and Mary Ann Hurn.
Exor: Isaac Hurn
Wit: Joseph Spengler, Joseph Zea and George Eberly
Dated: 15 June 1836   Proved: 13 March 1837

Will Book O - page 127

CHRISTIAN HAISEY, Shenandoah County. Wife: (not named). Sons: Daniel; Frederick; Henry; Joseph; David; John Haisey. Daus: Elizabeth; Christina, wife of Peter Miller.
Exor: Son, Daniel Haisey
Wit: George Shrum and Philip Jones
Dated: 4 March 1825

CODICIL to Will of CHRISTIAN HAISEY - Mentions: my plantation to be sold by my Exors. and money divided equally.
Wit: George Shrum and John Artz
Dated: 23 Feb. 1827   Proved: 11 June 1827

Will Book O - page 422

ROSANNA HAISEY, widow of Christian Haisey, dec'd., Shenandoah County. Brother: John Fultz. Mentions: William Philips.
Dau: Elizabeth Haisey.
No Exor. named
Wit: George Shrum and William Philips
Dated: 28 Sept. 1827   Proved: 13 Oct. 1828

Will Book A - page 472

JOHN HALL, Commonwealth of Virginia, County of Shanando and Parish of Beckford. Mentions: Rachael Whitson, dau. of Ruth Whitson. Mentions: Sum of 14 pounds 11 shillings in coin to be applied toward schooling the five daus. of Ruth Whitson. Mentions: John Whitson; Charles Barnes; Thomas Dodson; George White.
Exor: My good friend, Ruth Whitson
Wit: Charles Barnes and Nathan Smith
Dated: 30 July 1781   Proved: 30 June 1783

Will Book G - page 206

PETER HALLER, Shenandoah County. Son: Peter Haller - a certain plantation whereon he now lives. Son: Henry Haller - a certain plantation containing 141 acres whereon my said son, Henry, now lives, also, one tract of land containing 139 acres and one other of 30 acres. Son-in-Law: Andrew Finter, the husband of my dau. Margaret - a certain tract of land whereon the said Andrew Finter and my dau. Margaret now live. Daus: Barbara Haller; Catharine, now the wife of Jacob Surber; Margaret, wife of Andrew Finter; Elizabeth, wife of John Miller; Ann Mary, wife of George Moyer; Catharine Jr., wife of Peter Miller; Christina, wife of Philip Goetz; Eve, wife of John Shoemaker. Mentions: Children of my dau. Catharine by her first husband, Peter Coffeld (dec'd.), to wit: Peter Coffeld; Catharine, wife of John Dake and Elizabeth Coffeld. Mentions: Frederick Fernsler and Barbara, his wife to be Guardians of my dau. Barbara (she being dumb).
Exor: Peter Haller
Wit: Jacob Rinker, Andrew Kauffman and Christoph Kauffman
Dated: 21 Dec. 1796   Proved: 14 Jan. 1800

Will Book I - page 476

JACOB HALTIMAN, Shenandoah County. Wife: Elizabeth Haltiman. Children: Chinley Haltiman; John Haltiman; Esther Haltiman; Betsy Camel; Eve Bufsey; Daniel Haltiman; Peggy Whitehead; Stufle Haltiman. Mentions: Grandson, Joshua Stickler.
Exor: Jacob Funkhouser
Wit: Abraham Sonafrank and Cornelius Bufsey
Dated: 15 Nov. 1811   Proved: 12 Dec. 1814

Will Book Z - page 130

BARBARA HAMMON, widow and relick of John Hammon, dec'd., Shenandoah County. Daus: Rebecca Hammon; Flora Hammon; Susanna Bly, wife of William Bly. Son: Lawrence Hammon. Granddaus: Sarah Hammon and Barbara Hammon, heirs of my son, Elias Hammon, dec'd.
Exor: Son, Lawrence Hammon
Wit: William Baker and Henry Rosenberger
Dated: 1 March 1847   Proved: 11 Feb. 1850

Will Book E - page 180

MICHAEL HANNEGAN, Shenandoah County. Dau: Peggy Hannegan who lately married a certain James Murphey. Mentions: Peggy's daughter, Ann.
Exor: Neighbor, Joseph Young
Wit: Jacob Stiegel, Benjamin Sherfig and Jacob Good
Dated: 12 Aug. 1797   Proved: 11 April 1798

Will Book A - page 233

HENRY HARDING, SENIOR, County of Shanando. Wife: Wilmoth - one negro man named Toney and one negro girl named Lucy. Son: George Harding - 2 negroes to wit: Grace and Daniel. Son: Henry Harding, Jr. - 2 negroes to wit: Alex and Nell. Son: Nicholas Harding - 2 negroes to wit: Will and Lett, also, one thousand acres of land. Dau: Nanney Combs - one negro girl, Hoek. Dau: Wilmoth Smith.
Exors: Sons, George and Nicholas Harding
Wit: Edwin Young and William Saylors
Dated: 28 Sept. 1779   Proved: 25 Nov. 1779

Will Book D - page 474

WILLMOTH HARDING, Shenandoah County. Daus: Nancy Combs and Willmoth Smith. Mentions: one girl named Suchey is to be free woman at the end of 8 years from this date.
Exors: John Cavel and Robert McKay
Wit: James Mathew, Sen., Thomas G. Martin and Henry Harding
Dated: 14 Dec. 1794   Proved: 8 Dec. 1795

Will Book W - page 281

SUTTON I. HARNS, Shenandoah County. Wife: Maria Ann.
Mentions: Reuben Allen. Mentions: house and town lots
in Mount Jackson.
Exors: Raphael Conn and Rhesa Allen
Wit: Josh Snyder and Jacob Funkhouser
Dated: 9 Feb. 1843   Proved: 13 March 1843

Will Book F - page 290

PHILIP HARPINE, Shenandoah County. Wife: Mary (Catharine).
Son: Abraham - 246 acres of land adjoining lands of Reuben
Moore's heirs, Christian Moyer and others, being part of a
tract which contained 400 acres, the house whereon he now
lives, the Grist Mill, Saw Mill and other buildings. Son:
Philip - the remainder of the aforesaid tract of land.
Daus: Mary; Catharine; Magdalene; Margaret; Elizabeth;
Susanna.
Exors: Sons, Abraham and Philip
Wit: Jacob Miller and Jacob Guth
Dated: 2 Jan. 1801   Proved: 11 March 1805

Will Book B - page 399

DAVID HARROW, County of Shanando. Wife: Mary. Mentions:
Lands on Stoney Creek, purchased of Joseph Smith and where-
on Adam Holker now dwells - to be sold. That Adam Holker
have my oldest son, John, until he arrives of age to be
bound out to a trade. George Black to have my son, Henry,
until he arrives of age to be bound out to a trade.
Exors: Wife, Mary and Adam Holker
Wit: J. Williams, George Swartz, Mary Holker and Dorothy
Swartz.
Dated: 19 Sept. 1787   Proved: 25 Oct. 1787

Will Book R - page 494

AARON HAWKINS, Shenandoah County. Mentions: Aaron Hawkins, son of Jane Cally, sometimes called Jane Kearn, who now lives with me and Joseph Hawkins, son of Rebecca Bird, otherwise called Rebecca Hawkins. Aaron and Joseph I acknowledge and believe to be my illegitmate sons. Mentions: The said Joseph Hawkins and Aaron Hawkins, the two persons aforesaid named, I leave the whole of my estate - lots in town, woodlands which I purchased from the Exors. of the late Col. Abraham Bird of Kentucky (100 acres). Mentions: Edith Catharine Hawkins and Sarah Ann Hawkins (daus. of Rebecca Bird, otherwise called Rebecca Hawkins). Mentions: William Brinker, son of Barbara Brinker. My step-mother: Sarah Hawkins. Mentions: Hannah Cully, dau. of Betsey Ann.
Exor: Brother, James Hawkins
Wit: Joseph Samuels and Stark Samuels
Dated: 4 Sept. 1832   Proved: 8 April 1833

Will Book W - page 218

ANNA HAWKINS, of Hawkinstown, Shenandoah County. Three sons: Rhesa A. Hawkins; Joseph Hawkins; Samuel Hawkins. Two daus: Sarah Ann and Elizabeth Mary.
Exor: Rhesa Allen
Wit: Joseph Allen and Jack Ruby
Dated: 15 June 1842   Proved: 10 Oct. 1842

Will Book X - page 380

ELIZABETH HAWKINS, Shenandoah County. Grandchildren: Elizabeth Ann Funk and Joseph Funk (children of Samuel Funk, dec'd.) - the house and lot I now live in Hawkinsburg. Dau: Rebecca Byrd. Son: Cabin Lev Watten, in State of Ohio.
No Exor. named
Wit: Charles Moore, Sarah Allen and Samuel Moore
Dated: 12 Feb. 1841   Proved: 13 April 1846

Will Book Y - page 231

JAMES HAWKINS, Shenandoah County. Wife: Christina Hawkins - the whole of my real Estate. Nephew: Wellington Rush. Niece: Elizabeth Hup (whom I have raised). Mentions: Frances Hup.
Exors: Christina Hawkins and Wellington Rush
Wit: Joseph Samuels, Aaron Hawkins and Dennis Wilson
Dated: 23 Feb. 1847   Proved: 7 Feb. 1848

Will Book T - page 83

SARAH HAWKINS, Shenandoah County. Nephew: Samuel Moore (son of my brother, Aaron Moore) - all my Estate both real and personal. Mentions: Note I hold on Rhesa Allen. Sister: Dorcas Young. Mentions: grandson of my sister, Dorcas Young, viz: Harrison Gill. Sister's dau: Sarah Gill. Mention Deborah Newland, now the wife of Wesley Thompson and her dau., Mary Jane. Mentions: sister, Mary's two sons, viz: Thomas Moffett and Aaron Moffett.
Exor: Nephew, Samuel Moore
Dated: 24 June 1835   Proved: 11 Aug. 1835

Will Book Y - page 231

JACOB HAWN, Shenandoah County. Mentions: My black boy, Alfred Lee, my slave, shall be free.
Exor: Benjamin Harman
Wit: Ananias Borden, Andrew Bushong and John G. Schmitt
Dated: 21 Jan. 1840   Proved: 10 Feb. 1840

Will Book I - page 48

ALEXANDER HAY, Shenandoah County. Wife: Elizabeth - one negro woman named Caty. Children: Peter; David; John; Reuben; Mary; Barbara; Susannah.
No Exor. named
Wit: William R. Almond and Daniel Beaver
Dated: 6 June 1811   Proved: 8 Nov. 1813

Will Book H - page 154

PETER HEASTAND, SENIOR, Shenandoah County. Wife: Barbara.
Dau: Anna, wife of Michael Bixler - parcel of land conveyed
to me by my father, Henry Heastand, bearing date March 1777
containing 230 acres. Oldest dau: Elizabeth Ruffner (widow).
Son: Peter Heastand. Daus: Mary Huffman; Barbara Judd, wife
of Person Judd.
Exors: Son, Peter Heastand friend, Daniel Strickler
Wit: John Roads, _____ (Ger.) and Henry Mouser

CODICIL to Will of PETER HEASTAND, SENIOR - Mentions: Wife,
Barbara to have one horse creature, one cow and two sheep.
Dated: 30 Dec. 1811   Proved: 9 March 1812

Will Book B - page 2

HENRY HEESTANT, Dunmore County, Province of Virginia.
Five sons: Jacob (eldest); Daniel (only 2 named). Dau:
Barbara (eldest) - nothing of this Legacy so long as she
lives in Wedlock with that man but when she comes to be a
widow woman, then she shall have her share. Dau: Magdalene
(youngest). One dau. not named.
No Exor. named
Wit: John Krech, Jacob Heestant, Peter Heestant and Andrew
Genling.
Dated: 22 March 1777   Proved: 28 Aug. 1783

Will Book R - page 96

HENRY HEGAS (HIGGINS), Shenandoah County. Wife: (not named).
Children: (not named).
Exors: John Ott (of Henry) and Frederick Hisey
Wit: Joseph Evans and Aaron Evans
No date   Proved: 12 Dec. 1831

Will Book R - page 503

GEORGE JACOB HELSLEY, Shenandoah County. Wife: Rosina.
Sons: Nicholas; Philip; Jacob; Daniel. Daus: Rebecca
Helsley; Sebilla Helsley; Elizabeth, wife of Henry Helsley;
Caty, wife of John Coffman; Dorothy, wife of Henry Rinker.
Mentions: Dau., Rebecca Helsley - an idiot. Mentions: Joshua
Fultz, Jr. be appointed Guardian to my dau. Rebecca Helsley.
Exor: Joshua Fultz, Junior
Wit: John Rhodes, Sen., Joseph Andrick and A. Rinker
Dated: 18 April 1825   Proved: 13 May 1833

Will Book H - page 505

JACOB HELSLEY, Shenandoah County. Wife: Mary. Son: Peter Helsley - all my lands and plantation containing 300 acres. Sons: George Jacob Helsley; Christian Helsley. Daus: Dorothy, wife of Thomas Hudson; Livila, wife of Henry Lonas (of State of Tennessee); Catharine, wife of Henry Hollar, Jr.; Barbara (dec'd.), wife of George Lonas. Grandson: Joseph Helsley, son of my son Henry Helsley (dec'd.). Mentions: my negro boy Jim or James shall be sold. Mentions: Joshua Foltz to be Guardian of my grandson, Joseph Helsley.
Exors: Two sons, George Jacob Helsley and Peter Helsley
Wit: Jacob Rinker, George Mock and _____(Ger.)
Dated: 21 Nov. 1811

CODICIL to Will of JACOB HELSLEY - Mentions: wife to have house clock and 10 bushels of wheat which my son Peter oweth to me.
Wit: Jacob Rinker, Stephen Showman and _____(Ger.)
Dated: 3 Dec. 1813   Proved: 7 Feb. 1814

Will Book T - page 87

ROSINA HELSLEY, widow of George Jacob Helsley, Shenandoah County. Daus: Rebecca Helsley, Sibilla, wife of Joseph Baker. Sons: Philip Helsley and Niclas Helsley.
Exor: Son, Philip Helsley
Wit: Isaac Foltz and George Andrick
Dated: 11 May 1835   Proved: 12 Oct. 1835

Will Book Z - page 184

SOLOMON HENKEL, town of New Market, Shenandoah County. Wife: Rebecca - the house and lot where I now live (part of lot #4 and all of lot #5). Grandson: Silon Homer Henkel - the house and lot in Winchester, Frederick Co., Va., which my wife, Rebecca inherited from her father, Godfrey Miller. Sons: Samuel Godfrey Henkel; Siram Peter Henkel; Solomon David Henkel; Solon Paul Charles Henkel. Grandson: Solomon Peter Rupert - town lots. Dau: Hannah, now married to Lewis Zirkel - town lots. Dau: Helen Anna Maria - town lots.
Exors: Sons, Samuel G. Henkel and Solomon D. Henkel
No witnesses
Dated: 20 Feb. 1847

CODICIL to Will of SOLOMON HENKEL - Mentions: Exors. of Will, sons, Samuel and Solomon not requested to give Bond.
Dated: 19 March 1847   Proved: 9 Nov. 1847

Will Book F - page 174

MICHAEL HENLINE, Shenandoah County. Granddaughter: Gertrout Coffelt. Father of granddaughter: Jacob Coffelt. Dau: Elizabeth (now deceased), wife of Jacob Coffelt. Brother: John Henline.
Exor: Friend, Jonas Rinehart
Wit: George Dellinger, Robert Gaw and Jacob Rinker
Dated: 23 Nov. 1801   Proved: 12 Dec. 1803

Will Book W - page 111

WILLIAM HENRY, Shenandoah County, town of Strasburg. Wife: Sarah Henry. Son: Steward Henry - my wagon making tools. Other children: Mary Henry; Susanna Henry; Sarah Henry; Elizabeth Henry. Mentions: Bonds I hold against Richard and David Barton.
Exor: Son, Steward Henry
Wit: David Yost and Joseph Wattson
Dated: 19 March 1842   Proved: 11 April 1842

Will Book H - page 127

JOHN HEPNER, Shenandoah County. Wife: Anna - 100 acres of land I purchased of George Hepner. Brother: George Hepner.
Exors: George Hepner and Jacob Zirckle
Wit: William Good, Abraham Good and Henry Barb
Dated: 12 Nov. 1811   Proved: 9 Dec. 1811

Will Book I - page 466

PETER HERBAUGH, Shenandoah County. Son: Isaac Herbaugh - plantation I now live on (100 acres of woodland). Youngest dau: Hennah, Other children: (not named).
Exors: George Hottle and Isaac Herbaugh
Wit: Benjamin Williams, Jacob Lochmiller and Philip Orndorff, Junior.
Dated: 29 Aug. 1815   Proved: 12 Sept. 1815

Will Book E - page 65

BARBARA HERSHBERGER, Shenandoah County, widow and relick of Henry Hershberger, dec'd. and also late widow and rekick of Jacob Pence, dec'd. Five sons: Frederick; Lewis; Daniel; Emanuel and Jacob Pence. Daus: Barbary Rinker; Mary Hershberger; Susannah Nale and Eave Frees.
Exors: Daus., Eave Kevler and Elizabeth Fruase
Wit: John Swindler, Thomas Jones, Jesse Wood, Edward Almond and Jacob Baker
Dated: 4 Jan. 1794   Proved: 14 March 1797

Will Book F - page 330

CHRISTIAN HERSHBERGER, Shenandoah County, farmer. My nine children: Barbara; Daniel; Abraham; Henry; Anna; Maria; Elizabeth; Susanna; Christian.
Exors: Son, Daniel and son-in-law, John Maggert
Wit: John Roads, Christian Alshite, Martin Coffman and George Bufswell
Dated: 28 Feb. 1805   Proved: 10 June 1805

Will Book B - page 348

HENRY HERSHBERGER, Shenandoah County. Wife: (not named). Children: Anna; John; Henry; Abraham; Christian; Samuel; Daniel; David. Mentions: John and Henry shall be bound out until 16 years of age and then be brought to a Trade. Abraham and Christian sent to school until they learn to read and Abraham to write. Likewise, David and Daniel be sent to school. Guardians are hereby appointed - Martin Kauffman and John Hockman.
No Exor. named
Wit: Peter Fox and Jacob Hockman
Dated: 1782   Proved: 28 Feb. 1788

David Jordan sworn to the Translation

Will Book P - page 153

ISAAC HERSHBERGER, Shenandoah County. Wife: Molly Hershberge Dau: Ann Shenk, wife of John Shenk - tract of land lying around the Big Spring containing 311 acres. Dau: Mary Kelly, wife of Charles Kelly. Dau: Hestor Keyser, wife of George Keyser - tract of land whereon I now live containing 150 acres and another tract adjoining known as Green Castle containing 58 acres.
Exors: George Keyser and Isaac Shenk (son of John Shenk)
Wit: Benjamin Wood, Ambrose Borten and Joshua Jennings
Dated: 15 Sept. 1827   Proved: 8 June 1829

Will Book G - page 74

JOHN HERSHBERGER, Parish of Beckford, Shenandoah County.
Wife: Anna, Son: Isaac Hershberger - 160 acres with a Grist
Mill and Saw Mill thereon. Son: Jacob Hershberger. Son:
John Hershberger - 100 acres on the Hawksbill Creek. Son:
Samuel Hershberger - remainder of my land containing 162
acres, it being the old plantation whereon I now live.
Exor: Son, Jacob Hershberger
Wit: John Mufselman, Martin Coffman and Jacob Rinker
Dated: 20 May 1790   Proved: 8 June 1807

Will Book Q - page 143

SAMUEL HERSHBERGER, Shenandoah County. Wife: Anna Hershberger.
Daus: Mary Miller; Susannah Trumba. Son: Emanuel Hershberger -
tract of land whereon I now reside containing 200 acres. Other
children: Joseph Hershberger; Samuel Hershberger; Barbara
Varner; David Hershberger.
Exors: David Varner and Abraham Spitler
Wit: Emanuel Jeffries, Christian Grove and Maun Almond
Dated: 20 Dec. 1824   Proved: 11 Oct. 1830

Will Book U - page 480

SARAH HESLOP (HASLIP), Shenandoah County. Mentions: Mrs.
Smith, wife of Dr. John G. Schmidt - my white quilt. Mrs.
Ann Jones - my best carpet. Mrs. Polly Clower, wife of
Samuel Clower - my arm chair. Eliza Gore, alias Evans (now
living with me) - my house and lot whereon I now live.
Mentions: James M. Gray and his sister, Minerva M. Gray.
Mentions: Algernon Tibbs and my niece, Victoria Meng.
Exor: Isaac Trout
Wit: Mary E. Ferguson and P. Williams
Dated: 19 July 1838   Proved: 7 Jan. 1839

Will Book L - page 306

ABRAHAM HESS, Shenandoah County. Wife: Mary. Children:
Polly, wife of William Barb; Anne, wife of Philip Sayger;
John Hess; Peter Hess; Christena, wife of John Wisman;
Margaret Hess; Catharine Wolf. Mentions: Adam Wolf shall
not in any manner enjoy any part of legacies hereby given
to my said dau. Catharine.
Exors: Sons, John Hess and Peter Hess
Wit: A. Hoffman, P. Williams, Sen. and Philip Williams, Jr.
Dated: 18 Nov. 1820   Proved: 12 March 1821

Will Book T - page 2

CHRISTINA HETER, Shenandoah County. Grandsons: George Mack; John Louder and Philip Louder. Granddaughters: Christina Stoneburner; Sarah Folk and Catharine Grove. Mentions: my late husband, John Heter, of the County of Rockingham.
Exor: John Gyer
Wit: George Shrum and Philip Gibler
Dated: 25 Nov. 1833   Proved: 8 June 1835

Will Book W - page 196

CHRISTOPHER HICKLE, Shenandoah County. Wife: Elizabeth - certain plantation conveyed by heirs of Jacob Rinker, Sen., also, tract adjoining same conveyed to me by Henry Drummond, also, tract lying on or near Ryals granted to me by Patent containing 60 acres, also, plantation I now live on lying on Mill Creek. Also, old negro woman slave, Lucy and the following slaves, to wit: Edmond; Benjamin; Isaac and Isaac's sister, Maria and negro boy, Bill (son of Lucy). Mentions: friend, Levi Rinker and his wife, Margaret Jane - all my lands and plantation purchased from the heirs of John Morgan, dec'd. Mentions: My store be conducted and carried on by Levi Rinker. Brothers: Stephen Hickle; Jacob Hickle (dec'd.); George Hickle; Devault Hickle (dec'd.); Henry Hickle; John Hickle (dec'd.); Samuel Hickle (dec'd.). Sisters: Catharine Hickle (dec'd.); Elizabeth Reed (dec'd.); Sarah (dec'd.); Mary, wife of _____ Bleu. Mentions: friend, Robert Gaw - my negro girl, Fanny. Mentions: Jacob G. Rinker and Jacob Rinker (son of Henry). Mentions: Lemuel Hickle Rinker (son of my friend, Levi Rinker). Mentions: Eliza and Sarah Phau. Mentions: 500 dollars to German Reform Church toward one indigent student of Virginia for the Ministry.
Exor: Levi Rinker
Wit: Jeremiah Heller, William Tisinger, Aaron Hammon and A. Rinker
Dated: 28 April 1841

CODICIL to Will of CHRISTOPHER HICKLE - Mentions: After the decease of my wife, Elizabeth, stock in my store I give same to Lemuel Hickle Rinker.
Wit: Aaron Hammon and A. Rinker
Dated: 22 June 1841   Proved: 12 Sept. 1842

Will Book Z - page 111

ELIZABETH HICKLE, Shenandoah County. My grandnephew: Jacob Rinker, son of Samuel Rinker - the farm that belonged to my father and land I bought of Benjamin Hudson and farm of Erasmus Rinker, west of the big road. Mentions: My brother's and sister's children - but Samuel Rinker getting none. Nephew: Levi Rinker - the house in which I live, also, the Watt farm which Samuel Overholser now lives. Mentions: nephew, Robert Gaw. Mentions: Mary Windle. Mentions: Liberty unto all my slaves and each have a horse and 50 dollars.
Exors: Nephew, Levi Rinker and friend, Jacob Kagey
Wit: L. Triplett and Samuel Coile
Dated: 3 July 1849   Proved: 7 Jan. 1850

Will Book L - page 157

MARGARET HILBERT, Town of New Market, Shenandoah County.
Dau: Mary Mort. Three sons: George; Bernard; Michael.
Exor: John Shomo
Wit: Michael Blefsing, John Coffman and Jonathan McDaniel
Dated: 20 March 1819   Proved: 9 Nov. 1819

Will Book E - page 61

THOMAS HINTON, Shenandoah County. Wife: Ann. Sons: George Hinton and Thomas Hinton. Dau: Hannah. Daus. in Kentucky: Ann Copeland; Alice Samples; Pearces Boon; Ruth Rader.
Exors: Wife, Ann Hinton and son, George Hinton, Michael Waren
Wit: Joseph Young, Evan Jones and Daniel Walters
Dated: 27 Nov. 1796   Proved: 14 Dec. 1796

Will Book B - page 317

HENRY HISER, Shenandoah County. Wife: Eve. Daus: Eve Huddle, wife of Daniel Huddle; Catharina; Anna Maria; Elizabeth. Son-in-Law: Daniel Huddle - my plantation whereon I now live.
Exors: Wife, Eve and son-in-law, Daniel Huddle
Wit: Samuel Mills, Adam Durting and _____(Ger.)
Dated: 16 Feb. 1787   Proved: 23 Feb. 1787

Will Book D - page 314

JACOB HISER, Beckford Parish, County of Shenandoah. Wife:
Susanna. Five children: (not named) - is to be sent to
English skull and is to learn to rite and sifer.
Exors: Son, Jacob and Abraham Crabel
Wit: Adam Shearman, Jun. and _____ (Ger.)
Dated: 18 Nov. 1789   Proved: 31 Dec. 1789

Will Book F - page 108

JOHN HISY, Shenandoah County, yeoman. Wife: Maryann.
Children: Catharina; Christina; Elizabeth; Jacob; Mary;
Joseph; Abram; Jonathan.
Exors: Wife, Maryann, Philip Grandstaff and Abraham Gochenour
Wit: John Mourer, Peter Miller and John Haas
Dated: 6 March 1803   Proved: 12 April 1803

Will Book H - page 340

ALEXANDER HITE, of Strasburg, Shenandoah County. My children:
Mary Muck; Frederick Hite; Susanny Feagel; Jacob Hite;
Elizabeth Hite; Margaret Hite; Catherine Kurter; Ann Hite;
David Hite. Mentions: three tracts of land, that is, mountain
tract purchased of Cronomer Baker; other tract containing
150 acres purchased of Isaac Zane, now in possession of
Jonathan Evans; other tract in the forks of the Shenandoah
River, also, two out lots containing 5 acres each - to be
sold. Mentions: My mansion house in Strasburg with the
three Inn lotts be reverted for my three daus., Elizabeth,
Margaret and Ann.
Exors: Samuel Richardson and David Stickley
Wit: Samuel Gardner, Jacob Hershberger, Isaac Beakhim and
Jacob Sonner.
Dated: 7 Jan. 1813   Proved: 7 Feb. 1813

Will Book P - page 263

DANIEL HITE, SENIOR, Shenandoah County. Mentions: wife of
my dec'd. son, David Hite - tract of land on which I at
present reside joining Abraham Roadcap and Jacob Strickler,
also, tract of land I purchased of my son, Abraham Hite
(60 acres). Sons: Daniel Hite and Abraham Hite. Daus:
Ann Bare; Magdalin Hopewood. Mentions: heirs of my dec'd.
son, Joseph Hite and heirs of my dec'd son, Andrew Hite.
Exor: Abraham Spitler, Jr.
Wit: Isaac Spitler, David Rothgeb, Jr. and _____ (Ger.)
Dated: 17 March 1825   Proved: 9 Nov. 1829

Will Book O - page 357

FREDERICK HITE, Town of Strasburg, Shenandoah County. Wife:
Mary - the house and lot I now live in. My four children:
Catharine Houck; Sarah Hurn; Susan Eberly and Jacob Hite.
Exor: Son-in-Law, Philip Eberly
Wit: Will M. Bayly, Daniel Eberly and Jacob Miller
Dated: 8 July 1828　　　　　　　　　Proved: 11 Aug. 1828

Will Book L - page 61

ABRAHAM HOCKMAN (son of Christian), Shenandoah County.
Wife: Anna Hockman. Sons: Henry Hockman and Christian
Hockman. Two daus: Rebecca, wife of William Bauserman, Jr.
and Sarah, wife of Jacob Bauserman.
Exors: Wife, Anna Hockman, son, Henry Hockman and Henry Keller
Wit: Samuel R. Bader, Michael Roads and John Roth
Dated: 20 June 1809　　　　　　　　Proved: 13 April 1819

Will Book Z - page 484

ABRAHAM HOCKMAN (of Henry), Shenandoah County. Wife:
Catharine Hockman. Son: Henry Hockman - the whole home
farm or plantation. Six daus: Maria, wife of John Rickard;
Rebecca, wife of Henry Kerns; Ann, wife of Noah Funkhouser;
Catharine, wife of Cornelius Shaver; Sarah Hockman; Barbara
Hockman. Mentions: Benjamin Harman to manage my whole Real
Estate until my said son, Henry, attains the age to act.
Exors: Son, Henry Hockman and Benjamin Harman
Wit: Abraham Strickler, Henry Ridenour and Isaac Beydler
Dated: 11 Feb. 1851　　　　　　　　Proved: 7 April 1851

Will Book B - page 509

BENJAMIN HOCKMAN, Shenandoah County. Wife: Barbara.
Mentions: three daus. of my brother, Rudolph Hockman, dec'd.,
viz: Catharine Hockman, now the wife of Frederick Dull;
Barbara Hockman, now the wife of Henry Daring; Elizabeth
Hockman, now the wife of Henry Fravel, Jun. Mentions:
Rebecca Colvel, now the wife of Adolph Miller.
Exors: Wife, Barbara and John Hoover
Wit: Henry Fravel and Abraham Pidiler
Dated: 24 Aug. 1788　　　　　　　　Proved: 25 Dec. 1788

Will Book E - page 318

CHRISTIAN HOCKMAN, Shenandoah County. Wife: Catharina Hockman. Son: John Hockman - all the plantation whereon I now live containing 262 acres. Son: Abraham Hockman - all that plantation now in his possession containing 100 acres of land purchased of Nicholas Pitman. Daus: Magdelena, wife of Peter Smith; Catharina, wife of Philip Snapp.
Exors: Sons, John and Abraham
Wit: _____(Ger.), _____(Ger.) and Alexander Hite
Dated: 7 Feb. 1783   Proved: 25 Dec. 1788

Will Book L - page 417

CHRISTIAN HOCKMAN,(son of John), Shenandoah County. Wife: Christena. My children: (not named).
Exors: John Zehring and John Nicely
Wit: Peter Hockman and Christian Hockman (son of Abraham)
Dated: 1 Jan. 1822   Proved: 11 Feb. 1822

Will Book Y - page 115

GEORGE HOCKMAN, Shenandoah County. Wife: (not named). Two daus: Sara and Anna Maria - the small house so long as they remain single.
Exors: Son, Peter
Wit: Samuel Hockman and Joseph Hockman
Dated: 20 Aug. 1846   Proved: 12 July 1847

Said Will being writing in German - Charles Mourer was sworn to interpet same into English language.

Will Book P - page 104

HENRY HOCKMAN, near Woodstock, Shenandoah County. Wife: Elizabeth. Two sons: Joseph Hockman and Isaac Hockman - to have the plantation whereon I now live. Mentions: heirs of my son, Henry Hockman (dec'd.). Son: Jacob Hockman. Daus: Barbara Dellinger, wife of George Dellinger (dec'd.); Elizabeth Bowman, wife of Stephen Bowman; Catharine McCord, wife of Thomas McCord; Rebecca Meily, wife of Joseph Meily (dec'd.); Polly Farra, wife of John Farra.
Exor: Son, Joseph Hockman
Wit: Simeon Yager, John Wakeman and Henry Wakeman
Dated: 21 March 1829   Proved: 11 May 1829

Will Book Q - page 287

HENRY HOCKMAN, son of Abraham, dec'd., late of the County of Lancaster, State of Pennsylvania but now of Shenandoah County. Wife: Katharine Hockman - her lawful Dower in all the lands and either of the dwelling houses. Son: John Hockman - all that land and plantation I purchased of David Crabill whereon my said son now resides. Dau: Elizabeth Hockman. Son: Abraham Hockman - all my lands and plantation whereon I now reside.
Exors: Sons, John Hockman and Abraham Hockman
Wit: Samuel R. Bader and John Roth
Dated: 19 April 1828   Proved: 9 May 1831

Will Book M - page 39

JOHN HOCKMAN, Shenandoah County. Wife: Barbara Hockman. Son: Christian Hockman - my land and plantation that I now posses. Mentions: Mary Hockman, widow and relick of my son, George Hockman (dec'd.). Dau: Magdalene, wife of John Zehring.
Exors: Son-in-Law, John Zehring and son, Christian Hockman
Wit: Samuel R. Bader and _____ (Ger.)
Dated: 20 April 1816

CODICIL to Will of JOHN HOCKMAN - Mentions: My three children divide share of money by the last Will and Testament of Laurence Marty (dec'd.)
Wit: P. Williams and Joseph Irwin
Dated: 23 June 1821

SECOND CODICIL to Will of JOHN HOCKMAN - Mentions: Children of dec'd. son, George, viz: Abraham; Magdalene; John; Jacob; Catharine.
Wit: Samuel R. Bader, Peter Hockman and Christian Hockman
Dated: 11 Aug. 1821

THIRD CODICIL to Will of JOHN HOCKMAN - Mentions: Said son, Christian Hockman (dec'd.) - widow of said son could have the dower in said land - Christena Hockman, widow and relict of Christian Hockman (dec'd.).
Wit: Peter Hockman, George Hockman and John Zehring
Dated: 6 Feb. 1822   Proved: 10 June 1822

Will Book H - page 509

PETER HOCKMAN, Shenandoah County. Wife: Anna. Adopted son: George Hockman. Children: Barbara Bowman; Rebecca Golleday; Tekla Grikenberger; Anna Spieger; Catharine Reese.
Exors: Christian Greabill and David Greabill
Wit: Peter Eshelman, George Hockman (son of John Hockman) and _____(Ger.)
Dated: 11 April 1800   Proved: 7 March 1814

Will Book N - page 223

CHRISTIAN HOFFMAN, Town of Strasburg, Shenandoah County. Wife: (not named). My four daus: (three not named). Dau: Barbara - to have first choise of the female slaves namely, Betsy Ann and Cate. Son: Andrew Hoffman - second choise of my female slaves. Mentions: Slave, Mary to be free immediatly after my decease. Mentions: my wife shall make such provision for John Stover as she thinks proper after my decease.
Exor: Son, Andrew Hoffman
Wit: George Dosh, Isaac Longaire and John Marshall
Dated: 30 May 1824   Proved: 13 June 1825

Will Book I - page 363

GEORGE HOFFMAN, Shenandoah County. Sons: Lewis Hoffman; Daniel Hoffman; Henry Hoffman; Mathias Hoffman; David Hoffman; Jeremiah Hoffman. Daus: Elizabeth Fultz; Mary Hoffman; Anne Hoffman.
Exor: Son, David Hoffman
Wit: Christian Alshite, Rudolph Baker and Joseph Louderback
Dated: 9 Feb. 1813   Proved: 7 Aug. 1815

Will Book U - page 151

MARY HOFFMAN, Shenandoah County. Grandson: John Stover - my black boy named Isaac, about 15 years old. Mentions: deceased husband, Christian Hoffman.
No Exor. named
Wit: Leonard Balthis and William Eyster
Dated: 14 June 1834   Proved: 22 Sept. 1837
                              Licking Co. State of Ohio

Will Book S - page 309

PETER HOFFMAN, Shenandoah County. Wife: Mary Hoffman - all my Estate both real and personal. Youngest son: John Hoffman - my hatter tools.
No Exor. named
Wit: David Yost and Isaac Hurn
Dated: 17 June 1834 Proved: 8 Sept. 1834

Will Book Z - page 450

ROBERT M. G. HOFFMAN, of Woodstock, Shenandoah County. My mother (not named) - my two slaves, Milton and Ambrose and my house and lot in town of Wardensville, County of Hardy, Virginia. Mentions: Jacob R. Gaw.
Exor: My mother
Wit: William Ott and Jno. Hickman
Dated: 15 Jan. 1851

CODICIL to Will of ROBERT M. G. HOFFMAN - Mentions: sister, Elizabeth Haas' children. Mentions: my slaves to go to Liberia.
Wit: William A. Crawford and Jacob R. Gaw
Dated: 11 Feb. 1851 Proved: 10 March 1851

Will Book B - page 86

JACOB HOLEMAN, Shanando County, yeoman. Wife: Margaret Holeman - plantation whereon I now live containing 550 acres, also slaves. Son: Daniel Holeman - plantation whereon he now lives containing 420 acres, slaves. Dau: Elizabeth Dedkison - tract of land whereon she now lives, also slaves. Dau: Rachael Holeman - slaves. Son: Andrew Holeman - plantation whereon he now lives containing 400 acres, slaves. Dau: Rebecca Holeman - slaves. Dau: Mary Ann Holeman - slaves. Son: Jacob Herod Holeman - plantation adjoining Andrew Holeman's containing 150 acres, slaves.
Exor: Wife, Margaret Holeman
Wit: Samuel Mills, Thomas Lewis and William Cathey
Dated: 26 Oct. 1783 Proved: 25 March 1784

Will Book Q - page 129

AUGUSTINE HOLLER, Shenandoah County. Wife: Catharine.
Son: David Holler - tract of land whereon he now lives
conveyed to me by Peter Painter containing 99 acres. Sons:
Isaac and Abraham Holler - the plantation whereon my said
son, Isaac now lives conveyed to me by heirs of Thomas
Cunningham (dec'd.) and Henry Long (150 acres). Sons:
Augustine and Alexander Holler - plantation whereon I now
live containing 153 acres. Son: John Holler - tract of
land containing 70 acres conveyed to me by John Lesher.
Grandson: Henry Holler (base born child of my dau. Lidia).
Daus: Rachael, wife of Jacob Reedy; Lidia, wife of Isaac
Clindenst; Leah, wife of John Bowman; Mary Holler and
Catharine Holler.
Exors: George Lantz and Jacob Coffelt
Wit: Jacob Snapp, William Grubb and A. Rinker
Dated: 5 Oct. 1830   Proved: 13 Dec. 1830

Will Book N - page 267

HENRY HOLLER, SENIOR, Shenandoah County. Wife: Elizabeth.
Sons: Henry Holler; William Holler and Joseph Holler -
450 acres equally divided among them. Daus: Catharine
Holler; Polly Holler; Elizabeth Holler - all my rights
and title in the lands I purchased from the heirs of
Frederick Fansler (dec'd.) containing 100 acres.
Exors: George Lantz and Absalom Rinker
Wit: Jacob Lantz, George Miller and William Philips
Dated: 23 July 1825   Proved: 12 Sept. 1825

Will Book H - page 511

PETER HOLLER, Shenandoah County. Son: Peter - 100 acres
of land joining land of Peter Koffelt's heirs, Ferntzler's
heirs and others. Son: Henry - 100 acres of land together
with the Saw Mill. Son: John - the Grist Mill together
with 100 acres of land including my dwelling house. Son:
Jacob - remainder of land. Sons: Augustine and Elias.
Daus: Catharine, wife of Peter Helzel, Eva, wife of John
Seevy; Dorothy, wife of Martin Dellinger; Anna, wife of
Jacob Bowman; Elizabeth, wife of Adam Ollinger.
Exors: Absalom Rinker and William Philips
Wit: Peter Sine, William Ferntzler and John Wetzle
Dated: 22 Oct. 1813   Proved: 7 March 1814

Will Book A - page 536

CONRAD HOLVAH, Shenandoah County. Wife: Catherine. Sons: John Holvah (youngest); George Holvah; Conrad Holvah.
Exors: Sons, John and George Holvah
Wit: Thomas Lewis and Evan Jones
Dated: 26 July 1783   Proved: 28 June 1784

Will Book F - page 397

JOHN HOMMON, Shenandoah County. Wife: Maria. Mentions: children of my dau. Eve; children of my dau. Maria; children of my dau. Margaret, wife of Leonard Caufman.
Daus: Elizabeth; Susannah; Catharine; Barbara; Judith.
Sons: John; Thomas; George.
Exors: Sons, Thomas and George and friend, Samuel Walton
Wit: Peter Tusinger, George Shaver and _____ (Ger.)
Dated: 14 Dec. 1805   Proved: 13 Jan. 1806

Will Book A - page 41

PETER HOOP, Parish of Beckford, County of Dunmore, Colony of Virginia. Wife: (not named) - my house and Lot #122.
Sons: Peter and John. Dau: Susannah - lot aforesigned to me by George Deacot. Mentions: Lot #106 and Lot #11 in town - to be sold.
Exors: Cutlip Sink and Adam Funk
Wit: Will Webb and Samuel Gory
Dated: 8 June 1773   Proved: 22 June 1773

Will Book A - page 229

WILLIAM HOOVER, Shanando, Common Wealth of Virginia.
Wife: Margarett, Sons: Balfer (eldest); Jacob; William Hoover and John Hoover. Daus: Susanna, wife of Christopher Houts; Catherine, yet single; Barbary, wife of Benjamin Hockman; Margaret, wife of John Crockshan; Elizabeth, wife of Jacob Hotsinpiller; Christina, wife of David Bowman.
Exors: Son, Balfer and Jacob Bowman
No witnesses - Proved by oath of Jacob Rinker
Dated: 6 Feb. 1779   Proved: 25 Nov. 1779

Will Book I - page 160

HENRY HOSHOUR, SENIOR, Shenandoah County. Wife: Elizabeth. Step-dau: Lidia. Sons: Peter; Henry; Joseph; George; Samuel; Philip; Jacob. Daus: Elizabeth, wife of Joseph Ryman; Anna, wife of Jacob Shoemaker; Margarete, wife of Michael Shoemaker; Mary, wife of Daniel Rougel. Mentions: heirs of my son, John. Mentions: Henry Hoshour, son of my son, Henry; Henry Shoemaker, son of Jacob Shoemaker.
Exors: Absolam Rinker and Joshua Fultz, Jun.
Wit: John Beidleman, George Keller and George Feather
Dated: 24 Dec. 1812   Proved: 11 Oct. 1814

Will Book W - page 123

GEORGE HOTTEL, Shenandoah County. Wife: Rebecca. Son: Samuel Hottel. Mentions: Farm upon which my son, Samuel resides; mountain tract; tract of land adjoining Abraham Pitman (100 acres); land lying in Hardy Co. (304 acres); tract conveyed to me by Littleton Tazwell, Esq., Governor of Virginia (780 acres); tract name of Peer tract (163 acres); tract containing 852 acres conveyed to me by David Campbell, Esq., Governor of Virginia - to be sold. Daus: Kitty and Rebecca - part of my house and garden provided they remain unmarried. Dau: Sarah Hawn and her dau., Leah Hawn. Mentions: All my children except those named.
Exors: Son, William Hottel and son-in-law, William Baker
Wit: William Seiver, Abraham Keller, William G. Feller, Samuel G. Feller and James Seiver
Dated: 20 July 1841   Proved: 13 June 1842

Will Book O - page 170

JACOB HOTTEL, Shenandoah County, late Trumbull County, Ohio. Wife: Anna - all my real and personal Estate. Mentions: Joseph Allen and Lydia Carlems.
Exor: Anna Hottel
Wit: Lyman Potter and Peris Hiscock
Dated: 5 Jan. 1827   Proved: 8 Oct. 1827

An authenticated copy of last Will and Testament of Jacob Hottel was proved in Shenandoah County on 8 Oct. 1827

Will Book V - page 512

ROSINA HOTTEL, Shenandoah County. Mentions: Four children of my first husband, Christian Wohlgemoth (dec'd.) be excluded from all my Estate. My deceased father: Frederick Fox in Ohio. Children of my second husband, Daniel Hottel (dec'd.) : Christina, wife of Jacob Haun (of John); Sarah, wife of William Spiegle; Lydia, wife of Joseph Barton.
Exors: Two sons-in-law, William Spiegle and Joseph Barton
Wit: Charles Fisher and P. Williams
Dated: 14 Oct. 1837   Proved: 11 Oct. 1841

Will Book B - page 325

NICHOLAS HOUBURT, Shenandoah County. Wife: Catharine.
Sons: Peter and John. Dau: Cataron. Mentions: My father, Peter and his wife.
No Exor. named
Wit: Peter Lionberger and Jacob Strickel
Dated: 21 Oct. 1786   Proved: 26 April 1787

Will Book H - page 427

MICHAEL HOUDESHELL, Shenandoah County. Dau: Barbara Houdeshell - 125 acres of land. Other children: Elizabeth Shaver; Laurence Houdeshell; Michael Houdeshell; George Houdeshell. Mentions: heirs of John Houdeshell (dec'd.).
Son-in-Law: Adam Sine.
Exor: Adam Sine
Wit: James Sterrett, Nicholas Truck and George Miller, Jun.
Dated: 31 July 1812   Proved: 7 June 1813

Will Book E - page 392

BENJAMIN HOUSDON, Shenandoah County, yeoman. Wife: Nancy.
Sons: James; Benjamin; Edmon. Dau: Polly.
Exor: Wife, Nancy
Wit: Achory Berry, Mary Hanback and Ann Busserman
Dated: 25 June 1800   Proved: 13 Oct. 1800

Will Book D - page 403

HENRY HOUSER, Shenandoah County. Wife: Magdalene. Three daus: Elizabeth; Ann; Mary. Sons: Martin and Jacob.
Son-in-Law: Henry Hershberger.
Exors: Son, Martin and Samuel Strickler
Wit: Abraham Dust, Jacob Neff and Mary Sneider
Dated: 21 Feb. 1795   Proved: 14 April 1795

Will Book N - page 268

PETER HOUSHOUR, Shenandoah County. Wife: Julias. Mentions: Peter Houshour, son of my brother, Joseph Houshour. Mentions: late father, Henry Houshour, dec'd. Mentions: friend, David Wetzel. Mentions: James Wetzel, son of aforesaid friend, David Wetzel - one half of my plantation including my dwelling house I now live and containing 211 acres. Mentions: Leah Wetzel, now the wife of my aforesaid friend, David Wetzel- remainder half of my land.
Exors: David Wetzel and Absalom Rinker
Wit: Wendle Coffman and Adam Coffman
Dated: 16 June 1825   Proved: 12 Sept. 1825

Will Book E - page 181

WENDEL HOUTZ, Shenandoah County. Wife: Catharine Elizabeth. Dau: Catharine, wife of Augustine Cofman - two hundred and twenty acres of land surveyed by Jacob Rinker being part of 400 acres conveyed to me by Abraham Brubaker, also, 117 acres joining lands of Joseph Pugh and Peter Hoshour, conveyed to me by Traverner Beale and Betty his wife. Dau: Barbara, wife of Daniel Cofman. Mentions: Grandchildren, Catharine Elizabeth Cofman; John Cofman; Andrew Cofman; Wendel Cofman; Elizabeth Cofman; Daniel Cofman; and Henry Cofman - children of my dau., Barbara, wife of Daniel Cofman.
Exors: Wife, Catharine Elizabeth and son-in-law, Augustine Cofman.
Wit: Peter Coffelt and George Rinker
Dated: 14 Aug. 1797   Proved: 11 April 1798

Will Book A - page 284

JOHN HOY, Dunmore County and Colony of Virginia. Wife: Catharina. Children: (not named).
Exors: Edwin Young and Jonathan Langdon
Wit: William Murphy and Peter Holler
Dated: 17 March 1776   Proved: 25 March 1777

Will Book I - page 98

CHARLES HUDDLE, Shenandoah County, farmer .... was unlucky hit by the stroke of a horse and my body hurt. Wife: Barbara (dec'd.). Son: John Huddle (first born) - 285 acres of land. Son: Jacob Huddle - 215 acres of land. Son: Joseph Huddle - 250 acres of land. Son: Solomon Huddle - 204 acres of land. Son: Daniel Huddle - 201 acres of land. Dau: Magdalene Huddle - 163 acres of land. Daus: Elizabeth Huddle; Barbara Huddle; Mary Huddle; Ann Huddle; Susannah Huddle.
No Exor. named
Wit: John Snap, Jacob Funk and Frederick Altorffer
Dated: 10 June 1778 Proved: 9 Aug. 1814

Translation in the English language thereof was proved by the oath of Samuel R. Bader.

Will Book B - page 344

DAVID HUDDLE, Shenandoah County. Wife: Margaret. Four small children which I leave behind: Conrad; George; David and Mary Elizabeth.
Exors: Wife and brother, Jacob
Wit: Simon Harr, Jacob Keller, _____(Ger.) and Christian Copp
Dated: 25 Aug. 1785 Proved: 22 Feb. 1787

Will Book B - page 327

GEORGE HUDDLE, Shenandoah County. Mentions: Three grandsons (viz): Henry Huddle; Gideon Huddle; John Huddle, sons of my eldest son, John Huddle, dec'd. - two tracts of land, viz. 188 acres being part of land I bought of John McKenney and 14 1/2 acres being part of tract deeded by John Smith, Solomon Smith and Samuel Smith. Son: Henry Huddle - 218 acres. Dau: Elizabeth, wife of Christian Copp - 170 acres on Tom's Brook devised to me by George Keller by last Will and Testament of my father, John Huddle, dec'd. Son: Jacob Huddle - part of tract of land granted me from Proprietors Office of Northern Neck of Va. (253 acres). Son: David Huddle - remainder of last mentioned tract containing 292 acres. Son: George Huddle - 200 acres in Hampshire County deeded me from Proprietor of the Northern Neck of Va. Dau: Dorothy, wife of Jacob Funkhouser - tract of land (404 acres) in Co. of Hampshire granted by the Proprietors Office of Northern Neck. Son: Daniel Huddle - 220 acres in the aforesaid Co. of Hampshire. Dau: Anna, wife of Jacob Hammon - 409 acres on Trout Run, Hampshire County.
Exors: Sons, Henry Huddle and Jacob Huddle
Wit: Jacob Rinker, Jun., Henry Keller and Jacob Keller
Dated: 17 Aug. 1782 Proved: 26 April 1787

Will Book H - page 458

JACOB HUDDLE, SENIOR, Shenandoah County. Wife: Elizabeth Huddel. Brother: John Huddel (dec'd.). Son: Jacob Huddel - plantation and tract of land whereon I now live. Dau: Mary, wife of George Hutchinson - that plantation and tract of land whereon she now lives, also, land I purchased of Ulrick Bealer. Father: Charles Huddel (dec'd.).
Exor: Wife, Elizabeth Huddel
Wit: _____(Ger.), Samuel R. Bader and Joseph Sperry
Dated: 25 June 1813   Proved: 13 Sept. 1813

Will Book L - page 225

JACOB HUDDLE, SENIOR (HOTTEL), Shenandoah County. Wife: Dorotha Hottel. Son: George Hottel - two lots of land containing 10 acres whereon he now lives and has a tanyard, and another containing 90 acres. Son: Daniel Hottel - tract of land and plantation I bought of Henry Wilkin containing 178 1/2 acres. Son: John Hottel - tract of land and plantation containing 182 acres. Son: Jacob Hottel - tract of land and plantation I bought of Balzer Hoover containing 109 acres. Son: Andrew Hottel - tract of land and plantation I bought of Nicholas Bardeu containing 200 acres. Son: Henry Hottel - the land and plantation whereon I now live. Daus: Elizabeth, wife of Peter Swartz; Mary Hottel; Catharine Hottel; Rebecca Hottel. Mentions: Lot in town of Woodstock - to be sold.
Exors: Sons, George Hottel and Daniel Hottel
Wit: Samuel R. Bader, William Hottel and Samuel Weeks
Dated: 15 March 1817   Proved: 7 Aug. 1820

Will Book A - page 4

JOHN HUDDLE, County of Frederick and Colony of Virginia.
Wife: Elizabeth. Son: Henry.
Exors: Wife, Elizabeth and George Huddle
Wit: Samuel Mills, Michael Hayman and Henry Huddell
Dated: 18 March 1772   Proved: 26 May 1772

Will Book Y - page 289

DOROTHY HUDSON, Shenandoah County. Son: Benjamin Hudson. Other children: Richard; Elizabeth; Jacob; Barbara; Sarah; Nancy.
Exor: Son, Benjamin Hudson
Wit: Jacob Noel and Jacob Mumaw
Dated: 13 Jan. 1847   Proved: 10 April 1848

Will Book O - page 479

ALEXANDER HULVA, Shenandoah County. Eldest dau: Caty Ann.
Youngest dau: Helenah.
Exor: William Kerlin
Wit: Simon Nicholls, Richard Carryer and Samuel Good
Dated: 9 Nov. 1828   Proved: 8 Dec. 1828

Will Book F - page 291

THOMAS HUMES, Shenandoah County. Wife: Ann Humes. Mentions:
Jean Gooding, wife of William Gooding. Mentions: Enoch
Watkins and Archable Watkins.
No Exor. named
Wit: William Moreland, Thomas Sandsbury and James Blackwood
Dated: 10 March 1795   Proved: 11 March 1805

Will Book L - page 296

EDWARD HUNSTON, SENIOR, Shenandoah County. Son: Thomas
Hunston - one negro man named Benjamin, negro woman named
Hannah and her dau. Helen and their increase forever, also
one negro man named Joseph. Dau: Sarah Morehead - one dollar.
Son: Edward Hunston - one dollar. Heirs of my dau. Elizabeth
Cooper (dec'd). Son: John Hunston - one dollar. Dau: Ann
Berry - one horse. Heirs of my dau. Jane Eliott. Dau:
Susanna Morehead - one negro boy named Reuben. Dau: Lucy
Mallory - one horse. Son: Nathaniel Q. Hunston - one negro
man named Jacob and one negro woman named Amelia. Grand-
daughter: Mary W. Hunston - one negro boy named Thomas (son
of Hannah). Dau-in-Law: Lucy Hunston (wife of Thomas Hunston)-
one looking glass. Mentions: dau.-in-law, Matilda Hunston
(wife of John Hunston).
Exor: Son, Thomas Hunston
Wit: William F. Broadus, D. Downey, William Downey and
Eleazer Downey
Dated: 13 Dec. 1820

CODICIL to Will of EDWARD HUNSTON, SENIOR - Mentions: tract
of land being in State of Kentucky containing 2,009 acres.
Mentions: John Triplett - 500 acres of this said land. Residue
of said land to my son, Thomas Hunston and grandson, Edward
Hunston (son of Thomas Hunston).
Wit: same as above
Dated: 13 Dec. 1820   Proved: 13 Feb. 1821

Will Book A - page 322

WILLIAM HURST, Shanando County. Wife: Judith Hurst. Sons: John Hurst and William Hurst. Daus: Elizabeth Morgan; Judith Smith; Hannah Hoy and Nancy Byer.
No Exor. named
Wit: John Hancock, John Hoy and William Oweings
Dated: 15 Oct. 1780   Proved: 29 March 1781

Will Book G - page 17

FRANTZ JACOB, Shenandoah County. Daus: Susannah Jacob; Julianna Jacob; Mary, wife of Henry Boyer; Eve, wife of Felde Miller; Elizabeth, wife of Adam Seivert; Catharine Jacob; Magdelene Jacob; Anne T. Jacob. Son: Jacob Jacob (eldest) - my land and plantation I now live on. Son: Daniel Jacob (youngest) - 40 acres of unimproved land adjoining lands of Peter Munch, the Glebe and John Jordan.
Exor: Eldest son, Jacob Jacob
Wit: Samuel R. Bader and Eli Kuran
Dated: 19 July 1804   Proved: 9 March 1807

Will Book N - page 350

JULIAS JACOBS, Shenandoah County. Brothers: David Jacobs and Jacob Jacobs. Nephew: John Jacobs. Brother-in-Law: Henry Boyers. Sister: Dilly Jacobs. Mentions: Catharine Jacobs, wife of my brother, Jacob.
Exor: Brother, Jacob Jacobs
Wit: Jacob Hahn, David Bushong and Martin Hupp
Dated: 25 Nov. 1825   Proved: 9 Jan. 1826

Will Book F - page 29

JANE JENKINS, Shenandoah County. Two sons: Josiah Jenkins and Thomas Jenkins - all my part of land left me by my deceased husband, Samuel Jenkins. Four daus: Elizabeth; Ann; Jean; Sarah.
Exors: Son, Josiah and dau., Ann
Wit: Henry Finly, Mathias Deer and Margaret Jenkins
Dated: 25 April 1801   Proved: 13 Sept. 1802

Will Book C - page 18

WILLIAM JONES, Shenandoah County. Wife: Elizabeth - negro wench named Else. Dau: Elizabeth. Mentions: Westly White, grandson of my beloved wife.
Exors: Thomas Henton and Anderson Moffett
Wit: Thomas Lewis, John Roush and Benjamin Heinkle
Dated: 26 Dec. 1788   Proved: 30 April 1789

Will Book R - page 226

DAVID JORDAN, SENIOR, Shenandoah County. Wife: Eve Margaretha. Sons: Charles and heirs of son, David (dec'd.) - tract of land whereon I now dwell (236 acres). Son: John - house and lot in Woodstock #126 whereon he has eracted a Tanyard and that out Lott in the Spring Hollow. Sons: Lewis and Benjamin. Daus: Mary Magdalena, wife of Daniel Hottel; Elizabeth and Catharine. Mentions: 100 acres situated between Narrow Passage and Stony Creek; two out lotts or 10 acres situated in the Spring Hollow - to be sold. Also, Lot #118 in town of Woodstock - to be sold.
Exor: Son-in-Law, Daniel Hottel
Wit: Thomas McCord, Benjamin Fravel and Henry Wunder
Dated: 1 Feb. 1832   Proved: 9 April 1832

Will Book S - page 507

EVE MARGARETH JORDAN, Shenandoah County. Son: Charles Jordan. Grandchild: Margareth Jordan, dau. of John Jordan. Dau: Catharine. Mentions: Deceased brother, John Brunner's widow, residing in Frederick, Maryland.
Exor: Charles Jordan
Wit: Charles Fisher and Thomas McCord
Dated: 26 Sept. 1834   Proved: 11 May 1835

Will Book F - page 153

THEODIOCUS JORDINE (JORDAN), Shenandoah County. Wife: Rosey. Sons: Jeremiah Jordine; Theodiocus Jordine. Dau: Rosey.
Exors: Isaac Hershberger and John Basye
No witnesses
Dated: 29 Jan. 1803   Proved: 12 Sept. 1803

Will Book Q - page 1

ABRAHAM JUDY, Shenandoah County. Wife: Katharina - all my lands. All my children: (not named).
Exor: Abraham Spitler, Jun.
Wit: Daniel Rothgeb and David Dacker
Dated: 19 Jan. 1827   Proved: 9 Aug. 1830

Will Book S - page 506

CHRISTIAN KAGEY, Shenandoah County. Wife: Catharine.
Eight children: Martin Kagey; Isaac Kagey; Barbara Kagey, wife of Zachariah Shirley; Samuel Kagey; Christian Kagey; Mary Kagey, wife of Joseph Neff; Elizabeth Kagey; Daniel Kagey.
Exors: Son-in-Law, Zachariah Shirley and Joseph Neff
Wit: Adam Olinger, John Thomas and John Newman
Dated: 5 July 1834   Proved: 11 Aug. 1834

Will Book V - page 80

HENRY KAGEY, Shenandoah County. Wife: Elizabeth. Mentions: Catharine Gochenour, widow of Abraham Gochenour shall have privilage of living in house where she now lives, rent free. Mentions: three children of Abraham Gochenour, dec'd. viz: John Henry; Samuel; James Harvey.
Exor: Michael Neff
Wit: S. F. Newland, Mounce Byrd and Joel Pennybacker
Dated: 15 Aug. 1839   Proved: 7 Oct. 1839

Will Book W - page 200

JACOB R. KAGEY, Shenandoah County. Wife: Mary Kagey - all the lands that I now have.
Exors: David Crabill, Sen. and Abraham Crabill, Jun.
Wit: Peter Hockman and George Shaver
Dated: 5 Oct. 1826   Proved: 10 Oct. 1842

Will Book X - page 276

JOHN KAGEY, Shenandoah County. Wife: (not named). Son:
Abraham - all my lands that I own. Son: Henry. Daus:
Anna and Elizabeth. Mentions: Anthony Ryan; Washington
Mahaney; Cathia McMollin.
Exor: Son, Abraham
Wit: John R. Kagey, Peter Kagey and Joseph Gochenour
Dated: 1 March 1832   Proved: 10 Nov. 1845

Will Book Y - page 456

PETER KAGEY, Shenandoah County. Wife: (not named).
Children: (not named).
Exor: Brother, David Kagey
Wit: John Cline, John Geib and Joseph Houser
Dated: 2 Feb. 1849   Proved: 12 March 1849

Will Book B - page 33

HENRY KAGY, SENIOR, Shanando County. Wife: Barbara.
Oldest son: John - 100 acres. Sons: Henry; Jacob; Abraham;
Christian; Rudolph; Isaac; Martin. Daus: Ann; Barbara;
Elizabeth.
Exor: Son, John Kagy
Wit: Jacob Neff, Frances Neff and Joseph James
Dated: 18 Oct. 1783.   Proved: 25 Dec. 1783

Will Book M - page 263

JOHN ADAM KAUFFELD, Shenandoah County. Sisters: Margaret
and Clara. Brother: George Kauffeld - 100 acres held between
us by Deed from the widow Kell. Brother: Jacob. Mentions:
two plantations containing 500 acres to be sold and money
to be divided between my brothers and sisters.
Exor: Brother, George Cauffeld
Wit: Nicholas Druck, Henry Druck and Charles Helzel
Dated: 17 Dec. 1817   Proved: 8 Dec. 1823

Will Book G - page 79

DANIEL KAUFFMAN, Shenandoah County. Wife: Barbara. Nine children: (not named).
Exors: Wife, Barbara and Henry Hottel
Wit: David Fedle, Augustine Coffman and Charles Wetzel
Dated: 21 April 1807   Proved: 8 June 1807

Will Book L - page 18

AUGUSTINE KAUFMAN, Shenandoah County. Wife: Mary Catharine - my estate and slaves. Sons: John; Adam; Mathias. Daus: Mary Catharine, late wife of Henry Surber; Christina, wife of John Wetzel; Ann Mary, wife of Henry Riffey; Elizabeth, wife of David Fadley; Barbara, wife of John Haller; Mary, wife of Jonathan Fadley.
Exor: Absalom Rinker
Wit: Jacob Coffelt, _____ (Ger.) and George Feather
Dated: 7 Feb. 1817   Proved: 9 Nov. 1818

Will Book H - page 338

MARTIN KAUFMAN, Shenandoah County. Wife: Mary Kaufman. Son: Jacob Kaufman - the plantation I now live on except 3 acres of meadow and part of upper orchard. Son: Samuel - 3 acres of meadow and upper part of orchard. Mentions: Land on the Blue Ridge. Mentions: To the President of the United States, I give a Bond due me by Christian and Samuel Forrer for one hundred pounds.
No Exor. named
Wit: William Marye, Samuel Forrer and Daniel Mauck
Dated: 20 Sept. 1809   Proved: 8 Feb. 1813

Will Book N - page 222

MARY KAUFMAN, Shenandoah County. Mentions: Son, Samuel Kaufman's children, viz: Nancy; Mary; Katharine; Elizabeth; David Kaufman. Mentions: Son, Jacob Kaufman's children, viz: Mary; Nancy; Barbara; Fidiny; Martin Kaufman.
Exors: Abraham Strickler and Christian Maggot
Wit: Christian Forrer, Rhoda Nicholas, _____ (Ger.) and Susannah Kaufman
Dated: 2 Feb. 1815   Proved: 9 May 1825

Will Book P - page 25

RUDOLPH KEAGY, Shenandoah County. Wife: Barbara - my plantation whereon I now live including my mountain tract of land. Children by my said wife, Barbara: David; Anna; John; Mary; Peter; Magdalene; Eve. Son: Christley - 100 acres of land in Township of Bristol, County of Trambull, State of Ohio. Son: David - 100 acres in aforesaid County and State. Sons: Jacob and Henry - balance of my land in aforesaid County and State, equally divided. Son: John - one half of all my land in Shenandoah County. Son: Peter - other half of my lands in Shenandoah County.
Exor: Son, David Keagy
Wit: Moses Walton, John Kagey and Reuben Walton
Dated: 21 March 1822   Proved: 9 March 1829

Will Book Y - page 327

ELIZABETH KEENER, Shenandoah County. Mentions: Michael Scarbaugh - the house and lot whereon I now reside in town of Woodstock.
Exor: W. W. Magruder
Wit: Noah Burner and Samuel Painter
Dated: 4 April 1848   Proved: 10 July 1848

Will Book G - page 333

NICHOLAS KEFFER, Shenandoah County. Wife: Polly Keffer. My children: (not named).
Exors: William Richardson and Martin Hupp
No witnesses
Dated: 25 June 1809   Proved: 11 Sept. 1809

Will Book Y - page 154

ADAM KEISTER, Town of Strasburg, Shenandoah County. Wife: Catharine - all my personal and real property.
No Exor. named
Wit: Cyrus Spengler and George Brinker
Dated: 12 May 1847   Proved: 13 Sept. 1847

Will Book B - page 323

ABRAM KELLAR, Shenandoah County. Wife: Elizabeth.
Children: Joseph Kellar; William; John; Jose; Rachael; Elizabeth.
Exor: Joseph Kellar
Wit: Peter Miller, George McKay and Charles Catlett
Dated: 20 April 1787 Proved: 26 April 1787

Will Book F - page 252

ELIZABETH KELLER, Shenandoah County. Mentions: my negro woman Daphney and her dau. Leas shall be free after my death. Mentions: Step-dau., Rachael Roy's sons by her first husband, namely, Abraham Matthews; Isaac Matthews and William Matthews. Mentions: Step-dau., Rachael Roy's three daus. by her first husband, Benjamin Matthews, namely, Elizabeth Matthews; Rebeckah Matthews and Sarah Matthews.
Exors: Isaac Overall and John Overall
Wit: David Keener and Jacob Miller
Dated: 23 Sept. 1804 Proved: 8 Oct. 1804

Will Book A - page 487

GEORGE KELLER, Shanando County in Virginia. Wife: Barbary.
Sons: George Keller; Isaac Keller; Jacob Keller; Henry Keller. Daus: Elizabeth; Mary; Barbary. Mentions: son-in-law, Henry Fravel and son-in-law, Mathias Wilkin. Mentions: Ann Keller.
Exors: Sons, George and Jacob Keller
Wit: George Huddle and Augustine Wendle
Dated: 13 July 1779 Proved: 28 March 1783

Will Book B - page 418

GEORGE KELLER, Beckford Parish, County of Shenandoah. Wife: Barbara. Son: Jacob Keller. Daus: Elizabeth Snapp, wife of Joseph Snapp; Mary Shireman, wife of Adam Shireman, Junior; Magdalena and Barbara Keller.
Exors: Sons-in-law, Joseph Snapp and Adam Shireman, Jr.
Wit: Alexander Hite, Philip Windle and George Copp
Dated: 28 Dec. 1787 Proved: 31 Jan. 1788

Wills and Accts. (1809-1863) - page 66

GEORGE KELLER, Shenandoah County. Wife: Catharine Keller - all my land and plantation whereon I now live on Tom's Brook. Sons: Samuel Keller; Jacob Keller; John Keller. Daus: Susanna Keller; Elizabeth, wife of Cornelius Dysert; Sarah, wife of John Kern; Rebeah, wife of Gabriel Stickley; Mary, wife of David Crabill; Catharine, wife of Abraham Crabill; Rachel Keller; Hannah Keller; Barbara Keller.
Exors: Son, John Keller and son-in-law, Abraham Crabill
Wit: David Crabill, Isaac Dunnivan and Jonathan Kronck
Dated: 4 March 1819   Proved: 22 May 1820

Will Book T - page 429

GEORGE KELLER, Shenandoah County. Mentions: two friends, Philip Ruby and Philip Wilkin - all my land and plantation whereon I now reside containing 146 acres. Mentions: friend, Absalom Rinker. Mentions: three friends, Polly Shaver, widow of Philip Shaver, dec'd.; John Strout and Anna Betts - the remainder part of my Estate.
Exor: Absalom Rinker
Wit: Joshua Foltz, Thomas Corbin, Isreal Rinker and Lewis Fadley
Dated: 6 June 1836

CODICIL to Will of GEORGE KELLER - Mentions: Reuben Pence, son of Isaac Pence to share in Estate.
Wit: Joshua Foltz and Thomas Corbin
Dated: 19 Oct. 1836   Proved: 7 Nov. 1836

Will Book T - page 337

JACOB KELLER, Shenandoah County. Wife: Susannah Keller. Son: John Keller - tract of land and plantation whereon Adam Burner now lives, also, tract I purchased of John Nichols. Sons: Jacob and George - residue of my Estate, my books and surgical instruments, lands and plantation with the Grist Mill and Saw Mill - equally divided between them. Dau: Sarah, wife of John Shipe - one half tract of land (entire tract contains 200 acres). Dau: Polly, wife of James Burner - residue of above mentioned tract of land. Mentions: tract of land in Front Royal, 2 tracts of land in Powell's Fort - to be sold. Daus: Catharine, wife of Adam Lickliter; Rebecca, wife of Isaac Funk; Barbara, wife of Isaac Beydler; Susannah Keller; Mary Ann, wife of Adam Burner.
Exors: Son-in-Law, Isaac Beydler and friend, Henry Cullers
Wit: Jacob Ott, P. Williams and George Bowman
Dated: 13 Nov. 1836   Proved: 13 June 1836

Will Book N - page 343

JOSEPH KELLER, Shenandoah County. Wife: Leah - plantation whereon I now live. Son: George Keller - 295 acres of land (part of the 375 acres adjoining the place I now live). Dau: Elizabeth, wife of John Stickley - the remainder of said tract of 375 acres, adjoining lands of John Supinger and Jacob Windle. Dau: Esther Bly, mother of Joseph, John and Isaac Bly. Son-in-Law: John Bly - one dollar. Mentions: My fourth part of a tract of land containing 7,000 acres shall be equally divided between my son, George Keller, Elizabeth Stickley and my grandsons, Joseph Bly, John Bly and Isaac Bly. Mentions: William Martin and Jane Curry - two bound children.
Exor: Son, George Keller
Wit: Jacob Windle, Jacob Grove and William Martin
Dated: 24 March 1801

CODICIL to Will of JOSEPH KELLER. - Mentions: Son, George Keller and grandsons, Joseph, Isaac and John Bly.
Wit: Jonathan Pittman and Jacob Windle
Dated: 11 April 1815   Proved: 12 Dec. 1825

Will Book V - page 260

LEAH KELLER, widow of Joseph Keller, Shenandoah County. Son: George Keller - one half the money contained in a round box in my chest (gold). Granddaughter: Leah Keller - the round box and other half of the money. Daus: Esther Hudson and Elizabeth Stickley. Grandson: Jacob Keller.
Exor: Son, George Keller
Wit: Joseph Wattson and Jacob Windle
Dated: 11 July 1837   Proved: 10 Aug. 1840

Will Book M - page 194

SUSANNA KELP, Shenandoah County. Widow of William Kelp, dec'd. My sister's dau: Susanna Sine, wife of Peter Sine. Sister: Clara Coffeld, widow of George Coffeld (dec'd.).
Exor: My sister's son, Adam Coffeld
Wit: David Jordan, _____(Ger.) and John Meily
Dated: 12 March 1808   Proved: 9 June 1823

Will Book D - page 190

WILLIAM KELP, Shenandoah County. Wife: Susanna Kelp - plantation whereon I now live adjoining George Wisman and John Gibler. Mentions: Two brothers, John Adam Kelp and John Adam Kelp, Junior (surnamed, Jonathan Kelp). Youngest sister: Catharine Kelp (now living in Ephrata in Pennsylvania). Other three sisters: Catharine, wife to John Haus; Christina, wife to Christian Luther and Anna Maria, wife to John Martin.
Exor: Wife, Susanna
Wit: David Jordan, Mathias Zehring and _____ (Ger.)
Dated: 17 April 1792   Proved: 12 March 1793

Will Book A - page 467

ABRAHAM KENDRICK, Frederick County, Commonwealth of Virginia. Wife: Barbary - all my plantation that I purchased of Sam Vance. Son: Jacob Kendrick - plantation whereon he now lives. Son: Abraham Kendrick - plantation whereon he now lives. Sons: Benjamin Kendrick and Christopher Kendrick. Dau: Catharine - 540 acres I purchased of Delinger.
Exors: Alexander Hite and Philip Hufman
Wit: John Cordell, Alexander Hite, Philip Bush, Isaac Sittler, John Bushong and Abraham Crable.
Dated: 15 Nov. 1779   Proved: 27 Dec. 1782

Will Book L - page 385

MARY KENDRICK, Shenandoah County. Granddaughter: Lucy Robertson - my house and lot that I at present occupy.
Exor: Jacob Good (saddler), Washington Farra and Simeon Yager
Dated: 17 April 1820   Proved: 8 Oct. 1821

Will Book P - page 314

MARY KENNEDY, Town of Woodstock, Shenandoah County. Mentions: Christena Wisman, Lydia Wisman and Dociam Wisman - the house and lot I now occupy. Mentions: Rents owing me from Estate of George Fravell, dec'd.
Exor: Nephew, George Wisman, Jr.
Wit: Philip Miller and Samuel Clower
Dated: 13 Nov. 1828   Proved: 11 Jan. 1830

Will Book B - page 363

CHRISTIAN KIBLER, County of Shanando. Wife: Mary Magdelene Kibler. Sons: William; Philip; Christian; John; Lewis.
Daus: Catharina and Magdalene.
Exors: Mathis Smutz and John Cook
Wit: Samuel Mills, John William Sign and Ann Mary Sign
Dated: 12 Aug. 1786　　　　　　　　Proved: 21 July 1787

Will Book F - page 292

WENDLE KIBLER, Shenandoah County. Wife: Agata - the whole of all that I am worth and all that I possess.
Exor: John Hockman
Wit: Mathias Gleiser and Peter Nagle
Dated: 31 March 1804　　　　　　　　Proved: 11 March 1805

This last Will and Testament in the German language (with translation thereof in English) was proved by the oathes of the witnesses and the translation by the affirmation of John Roads.

Will Book E - page 109

DANIEL KIBLINGER, Shannadoh County, yeoman. Wife: Catharin. Sons: John; Jacob; Adam. Daus: Catharin; Anna Mary; Elizabeth; Eve; Susana.
Exor: Son, John
Wit: Philip Summer, Joseph Roth and John Bentz
Dated: 12 Aug. 1797　　　　　　　　Proved: 12 Sept. 1797

Will Book F - page 426

DANIEL KINGERY (KINGAREE), Shenandoah County. Wife: (not named). Son: Solomon - land and plantation whereon he now lives. Son: John - land and plantation whereon I now live. Sons: Henry and Abraham. My daus. who are married: Elizabeth Anna; Caty; Mary; Rebecca.
Exor: Son, Solomon
Wit: William Byrd, Samuel Coffman and _____ (Ger.)
Dated: 6 May 1803　　　　　　　　Proved: 8 April 1808

Will Book Y - page 486

JACOB KIPPS, Shenandoah County. Wife: Elizabeth. Sons: George and Henry. Daus: Eve; Catharine, wife of John Cline; Mary, wife of Samuel Hupp. Son: Jacob - a lot of land whereon a dwelling house, stable, well and milk house now stand. Dau: Elizabeth, wife of Benjamin Landis - tract of land in Main County, State of Indiana containing 80 acres. Son: Moses - my farm whereon I now live (100 acres).
Exor: Reuben Walton
Wit: Moses Walton, Michael Nefs and John Shomo
Dated: 26 April 1830

CODICIL to Will of JACOB KIPPS - Mentions land to sons, Jacob Kipps, Henry Kipps and Moses.
Wit: Joel Pennybacker, Jno. Zirkle and Aaron Nefs
Dated: 27 April 1838   Proved: 7 May 1849

Will Book O - page 357

JOHN KIPS, Shenandoah County. Wife: (not named). All my children: (not named). Mentions: My wife and brother, Jacob Kips to keep the house which I now occupy open as a Wagon Stand. Mentions: sell my negro woman by name of Diana.
Exor: Jacob Williamson
Wit: S. Coffman, Francis Sibert and John Shomo
Dated: 20 June 1828   Proved: 11 Aug. 1828

Will Book I - page 50

JACOB KIRLIN, Shenandoah County. Sons: Samuel and William - my plantation whereon I now live containing 200 acres. Sons: John Kirlin and David Kirlin. Dau: Elizabeth.
Exors: Son, William and friend, Jacob Good
Wit: George Mourey, Martin Garber and Barbara Gets
Dated: 17 March 1814   Proved: 12 April 1814

Will Book I - page 143

JOHN KLICK (CLICK), SENIOR, Shenandoah County. Wife:
Barbara (dec'd.). Present wife: Mary. Son: John - all the
plantation whereon I now live adjoining lands of Abraham
Hefs, William Good and Henry Baughman containing 314 acres.
Daus: Elizabeth; Barbara; Ann; Catharine. Children of my
deceased wife, Barbara and her former husband, Henry Baughman:
Jacob Baughman (wife was formerly Catharine Neff) and other
children (not named).
Exors: Son, John, Jacob Gerber and John Kagy
Wit: Frances Neff, J. Steigel, Peter Zimmerman and Jacob
Rinker
Dated: 19 March 1805   Proved: 9 March 1814

Will Book L - page 444

JOHN KLICK (CLICK), JUNIOR, Shenandoah County. English
translation to this Will is missing. A copy of the German
Will can be ordered from the Shenandoah County Courthouse,
Woodstock, Virginia.

Will Book L - page 46

GEORGE KNEISLEY, Shenandoah County. Wife: Susannah.
Sons: John and Jacob. Other children: (not named).
Exors: David McIntuf, Sen. and George Bowman
Wit: David Clem and Henry Lichliter
Dated: 28 Jan. 1819   Proved: 8 March 1819

Will Book W - page 124

JACOB KNEISLEY, JUNIOR, Shenandoah County. Father: Jacob
Kneisley. Brother: Chapman Kneisley. Mother: Barbara
Kneisley. Brothers-in-Law: Henry Gochenour and James
Ruddell.
Exor: Samuel Williams
Wit: Conrad Lichliter and Henry Gochenour
Dated: 29 March 1842   Proved: 13 June 1842

Will Book F - page 284

JOHN KNISLY, Shenandoah County. Wife: Magdalene. Son: George Knisly - tract of land whereon he now lives situated in Powel's Fort, I purchased from Calop Odell containing 268 acres. Son: David Knisly - tract of land whereon he now lives situated in Powel's Fort, I purchased from Isaac Odell containing 56 acres. Sons: John; Jacob; Henry. Dau: Elizabeth, wife of John Middleton - 5 acres of land which he, John Middleton, now lives. Mentions: children of my dau. Margretha, wife of John Evans - one certain Lot in town of Woodstock. Daus: Magdalene, wife of John Wood and Catharina.
Exors: Wife, Magdalene, David Jordan, Jackman Felzer and David Beaver
Wit: Henry Conrad, George Dellinger and _____(Ger.)
Dated: 22 May 1804　　　　　　Proved: 9 July 1804

Will Book I - page 507

JOHN KNOP, Shenandoah County. Wife: Mary - the house which I now live in, in town of Woodstock. Mentions: land and plantation on Narrow Passage Creek adjoining land of John Thompson and John Rufsell and Lot #91 adjoining the town of Woodstock - to be sold.
Exor: Jacob Rinker, Jr.
Wit: _____(Ger.), Samuel Bare and John Effinger
Dated: 16 Nov. 1815　　　　　Proved: 11 Dec. 1815

Will Book T - page 125

MARY KNOPP, Shenandoah County. Dau: Elizabeth Donnelson - my five acre lot adjoining William Ott and my house and lot in Town of Woodstock I now live in. Son: John Seller. Dau: Catharine Mills.
No Exor. named
Wit: John Haynes, Samuel Few and Samuel Bare
Dated: 14 May 1835　　　　　Proved: 7 Dec. 1835

Will Book O - page 34

GEORGE KOONTZ, Shenandoah County. Wife: Elizabeth.
Children: John Koontz; Mary Koontz; Eveline Koontz;
Henry Koontz; William J. Koontz; George Koontz.
Exor: John Koontz
Wit: William Payne, William Thompson and Peter Bushong
Dated: 9 April 1819   Proved: 12 Feb. 1827

Will Book T - page 529

MICHAEL KOONTZ, SENIOR, Shenandoah County. Wife: Mary.
Twelve children: Michael; Catharine; Sarah; Polly; Anna;
Susan; Mary; Lydia; Samuel; John; Barbara; Christina.
Exors: Wife, Mary Koontz and son, Michael Koontz
Wit: Levi Rinker and George Tarkleson
Dated: 17 Dec. 1836   Proved: 13 March 1837

Will Book D - page 391

CONRAD KUHL (COOL), Shenandoah County. Wife: Catharine.
Youngest son: Ernest. Son: John. Other children: (not named).
Exors: Son, John and Michael Branner
Wit: Abraham Harpine, Jacob Stiegle and _____(Ger.)
Dated: 4 Dec. 1794   Proved: 12 Jan. 1795

Will Book W - page 67

EVE LAMBERT, of Woodstock, Shenandoah County. Sister:
Sally Anspauck - my part of the house and lot in Woodstock.
Nephew: Henry Trout (son of Henry Trout, dec'd.). Ten
Nieces: Mary Trout; Elizabeth Trout; Rebecca Trout (daus.
of Philip Trout, dec'd.); Elizabeth Trout, Rebecca Hickman;
Mary Myers (daus. of Henry Trout, dec'd.); Mary Yager;
Sarah Yager; Rebecca Yager; Elizabeth Yager (daus; of
Simeon Yager).
No Exor. named
Wit: Samuel Myers and Isaac Trout
Dated: 22 Sept. 1828   Proved: 7 Feb. 1842

Will Book W - page 282

HENRY LAMBERT, Shenandoah County. Wife: Elizabeth Lambert.
Grandson: Robert Miller, son of Samuel Miller. My four
children: Julia Marshall; David Lambert; Henry Lambert;
Elizabeth Grandstaff.
Exors: Son, David Lambert and Henry Marshall
Wit: John Coffelt, John Maurer and Joseph Ludwick
Dated: 8 Jan. 1843   Proved: 14 March 1843

Will Book R - page 235

MARY LAMBERT, Shenandoah County. Sons: William Lambert
and Isaac Lambert - divide the land equally as their father,
Abraham Lambert, requested. Son: John Harrow. Dau: Sarah
Artz, formerly Sarah Lambert.
Exor: Son, Isaac Lambert
Wit: Simeon Yager and Isaac Trout
Dated: 30 Aug. 1831   Proved: 7 May 1832

Will Book D - page 193

GEORGE LANTZ, Shenandoah County. Sons: George; Jacob;
John; Andrew. Mentions: five children of my dau,,
Margaretha (dec'd.).
Exor: Youngest son, Jacob Lantz
Wit: William David, Charles Smith and Samuel Hoshour
Dated: 27 Dec. 1792   Proved: 12 March 1793

Will Book T - page 525

JACOB LANTZ, Shenandoah County. Dau: Mary, wife of John
Bowman - two tracts of land, one whereon said Bowman now
resides conveyed to me by heirs of Jacob Ruby, dec'd.
(192 acres); the other containing 200 acres conveyed to
me by Jacob Coffelt. Son: George Lantz - my plantation
whereon I now live containing 470 acres and my negro girl,
Sinah.
Exor: Son, George
Wit: A. Rinker, John Painter (of George) and George Bender
Dated: 13 Oct. 1836   Proved: 13 Feb. 1837

Will Book B - page 427

BENJAMIN LAYMAN, County of Shanando. Wife: Catharine - 35 acres of land. Dau: Elizabeth Shireman - 150 acres. Son: Joseph Layman - 95 acres adjoining lands of Nicholas Saum and Daniel Huddle. Son: John Layman - 110 acres. Son: Benjamin. Son: Isaac - one shilling. Daus: Mary Boughman; Barbara Funkhouser; Catharine Wilkin; Ann; Susannah; Christena; Roseanah; Sarah.
Exors: Godfrey Wilkin and Frederick Woodford
Wit: George Wetzel, Henry Daring, Frederick Woolford and John Williams
Dated: 9 Jan. 1787   Proved: 28 Feb. 1788

Will Book G - page 415

EDWARD LEAVELL, Shenandoah County. Wife: Mary Ann. Son: Edward. My other children: (not named).
Exor: Son, Edward
Wit: Peirson Judd and Frederick Oldher
Dated: 12 Jan. 1810   Proved: 12 Feb. 1810

Will Book V - page 8

RICHARD LEE (a man of color), Shenandoah County. Wife: Rachael Lee - all my lands and tenements. My children: (not named).
Exor: Daniel Hottle
Wit: John G. Schmitt and George Shrum
Dated: 12 April 1839   Proved: 13 May 1839

Will Book F - page 480

JAMES LEETH, Shenandoah County. Wife: Lydia - my negro woman, Sarah. Son: George Leeth - all my lands that I now hold and two negro boys named Joseph and Soloman. Dau: Polly Terrce - mulatto boy named Dick. Dau: Nancy Leeth - to have youngest child of negro, Sarah (Lucy). Dau: Hannah Overall.
Exor: Son, George Leeth
Wit: Jeremiah McKay, William McKay and Abraham Odell
Dated: 13 July 1806   Proved: 13 Oct. 1806

Will Book E - page 107

LEAH LEETH, widow, Parish of Beckford, County of Shenandoah.
Son: William Tyler - all my rights, title and claim of the
plantation whereon I now live, willed to me by my father,
Robert McKay. Mentions: granddaughter, Margaret Whitson;
Grandsons: Joseph Whitson and James Whitson. Dau: Leah.
Exor: Son, William Tyler
Wit: Jeremiah McKay, James Johnston and Samuel Odell
Dated: 9 Oct. 1794   Proved: 12 Sept. 1797

Will Book K - page 208

HENRY LENARD, Shenandoah County. Wife: Catherine - the
plantation I now live on. Mentions: Michael Lenard, son
of John Lenard. Mentions: land lying in Rockingham County,
Virginia - to be sold.
Exor: Jacob Knupp
Wit: George Mourey, Jonathan Harpine and _____(Ger.)
Dated: 1 Sept. 1816   Proved: 13 Jan. 1817

Will Book E - page 6

GEORGE LENTZ, Shenandoah County. Wife: Anna Catherina.
Sons: George Adam Lentz; Henry Lentz; Jacob Lentz and
George Lentz (dec'd.). Daus: Anna Maria (dec'd.);
Catharina (dec'd.) and Elizabeth.
Exors: Wife, Anna Catharine and Henry Lentz
Wit: George Fravel, David Jordan and John Geyer
Dated: 6 Nov. 1789   Proved: 8 March 1796

Will Book H - page 438

HENRY LENTZ, Shenandoah County. Wife: Mary Lentz. Sons:
George Lentz and Philip Lentz.
Exors: Mathias Smutz, Sen. and Henry Kevrans
Wit: George Bauhman, John Kline and Simeon Yager
Dated: 9 May 1813   Proved: 12 July 1813

Will Book O - page 21

ADAM LICHLITER, Shenandoah County. Wife: Catharine Lichliter. Son: Henry Lichliter - tract of land whereon he now lives containing 109 acres which I purchased of Henry Franz, and part of tract which I purchased of John Dilly containing 104 acres. Son: Adam Lichliter - remainder of above mentioned tract, also, tract I purchased of my brother, John Lichliter, containing 95 acres, also, small tract I got a Warrent for containing 15 acres and the land I now live on containing 84 acres. Other children: Conrad Lichliter; Catharine, wife of Henry Sibert; Jacob Lichliter; Daniel Lichliter; Barbara Knisley, wife of John Knisley; David Lichliter; Magdalene Smith, wife of Solomon Smith.
Exors: Sons, Jacob Lichliter and Henry Lichliter
Wit: John Shipe, Daniel Shipe and John Jones
Dated: 8 Dec. 1826   Proved: 8 Jan. 1827

Will Book R - page 124

CHRISTENA LINDAMOOD, Shenandoah County, widow and relick of Andrew Lindamood, dec'd. Granddaughter: Magdelene Fry. Mentions: John Albright, son of my granddaughter, Magdelene Fry. Grandson: Samuel McWay. Mentions: Andrew McWay, son of Samuel McWay. Daus: Caty Fry; Elizabeth Foltz, Barbara Smith; Christena Bender; Mary Fry.
Exor: John Bender, Senior
Wit: George Lindamood, Jacob Noel and Samuel McQuay
Dated: 27 May 1831   Proved: 12 Dec. 1831

Will Book S - page 307

MICHAEL LINDAMOOD, Shenandoah County. Wife: Mary - the mansion house. Son: Joseph - 5 acres to be laid off next to his place. Sons: Elijah and Jacob - all the residue of my land to be divided equally. Daus: Mary; Christina; Magdalene; Regina. Mentions: Dau. Catharine's child. Unfortunate dau: Rachael - one dollar.
Exor: Son, Elijah
Wit: William Fry and Michael Fry

CODICIL to Will of MICHAEL LINDAMOOD - Mentions: Son, Elijah to give son, Jacob one half of the barn.
Dated: 28 July 1834   Proved: 8 Sept. 1834

Will Book M - page 341

ANDREW LINDAMUDE, Shenandoah County. Wife: Christena Lindamude - my dwelling house wherein I now live. Sons: Michael Lindamude and Andrew Lindamude - plantation whereon I now live containing 225 acres, also, tract of land containing 81 acres which I purchased of Joseph Ryman. Daus: Barbara, wife of John Smith; Elizabeth, wife of Joshua Fultz, Jr.; Christena, wife of Henry Fry; Catharine, wife of Jacob Fry; Mary, wife of John Fry. Grandson: Samuel, son of my dau. Barbara. Granddaughter: Magdalene, dau. of my dau. Barbara.
Exor: Jacob Rinker, Sen.
Wit: _____(Ger.), John Bainder and John Emswiller
Dated: 11 Feb. 1816   Proved: 10 May 1824

Will Book N - page 142

CHRISTOPHER LINDAMUDE, Shenandoah County. Wife: Frainey. Two sons: Michael Lindamude and George Lindemude - all my lands containing 591 acres. Daus: Elizabeth, wife of Michael Fedley; Hannah Grove; Mary, wife of George Painter; Susannah, wife of Jonathan Harpine; Rachael, wife of Philip Painter; Christina Lindemude.
Exors: Henry Frye and George Painter (son of John)
Wit: Jacob Rinker, Nancy Williams and Ephraim Rinker
Dated: 23 May 1818   Proved: 7 March 1825

Will Book S - page 320

JACOB LINEWEAVER, Shenandoah County. Wife: Margaret Lineweaver (later called Catharine). Sons: John Lineweaver and Philip Lineweaver - all my lands consisting of two surveys (125 acres). Six daus: Catharine; Mary; Margaret; Christena; Sarah; Elizabeth.
Exors: John Saum and Jacob Gochenour
Wit: Phineas Orndorff and Henry Wolfe
Dated: 4 Sept. 1828   Proved: 13 Oct. 1834

Will Book E - page 307

CATHARINE LINK, Shenandoah County. Son: Henry Hiser.
No Exor. named
Wit: John Bathis and Solomon Spangler
Dated: 21 April 1799   Proved: 10 Sept. 1799

Will Book F - page 506

JOHN LIONBERGER, JUNIOR, Shenandoah County. Wife: Susannah - shall keep full possession of all my Estate if she remains unmarried. Children: Reuben; Daniel; Ann; John (youngest).
Exors: Brother, David Lionberger and Joseph Roads
Wit: William Almond, Alexander Hay and Samuel Forrer
Dated: 11 Oct. 1806   Proved: 8 Dec. 1806

Will Book T - page 449

JOHN LOCK, Shenandoah County. Wife: Dycia - tract of land containing 60 acres. Mentions: Bond given by George Bird, dec'd. to Dycia Murphy in year 1825, in hands of Reuben Bird. Mentions: William Fitch, who married my dau. Polly; Jacob Fravel, who married my dau. Milly; Jacob Howbert who married my dau. Margaret; William Crow, who married my dau. Betsy.
Exor: George Will
Wit: Reuben Miller, Henry Tutt and Reuben Bird
Dated: 9 Feb. 1833   Proved: 12 Dec. 1836

Will Book B - page 512

GEORGE LOCKMILLER, Gentleman, Shenandoah County. Wife: Catharina. Four sons: (only three named)Jacob Lockmiller; George Lockmiller; John Lockmiller. Three daus: (only one named) Barbra.
Exor: John Blye
Wit: Jacob Bly, Catharina Lockmiller and Peter Hurbough
Dated: 3 Oct. 1788   Proved: 25 Dec. 1788

Will Book L - page 326

JACOB LOCKMILLER, Shenandoah County. Wife: Catharine Lockmiller. Dau: Solina Lockmiller. Sons: William and John Lockmiller. Rest of children: (not named). Mentions: Joseph Spencer.
Exor: George Hottel, Esq.
Wit: Elijah Richards, Isaac Hurbough and Polly Hurbough
Dated: 16 Dec. 1820   Proved: 11 June 1821

Will Book I - page 416

JOHN LOINBERGER, SENIOR, Shenandoah County. Wife: Barbara. Four sons: Samuel; Abraham; Joseph and Jacob - the plantation whereon I now live equally divided amongst them after Jacob arrives of lawful age. Daus: Mary; Leah; Magdalene; Barbara; Susannah; Rebecca. Mentions: David and Peter, heirs of son, John. Also, leaves his Black Smith tools to his four sons.
Exors: William Marye and William Almond
Wit: Ambrose Booten, John Whiting and William Mourer
Dated: 15 Jan. 1813   Proved: 11 Sept. 1815

Will Book D - page 199

GEORGE LONAS, Shenandoah County. Wife: Rosina. Son:Henry Lonas - all my plantation whereon I now live containing 320 acres. Son: Adam Lonas. Daus: Margaret, wife of George Bower of the City of Philadelphia. All my children: (not named).
Exor: Son, Henry Lonas
Wit: Jacob Rinker, George Delinger and Ulrick Nease
Dated: 4 June 1789   Proved: 12 March 1793

Will Book Y - page 334

ELIZABETH LONG, Shenandoah County. Sons: John Long and Jacob Long - all my land (120 acres) and the plantation I now live on. Daus: Susannah, wife of Daniel Wambler; Catharine, wife of Jonas Wambler; Sarah, wife of Daniel Stoner.
Exors: Sons, John and Jacob Long
Wit: Jacob Noel, John Wine and Isaac Myers
Dated: 8 Sept. 1842   Proved: 7 Aug. 1848

Will Book I - page 47

LEWIS LONG, Shenandoah County. Mother and Father: James and Mary Long. Sister: Frankey Long.
Exor: Father, James Long
Wit: Philip Spengler and Jacob Coffman
Dated: 27 July 1813   Proved: 8 Nov. 1813

Will Book N - page 379

PHILIP LONG, SENIOR, Shenandoah County. Son: Reubin Long - 700 acres of land I purchased of John Strickler and Michael Rader, also, two negroes namely, Ned and Cate. Son: Philip Long - certain tract of land containing 289 1/2 acres which I purchased of C. Auld, also, three negro slaves, namely George, Ben and Nance. Son: Adam Long - certain tract of land lying in Mason County purchased of John Thornton, also, another containing 400 acres. Son: Nathan Long - balance of the tract of land of 1,100 acres in Mason County and two negro slaves named John and Abraham, also, another tract of land of 447 acres. Son: Jonas Long - tract of land in Cabell County containing 400 acres and three negro slaves namely, Pat Ned and Susanna. Son: Isaac Long - land on which he now lives containing 864 acres and two negroes, namely, Newman and Barbara. Dau: Mary Secrist, wife of Michael Secrist - negro woman named Winney.
Exor: Son, Isaac Long
Wit: Nancy Painter, William Mayer and George Dediman
Dated: 12 Feb. 1823   Proved: 13 Feb. 1826

Will Book D - page 286

DAVID LOUDERBACK, Shenandoah County. Wife: Elizabeth. Sons: David; John; Mathias; Joseph; Daniel; Abraham. Daus: Christina; Susanna; Elizabeth; Sarah; Eve; Barbara.
Exors: Son, Mathias and John Foby
Wit: John Foby, John Foby, Jr. and George Koontz
Dated: 14 Feb. 1792   Proved: 11 Dec. 1793

Will Book O - page 464

JOSEPH LOUDERBACK, Shenandoah County. Son: David - my
home place. Son: Joseph - land in State of Ohio (164 acres).
Dau: Elizabeth - five acres.
Exor: Jacob Stroht
Wit: Jacob Foltz and Reuben Foltz
Dated: 8 Oct. 1828   Proved: 11 Nov. 1828

Will Book F - page 519

MATHIAS LOUDERBACK, Shenandoah County. Wife: Magdalene.
Son: David - already received his portion. Sons: Philip
and Rubin - the plantation of 216 acres whereon I now
live. Sons: Daniel and Abraham - land in Rockingham Co.
of 164 acres. Daus: Sarah; Barbary; Eve, wife of Abraham
Camel; Magdalene, wife of Joromya Hufman.
Exor: Son, Philip
Wit: Jacob Kiser, Joseph Louderback and John Cochenour
Dated: 29 Dec. 1806   Proved: 13 Jan. 1807

Will Book E - page 355

DANIEL LOVE, Shenandoah County. Wife: Tabitha Love - lot
in Shenandoah County containing 150 acres. Daus: Tabitha
Love; Polly Love; Sarah Love; Elizabeth Love. Mentions:
My estate lying in County of Culpeper consisting of 11 acres.
Exors: William Allen and Thomas Hickman
Wit: John Remy, Benjamin Hally; Enoch Weekley and John Hickman
Dated: 10 Feb. 1799   Proved: 11 Dec. 1799

Will Book O - page 336

JOHN LUTHER, Village of New Holland, County of Lancaster,
State of Pennsylvania. Wife: Elizabeth. Dau: Louisa.
Wife's father: Peter Diller, dec'd. Two sons: Diller and
John Weaver - my surgical and obstetrical instruments and
my entire Library.
Exors: Brother-in-Law, Roland Diller and son, Diller Luther
Wit: Henry Roland and Levi Diller
Dated: 6 April 1827

CODICIL to Will of JOHN LUTHER- Mentions: Dau. Louisa has
been engaged and bespoken for - changes legacy.
Dated: 7 Feb. 1828   Proved: 24 March 1828
                                  Lancaster Co. Pa.
                                       9 July 1828
                                  Shenandoah Co., Va.

Will Book B - page 266

JONAS LUTZ, Strasburg, Shenandoah County. Dau: Margaret
Lutz - house and lot in town of Strasburg obtained by Deed
from Alexander Machir, Esq. Dau: Clara, wife of Thomas
Welsh. Sons: Joseph Lutz and Jacob Lutz.
Exor: Alexander Hite
Wit: Philip Huffman, Jacob Yost and _____(Ger.)
Dated: 13 Sept. 1783   Proved: 28 Sept. 1786

Will Book I - page 259

MICHAEL LUTZ, Shenandoah County. Wife: Susannah. Sons:
Jacob; George; John Lutz. Daus: Mary Lutz; Susannah Lutz;
Caty Lutz; Modleen Lutz.
Exors: George Lindamude and George Funkhouser
Wit: _____(Ger.), Jacob Groves, Michael Filsmoyer and
Jacob Lindamood
Dated: 2 Aug. 1812   Proved: 7 Sept. 1812

Will Book A - page 250

JOHN MACANTUR, SENIOR, Shanando County, Colony of Virginia.
Wife: Rozeanah. Sons: John; Frederick; Daniel; David;
Casper and Christopher. Daus: Mary and Margret.
No Exor. named
Wit: John and Frederick McEntor
Dated: 25 June 1799   Proved: 29 July 1799

Will Book C - page 176

ALEXANDER MACHIR, Strawsburg, County of Shenandoah. Wife:
Magdalena. Children: Scota Machir; Margaret Machir: Betsy
Machir; Sarah Machir; Angus Machir; Henry Machir and John
Machir. Mentions: Kinsman, James Carnagy, dec'd.
Exors: John Croudson of Woodstock, John Machir of District
of Kentucky, James Machir of Moorefield and William Clayton
Williams - also jointly guardians of my children.
Wit: George Lind, Philip Huffman and George Cooper
Dated: 2 March 1790   Proved: 24 June 1790

Will Book Y - page 313

ELIZABETH MACHIR, Shenandoah County. Mentions: Estate to be divided equally in three parts. Son: Philip Machir; Dau: Catharine S. Frank. Mentions: other third to son, Philip A. Machir in trust for use of Harriet Machir, wife of my son, Joseph S. Machir.
Exor: My brother, Joseph S. Spangler
Wit: George Brinker, Joseph Zea and John Pirkey
Dated: 30 Oct. 1847   Proved: 12 June 1848

Will Book U - page 375

DAVID MAFIUS, Shenandoah County. Wife: Barbara. Sons: John Mafius; George Mafius; Samuel Mafius; Jacob Mafius; Joseph Mafius. Daus: Sarah, now Sarah Swartz; Barbara Mafius; Catharine Mafius; Elizabeth Mafius. Mentions: brothers and sisters (not named).
Exors: Son-in-Law, Joseph Swartz and son, John Mafius
Wit: Simeon Yager, Samuel Maphies and Joseph Wisman
Dated: 23 Nov. 1832   Proved: 8 Oct. 1838

Will Book O - page 310

CHRISTIAN MAGART, Shenandoah County. Wife: Mary - the place upon which I now live containing about 201 acres during her natural life. Son: Isaac - the above place after her death. Dau: Mary Rothgeb. Mentions: land purchased of John Mauck adjoining land of David Rothgeb, Sen. Grandchildren: (the children of my deceased dau. Barbara Kaufman), Mary Gander; Anna Kaufman; Barbara Kaufman; Frances Kaufman; Martin Kaufman.
Exor: John Varner
Wit: W. C. Lauck, Henry Strickler and David Strickler
Dated: 25 March 1828   Proved: 12 May 1828

Will Book A - page 78

DAVID MAGERT, Colony of Virginia, in Frederick County. Wife: Margaret. Children: David (oldest); Bence; Daniel; John; Henry; Jacob; Rudolph and Elizabeth.
Exors: Jacob Sheafer and Henry Mauk
Wit: George Kuntz, John Magert and Peter Roadcap
Dated: 23 Dec. 1770   Proved: 23 May 1775

Will Book F - page 384

BENJAMIN MAGGERT, Shenandoah County. Wife: Susana Maggert.
Children: (not named).
Exors: Christian Alshite and Thomas Newman
Wit: _____(Ger.), Jacob Maggert and Barbara Newman
Dated: 5 Sept. 1805   Proved: 9 Dec. 1805

Will Book W - page 258

RACHEL MAHANEY, widow of Stephen Mahaney (dec'd.), Shenandoah
County. My mother: Mary Parkins (dec'd.). My father:
Isaac Parkins. Daus: Isabella Mahaney and Hannah Marker,
wife of Amos Marker - lot of land lying in Frederick Co.,
Va. near Winchester left to me by my mother (30 acres).
Mentions: Vastine Colville and Mary his wife of Licking
County, Ohio. Mentions: Nathan Parkins.
Exor: Son-in-Law, Amos Marker
Wit: Joseph Wattson, Herbert Hiner and John Cooper
Dated: 24 Feb. 1842

CODICIL to Will of RACHEL MAHANEY - Mentions: Isabella
Mahaney (now Isabella Bayly) - I give young mare, Abby.
Wit: Joseph Wattson and John Cooper
Dated: 4 Aug. 1842   Proved: 13 Feb. 1843

Will Book V - page 447

STEPHEN MAHANEY, Shenandoah County. Daus: Isabela Mahaney;
Hannah Marker, wife of Amos Marker; Mary Colville, wife of
Vastine Colville. Sons: Lewis Mahaney; Elisha Mahaney;
Joseph P. Mahaney and Stephen M. Mahaney.
Exor: Son-in-Law, Amos Marker
Wit: Joseph Wattson and John Cooper
Dated: 4 Jan. 1841   Proved: 10 May 1841

Will Book L - page 3

ISAAC P. MAHONEY, Shenandoah County. Mother: (not named).
Sisters: Isabella and Hannah.
Exor: Brother, Thomas L. Mahoney
Wit: John Colville and James Colville
Dated: 13 Aug. 1818   Proved: 12 Oct. 1818

Wills and Accts. (1809-1863) - page 221

ADAM MAPHIS, Shenandoah County. Son: Philip Maphis -
my plantation on which I now reside. Daus: Anna Maphis;
Regina, wife of Isaac Richards. Mentions: negro man
named John. Mentions: son, Philip Maphis to be guardian
for my said dau. Anna Maphis.
Exor: Son, Philip Maphis
Wit: Benjamin Harman, Abraham Smootz and Daniel Hottel
Dated: 6 Jan. 1844   Proved: 5 April 1845

Will Book X - page 248

GEORGE MAPHIS, Shenandoah County. Sons: William Maphis;
John Maphis; Jacob Maphis. Grandson: Cornelius Painter
(late my ward). Grandson: Noel Hockman, son of my dec'd.
dau. Mary Hockman. Dau: Betsy Strickler, wife of Daniel
Strickler.
Exors: Son, John Maphis and son-in-law, Daniel Strickler
Wit: W. W. Magurder, John Sibert and Jacob Fravel
Dated: 4 Jan. 1843   Proved: 8 Sept. 1845

Will Book O - page 494

JOHN MAPHIS, Shenandoah County. Wife: Catharine Maphis.
Son: George Maphis. Son: Samuel Maphis - the plantation
and land whereon he now lives adjoining George Wisman.
Daus: Christina, wife of George Lantz; Eva, wife of
Christian Funkhouser; Hanna Maphis. Granddaughter: Catharine
Gochenour (dau. of my dau. Sally, dec'd.). Grandson:
Philip Funkhouser (son of my dau. Mary, dec'd.). Mentions:
My plantation and land adjoining the town of Woodstock be
equally divided between my daus, Eva Funkhouser and Christina
Lantz. Mentions: My plantation and land adjoining Jacob
Gochenour, Jacob Rodeheffer and George Maphis, Sen. and
also 10 acres unto my dau, Hannah Maphis. Mentions: My
plantation and lands in County of Hardy to my two grand-
children, Philip Funkhouser and Catharine Gochenour.
Exors: Sons, George Maphis and Samuel Maphis
Wit: George Shrum, Jacob Peer and Philip Maphis
Dated: 26 Aug. 1828   Proved: 12 Jan. 1829

Will Book F - page 479

THOMAS MARKS, Shenandoah County. Wife: Mary Marks. Sons:
John Marks; James; Thomas. Daus: Mary Marks; Jane Marks.
Exors: Wife, Mary Marks and son, James Marks.
Wit: John Blackwood and Thomas Perry
Dated: 28 Aug. 1805   Proved: 9 Oct. 1806

Will Book U - page 46

EDWARD MARSH, Shenandoah County. Wife: Catharine.
Mentions: Edward Marsh Fry, son of Samuel Fry - my silver
watch. Mentions: Mrs. Elizabeth Fry of Woodstock and
friend, Philip Williams, Sen.
Exors: Wife, Catharine and Philip Williams, Jr.
Wit: David Crawford and Lorenzo Sibert
Dated: 9 Dec. 1834   Proved: 13 June 1837

Will Book E - page 81

BENJAMIN MATHES, Shenandoah County. Wife: Rachel Mathes -
one third part of land (100 acres) lying next to James
Stenson's. Son: Abraham - 100 acres of land next to my
beloved wife. Son: Isaac - 100 acres on north side of his
brother, Abraham. Son: William. Daus: Betty; Rebeckah;
Sally.
Exors: Wife, Rachel Mathes and friend, Henry Mathes
Wit: James Mathes, Sen., John Lockhart and James Stenson
Dated: 9 Sept. 1796   Proved: 11 April 1797

Will Book B - page 499

ALEXANDER MATHEWS, Shanendoh County, Colony of Virginia.
Wife: Gressel. Sons: James; John; Alexander; Jeremiah;
Benjamin; George.
Exors: Sons, James and Benjamin
Wit: Abraham Keller, John Hutchison and John Wetherton
Dated: 5 Sept. 1783   Proved: 30 Oct. 1788

Will Book G - page 128

CATHARINE MAUCK, Shenandoah County, single woman. Brother-
in-Law: Jacob Niberger. Sister: Christina Niberger.
No Exor. named
Wit: George Cooper, Jacob Cooper and John Machir, Jun.
Dated: 13 Aug. 1807   Proved: 12 Oct. 1807

Will Book F - page 59

DANIEL MAUCK, Shenandoah County, farmer. Wife: Rebecka - the homeplace where I now live, plantations, Stills and Mills for five years. Son: Joseph Mauck - the said homeplace which I bought of John Kountz at the expiration of five years. Sons: Abraham Mauck; David Mauck; Robert Mauck; Daniel Mauck; Jacob Mauck. Daus: Catharina Mauck; Elizabeth Mauck; Maria Mauck; Barbara Mauck; Anna Mauck (their maiden names). Mentions: All the plantations down by the river which I bought from Joseph Barns, Ruth Whitson, Williams and Clark and that which lies in the Blue Ridge - to be rented out.
Exors: John Roads and son, Joseph Mauck
Wit: Levi Keenan, Joseph Strickler and _____(Ger.)
Dated: 6 Oct. 1802

CODICIL to Will of DANIEL MAUCK - Mentions: My dau. Maria's portion to fall under her own hand and not any part thereof into the hands of George Pence, her present husband.
Wit: Levi Keenan, George Houserman, Jr. and John Bushwell
Dated: 2 Jan. 1803   Proved: 10 Jan. 1803

Will Book F - page 301

REBECKA MAUK, Shenandoah County. Sons: Robert Mauk; Daniel Mauk; Jacob Mauk.
Exors: Sons, Joseph Mauk and Robert Mauk
Wit: Daniel Beaver, _____(Ger.) and George Houseman, Jr.
Dated: 5 Jan. 1805   Proved: 11 March 1805

Will Book W - page 177

ROBERT MC ALLISTER, of Mount Jackson, Shenandoah County, blacksmith. Wife: (not named). Mentions: Isaiah Allen be appointed guardian for my children (not named).
Exor: Brother-in-Law, Isaiah Allen
Wit: W. D. Farra, John N. Hill and Sutton J. Harris
Dated: 22 Feb. 1840

CODICIL to Will of ROBERT MC ALLISTER - Mentions: my mother, Lucy McAllister.
Wit: Sutton J. Harris and John N. Hill
Dated: 30 Nov. 1840   Proved: 8 Aug. 1842

Will Book B - page 544

JAMES MC CARTH, Shanando County. Wife: Sarah. Son: Jonas.
Daus: Dianah; Mary; Hannah; Elizabeth; Sarah; Margaret.
Exors: Son, Jonas and George Adam Zirckle
Wit: Mathew Fasmer, Daniel Darst, Abraham Brannaman, Sen.
and Jacob Neff
Dated: 22 Oct. 1788   Proved: 26 Feb. 1789

Will Book U - page 332

WILLIAM MC CORD, Shenandoah County. Wife: Sarah - the house
in which I now live, also, 8 acre lot below town. Children:
(not named).
Exor: Daniel Stickley
Wit: Thomas Miller, John W. Farra and George Dosh
Dated: 11 May 1838   Proved: 11 June 1838

Will Book E - page 504

JOHN MC GOWAN, Shenandoah County. Wife: Phoebe McGowan -
parcel of land containing 56 acres which I bought of Benjamin
Greigsby. Mentions: sister, Jane McGowan.
Exors: Isaac Strickler and David Tyler
Wit: Abraham Reed, Peter Brubaker, Augustus John Pryce and
John Brubaker
Dated: 16 Dec. 1801   Proved: 8 March 1802

Will Book X - page 173

DAVID MC INTURFF, Shenandoah County. Step-son: Jacob
Taylor. Mentions: my own children (not named).
No Exor. named
Wit: Daniel Cullers and Henry Cullers
Dated: 29 Dec. 1827   Proved: 10 March 1845

Will Book E - page 183   NUNCUPATIVE WILL

GEORGE MC KAY, Shenandoah County. Wife: Mary McKay - one negro man named Joe. Son: William. All my children both male and female alike: (not named).
The above Will entered down from testators own mouth in his presence a few hours before his death by us the subscribers who were called upon by the testator to write the same but was not signed by him, the testator.
Wit: Jeremiah McKay and James Mathes, Senior
Dated: 3 Dec. 1797   Proved: 12 June 1798

Will Book E - page 105

JAMES MC KAY, Parish of Beckford, County of Shenandoah, Colony of Virginia. Wife: Mary. Eldest son: James - part of plantation (300 acres) being part of 400 acres on road that leads to Weaver's Mill. Son: Robert - that part of plantation where I now live (127 acres) adjoining Thomas Buck's land and Isaac Hite's line. Son-in-Law: John Coile - that parcel of land whereon he now lives. Dau: Susanah Coile, wife of John Coile. Daus: Nancy and Lidia. Mentions: tract of land jointly owned with Andrew McKay, to be sold. Mentions: mulatto man named Sam - his freedom. Mentions: Sarah Harett - 3 acres of land (the Nathan meadow).
Exors: Son, Robert McKay and son-in-law, John Coile
Wit: James Mathes, Jun., James Miller and William Allen
Dated: 18 July 1797   Proved: 12 Sept. 1797

Will Book F - page 203

ELIZABETH MERCER, of Strasburg, Shenandoah County.
Mentions: John Campbell.
Exor: John Roger
Wit: John Batthiz and James Crawford
Dated: 18 Jan. 1804   Proved: 12 March 1804

Will Book E - page 142

HENRY MEYER, Shenandoah County. Wife: Barbara. Sons: John Meyer and Michael Meyer. Seven other children: (not named).
Exors: Sons, John and Michael Meyer
Wit: David Jordan, John Stover and John Albright
Dated: 28 May 1787   Proved: 12 Dec. 1797

Will Book W - page 25

MARTIN MILEY, Shenandoah County. Mentions: I have this day sold my land to Samuel Wisman. Four daus: Elizabeth, wife of Benjamin Fravel; Rachel, wife of Jacob Winterholder; Rebecca McClanahan; Mary Miley. Grandson: Joseph Veach, son of my dau. Rachel Winterholder. Late son: Joseph Miley.
Exor: Samuel Wisman
Wit: George Bowman, Harrison Nickels and Philip Wisman
Dated: 25 April 1840   Proved: 13 Dec. 1841

ARTICLE OF AGREEMENT between Martin Miley and Samuel Wisman. Sold land inherited partly by his father, Daniel Miley and partly by purchase from his brother, John Miley and his sisters, Catharine Wisman and Christina Hockman containing 134 acres.
Dated: 25 April 1840

Will Book A - page 40   NUNCUPATIVE WILL

ABRAHAM MILLER, SENIOR, County of Dunmore. Eldest son: (not named - Jacob). Wife: (not named- Christina).
Exors: George Keller and Ulrick Supinger
Wit: Ulrich Miller and Jeremiah Kefferry
Dated: 23 April 1773   Proved: 22 June 1773

Oral Will presented the night before he died and not being capable to make a Will.

Will Book D - page 209

CATHARINE MILLER, Shenandoah County. Son: Joseph Hopewell - my negro man named James. Mentions: grandsons, George Miller; William Miller; Joseph Miller; James Miller; Isaac Miller (sons of James Miller).
Exors: Son, Joseph Hopewell and son-in-law, Thomas Allen
Wit: Isaac Miller, William Reynolds and Robert S. Rufell
Dated: 24 Oct. 1788   Proved: 26 July 1792

Will Book Y - page 481

CHRISTIAN MILLER, Shenandoah County. Mentions: I give and devise unto Samuel C. Williams in trust for Nancy Miller, wife of my son, Reuben Miller, the house and lot in town of Woodstock, number 136. Dau: Cofsanda Hickman - my personal estate.
Exor: Benjamin Hickman
Wit: G. B. Samuels and Mark Bird
Dated: 3 May 1848   Proved: 9 April 1849

Will Book T - page 343

CHRISTIAN MILLER, SENIOR, Shenandoah County. Wife: Catharine. Son: Philip Miller; Jacob W. Miller; John Miller; Henry. Daus: Catharine Ligget (dec'd.); Polly, wife of John Gaw; Elizabeth, wife of John Bare. Son-in-Law: George Shroffe and his wife, Barbara. Mentions: grandchildren of my dau. Catharine Ligget, dec'd.
Exors: Son, Philip Miller and son-in-law, John Bare
Wit: Jno. Crousdon, P. Williams and P. Williams, Jr.
Dated: 6 March 1820

CODICIL to Will of CHRISTIAN MILLER, SENIOR - Mentions: my land and personal property except the third divised to my wife during her natural life, to be sold by my Exors. as soon as convenient.
Wit: Joseph Irwin and James C. Williams
Dated: 29 July 1822   Proved: 14 June 1836

Will Book E - page 485

GEORGE MILLER, SENIOR, Shenandoah County, Blacksmith. Wife: Eve. Four oldest sons: John Miller; George Miller; Philip Miller; Frederick Miller - my plantation containing 340 acres. Four oldest daus: Salome Miller; Barbara Miller; Catharine Miller; Elizabeth Miller. Mentions: Money owing me from said Stephen Mahoney. Mentions: small children (not named) of my present wife, Eve, she being big with her sixth child.
Exors: Sons, John Miller, George Miller, Philip Miller and Frederick Miller
Wit: James Crawford, Philip Sonnar, Philip Road, Jacob Windle, Alexander Hite, Jacob Grove and _____ (Ger.)
Dated: 23 Nov. 1801   Proved: 11 Jan. 1802

Will Book B - page 538

HENRY MILLER, Shenandoah County. Wife: (not named).
Sons: Mark Miller and Edward Miller.
Exor: Son, Mark Miller
Wit: Michael Spigle, Jacob Huddle and Nicholas Dull
Dated: 10 Nov. 1788   Proved: 29 Jan. 1789

Will Book D - page 58

HENRY MILLER, Shenandoah County. Wife: Dorothea Miller.
Eight children - 6 daus. and 2 sons (not named).
Exor: Michael Clipple
Wit: Simon Harr, Lewis Miller and _____(Ger.)
Dated: 5 Sept. 1791   Proved: 27 Oct. 1791

Will Book A - page 116

JACOB MILLER, Dunmore County. Wife: Rebecca - my Lot in Town of Woodstock, number 72. Sons: Joseph and Henry.
Daus: Susana; Barbara and Rebecca.
Exors: Henry Ott and Joseph Yeager
Wit: John Brown, Antony Nisely and Thomas Dempsey
Dated: 1 Nov. 1776   Proved: 25 March 1777

Will Book A - page 344

JACOB MILLER, County of Shanando. Wife: Elizabeth - all my lands which I hold by Deed from Jacob Kellrick containing 235 acres. Son: Godfrey - my large German Bible. Son: John - my sermon book. Sons: Philip and Adam - one horse creature each. Other children: (not named).
Exor: Jacob Moyer
Wit: Jacob Rinker, Jr., Jacob Surber and Richard Hudson
Dated: 9 Sept. 1781   Proved: 25 Oct. 1781

Will Book I - page 418

JACOB MILLER, Shenandoah County. Wife: (not named) - the new house. Son: Samuel Miller - old plantation whereon I live (211 acres), also, 144 acres of mountain land. Son: Abraham Miller - 200 acres of land in Augusta County whereon he lives. Son: Jacob Miller - remainder of land on North River in Augusta County (198 acres). Other children: Martin Miller and Nancy Miller. Mentions: David Miller. Susanna and Barbara who departed this life. Mentions: Daniel Garber to have Susanna's share. My grandchildren: Jacob Sager; Mary Sager; Abraham Sager; Samuel Sager.
Exors: Daniel Garber and Jacob Garber
Wit: Jonathan Harpine, _____(Ger.) and Michael Wine

CODICIL to Will of JACOB MILLER - Mentions: wife's youngest dau. Catharine. Wife's other daus: Elizabeth and Polly - shall have legacies with my children.
Wit: same as above
Dated: 5 May 1815   Proved: 11 Sept. 1815

Written in the German language and a translation thereof in the English language was proved by the oath of Jacob Rinker.

Will Book K - page 23

MARK MILLER, Shenandoah County. Wife: Anna Miller. Sons: David Miller; George Miller; Abraham Miller; Joseph Miller. Daus: Magdalene Miller; Catharine Miller; Sarah Miller; Rebecca, wife of Philip Rodeheffer. Mentions: land and plantation (216 acres) - to be sold.
Exors: Henry Hockman (son-in-law of Abraham Beydler, dec'd.) and Henry Artz, Senior
Wit: Samuel R. Bader, Henry Baserman and David Jordan
Dated: 26 Dec. 1815   Proved: 11 March 1816

Will Book M - page 339

PHILIP MILLER, Shenandoah County. Wife: Sarah. Sons: Philip and Henry. Daus: Barbara; Salome and Sereptia.
Exor: Wife, Sarah
Wit: Philip Bafsard, John Miller, John Colville and William Keil
Dated: 13 April 1824   Proved: 10 May 1824

Will Book Y - page 411

REBECCA MILLER, Shenandoah County. Mentions: Samuel Zehring - one set of Windsor chairs. Mentions: Mary Harriet, dau. of Andrew Funkhouser. Mentions: full sisters and brothers and half sisters and brothers (not named).
Exor: Andrew Funkhouser
Wit: Levi Rinker and Jacob Lutz
Dated: 19 Dec. 1848   Proved: 12 Feb. 1849

Will Book S - page 508

ROBERT MILLER, of the City of Baltimore, Merchant. Sister: Mrs. Margaret Henderson. Mentions: Mrs. Sarah Miller, relick of my brother, John and her dau. Mrs. Ege. Niece: Mary Bullett, formerly Denison. Mentions: Children of my late niece, Sally West - the land in Perry Co., Pennsylvania. Mentions: a deed of gift of all my right interest and Estate in Union Forge in Shenandoah County, Va. of Arthur & Miller to Robert Miller Dennison in trust for his mother, Mrs. Elizabeth Dennison. Mentions: tracts of land in Union Co., Ohio containing 2, 464 acres to children of John S. Webster and his present wife, Elizabeth. Mentions: Andrew McDowell, husband of my niece, Rebecca. Mentions: William Henderson - tract of land in Ohio. Mentions: nieces, Mifs Jane Wilson; Mrs. Rebecca McDowell; Mrs. Elizabeth Webster; Mifs Margaret Thornburgh; Mrs. Sarah McCauley.
Exors: Edward Denison (atty. at law) and Patrick McCauley, M.D
Wit: John McClellan, George C. Munson and Jno. McKean, Jr.
Dated: 11 April 1834   Proved: 11 May 1835

Will Book U - page 24

SAMUEL MILLER, Shenandoah County. Wife: Bettsy. Three oldest children: Mary; Anthony; John. Dau: Caty. Younger children: (not named).
Exor: Son-in-Law, David Kagey
Wit: Michael Wine, Jacob Garber, Sutton I. Harris and
_____ (Ger.)
Dated: 15 Feb. 1837   Proved: 12 June 1837

At a Court held for the County of Shenandoah on Monday, the 7th day of August 1837, Elizabeth Miller, widow of Samuel Miller, dec'd. came into Court and openly renounced and relinquished the provisions of the Will of said Samuel Miller, dec'd. her said husband, which is ordered to be certified.

Will Book A - page 191

WILLIAM MILLER, Dunmore County. Wife: Catharine Miller. Son: William - part of plantation I now live on joining Henry Cloud. Son: Isaac Miller - tract of land in Hampshire County deeded to me by his Lordship (433 acres). Dau: Rebecca Miller - land I bought of John Dunbar in Hampshire County (412 acres). Dau: Elizabeth Miller - remainder part of lands. Daus: Sarah Miller, wife of James Miller; Abagail, wife of Thomas Allen. Mentions: Stepson, Joseph Hopewell. Exors: Son, Isaac and Son-in-Law, Thomas Allen
Wit: William Calfee, William Jennings and Joseph Hopewell
Dated: 1 Oct. 1776   Proved: 24 Sept. 1778

Will Book F - page 71

SAMUEL MILLS, Town of Strasburg, Shenandoah County, single man - whereas my family relation in England being all deceased and having not any other relation there and not any in America, I do hereby adopt the following children to be my Lawful heirs: Joseph Stover Spangler; Elizabeth Spangler; Catharine Spangler; Margaret Spangler (son and daus. of Philip Spangler and Regina his wife of Strasburg). Brother: W. James Mills (dec'd.), late of Beules in County of Suffolk in England, Great Britain.
Exor: Philip Spangler
Wit: Isaac Bowman, Anthony Spangler and Augustine Shoe
Dated: 6 Jan. 1801 .   Proved: 11 Oct. 1802

Will Book I - page 365

MOSES MOODEY, Shenandoah County. Sons: Moses Moodey; William Moodey; Bryant Moodey; John Moodey. Three daus: Margaret Homer; Rachael Wood; Sarah Homer.
Exors: Son-in-Law, John Wood and friend, Isaac Hershberger
Dated: 8 Oct. 1814   Proved: 7 Aug. 1815

Will Book W - page 334

AARON MOORE, Shenandoah County. Son: Samuel Moore - all the plantation on which I live (except 25 acres). Son: Charles Moore - 25 acres, two other shares of land which I purchased of William Allen (dec'd.). Sister: Darcus Young.
Exors: Sons, Samuel Moore and Charles Moore
Wit: James Hawkins, Jacob Funk and Joseph Samuels
Dated: 11 April 1843   Proved: 12 June 1843

Will Book R - page 395

CHARLES S. MOORE, Shenandoah County. Wife: Elizabeth - the plantation whereon I now live adjoining lands of William Steenberger until my youngest son, Charles, arrives at the age of 19. Son: Charles - when he arrives at the age of 19, the house with the cellar under it. Son: Abraham - three hundred dollars because of a crippled hand. Other children: Catharine, wife of Andrew Byrd; Jacob; Sarah Catharine; Elizabeth Mary; Lydia.
Exor: Isaac Thomas of Rockingham County
Wit: Isaac Thomas, Wesley Neuham and Morgan Moore
Dated: 27 July 1830   Proved: 10 Dec. 1832

Will Book S - page 150

HELENA MOORE, Shenandoah County. Sister: Polly Ann Moore. Mother: Lydia Moore.
Exor: My mother, Lydia Moore
Wit: William Shomo, Henry Spitzer and Daniel Shomo
Dated: 9 Nov. 1833   Proved: 10 Feb. 1834

Will Book E - page 465.

JACOB MOORE, Parish of Beckford, Shenandoah County. Wife: (not named). Sons: George; Charles; Elijah; David and Jonathan. Daus: Sarah; Lydia; Mary.
Exor: Son, Charles
Wit: Samuel Mills and Solomon Kingree
Dated: 8 June 1795   Proved: 12 Oct. 1801

Will Book L - page 221

JOSEPH MOORE, Shenandoah County. Wife: Phebe. Son: Reuben Moore - all my plantation and lands whereon I now live on Holeman's Creek. Son: George Moore - tract of land containing 172 acres; two other tracts of land, one containing 40 acres adjoining Philip Harpine, Jacob Garber, John Wine and Jonathan Harpine. The other containing 4 acres adjoining Jacob Good, conveyed to me by Jacob Ludwig. Son: Strother Moore - all my lands in Rockingham County containing 276 acres, part I purchased of John Thomas' heirs and part I purchased from Michael Yankey and part from Alexander Gordon. Daus: Polly, wife of John Newman; Phebe, wife of Reuben Skeen.
Exor: Son, Reuben Moore
Wit: Moses Walton, Abraham Jones and John Jones
Dated: 12 May 1820   Proved: 12 June 1820

Will Book W - page 511

REUBEN MOORE, Shenandoah County. Wife: Sarah. My father: Joseph Moore (dec'd.). Sons: George; Joseph; John; Solomon - all my lands be kept together until first day of Sept. 1852 then divided among my sons. Dau: Frances Allen (dec'd.). Dau: Elizabeth Wander - my black boy named George and black girl, Catharine (both slaves). Dau: Catharine Moore - my black girl named Amanda.
Exors: Son, Joseph and Charles Wunder
Wit: Jno. Rice, Joseph Moore and Bernard Hall
Dated: 9 April 1844   Proved: 12 Aug. 1844

Will Book O - page 68

REUBIN MOORE, Shenandoah County. Nephew: Abraham Miller - my house and barn with all the land on the opposite side of Mill Creek except what I have reserved for the use of a school house and meeting house, also, part of my 200 acre tract. Nephew: Reubin Miller (son of Ann Miller) - the plantation I now live on and 100 acres and a second tract of 60 acres, a third tract of 100 acres purchased of John Penewit and part of the 200 acre tract which I have given his brother, Abraham Miller.
Exor: Thomas Moore, Sen.
Wit: John Morgan, Christopher Hinkle and Ephraim Rinker
Dated: 16 June 1822   Proved: 12 March 1827

Will Book C - page 244

THOMAS MOORE, Shenandoah County. Wife: (not named) - one third part of that plantation whereon I now live containing 400 acres; one third part of 200 acres lying on Shenandoah River in Rockingham County. Son: John Moore - plantation whereon he now lives containing 200 acres, also, tract in Rockingham County containing 300 acres. Son: Reubin Moore - tract of land in Rockingham County containing 300 acres. Son: Joseph Moore - tract of land whereon I now live containing 400 acres. Daus: Lydia; Anne; Elizabeth and Hannah. Nephew: Thomas George.
Exors: Sons, John, Reubin and Joseph
Wit: George Bird, Abraham Harpine and Philip Harpine
Dated: 10 May 1785   Proved: 30 Dec. 1790

Will Book F - page 269

LYDIA MORE (MOORE), Shenandoah County, widow. Sons:
Jonathan; David; Charles. Daus: Lydia and Polly.
Exors: Sons, Charles and Jonathan
Wit: Isreal Allen, Rebecca Thomas and J. Stiegel
Dated: 15 Oct. 1804   Proved: 10 Dec. 1804

Will Book X - page 270

ELIZABETH MORGAN, Shenandoah County. Children: Amanda
M. Morgan; Elizabeth Pennybacker; Maureen Morgan; John
Morgan; Mary E. Sigler; Hannah McMichael; Nancy M. Gandy;
Louisa A. Funkhouser.
Exor: John Morgan
Wit: Rhesa Allen, Whiting D. Farra and James McCann
Dated: 10 July 1845   Proved: 13 Oct. 1845

Will Book K - page 307

JONAS MORGAN, Shenandoah County. Wife: Ann Morgan - all
my real and personal property.
Exor: Wife, Ann Morgan.
Wit: Sehanah Ward, Ann Sehue and George Oakley
Dated: 20 Sept. 1816   Proved: 8 Sept. 1817

Will Book O - page 404

MARTIN MORLEY (MEILY), SENIOR, Shenandoah County. Wife:
Christena - the new house wherein Samuel Funkhouser now
resides. Mentions: children of my dau. Magdalene Mafius,
wife of George Mafius, Jr. Mentions: David Funkhouser,
son of Samuel Funkhouser and my late dau. Elizabeth
Funkhouser. Son-in-Law: George Mafius, Jr. - the plantation
whereon I now reside near the North Mountain. Mentions:
appoint David Meiley guardian for my infant grandson, David
Funkhouser.
Exor: Son-in-Law, George Mafius, Junior
Wit: Robert Turner, William Cahorn and W. W. Payne
Dated: 8 Sept. 1825   Proved: 10 Sept. 1828

Will Book A - page 100

GEORGE MOURER, Dunmore County. Wife: Ann Mary. Sons: Lennerd; Vollentin (Valentine); John; George; Philip; Mickel (Michael). Daus: Barbary and Mary.
Exors: Martin Foltz, wife, Ann Mary and John Hoy
Wit: Martin Foltz and John Hoy
Dated: 15 Nov. 1775   Proved: 28 May 1776

Will Book S - page 128

JOHN MOURER, SENIOR, Shenandoah County. Sons: John Mourer, Jr.; George Mourer; Jacob Mourer. Daus: Mary Mourer; Elizabeth Mauck, wife of George Mauck. Mentions: Rebecca, dau. of my dau. Mary.
Exor: Son, John Mourer
Wit: Robert Turner and William Philips
Dated: 29 June 1822   Proved: 13 Jan. 1834

Will Book B - page 181

MARY MOURER, Shenandoah County. Sons: Leonhart Mourer (youngest son); Vallintinello (Valentine) Mourer.
No Exor. named.
Wit: Abraham Cockerour and Jacob Ullander
Dated: 22 Aug. 1785   Proved: 28 Oct. 1785

Will Book N - page 214

HENRY MOUSER, Shenandoah County. Wife: Mary Mouser. Mentions: My faithful servant girl, Hannah Procter - three hundred dollars. Mentions: Brothers and sisters of me and my wife (not named).
Exors: Abraham Stover, Ulrick and Philip Borden, Sen.
Wit: Phines Orndorff and Samuel Borden
Dated: 1 Jan. 1825   Proved: 9 May 1825

Will Book Y - page 47

MARY MOUSER, Shenandoah County. Mentions: faithful servant girl, Elizabeth Jobb - fifty dollars. Mentions: Jacob Rickard and his wife, Mary (the dau. of my sister, Franny Hockman) - all of my Estate. Mentions: David Stover's children. Mentions: Franny Hockman's children. Mentions: children of George Shafer, Sen. Brother: Abraham Stover (dec
Exor: Philip Borden, Senior
Wit: David Roads and Christian Saum
Dated: 3 May 1834

CODICIL to Will of MARY MOUSER - Mentions: an extra 150 dollars to be paid to servant girl, Elizabeth Jobb.
Dated: 15 May 1834　　　　　Proved: 9 March 1847

Will Book F - page 223

JOHN MOYER, Shenandoah County. My beloved mother: Barbara Summer. Brother: Martin Moyer.
Exor: Brother, Martin Moyer
Wit: Samuel R. Bader and John Jordan
Dated: 20 May 1804　　　　　Proved: 11 June 1804

Will Book G - page 309

JOHN MOYER, Shenandoah County, yeoman. Mentions: Daniel Baker - all the property.
Exor: Daniel Baker
Wit: David Griffy and William Griffy
Dated: 2 April 1809　　　　　Proved: 12 June 1809

Will Book M - page 60

CHRISTIAN MOYERS, SENIOR, Shenandoah County. Wife: Barbara the plantation whereon I now live. Sons: Christian and Michael. Other children: (not named). Mentions: sell the land deeded to Jacob Miller and myself by John Utinger and 125 acres in County of Rockingham, bought of Abraham Sap.
Exors: George Mourey and son, Isaac Moyers
Wit: Michael Wine, Sen., Michael Wine, Jr. and _____(Ger.)
Dated: 14 June 1822　　　　　Proved: 8 July 1822

Will Book F - page 212

GEORGE MOYERS, Shenandoah County. Wife: Maryann. Sons: John Moyers; George Moyers; Henry Moyers; Jacob Moyers; Frederick Moyers. Daus: Dougherty, wife of Christian Weaver; Maryann Moyers.
Exor: Jacob Lantz
Wit: Jacob Rinker, Jacob Surber and Peter Coffelt
Dated: 5 Jan. 1802   Proved: 10 April 1804

Will Book G - page 20

MAGDALENA MUNCH, Shenandoah County. Children which are home with me at this time: Caty; Mary; Betsy; George and John Munch.
Exors: Son, Peter Munch and David McInturf
Wit: Jefse Veach, Henry Carryer and Jacob Donner
Dated: 2 Feb. 1807   Proved: 4 March 1807

Will Book E - page 62

PHILIP MUNCH, Shenandoah County. Wife: (not named). Children: (not named).
Exor: Magdalena Munch
Wit: Jacob Kowenstein, David McInturf, Henry Walther and Jacob Lichliter.
Dated: 2 Oct. 1796   Proved: 14 Dec. 1796

A true translation from the German original made by me - David Jordan.

Will Book L - page 24

MARY MYER (MOYER), Shenandoah County, widow of George Moyer. Son: John - all my estate. Son: George - one dollar. Son: Frederick - one dollar. Three grandchildren, heirs of my dau. Doradey, viz: George, Elizabeth and John. Granddaughter: Mary Weaver. Dau: Mary, wife of Henry Long. Grandson: George Long (son of Henry Long).
Exor: George Lantz
Wit: Jonathan Featly, Daniel Beidleman, George Feather and Jacob Coffeld
Dated: 2 April 1814   Proved: 7 Dec. 1818

Will Book Y - page 307

ISAAC MYERS, Shenandoah County. Wife: (not named). Two youngest sons: Samuel and Jonas. Sons: Peter and Christian. Daus: Catharine; Polly; Rebecca. Mentions: 216 acres I bought of the heirs of Samuel Myers, dec'd. Mentions: Farm which I now live, deeded to me by my father, Christian Myers. Mentions: Dau. Rebecca's son, John Isaac Myers.
Exors: Sons, Christian and Peter Myers
Wit: William Whisler, Lewis Wills and Joseph Barkett
Dated: 7 Jan. 1848

CODICIL to Will of ISAAC MYERS - Mentions: Children, Christia Peter, Samuel and Polly.
Dated: 30 March 1848   Proved: 13 June 1848

Will Book E - page 156

ADAM NEAS, Shenandoah County. Wife: Elizabeth. Two sons: John and Michael. Dau: Dolly.
Exors: Brother, John Neas and friend, Jacob Stiegel
Wit: Jacob Sairfas, Philip Harpine, John Brenner and Abraham Harpine
Dated: 29 Aug. 1797   Proved: 10 Jan. 1798

Will Book M - page 169

JACOB NEES, Shenandoah County. Wife: Mary Nees. Son: Joseph Nees. My seven children: (only one named).
Exor: George Mourey
Wit: Michael Nees, Jacob Bower and _____ (Ger.)
Dated: 7 April 1819   Proved: 8 April 1823

Will Book H - page 238

ABRAHAM NEFF, Shenandoah County. Nephew: Christian Neff, son of my brother, Christian - all my lands and plantation whereon I now live, Willed to me by my father, John Henry Neff, dec'd. My brothers and sisters: John Neff (dec'd.); Catharine; Francis; Jacob; Christian.
Exors: Nephews, John Neff, Sen. and John Neff, Jr.
Wit: Abraham Kagy, Abraham Neff, Jun. and Abraham Boehm, Jr.
Dated: 5 Feb. 1812   Proved: 10 Aug. 1812

Will Book V - page 335

BARBARA NEFF, Shenandoah County. Sons: Samuel Neff; John
Neff; Michael; Joseph; Jacob; Henry; David Neff. Daus:
Mary, widow of Emanuel Hupp, dec'd.; Anna, wife of Conaway
Rector; Catharine, wife of Abraham Gochenour. Granddaughter:
Catharine Hupp. Grandsons: Henry Neff and Daniel Neff (sons
of my son, Daniel Neff, dec'd.). Son-in-Law: Joseph Gochenour.
Exor: Son, John Neff
Wit: C. Hickle, Samuel Youst and Levi Rinker
Dated: 24 Nov. 1837   Proved: 9 Nov. 1840

Will Book I - page 93

CHRISTIAN NEFF, SENIOR, Shenandoah County. Wife: Mary.
Daus: Barbara and Catharine, wife of Christian Kagey.
Son: Abraham - all my land and plantation. Son: Christian.
Brother: Abraham Neff (dec'd.).
Exors: Son, Abraham and son-in-law, Christian Kagey
Wit: Joseph Gochenour, Abraham Kagey and Jacob Whitmyer
Dated: 2 July 1814   Proved: 8 Aug. 1814

Will Book H - page 268

FRANCIS NEFF, Shenandoah County. Son: John Neff - my lands
and plantation whereon I now live, Willed to me by my father,
John Henry Neff (dec'd.). Daus: Elizabeth; Mary; Magdalena,
wife of Benjamin Gaines. Mentions: George Grabil, husband
of my oldest dau. Anna. Mentions: children of my eldest
son, Jacob Neff (dec'd.).
Exors: Son, John Neff and Benjamin Gaines
Wit: Samuel Hupp, Aaron Gaines and Peter Good
Dated: 14 Sept. 1812   Proved: 12 Oct. 1812

Will Book L - page 234

JACOB NEFF, SENIOR, Shenandoah County. Wife: Anna. Late
husband of wife: John Backman, dec'd. Wife's children:
(not named). My son: David - my land and plantation where-
on I now live, together with 30 acres of woodland. Son:
John - the land and plantation whereon he now lives, together
with two other tracts. Son: Henry. Two daughter's husbands:
Frederick Huffman and Abraham Kagy.
Exor: Son, David
Wit: Samuel Strickler, Isaac Kagy, Rudolph Kagy and Abraham
Strickler
Dated: 27 March 1819   Proved: 11 Sept. 1820

Will Book B - page 101

JOHN HENRY NEFF, Shenandoah County. Wife: Anna. Sons:
John (oldest); Francis; Jacob; Christley; Abram. Dau:
Elizabeth (unhealthy). Mentions: Son-in-Law, Jacob
Baughman, married to my dau. Catherine - land I own here
and where Jacob Baughman lives.
Exors: Sons, John and Jacob
Wit: Adam Neff, Aaron Solomon, John Miller and Margaret Gabrie
Dated: 1 June 1784   Proved: 29 July 1784

Will Book H - page 197

GEORGE NEFS (NEASE), Shenandoah County. Wife: Elizabeth.
Sons: George Nefs; Michel Nefs; Jacob Nefs; Samuel Nefs.
My ten children: (only 4 sons named).
Exor: Wife, Elizabeth
Wit: Thomas Hudson, John Kaufman and George Hammon
Dated: 14 Oct. 1811   Proved: 12 April 1812

Will Book F - page 106

THOMAS NEWELL, Shenandoah County. Wife: Margaret Newell.
Sons: Thomas Newell and Samuel Newell. Daus: Margaret
Dould; Anne Willson; Elizabeth Martha Reder.
Exors: Wife, Margaret Newell and son, Thomas Newell
Wit: John Colville and John Setzer
Dated: 29 Jan. 1803   Proved: 12 April 1803

Will Book R - page 136

THOMAS NEWELL, Shenandoah County. Son: Robert Newell -
225 acres of land. Dau: Isabella Ireland - 218 acres of
land. Children of son, William Newell (dec'd.): Nancy
B. Newell; Sarah C. Newell; Elizabeth Newell; Jane Newell;
Rebecca Newell. Mentions: negro girl, Milly, remain with
widow and children of my son, William Newell, dec'd. until
Milly is 24 then she shall be free. Mentions: Rachel Thomas
(my wife's dau.) - 15 acres. Mentions: negro boy, Tom and
negro woman, Patsy. Mentions: William L. Newell and Catharin
Lee (children and heirs of my son, John Newell, dec'd.) - 225
acres.
Exor: Joseph Wattson
Wit: Martin Boehm and David N. Newell
Dated: 25 July 1827

CODICIL to Will of THOMAS NEWELL - Mentions: Rebecca Newell,
widow of my son, William Newell, dec'd.
Wit: George F. Hupp and Martin Boehm
Dated: 5 Oct. 1831   Proved: 13 Feb. 1832

Will Book Z - page 180

JOHN NEWLAND, Shenandoah County. Wife: (not named).
Children: Anne; Isaac; Rebecca; Margaret; Elizabeth
Newland (by my present wife). Children by my first
wife: Andrew; Polly; Susannah. Wife's son: Moses.
Exor: Samuel Hawkins
Wit: Alexander Doyle, Richard Winfield and Samuel Tidler
Dated: 3 March 1821   Proved: 12 March 1850

Will Book E - page 521

DANIEL NEWLEN, Hawkins town, Shenandoah County. Wife:
Elizabeth. Sons: Daniel Newlen; John Newlen; Joseph
Newlen; William Newlen. Son-in-Law: James Murphy, former
husband of my dau. Magdalena - 25 cents. Dau: Susanna,
wife of Richard Weaks - 50 cents. Dau: Catharine, wife
of John Gyger - 5 pounds of Virginia currency. Dau: Mary.
Exors: Sons, John and Joseph
Wit: Abraham Bird, Joseph Hawkins and George Feather
Dated: 3 May 1802   Proved: 7 June 1802

Will Book V - page 45

JOHN NEWMAN, Shenandoah County. Wife: Mary Newman -
all my lands, negroes and personal Estate during her
natural life. Son: Joseph M. Newman - received a medical
education at my expence. Son: George Newman - has
commenced the study of medicine. Other six children:
Catharine M. Williams; Francis M. Newman; Walter N. Newman;
Sarah Ann Newman; Phebe Ann Newman; John P. Newman.
Exor: Wife, Mary Newman
Wit: Moses Walton, Samuel Newman, Ann Newman and Jno. W. Rice

CODICIL to Will of JOHN NEWMAN - Mentions: Provisions made
for my wife presuming she will not marry.
Wit: same as above
Dated: 27 Nov. 1836   Proved: 12 Aug. 1839

Will Book I - page 391

WALTER NEWMAN, Shenandoah County. Wife: Catharine Newman - use and services of negro woman, Lucy and her son, Peter. Son: John Newman - land which I own (390 acres). Sons: Jonathan Newman; Samuel Newman; Walter Newman. Daus: Mary Moffett, wife of Daniel Moffett; Elizabeth Hoy, wife of Zahariah Hoy; Catharine, wife of Berman Peal; Ann Newman; Lydia Hupp, wife of Benjamin Hupp; Margaret Ruffner, wife of Martin Ruffner (dec'd.).
Exors: Sons, John Newman and Samuel Newman
Wit: Jacob Hershberger, Joseph Strickler and James Allen
Dated: 9 Dec. 1812 Proved: 7 Aug. 1815

Will Book D - page 140

RICHARD NICHOLAS, Shenandoah County. Wife: Jamime. Children: Daniel; John; Nancy; Moley; Abigale; Richard; and Thomas.
Exor: Son-in-Law, David Markenturfh (McInturf)
Wit: John Newman, John Woolen and Job Combs
Dated: 25 April 1792 Proved: 28 June 1792

Will Book B - page 99

ULRICK NIE, Shanando County. Province of Virginia. Wife: Margaret. My children: (not named).
Exor: Wife, Margaret
Wit: Jacob Wolande and Tevel Bish
Dated: 20 Jan. 1784 Proved: 24 June 1784

Will Book B - page 350

CHRISTIAN NIEBERGER, SENIOR, Town of Strasburg, Shenandoah County. Wife: Ann Mary. Son: Christian Nieberger - 2 half acre lotts lying in town of Strasburg. Sons: Jacob Nieberger; John and Christopher. Daus: Catharine, wife of Alexander Hite; Margaret; Magdeline and Elizabeth (youngest).
Exor: Son, Christian Nieberger
Wit: George Cooper (sadler); George Cooper (shoemaker) and Adam Shirman
Dated: 11 Dec. 1785 Proved: 28 June 1787

Will Book A - page 183

ANTHONY NISELY, Dunmore County, Colony of Virginia. Wife:
Barbara Nisely - house and lotts in town of Woodstock #18
and #47. Son: John Nisely - sold to him 100 acres. Son:
Jacob Nisely - sold to him 200 acres. Other children:
(not named). Mentions: 60 acres sold to Abraham Brubaker.
Exors: Wife, Barbara, John Brown and Frederick Woodford
Wit: John Brown, Will Webb and _____(Ger.)
Dated: 20 Feb. 1777   Proved: 28 Aug. 1778

Will Book Z - page 129

JACOB NOEL, Shenandoah County. Wife: Elizabeth. Son:
Jacob - land on the south side of Mill Creek (8 or 9
acres). Son: Samuel - balance of farm. Dau: Catharine
Ann. Son: William - the farm I purchased of Steenberger's
trustees (212 acres).
Exors: Sons, Samuel and William Noel
Wit: Moses Getz and Jacob Painter
Dated: 9 Dec. 1850   Proved: 11 Feb. 1850 (?)

Will Book B - page 449

DANIEL NULEN, Shenandoah County. Son: Daniel Nulen. Daus:
Rebeckah Nulen and Elizabeth Kesterson. Mentions: grandson,
Daniel Nulen - my plantation where I now live.
Exor: Son, Daniel Nulen
Wit: Abraham Bird and John Wyatt
Dated: 19 Oct. 1782   Proved: 28 Feb. 1788

Will Book B - page 39

SAMUEL OBERHOLDSER, Dunmore County, Colony of Virginia.
Wife: Eaff. Sons: Peter (oldest); Samuel. Daus: Barbara
and Eaff.
Exors: Wife, Eaff and Casper Hoop
Wit: Jacob Neff and _____(Ger.)
Dated: 29 May 1772   Proved: 25 Dec. 1783

Will Book E - page 177

ELIJAH ODELL, Shenandoah County. Wife: (not named). Sons: Andrew; Stephen; Silvanes; Jeremiah and Elijah. Daus: Ann; Sary and Abigal.
Exor: Son, Stephen
Wit: _____ (Ger.), John Smith and William Cunningham
Dated: 2 March 1796   Proved: 10 April 1798

Will Book F - page 461

JAMES ODELL, Shenandoah County. Sons: James Odell; Abraham Odell; Samuel Odell; Jeremiah Odell; John Odell; Isaac Odell. Daus: Jamina Job and Elizabeth Barnett.
Exors: Sons, Samuel Odell and Jeremiah Odell
Wit: James Kendal, Joshua Lampton and Jonathan Odell
Dated: 29 May 1806   Proved: 7 July 1808

Will Book A - page 127

JEREMIAH ODELL, Dunmore County. Wife: Leah - all land I now live on, also, one negro man as long as she liveth, then said negro to be free. Mentions: William Tyler. Brothers: Benjamin; James; Jonathan.
Exors: Brother, Benjamin and William Tyler
Wit: Isaac McKay, Abraham McKay and William Tyler
Dated: 24 June 1777   Proved: 22 July 1777

Will Book A - page 404

SAMUEL ODELL, County of Shenandoah, Colony of Virginia. Wife: Elizabeth. Sons: James Odell; Jonathan Odell and Samuel Odell.
Exors: Elizabeth Odell and James Odell
Wit: Samuel Odell, John Connery and Moses Shelton
Dated: 10 Oct. 1779   Proved: Aug. 1780

Will Book P - page 313

JOHN OFENBACKER, Shenandoah County. Wife: Rachel
Ofenbacker - the plantation whereon I now live. My
brothers: Frederick; Peter and the heirs of Jacob.
Sisters: Christina's heirs; Rosanna and Eve. My two
bound boys, George Parks and John Flemings.
No Exor. named
Wit: Ambrose C. Booten, John Kibler and Michael Shuler
Dated: 18 Jan. 1813   Proved: 11 Jan. 1830

Will Book R - page 331

DENNIS O'FERRELL, of Powell's Fort, Shenandoah County.
My housekeeper: Mary Ann Jones - all my personal property
and tract of land upon which I now reside. Mentions: a
child of the aforesaid Mary Ann Jones, by me, the child
now being in his eighth year.
Exor: Col. Samuel Bare
Wit: D. Smoot, James G. Fravel and P. Williams, Jr.
Dated: 30 Oct. 1828   Proved: 10 Sept. 1832

Will Book A - page 82

JACOB OFFENBACKER, Dunmore County, yeoman. Wife: Barbara.
Sons: Frederick; Jacob; John. Son: Peter - 310 acres.
Daus: Christina (oldest); Barbara; Rosina; Eva.
Exor: Wife, Barbara
Wit: Jacob Pence and Frederick Stonebarger
Dated: 28 April 1775   Proved: 26 Sept. 1775

Will Book A - page 484

JACOB OFFENBOCKER, Schannathae County, Province of Virginia.
Yeoman. Wife: Magdalena. Dau: Barbary - land whereon I
lef witch is sevendy-five ackers. Bruder: John Offenbocker.
Exor: John Offenbocker
Wit: (three witnesses - all signed in German)
Dated: 2 Dec. 1782   Proved: 27 March 1783

Will Book B - page 293

DANIEL OLDENBROUCK, Town of Woodstock, County of Shenandoah.
Wife: Hannah Oldenbrouck - half of tract of land containing
150 acres, divided between myself and Jacob Morley, dec'd.,
lying in Cumberland County, State of Pennsylvania. Son:
Daniel Oldenbrouck - to be bound to Dr. Augustine of the
town of Carlile in State of Pennsylvania in order to study
physick. Daus: Lewisee Oldenbrouck and Eleonoraw Oldenbrouck - property their deceased Mother left in possession
of Mr. Crawford, tavern keeper, in town of Lancaster, State
of Pennsylvania. Son: Jacob Oldenbrouck. Mentions: my
friend, Col. John Brown and William Dennis. Mentions:
Prises drawn in the United States Lottery - a certificate
left in possession of Jacob Swiler in City of Philadelphia.
Exor: Wife, Hannah Oldenbrouck
Wit: John Brown, Henry Brown and John Williams
Dated: 18 Oct. 1785   Proved: 25 Nov. 1785

Will Book Z - page 345

ADAM OLINGER, Shenandoah County. Wife: Eve Olinger - all
my lands and personal Estate until my youngest child
arrives at age 21 years (children born of my wife, Eve).
Son: Isaac Olinger. Dau: Rebecka Hosler, wife of George
Hosler.
No Exor. named
Wit: Philip Olinger and Benjamin Clem
Dated: July 1847   Proved: 9 Dec. 1850

Will Book Y - page 19

DAVID OLINGER, Shenandoah County. Son: William - the home
farm and all the property that is on it. Sons: David and
Philip. Daus: Catharine; Sarah; Rebecca; Polly. Son-in-Law: Benjamin Clem - 15 acres. Two married daus: Elizabeth
and Phibo Clem.
Exors: Sons, William and Philip
Wit: Michael Nefs, Philip Zirkle and John G. Zirkle
Dated: 5 Jan. 1847   Proved: 8 Feb. 1847

Will Book V - page 468

ANNA O'NIEL, Town of New Market, Shenandoah County.
Mentions: John Coffman (of John and his wife, Mary) -
all my real and personal Estate.
Exor: John Coffman
Wit: Jonathan McDaniel, Martin Meyers and Samuel G. Henkel
Dated: 27 Feb. 1841   Proved: 7 June 1841

Will Book Y - page 41

SAMUEL OSWALD, Town of New Market, Shenandoah County.
Wife: Caroline Oswald - my house and lot in town of New
Market and the family of negroes that I hold. Mentions:
Partner in firm of Neff, Walton and Company.
Exor: Wife, Caroline Oswald
Wit: Joseph R. Sibert, Samuel Tiller and Charles Spitzer
Dated: 7 Jan. 1847   Proved: 8 March 1847

Will Book K - page 434

PETER OVERHOLSER, Shenandoah County. Wife: Anna. Sons:
John Overholser and Christian Overholser - all my plantation
and lands whereon I now live containing 314 acres adjoining
lands of Abraham Hup and Abraham Good. Sons: Samuel Over-
holser; Jacob Overholser; Moses Overholser; Adam Overholser;
Benjamin Overholser. Daus: Mary Overholser and Susanna
Overholser. Sister: Eve Reefer.
Exors: Two sons, John Overholser and Christian Overholser
Wit: Jacob Rinker, George Weaver and _____(Ger.)
Dated: 14 Feb. 1818   Proved: 12 May 1818

Will Book Y - page 345

ADAM PAINTER, Shenandoah County. Son: Jacob Painter - all
my lands on Mill Creek containing 175 acres, the same my
said son now resides. Dau: Rebecca Trooke, wife of Philip
Trooke - 50 acres same whereon said Philip Trooke now resides.
Son: Joseph Painter - lands whereon I now reside known as
the home farm. Daus: Magdalene Painter, wife of John Painter;
Mary Fravel, wife of Samuel Fravel. Mentions: John Painter,
Jr., son of my dau. Magdalene Painter. Mentions: Lucinda
Painter, child of my dau. Christina Painter, dec'd.
Exors: Son, Jacob Painter and son-in-law, Samuel Fravel
Wit: Raphael Conn and Andrew Wench
Dated: 1848   Proved: 11 Sept. 1848

Will Book R - page 506

GEORGE PAINTER, Shenandoah County. Wife: Mary - my home plantation whereon I now live until my youngest son, William Painter attains the age of 21 years. Son: Abraham Painter - 100 acres, part of home plantation including house now occupied by Abraham Lutz. Daus: Mary, wife of John Foltz; Lidia, wife of Thomas Miller; Elizabeth Painter; Barbara, wife of William R. Rhinehart; Anna Painter. Son: Isaac Painter - 100 acres whereon my said son, Isaac now lives. Son: George Painter. Mentions: Plantation containing 186 acres - to be sold.
Exors: Son, Isaac Painter and son-in-law, John Foltz
Wit: Levi Rinker and A. Rinker
Dated: 26 April 1833   Proved: 13 May 1833

Will Book G - page 62

JOHN PAINTER, Shenandoah County. Wife: Philbina Catharin. Sons: George Painter; John Painter; Philip Painter; Mathias Painter. Daus: Elizabeth, wife of Philip Good; Catharine, wife of Jacob Rubey; Mary, wife of Michael Lindaimuth; Christina, wife of George Lindaimuth.
Exors: Jacob Lantz, Esq., and Philip Painter (son of Mathias)
Wit: _____ (Ger.), George Painter and Lewis Trout
Dated: 9 Sept. 1806

CODICIL to Will of JOHN PAINTER - Mentions: Sons, Philip and Mathias.
Wit: Adam Painter and _____ (Ger.)
Dated: 9 Sept. 1806   Proved: 14 April 1807

Will Book U - page 373

JOHN PAINTER, SENIOR, Shenandoah County. Wife: Elizabeth. Dau: Rosena, wife of Joseph Ozburn - my plantation whereon they now live (10 acres). Dau: Philbena, widow of John Frye, dec'd. - my plantation purchased from George Lindamood. Three grandchildren: children of my dau. Polly, dec'd., late the wife of Christian Funkhouser, viz: Rebecca Funkhouser; Isaac Funkhouser; William Funkhouser. Daus: Elizabeth, wife of John Nease; Rebecca, wife of George Craig; Lidia, wife of George Hammon; Catharine, wife of Jacob Lutz; Mary, wife of Philip Lindamude; Anna, wife of Abraham Dipboy.
Exor: Son-in-Law, Jacob Lutz
Wit: Peter Coil, Henry Frye, Tobias Stickley and A. Rinker
Dated: 1 Sept. 1838   Proved: 8 Oct. 1838

Will Book Y - page 457

MARY PAINTER, relick of George Painter, dec'd., Shenandoah County. Sons: George; Abram; Isaac. Four daus: Barbara, wife of William Rhinehart; Mary, wife of John Foltz; Anna, wife of Christopher Hickle; Elizabeth, wife of Jacob Minceer. Son-in-Law: Thomas Miller.
Exor: Son, George W. Painter
Wit: John Ewing and Andrew Werick
Dated: 10 Feb. 1847   Proved: 12 March 1849

Will Book Q - page 281

JAMES PARKS, Shenandoah County. Wife: Julia Parks - all the property, both real and personal.
No Exor. named
Wit: William S. Marye, Duana Marye and Mary Marye
Dated: 14 Sept. 1822   Proved: 11 April 1831

Will Book T - page 281

JOHN PEER, Shenandoah County. Sons: David Peer; Joseph Peer; Samuel Peer. Daus: Elizabeth Swaynie; Susan Harmon; Christina Orndorff. Son-in-Law: Philip Orndorff - land conveyed to me by Jonathan Peer.
Exor: Son-in-Law, Philip Orndorff
Wit: John Swaynie and James Connor
Dated: 25 March 1835   Proved: 9 May 1836

Will Book I - page 211

CONRAD PENCE, Shenandoah County. Wife: Eve. Son: John Pence - all that plantation and parcel of land containing 216 acres whereon he now lives. Son: Philip Pence - plantation and tract of land whereon I now live containing 200 acres. Dau: Rachael, wife of Solomon Shutters - land containing 88 1/2 acres which I purchased from George Henton adjoining Bernard Goetz and George Bower. Dau: Catharine Pence - remainder of tract of land purchased of George Henton containing 116 acres. Daus: Betty Funkhouser; Salome, wife of Andrew Boit; Susanna Pence; Lydia Pence. Mentions: female child of dau. Catharine Pence, Betsy.
Exors: Sons, John Pence and Philip Pence
Wit: Jacob Rinker, _____(Ger.) and Lewis Zirkle
Dated: 18 March 1814   Proved: 11 April 1815

Will Book W - page 312

JACOB PENCE, Shenandoah County. Mentions: Son, Jacob Pence and son-in-law, John Foltz - all my land. Mentions: William, my son by Magdalene Fry. Mentions: Heirs of my son, David Pence, viz: Morgan and Mary Catharine. Dau: Margaret, wife of John Foltz. Dau: Susannah, deaf and dumb, wife of Abraham Moyer, who has left her. Sons: John Pence and Joseph Pence.
Exor: Son-in-Law, John Foltz
Wit: Jno. Allen and Philip Pitman
Dated: 25 June 1842   Proved: 12 June 1843

Will Book I - page 112

NICHOLAS PENCE, Shenandoah County. Wife: Margaret. My six children: Catharina, wife of John Wynat of Pennsylvania; Peter; Jacob; John; George; Rebecca, wife of Frederick Stover.
Exors: Peter Snyder and Jacob Fravel
Wit: John Luts, James Barnell and George Feather

CODICIL to Will of NICHOLAS PENCE - Mentions: Wife and granddaughter, Catharine Stover.
Wit: John Hisey and George Feather
Dated: 13 Oct. 1813   Proved: 13 Sept. 1814

Will Book L - page 278

BENJAMIN PENNYBACKER, Shenandoah County. Wife: Sarah. My ten children: George; Nancy; Nathan; Joel; Charlot; Mark; Rebecca; Isaac; Sarah; Samuel. To my sons, George and Nathan - entire management of my real and personal estate consisting of my forge and all my lands and buildings and all that part of my real estate purchased from Samuel Coffman, together with my mountain land, slaves, horses and other stock.
Exors: Sons, George and Joel
Wit: William Steenberger, Benjamin Miller and Derick Pennybacker
Dated: 15 Dec. 1820   Proved: 12 Feb. 1821

Will Book Z - page 267

SAMUEL PENNYBACKER, Shenandoah County. Mentions: Margaret
P. Pennybacker, wife of my brother, Joel - all my property.
No Exor. named
Wit: William Sigler and R. Branham
Dated: 6 May 1850   Proved: 8 July 1850

Will Book T - page 1

MARGARET PENNYWIT, widow and relick of Jacob Pennywit, dec'd.
Shenandoah County. Daus: Catharine, wife of Jacob Funkhouser;
Maria, wife of David Goetz; Rosina Pennywit; Anna Pennywit;
Elizabeth, wife of Abraham Hockman. Sons: John Pennywit;
Jacob Pennywit; Samuel Pennywit.
Exor: Son-in-Law, Abraham Hockman
Wit: A. Rinker, Levi Rinker and C. Hickle
Dated: 31 July 1832   Proved: 8 June 1835

Will Book H - page 337

JACOB PENNYWITZ, Shenandoah County. Wife: Margaret.
Son: John Pennywitz - 50 acres of land to include the
Smith Shop where George Wetzel now works, joining the
land of Jonas Rinehart (dec'd.). Sons: Jacob Pennywitz
and Samuel Pennywitz - all the remainder of my lands.
My three single daus: Rosina; Ana; Elizabeth. Daus:
Catharine, wife of Jacob Funkhouser; Magdalene, wife of
David Goetz.
Exors: Wife, Margaret and son, John Pennywitz
Wit: Jacob Rinker, George Funkhouser and Abraham Funkhouser
Dated: 3 Jan. 1813   Proved: 8 Feb. 1813

Will Book R - page 256

GEORGE PHILIP PENTZ, Shenandoah County. Wife: Mary Pentz.
Sons: Jacob Pentz; Philip; John. Daus: Elizabeth, wife of
John Crage; Sally, wife of John Dellinger; Molly, wife of
John Zerfas; Mary, wife of Peter Crage.
Exors: Wife, Mary Pentz and son-in-law, John Crage
Wit: _____(Ger.) and George Mourey
Dated: 1832   Proved: 11 June 1832

Will Book D - page 440

SAMUEL PERRY, Shenandoah County. Daus: Elizabeth, Margarite;
Mary and Nancy. Sons: James and William.
Exors: John Coile, William Bailey and William Perry
Wit: James Matthews, Sen., Joseph Howey and Amos Brown
Dated: 23 Aug. 1795   Proved: 8 Sept. 1795

Will Book A - page 103

ULRICK PETERS, County of Dunmore, Colony of Virginia.
Wife: Catharain. Children: (not named).
No Exor. named
Wit: John Wyatt and Griffeth Dobbin
Dated: 7 March 1776   Proved: 24 Sept. 1776

Will Book E - page 457

AUGUSTINE PFEIFFER, Shenandoah County. Wife: Anna Mary.
Dau: Catharine, wife of John Wise - one negro girl. Dau:
Barbara, wife of Adam Wise - one negro girl. Son: Godlove -
the land whereon he now lives and two negroes. Dau: Eve,
wife of John Pence - the land whereon I and himself now
live and land whereon Jacob Judy now lives and one negro.
No Exor. named
Wit: Jacob Pence, David Pence and Philip Summer
Dated: 30 Sept. 1801   Proved: 12 Oct. 1801

This translation thereof by Simeon Yager, was sworn to
by him.

Will Book A - page 195

HENRY PFIFER, SENIOR, Shenandoah County. Sons: Henry Pfifer
and David Pfifer. Daus: Magdalen Bucher; Elizabeth Spenglar;
Catharine Stickly (dec'd.); Mary Miller; Ann Grove; Marget
Blint; Barbara Pfifer.
Exors: Son, Henry Pfifer and Stephen Deetheweck
Wit: Alexander Hite, Hieronomus Baker and Lawrence Snapp
Dated: 16 Sept. 1778   Proved: 29 Oct. 1778

Will Book U - page 36

WILLIAM PHILIPS, Shenandoah County. Son: John Philips - my plantation whereon I now live, the same bequeatht to me by John Fultz. Granddaughter: Rebecca, wife of David Huver. Daus: Catharine Sheetz; Rebecca Coffman; Elizabeth Haller; Mary Haas.
Exors: George Grandstaff, Esq. and Philip Haas
Wit: George Shrum and John Maurer
Dated: 13 Jan. 1837   Proved: 12 June 1837

Will Book P - page 458

JOSEPH PINGLEY, Shenandoah County. Son: Samuel Pingley - the plantation whereon he now lives. Two Granddaughters: Elizabeth Pingley and Harriet Pingley (daus. of David Pingley, dec'd.). Daus: Rachael Crofs; Barbara Wilson, (dec'd); Mary Wilson; Susanna Roads; Elizabeth Wilson; Sarah Piseler.
Exor: Son, Samuel Pingley
Wit: Joseph Wattson, Joseph Evans and William Gilham
Dated: 23 Feb. 1827   Proved: 7 June 1830

Will Book Y - page 255

SAMUEL PINGLEY, Shenandoah County. Wife: Mary Pingley. Grandsons: John William Pingley; David Pingley; James Atwell Pingley (children of my son, Joseph Pingley, dec'd.). Daus: Rachael, wife of Jacob Hinkins; Elizabeth, wife of John S. Mourey; Mary. Sons: David Pingley; John Pingley; Jeremiah Pingley.
Exors: David Pingley and John Pingley
Wit: Joseph Wattson and Levi Funkhouser
Dated: 15 Feb. 1848   Proved: 13 March 1848

Will Book P - page 312

DAVID PIPER, Shenandoah County. Wife: Barbara. Son: Joseph - my plantation where I now live. Dau: Catharine, wife of Isaac Funk. Son: David - 25 acres of land.
Exor: Son-in-Law, Isaac Funk
Wit: _____(Ger.), George Hinkins and David Stickley
Dated: 18 May 1824   Proved: 11 Jan. 1830

Will Book Z - page 233

EMANUEL PITMAN, Shenandoah County. Wife: Esther - the farm upon which I now reside. Mentions: to be buried in the grave yard upon the lands of Lawrence Keller. Mentions: Land I own in Harrison Co., Indiana - to be sold. My several sons and daus: (not named). Grandson: William Miller, son of my dau. Mary.
Exor: Son-in-Law, Moritz Heller
Wit: Henry Peer and G. A. Hupp
Dated: 7 July 1848

CODICIL to Will of EMANUEL PITMAN - Mentions: Dau. Mary's several children.
Dated: 25 Feb. 1850   Proved: 13 May 1850

Will Book Z - page 334

LAWRENCE PITMAN, Shenandoah County. Children: Andrew Pitman; Susan Carter; Elizabeth Carter, wife of John A. Carter; Mary Ripley, wife of W. Ripley; Catharine Carter, wife of William A. Carter; Joseph Pitman; Lawrence Pitman; Philip Pitman. Grandson: John Carter Dickinson.
Exor: Mark Bird
Wit: George Filsmoyers and George Maphis
Dated: 24 April 1850   Proved: 11 Nov. 1850

Will Book H - page 487

ADAM POKE, Shenandoah County. Wife: Elizabeth. Children: (not named).
Exors: John Hunnehouser and Leonard Lonas
Wit: Peter Barb, Andrew Bergman and Adam Seger
Dated: 15 Sept. 1813   Proved: 11 Oct. 1813

Will Book B - page 366

EDWARD PRICE, Shenandoah County. Brother: Zackeriah - my land to be maintained for my mother as long as she shall live. Sister: Nancy.
No Exor. named
Wit: William Bolson, William Tyree and Thomas Price
Not dated   Proved: 26 July 1787

Will Book B - page 95

JOHN PRICE, SENIOR, County of Shanando. Wife: Sarah.
Son: Edward Price - 120 acres. Son: John Price - 100 acres.
Son: Thomas Price - place whereon I now live. Sons: Samson
Price and Zackeriah Price. Dau: Ann (youngest).
Exors: Wife, Sarah and son, Edward Price
Wit: Joseph Fawsett, William Price and Solomon Ryan
Dated: 13 April 1780   Proved: 25 June 1784

Will Book D - page 425

PHILIP PRINCE (BRENTZ), Shenandoah County. Wife: Maria.
Oldest son: Philip - 50 acres. Son: Godlip - the Bible
and the old place he do dwell on. All my children: (not
named).
No Exor. named
Wit: Philip Somer, Bolser Somer and Daniel Brubaker
Dated: 6 Dec. 1793   Proved: 9 June 1795

Translation by David Jordan

Will Book F - page 427

PHILIP PRINCE, Shenandoah County. Wife: Elizabeth.
Son: Henry. Daus: Magdalene; Susanna; Elizabeth;
Catharin.
Exor: Son, Henry
Wit: Palser Seiver and George Prince
Dated: 27 Dec. 1802   Proved: 8 April 1808

Will Book L - page 46

BARBARA PRINTZ, Shenandoah County. Mentions: my loving
sweetheart, Jacob Altar, son of John Altar.
Exor: Jacob Altar
Wit: John Altar and John Shenk
Dated: 31 Jan. 1819   Proved: 8 March 1819

Translated by me, Jacob Rinker, Junior

Will Book M - page 374

THEODORE CONRAD PROBSTING, City of Baltimore, State of Maryland. Brothers and sisters: Frederick, now married to Caroline Bergfield; P. A. Probsting, now married in Hamburg; Eleanor Probsting, now late intermarried with J. Vorster; Julia Probsting, now late intermarried with S. Wever; Antoinetta Probsting, now intermarried with Theodore Pilgram. Mentions: Children of my deceased brother, Christian Probsting. Mentions: Friends, Adams and Jones who are my sureties on certain custom-house Bonds.
Exors: William Frick, Charles Bohm and F. W. Bumd (all of the City of Baltimore)
Wit: John C. Smith, John K. Law and Jno. Gill
Dated: 14 Sept. 1821

CODICIL to Will of THEODORE CONRAD PROBSTING - Mentions: my negro woman slave named Cafsandra Lewis shall be free.
Wit: Jon. Gill, Andrew Fedtzer and John P. Becktel
Dated: 23 Oct. 1821   Proved: 8 June 1824
(Shenandoah County, Va.)

Will Book E - page 235

JOSEPH PUGH, Shenandoah County. Mentions: children of my dau. Rebecca, wife of William Richardson - half of 5 acre lot adjoining town of Woodstock, also, small place that I have at Elks Run and tract of 200 acres lying near Funkhousers on the waters of Stoney Creek.
Exor: John Effinger
Wit: George Fravel, Abraham Lambert and George Swartz
Dated: 15 Jan. 1799   Proved: 12 March 1799

Will Book A - page 43

SUSANNA RANTZ, late of Virginia, now of Baltimore County, Maryland. Dau: Mary Reagan - one shilling sterling money of Great Britain. Dau: Catharine Swan. Mentions: children of Mary Reagan, viz: John Reagan and Susanna. Mentions: children of Mary Woolman and children of Susanna Keller. Mentions: Godfreth Woolmore be set free after my decease. No Exor. named
Wit: David Tate, Andrew Tate and Joseph Ashmead
Dated: 2 Dec. 1772   Proved: 5 April 1773

Will Book L - page 276

AUGUSTINE REEDY, Shenandoah County. Son: John Reedy -
all my land that I own. Son-in-Law: George Grandstaf.
Dau: Polly Grandstaf. Dau: Elizabeth, wife of George
Koontz - my negro girl, Sall.
Exors: Son, John Reedy and son-in-law, George Grandstaf
Wit: P. Williams, Henry Artz and Adam Ridenour
Dated: 27 Dec. 1820   Proved: 8 Jan. 1821

Will Book L - page 2

ESTHER REESE, Shenandoah County. Sons: Joseph Reese and
Isaac Reese. Sons: Daniel Stockslager and Jacob Stockslager.
Daus: Mary, wife of Jacob Beard; Esther, wife of Henry Baker;
Anna Zea, wife of Martin Zea; Magdalene Miller. Mentions:
children of my dau. Barbara, wife of Lewis Miller, dec'd.
Exors: Son-in-Law, Martin Zea and Philip Spengler
Wit: William M. Bayly, George Dosh and David Yost
Dated: 19 Sept. 1818   Proved: 12 Oct. 1819

Will Book B - page 351

THOMAS REMY, Shanandore County. Wife: (not named) - the
plantation that I now live on that I purchased of Benjamin
Smith. Sons: Elijah Remy and John Remy. Three daus: (not
named). Mentions: Plantation on Cabbin Run that I purchased
of John Runty - to be sold.
Exors: John Buck and John C. Richardson
Wit: Thomas Smith, Thomas Elzee and Mary McKenny
Dated: 7 Nov. 1786   Proved: 28 June 1787

Will Book N - page 225

MARY RHINEHART, Shenandoah County, widow and relick of Jonas
Rhinehart (dec'd.). Daus: Mary, wife of George Painter and
Barbara, wife of George Funkhouser. Sons: Jonas Rhinehart
and Andrew Rhinehart.
Exor: Willaim R. Rhinehart
Wit: William R. Rhinehart
Dated: 27 April 1825   Proved: 13 June 1825

Will Book U - page 234

ANNA RHODES, Shenandoah County. My brother: Daniel Rhodes. My father: Michael Rhodes. Sister: Rebecca Hockman, wife of Peter Hockman. Mentions: Maria Rhodes (dau. of my brother, Daniel Rhodes) and Mary Ann Rhodes (dau. of my brother, John Rhodes).
No Exor. named
Wit: John Thornberry and John Bowman
Dated: 23 Dec. 1835   Proved: 11 Dec. 1837

Will Book Y - page 537

ISAAC RHODES, Shenandoah County. Sister: Maria Maphias. Brother-in-Law: Joseph Maphias. My mother: Susana Rhodes - my house and lot in town of Edinburg, Virginia.
Exors: Mother, Susana Rhodes and John Rhodes, Jr.
Dated: 21 May 1849   Proved: 9 July 1849

Will Book A - page 407

HENRY RICABOHER, Shenandoah County, Province of Virginia. Wife: Magdaline. Sons: John (oldest); Adam; Henry and Peter. Daus: Barbara and Marget.
Exors: Son, John and Peter Lineberger
Wit: John Odell, John Snyder and George Coontz
Dated: 2 June 1780   Proved: Aug. 1780

Will Book G - page 152

CHARLES RICHARDS, Town of Woodstock, Shenandoah County. Wife: Elizabeth - all my real and personal Estate ...... as it has pleased God not to leave me any children in this world.
Exor: Wife, Elizabeth
Wit: David Jordan, Jacob Knisly and Philip Miller
Dated: 7 July 1807   Proved: 7 Dec. 1807

Will Book E - page 81

ISABELLA RICHARDSON, Shenandoah County. Son: Marquis Richardson - my whole estate and my negro man, Harry. Daus: Elizabeth Price; Sarah Combs, Mary Buck and Miriam Buck. Mentions: that Tom is to be free.
No Exor. named
Wit: John Buck and Peter Buck
Dated: 15 Oct. 1794　　　　　Proved: 15 March 1797

Will Book Q - page 192

SAMUEL RICHARDSON, Shenandoah County. Wife: Catharine Richardson. Mentions: faithful servant, Silvy, shall be free from involuntary servitude after my decease. Children: John C. Richardson; William H. Richardson; Marcus C. Richardson; Samuel B. Richardson; Ann H. Miller.
Exors: All of my above named children
Wit: Thomas F. Buck, T. C. Chrisman and J. N. Buck, William Richardson and Thomas P. Bayly

CODICIL to Will of SAMUEL RICHARDSON - Mentions: one thousand dollars in the State of Ohio, Franklin Co. for and Acadamy suitable also for a House of Worship.
Wit: Thomas Buck, Jr., Thomas F. Buck, Henry Hockman, and Will R. Ashby
Dated: 10 Dec. 1829　　　　　Proved: 7 March 1831

Will Book A - page 339

ABRAHAM RICKENBERGER, Shanando County. Wife: Elizabeth. Eldest son: Jacob Rickenberger - plantation whereon I now live. Son: Abraham - 150 acres. Sons: Peter; John and Philip. Dau: Anny.
Exors: Wife, Elizabeth and Mathias Painter
Wit: George Rinker, Nicholas Helmick and _____(Ger.)
Dated: 12 April 1781　　　　　Proved: 31 Aug. 1781

Will Book N - page 496

ANTHONY RICKETTS, Shenandoah County. Wife: Margaret.
Late son: Jarrid. Children: Mary Ann Case; John
Ricketts and Elijah Ricketts.
Exor: Son, John Ricketts
Wit: William Carson and William H. Triplett
Dated: 12 June 1826   Proved: 13 Nov. 1826

Will Book U - page 331

HENRY RIDENOUR, of Powell's Fort, Shenandoah County.
Wife: Magdalene Ridenour. Sons: John; David; Jonas.
No Exor. named
Wit: David McInturff, Jr., Henry McInturff and David
McInturff, Sen.
Dated: 26 Jan. 1838   Proved: 11 June 1838

Will Book R - page 428

MARY RIFFEY, widow and relick of Andrew Riffey, dec'd.,
Shenandoah County. Dau: Ann Riffey.
No Exor. named
Wit: _____(Ger.) and Peter Helsley
Dated: 28 April 1821   Proved: 11 Feb. 1833

Will Book G - page 302

JONAS RINEHART, Shenandoah County. Wife: Mary. Son:
Andrew Rinehart - all my lands and plantation in county
of Augusta, containing 200 acres. Sons: Jonas and Adam -
land lying in county of Fairfield in State of Ohio. Two
sons: John Rinehart and Michael Rinehart - all that plantation and tract of land whereon I now live containing 408
acres. Grandchildren: Magdalene and Rosina Rinehart
(children of my son, George Rinehart, dec'd.). Daus:
Mary, wife of George Painter; Barbara, wife of George
Funkhouser; Christina, wife of David Funkhouser. Granddaughter: Betsy David (dau. of my dau. Catharine dec'd.).
Exors: Two sons-in-law, George Painter and George Funkhouser
Wit: Jacob Coffelt, George Coffelt and Jacob Rinker
Dated: 21 Feb. 1809   Proved: 10 April 1809

Will Book H - page 261

LUDWICK RINEHART, SENIOR, Shenandoah County. Wife: Catharine.
Son: Ludwick Rinehart - my land and place whereon I now
live (373 acres). Son: John Rinehart. Daus: Magdalena;
Elizabeth; Catharine; Barbary.
Exors: Son, Ludwick Rinehart and John Kagy
Wit: John Glick, Martin Gerber, John Bertz and John Nehr
Dated: 16 Dec. 1811   Proved: 7 Sept. 1812

Will Book Q - page 125

EPHRAIM RINKER, Shenandoah County. Wife: Anna. Children:
Mary Catharine Rinker; Elizabeth Ann Rinker; Erasmus
LaFayette Rinker. Mentions: slave, Willoughby.
Exors: David Kerlin and Jacob Noel
Wit: Joseph Ryman, Samuel Mohler and A. Rinker
Dated: 10 Aug. 1830   Proved: 13 Dec. 1830

Will Book O - page 35

GEORGE RINKER, Shenandoah County. Wife: Dorothea. Children:
John; Joseph; Isaac (dec'd.); William; Mary, now intermarried
to Isaac Newland; Eleanora; Elizabeth; George.
Exor: Brother, Absalom Rinker
Wit: George Zimmerman
Dated: 14 June 1826   Proved: 12 Feb. 1827

Will Book A - page 114

JACOB RINKER, SENIOR, Shenandoah County. Oldest son: Jacob
Rinker - 186 acres whereon my said son now lives being lower
part of tract of 386 acres granted to me by deed from Honorable
Thomas Lord Fairfax bearing date 9 Jan. 1764 and one tract of
50 acres, part of tract of 200 acres granted by patent bearing
date 13 Aug. 1789. Also, tract of 278 acres granted by deed
from Lord Fairfax bearing date 24 April 1779 and tract of 170
acres granted by patent bearing date 23 July 1787. Son: Henry
Rinker - 150 acres of land. Son: George Rinker. Mentions:
Grandchildren: (children of my son, Jacob Rinker) namely:
Catharine Rinker; George Rinker; Barbara, wife of Robert Gaw;
Elizabeth Rinker; Jacob Rinker; Absalom Rinker; Ephraim Rinker.
(children of my son, George Rinker) namely: Magdalene, wife of
Jacob Keller, Jun.; George Rinker; Henry Rinker; Jacob Rinker;
Catharine Rinker; Philip Rinker; Elizabeth Rinker. (children
of my son, Henry Rinker) namely: Barbara Rinker; Catharine
Rinker; George Rinker; Henry Rinker.
Exor: Son, Jacob Rinker
Wit: Jacob Helsle, Philip Sink and Daniel Webb
Dated: 24 May 1797   Proved: 12 Sept. 1797

Will Book R - page 17

JACOB RINKER, JUNIOR, Shenandoah County. Mentions: the partnership in the mercantile business with John N. Hill. Mentions: Wife and children (not named) divide my Estate as if I should die Intestate.
Exors: James G. Fravel and Philip Williams, Jr.
Wit: Joseph Irwin, James G. Fravel and P. Williams, Jr.
Dated: 11 July 1831 Proved: 8 Aug. 1831

Will Book X - page 24

JACOB G. RINKER, Shenandoah County. Wife: (not named). Brother-in-Law: Jacob Smith. Son: Fenton Theodore Rinker. Brother: Henry St. John Rinker - appointed guardian to my infant son, Fenton Theodore Rinker.
Exor: Henry St. John Rinker
Wit: Mark Bird and Conrad Lichliter
Dated: 19 July 1844 Proved: 7 Oct. 1844

Will Book H - page 19

CHARLES ROBERTSON, County of Frederick, State of Virginia. Brother: Gary Robertson. Four sons: John; Edward; William; Gary. Three daus: Betsey; Polly; Katy.
No Exor. named
Wit: James Moore and Jacob Lucas
Dated: 10 Feb. 1807 Proved: 13 Aug. 1810

Will Book M - page 170

SAMUEL RODEHEFFER, SENIOR, Shenandoah County. Wife: Mary Rodeheffer. Sons: Philip Rodeheffer; John Rodeheffer; Jacob Rodeheffer; George Rodeheffer; Samuel Rodeheffer. Daus: Catharine, wife of Henry Ruby; Mary, wife of Gabriel Sager; Elizabeth, wife of Emanuel Brubaker; Magdalene Ohaver, widow of Isaac Ohaver, dec'd. Mentions: 93 acres of land.
Exor: Henry Kern
Wit: Samuel R. Bader and Jacob Peer
Dated: 5 April 1823 Proved: 12 May 1823

Will Book R - page 504

JOHN RODES, Shenandoah County. Wife: Margaret Rodes.
Two sons: Absalom Rodes and Vallentine Rodes - my
plantation whereon I live. Daus: Catharine, wife of
Daniel Bidlerman; Rebecca, wife of Philip Albert; Rosanah,
wife of William Estep; Christina Rodes; Barbary Rodes;
Elizabeth Rodes; Susanah. Son: John Rodes. Mentions:
Grandchildren (sons and daus. of my dau. Mary Sine, dec'd.).
Exor: Absalom Rinker, Esq.
Wit: George Shrum and Joseph Andrick
Dated: 14 May 1832   Proved: 13 May 1833

Will Book D - page 49

JAMES ROGERS, Shenandoah County. Mentions: Personal Estate
to be sold at publick sale and divided equally amonge
Sarah Calfee's three sons, namely: John, William and Henry.
Exors: Charles Calfee and Sarah Calfee
Wit: Robert Townsend, Joseph Townsend and Ruth Townsend
Dated: 19 Sept. 1791   Proved: 29 Sept. 1791

Will Book A - page 32

JACOB ROHRER, County of Frederick, Colony of Virginia.
Wife: Urshula. Sons: Jacob Rohrer; Daniel Rohrer and
Henry Rohrer. Daus: Anna and Elizabeth (younger).
Exors: Alexander Hite and Adam Beardback
Wit: _____(Ger.) and W. Hite
Dated: 29 April 1771   Proved: 27 April 1773

Will Book L - page 237

ANNA ROOF (RUFF), Shenandoah County. Sons: Martin Roof
and Samuel. Daus: Barbary Rush; Christenah Hawkins;
Elizabeth; Fanny; Mary Hefs. Grandchildren by my dau.
Mary Hefs, namely: John Martin; Anna; Samuel; Mary Elizabeth;
William. Son-in-Law: William Hefs.
Exor: Moses Walton
Wit: Charles M. Schroffe and Reuben Walton
Dated: 20 Sept. 1820   Proved: 9 Oct. 1820

Will Book I - page 44

JACOB ROOF (RUFF), Shenandoah County. Wife: Anna Roof.
Sons: Jacob Roof; John Roof; Martin Roof; Samuel Roof.
Daus: Catharine Ryan; Anna Hoffman; Barbara Roof; Mary
Hep; Christianny Roof; Elizabeth Roof; Fanny Roof.
Deceased dau: Eve Kagy. Children of dec'd dau., Eve
Kagy, viz: Jacob Kagy; Henry Kagy; Barbara Blofser and
Christian Kagy.
Exors: Samuel Strickler and John Zirkle
Wit: James Shipley, John Gaw and E. E. Rufsell
Dated: 24 April 1813   Proved: 11 April 1814

Will Book E - page 428

MARTIN ROOP, Shenandoah County. Wife: Margarett. Son:
Henry Roop - my plantation whereon I now live containing
157 acres. Sons: John Roop; Michael Roop; Martin Roop;
George Roop; Jacob Roop. Dau: Margaret - 200 acres.
Exors: Martin Garber and Jacob Garber
Wit: Martin Garber, Michael Crouse, Jacob Good and John
Hulvey
Dated: 2 June 1800   Proved: 8 June 1801

Will Book U - page 14

HENRY RORER, Shenandoah County. Mentions: Catharine Steel -
the house in which I now live. Mentions: William Elbern
to have the balance of my real Estate. Mentions: Elizabeth
Rorer. Mentions: two sisters (not named).
No Exor. named
Wit: Thomas J. Miller, J. W. Farra and Abraham Stoner
Dated: 29 April 1837   Proved: 8 May 1837

Will Book M - page 253

GEORGE ROTECAP, SENIOR, Shenandoah County. Wife: Barbara.
Son: David Rotecap - to have my Dutch Bible. Sons: Michael;
Reuben; George; Abraham; Joseph; Isaac; Jacob; Christian;
Samuel; John. Daus: Elizabeth; Barbara; Anna; Ester; Mary.
Exors: Abraham Strickler and George Buswell
Wit: Jacob Rinker, Jun., Jacob Sadler, Michael Effinger
and Abraham Fravel
Dated: 1817   Proved: 11 Nov. 1823

Will Book A - page 39

DAVID ROTHEHEFFER, Shenandoah County. Wife: Catherine.
Sons: David; John; Anthony; Samuel. My girls: (not named).
No Exor. named
Wit: George Mourer and George Mavis
Dated: 20 Feb. 1773   Proved: 22 June 1773

Will Book H - page 418

JOHN ROY, Shenandoah County. Wife: Jean Roy. Third son:
James Roy - all my land and Plantation that I now live on
with 87 acres under the Fort mountain adjoining William
Roy and land that James Roy bought of Daniel Cloud. Also,
three negroes named Lelah and her two children, Dick and
Nancy. Eldest son: Elijah Roy - two negroes named Hannah
and Lewis. Second son: John Roy - one negro named Jeremiah.
Youngest son: William Roy - one negro girl named Betty.
Daus: Betsy Atwood (oldest) and Cokey Grubbs (2nd dau.).
Exor: Son, James Roy
Wit: Lewis Lawrence, William Martin and James Stinson, Jr.
Dated: 12 Feb. 1813   Proved: 13 April 1813

Will Book C - page 248

JACOB RUBY, Shenandoah County. Wife: Elizabeth. Children:
Jacob; Elizabeth; Magdalena; John; Catharine; Henry and
Barbary.
No Exor. named
Wit: Michael Henline and George Feather
Dated: 25 June 1788   Proved: 27 Jan. 1791

Will Book B - page 381

ARCHIBALD RUDDELL, Shenandoah County. Wife: Elizabeth.
Sons: James Ruddell and Isaac Ruddell - all my lands at
Kentucky. Son: George - all lower part of my plantation.
Son: Archible - all the rest of my land and plantation.
Dau: Mary - received her part of Estate before. Other
daus: (not named).
Exors: Wife, Elizabeth and son, James Ruddell
Wit: John Newman, Ulrick Keener and George Sharp
Dated: 20 May 1786   Proved: 27 Sept. 1787

Will Book Z - page 336

GEORGE RUDDELL, Shenandoah County. Daus: Catharine Ruddell and Rebecca Goodrick. Granddaughter: Ann Wilson. Son: John Ruddell. Grandchildren: James Painter and Catharine Painter.
Exors: Samuel Painter and Philip Stover
Wit: Andrew Hoffman, Isaac Bowman and Samuel C. Williams
Dated: 20 June 1845   Proved: 11 Nov. 1850

Will Book A - page 338

JOHN RUDDELL, SENIOR, County of Shanando, Colony of Virginia. Wife: Mary Ruddell. Mentions: her children (not named).
Exor: Son-in-Law, Mounce Bird
Wit: Archible Ruddell, Rubin Dobbin and Daniel Brannaman
Dated: 20 March 1781   Proved: 31 May 1781

Will Book S - page 84

ISAAC RUDDLE, Shenandoah County. Wife: Susan. Sons: John Ruddle; James Ruddle; George Ruddle. Daus: Sarah, widow of David Jordan, Jr. (dec'd.); Catharine, wife of Reuben Hoover; Susan Ann Ruddle. Mentions: 219 acre tract of land.
Exor: Son, James Ruddle
Wit: Robert Turner, Thomas McCord and Jacob Farra
Dated: 3 Aug. 1833   Proved: 7 Oct. 1833

Will Book W - page 325

SUSAN RUDDLE, Shenandoah County. Sons: James Ruddle; George Ruddle. Mentions: Rebecca Ruddell, wife of my son, James Ruddell, who I have lived with. Dau: Susan Ann, wife of Philip Stover.
Exor: Son, James Ruddell
Wit: Andrew Huffman and Abraham Nicholas
Dated: 6 Sept. 1842   Proved: 12 June 1843

Will Book F - page 456

BENJAMIN RUFFNER, Shenandoah County. Wife: Elizabeth.
Sons: Peter and Benjamin. Other children: Mary; Reginia;
Martin; Anna; Emanuel; Barbara; Abraham; Reuben; Catharine;
Michael; Elizabeth. Two youngest children by my first
wife: Martin and Anna - Estate due in right of their mother
from the Estate of Jacob Burner. Mentions: Dau. of my
dau. Anna, Susanna Ruffner.
Exors: Christian Fover and John Roads
Wit: Joshua Ruffner, Peter Heastant and Isaac Wright
Dated: 9 May 1808   Proved: 7 July 1808

Will Book A - page 152

PETER RUFFNER, SENIOR, Parish of Beckford, County of Dunmore.
Wife: Mary Ruffner. Sons: Peter Ruffner; Manuel Ruffner;
Joseph Ruffner; Benjamin Ruffner; Ruben Ruffner. Mentions:
son-in-law, Jacob Stover - 150 pounds.
Exors: Wife, Mary Ruffner, son, Joseph Ruffner and friend,
Benjamin Strickler
Wit: Edwin Young, Selby Foley, Christian Grove and Jacob
Burner.
Dated: 15 Jan. 1778   Proved: 28 May 1778

Will Book W - page 379

JOHN RUPERT, Shenandoah County. Wife: Mary Rupert - the
plantation I bought of Philip Haas lying on the Passage
Creek. Dau: Elizabeth - one dollar and no more. Mentions:
two daus. of my dau., Elizabeth (not named). Mentions:
Gideon and Elizabeth, son and dau. of my dau., Margaret
Rupert. Sons: Moses Rupert (dec'd.); Adam Rupert; Christian
Rupert; Daniel Rupert; Peter Rupert; John Rupert.
Exor: Jacob Noel
Wit: Jacob Noel, Joseph Ozburn and Samuel Noel
Dated: 2 Nov. 1842   Proved: 9 Oct. 1843

Will Book B - page 59

EDWARD RYAN, Frederick County, Colony of Virginia. Son:
Thomas Ryan - all my plantation lying on a branch of Stony
Creek called Sorrel Run. Dau: Eleanor Ryan. Mentions:
grandsons, Henry and John Coffehel
Exor: Son, Thomas Ryan
Wit: Jacob Rinker, Jr., Jacob Rinker, Sen. and George Rinker
Dated: 13 Jan. 1772   Proved: 26 Feb. 1784

Will Book I - page 244

CHRISTIAN SAGER, Shenandoah County. Six children: Jacob; Chrisla; Abraham; Samuel; Mary; John. Mentions: plantation whereon I now live shall be leased or rented yearly as long as my mother should live.
Exors: George Mourey and Christian Omarte
Wit: Jacob Ohmart, George Omarte and _____(Ger.)
Dated: 15 March 1815   Proved: 12 June 1815

Will Book P - page 498

GABRIEL SAGER, Shenandoah County. Wife: (Sarah) Mary Sager. Sons: Ely and John. Mentions: Joseph Cauffman and Reuben Coffman - my dau. Mary's legacy. Daus: Elizabeth, wife of Peter Dull, Barbara, wife of Abram Smutz; Lidia, wife of John Currey; Susannah; Ann; Esther; Delila.
Exor: David Crawford
Wit: George Shrum, Philip Rodeheffer and Mathias Smutz
Dated: 6 Dec. 1827

CODICIL to Will of GABRIEL SAGER - Mentions: divide land among children.
Wit: George Shrum, Jacob Cook and John Cook
Dated: 8 Dec. 1828   Proved: 12 July 1830

Will Book X - page 249

CATHARINE SALVAGE, town of New Market, Shenandoah County. Mentions: Great-granddaughters, Mary Frances Calvert and Catharine Ann Calvert, infant children of John S. Calvert and Catharine Ann Calvert, his wife - all my Estate. Mentions: son-in-law, Richard Winfield.
Exor: John D. Zirkle
Wit: Philip Leggett, John Coffman and Grafton Weeks
Dated: 27 June 1845   Proved: 8 Sept. 1845

Will Book M - page 450

ELIZABETH SAMUELS, Shenandoah County. Children: Green; Isaac; Rutha; Mary.
Exor: Son, Isaac
Wit: Samuel Hawkins, William Byrd, Jr. and George Pennybacker
Dated: 11 May 1824   Proved: 11 Oct. 1824

Will Book N - page 213

MARY SAMUELS, Shenandoah County. Sister: Ruth Byrd - my negro girl name of Manda. Late father: Isaac Samuels. Late sister: Sarah Samuels. Brothers: Joseph; Abraham; John; Isaac; Green. Sisters: Nancy Mayberry; Rebecca Byrd.
Exor: Brother, Isaac Samuels
Wit: Mark Cauldwell, Reubin Branham and George Pennybacker
Dated: 22 March 1825   Proved: 9 May 1825

Will Book X - page 319

EMANUEL SANLAW, Shenandoah County. Wife: Anna Sanlaw - all the residue of my Estate.
Exor: Wife, Anna Sanlaw
Wit: Michael Kontz, Eliza Lindamood and R. M. Conn
Dated: 27 May 1845   Proved: 9 Feb. 1846

Will Book N - page 224

MARY ANN SAUM, Shenandoah County. Four children: John Saum; Daniel Saum; Eve, wife of John Roads; Christian Saum. Step-son: Adam Saum.
Exor: John Saum
Wit: P. Williams, Robert Turner and James Williams
Dated: 7 April 1821   Proved: 13 June 1825

Will Book G - page 305

NICHOLAS SAUM, Parish of Beckford, Shenandoah County. Wife: Anna Mary. Three youngest sons: John Saum; Daniel Saum; Christian Saum - the plantation whereon I now live containing 120 acres adjoining land of Martin Wiley and another tract containing 60 acres. I purchased of Augustine Reedy. Other children: Frederick Saum; Jacob Saum; Catharine Bower, widow of Nicholas Bower; Magdalene Bowman, wife of Benjamin Bowman; Adam Saum and Eve Saum.
Exors: Son-in-Law, Benjamin Bowman and wife, Anna Mary Saum
Wit: Jacob Lineweaver and Simeon Yeager
Dated: 18 Feb. 1809   Proved: 10 April 1809

Will Book L - page 438

BALSAR SAUR, Shenandoah County. Wife: Barbara Saur. Son: Isaac - the plantation on which I at present reside which I purchased of Peter Lionberger, together with all the Slaves except one. Dau: Susanna Saur - plantation which I bought of John Crumb on which John Smith at present lives and choice of one slave. Dau: Barbara Summers - plantation adjoining the lands of my brother, Frederick Saur. Mentions: Brother-in-Law, Samuel Wise (son of Michael Wise). Mentions: Jacob Shenk.
Exors: Son, Isaac Saur and friend, John Varna
Wit: William R. Almond, Edward Almond and Marm Almond
Dated: 11 July 1821   Proved: 7 Jan. 1822

Will Book V - page 391

PETER SAYGER, Shenandoah County. Wife: Anna. Mentions: Jacob Barb, Jr., son of Jacob Barb. Mentions: Stephen Strotherman. Mentions: Absalom Sager, son of my brother, Conrad Sayger. Mentions: Thomas Davis and Anna Barb, dau. of Jacob Barb, Jr.
Exor: Edward Walton
Wit: John Foltz, Peter Baker, Jr. and Jacob Baker
Dated: 26 Oct. 1840   Proved: 8 Feb. 1841

Will Book Q - page 110   NUNCUPATIVE WILL

FIELDING SCANLAND, Shenandoah County.
    The following words is the substance of the last Will and Testament of Fielding Scanland, dec'd. His last desire was that his son, Benjamin Scanland should have all that he was worth at his death.
Wit: Peter Price and Catharine Tett
Dated: 2 Oct. 1830   Proved: 10 Nov. 1830

Will Book W - page 183

PHILIP HENRY SCHICKENDANTZ, Shenandoah County. Wife: Christina Schickendantz. Mentions: Joseph Supinger; Rhoda Pangle, wife of William Pangle; Sarah Supinger. Mentions: children of Rebecca Pfiffer, dec'd., viz: Elizabeth; Levi and Rebecca.
Exor: Joseph Pfiffer
Wit: Joseph Wattson and Obed Hockman
Dated: 24 Aug. 1841   Proved: 8 Aug. 1842

Will Book F - page 470

MATHIAS SCHMOOTZ (SMOOTZ), SENIOR, Shenandoah County.
Wife: Regina Smootz. Son: Abraham Smootz - part of my
plantation whereon I now live conveyed to me by Christian
Stover (210 acres). Son: Mathias Smootz - remaining part
of plantation (215 acres). Daus: Barbara, wife of Michael
Stover; Magdalene, wife of Lewis Keebler; Elizabeth, wife
of Henry Gochenour; Anna, wife of John Miller; Rosina, wife
of Gabriel Sager; Mary, wife of Adam Mavis.
Exors: Sons, Abraham Smootz and Mathias Smootz
Wit: Samuel Rodeheffer, Samuel R. Bader and John Gochenour
Dated: 24 June 1800   Proved: 8 Sept. 1800

Will Book O - page 260

ABRAHAM SCHMUTZ (SMOOTZ), Shenandoah County. Wife: Anna.
Children: Mary, wife of Paul Hammon; Barbara; Elizabeth;
Mathias; Jacob; Abraham; Anne; John.
Exors: Sons, Mathias Schmutz and Jacob Schmutz
Wit: _____(Ger.), Jacob Wilkin, Philip Swartz and George Shrum
Dated: 19 Jan. 1816   Proved: 10 March 1828

Will Book E - page 518

CONRAD SEAGER, Shenandoah County. Wife: Mary. Son: Abraham,
who is lame. Other children: Gabriel; Christian; Samuel;
Mary; Catharine. Mentions: two children of my dau. Catharine
(not named).
Exors: Sons, Gabriel and Christian
Wit: Jacob Neff, Michael Bright, Joseph Taylor and I. Stiegel
Dated: 24 Aug. 1800   Proved: 12 April 1802

Will Book F - page 204

CONRAD SEIPLE, Shenandoah County. Wife: Hannah. Son:
Conrad - 150 acres of land whereon he now lives adjoining
lands of George Zirkle (dec'd.) and Ollinger line being
part of a tract of 400 acres which I purchased from heirs
of James Cunningham. Son: Frederick - 150 acres taken
from aforesaid tract, including dwelling house wherein I
now live. Dau: Elizabeth - 50 acres of aforesaid tract of
land, including house where Elizabeth and husband now live.
Dau: Hannah - 50 acres of aforesaid tract of land. Dau:
Catharine.
Exors: Sons, Conrad and Frederick
Wit: Jacob Ollinger, Jacob Stegle and Michael Bright
Dated: 28 Jan. 1801   Proved: 12 March 1804

Will Book M - page 208

JACOB SEIVER, Shenandoah County. Wife: Jarida Seiver.
Dau: Sarah, wife of John Marker - 50 acres of land conveyed to me by Philip Snapp and my female negro slave, Lucy with her two children. Son: John Seiver - 50 acres of land same he now lives on that I purchased of my brother, Isaac Seiver. Dau: Elizabeth, wife of Lawrence Keller - 50 acres of land, the same I purchased of my brother, Moses Seiver. Son: William Seiver - one half of that tract of land conveyed to me by my father, Bernhard Seiver, whereon I and he now live, also, 12 1/2 acres of woodland purchased of my brother, Bernhard Seiver. Son: Lawrence Seiver - other half of land conveyed to me by my father.
Exors: Son, William Seiver and son-in-law, Lawrence Keller
Wit: Samuel R. Bader and Emanuel Pittman
Dated: 10 Sept. 1822   Proved: 11 Aug. 1823

Will Book I - page 41

MOSES SEIVER (SCIBERT), Shenandoah County. Wife: Mary.
Son: George Scibert - I have made Deed for a tract of land which is his full share. Son: Henry Scibert - tract of land I purchased of Mary Grove containing 200 acres. Son: John Scibert - balance of three tracts of land called the home place (after taking off 100 acres adjoining Copperstone, Michael Clem and Wiseman land). Son: Abraham Scibert - 100 acres of land. Mentions: children of my dau. Elizabeth Wiseman. Mentions: Frederick McInturf, trustee for my wife, Mary. Mentions: balance of my Estate shall be sold by my Exor. Mentions: children of my dau. Marty Bechtel, dec'd.
Exor: John Roads
Wit: John Gaw, Philip Williams and Charles O'Neil
Dated: 27 Feb. 1810   Proved: 11 April 1814

Will Book G - page 169

DANIEL SHAEFFER (SHAVER), Town of Woodstock, Shenandoah County. Wife: Catharine. Mentions: 25 pounds currency be paid toward building or repairing the German Lutheran Church at Stover Town and 25 pounds to the German Lutheran Church at Woodstock. Also, 25 pounds to the German Reformed Church at Woodstock. Mentions: Henry Shaeffer, son of my brother, Henry B. Shaeffer (dec'd.) of York County, Pennsylvania. Mentions: Peter Hull, brother of my late wife, Margaretha (dec'd.) and Catharine Hull, sister of the same, both of Lancaster County, State of Pennsylvania. Mentions: Frederick Fry, son of my sister, Christina (dec'd.). Mentions: Wife of Conrad Lear who is dau. to my sister, Catherine (dec'd.) of Shenandoah County. Mentions: my three dec'd. brothers, viz: Henry, Paul and Christopher Shaeffer. Sisters: Christina, wife of Frederick Fry; Catharina Conn; Anna Mary Caldreider, all of York County, Pennsylvania.
Exors: Jacob Fry, Nicholas Keffer and Henry Hockman
Wit: Henry Cline, George Mavius and Jacob Bushong
Dated: 27 May 1805   Proved: 7 March 1808

Will Book F - page 201

MARTIN SHANK, Shenandoah County. Wife: Corlena. Sons: Martin and John - 800 acres of land each. Daus: Ann Mary, wife of John Oldhare; Barbara, wife of Isaac Breedlofe. Children of the said Breedlofe's first wife: Martin; George and John. Dau. Barbara's son: George Stomback.
Exors: Sons, Martin and John
Wit: Philip Somer and Jacob Boehm
Dated: 2 Oct. 1801   Proved: 12 March 1804

Will Book U - page 537

GEORGE SHAVER, SENIOR, Shenandoah County. Son: George Shaver - tract of land whereon I now live (180 acres). Dau: Katharine, wife of John Gochenour - all the tract of land and plantation whereon she and her husband now live. Dau: Franey, wife of Jonathan Gochenour - 226 acres of land. Dau: Magdelene, wife of William Kronk - 136 acres of land. Dau: Barbara, wife of John Copp - tract of land whereon she and her husband now live. Dau: Sarah, wife of Anthony Funkhouser - several parcels of land which makes her equal with her brother and sisters.
Exors: Son, George Shaver and son-in-law, John Gochenour
Wit: Samuel R. Bader and Henry Baserman
Dated: 20 Oct. 1824

CODICIL to Will of GEORGE SHAVER, SENIOR - Mentions: Son, George Shaver.
Wit: same as above
Dated: 11 July 1828   Proved: 8 April 1839

Will Book G - page 127

JACOB SHAVER, Shenandoah County. Wife: Eve. Youngest dau: Eve. All my daus: (not named).
Exors: Philip Summer and George Pence
Wit: George Gander and Frederick Sower
Dated: 12 March 1807   Proved: 12 Oct. 1807

Will Book I - page 242

JACOB SHAVER, Shenandoah County. Wife: Otilla. Son: George - to have the land whereon he now lives along John Byrd's line to Pence line. Son: Henry - to have land he now lives, that is, 50 acres. Son: Philip - to have land and plantation whereon I now live. Son: Jacob. Dau: Mary Beavers. Mentions: My 13 children - children of my last wife and children from my first wife. Son-in-Law: Peter Byrd. Son-in-Law: Thomas Hammon. My two youngest sons: Jonas and Solomon.
Exors: Son, Philip and friend, George Mourey
Wit: John Bort and George Bird
Dated: 30 Oct. 1813   Proved: 12 June 1815

Will Book E - page 152

ADAM SHEARMAN, SENIOR, of Strasburg in Shenandoah County.
Wife: Catharina. Son: Adam Shearman. Dau: Susannah.
Mentions: Money owing me in State of North Carolina from Henry Hergelrole.
Exor: Son, Adam Shearman
Wit: Alexander Hite, Jacob Funk and _____ (Ger.).
Dated: 3 May 1797   Proved: 12 Sept. 1797

Will Book I - page 90

ADAM SHEARMAN, Shenandoah County. Wife: (not named).
Son: John - all my land on the side Creek (40 acres).
Son: Jacob - the Mills and dwelling house and land on other side of Creek (30 acres). Son: Adam. Daus: Sally; Polly and Bevey. Mentions: Exors. to bring suit against John Machir for money coming for the land sold him. Mentions: 197 acres of land now claimed by Ridenour and in dispute.
Mentions: Brother-in-Law, Peter Boyer as guardian to son, Adam.
Exors: Brother-in-Law, Jacob Keller and John Westley Abbott
Wit: Malow Roach, Adam Cyford, Samuel Danner, Bennett Penkine, Jacob Golladay and George Keller
Dated: 23 July 1814   Proved: 8 Aug. 1814

Will Book V - page 47

HENRY SHEETZ, SENIOR, Shenandoah County. Sons: Henry Sheetz; Daniel Sheetz; John Sheetz - divide my plantation in three equal parts. Daus: Christiana Sheetz; Elizabeth Row, wife of Henry Row; Susannah Rode, wife of George Rode. Mentions: children of my dau. Barbary, wife of David Row, dec'd., to wit: Henry, David and Elizabeth.
Exors: Sons, Henry and Daniel Sheetz
Wit: George Shrum and Adam Bly
Dated: 9 Aug. 1833   Proved: 12 Aug. 1839

Will Book O - page 423

JACOB SHEETZ, Shenandoah County. Wife: Eve Sheetz.
Sons: Mathias Sheetz; Philip Sheetz; George Sheetz;
Joseph Sheetz. Granddaughter: Ann Hoover. Mentions:
Slave named Gilbert - to be sold.
Exors: Sons, Mathias Sheetz and Philip Sheetz
Wit: George Shrum, William Philips and Daniel Sheetz
Dated: 14 Aug. 1828   Proved: 13 Oct. 1828

Wills and Accts. (1809-1863) - page 156

JOHN SHEETZ, Shenandoah County. Wife: Margaret. My
children: George; Polly; Henry; Peter; John; Jacob;
Sophia; Betsy. Mentions: granddaughter, Leah, dau. of
my dau. Polly.
Exor: Adam Barb
Wit: Alexander Doyle, Jacob Funkhouser and Abraham Funkhouser
Dated: 30 Nov. 1826   Proved: 27 Sept. 1830

Will Book S - page 14

MATHIAS SHEETZ, Shenandoah County. Wife: Catharine Sheetz.
My children: (not named).
Exor: Philip Sheetz
Wit: Henry Winder and George Sheetz
Dated: 16 Sept. 1829   Proved: 7 Dec. 1829

Will Book M - page 224

HENRY SHEFFER, Shenandoah County. Wife: Magdalena - all
my household and real Estate. Daus: Elizabeth and Catharine.
Son: Joseph. Mentions: Remaining infant children which
have not yet got any learning that they should be learned
to read as well as necessary.
Exors: Son, Joseph Sheffer and brother, James Sheffer
Wit: George Will (of George), Abraham Sheffer and Solomon
Sheffer.
Dated: 21 April 1823   Proved: 8 Sept. 1823

Will Book D - page 221

MICHAEL SHEFFER, Shenandoah County. Wife: (not named).
My oldest son: Michael Sheffer, Mentions: wife's two
sons, Henry and Jacob Moatz. Mentions: John Walker.
Exor: Wife, Catharine Sheffer
Wit: James Cunningham, Michael Moatz and Michael Zirkle
Dated: 13 Dec. 1780   Proved: 11 June 1793

Will Book K - page 207

JOHN SHELTON, SENIOR, Shenandoah County. Wife: Catharine
Shelton - one negro girl named Betsy. Sons: Isaac Shelton;
William; John; Jeremiah; Samuel; Joseph (dec'd.).
Exor: Son, Isaac Shelton
Wit: William S. Marye, Cornelius Gaines and Valentine Ramey
Dated: 13 Nov. 1816   Proved: 13 Jan. 1817

Will Book I - page 169

CAROLINE SHENK, Shenandoah County. Sons: Martin and John
Shenk. Son: George Shenk alias Stanback. Children of my
deceased dau., Eve Breedlove: Martin; George and John
Breedlove. Daus: Mary Altherr and Barbara Breedlove.
Grandson: George Shenk, alias Stanback.
Exors: John Roads and John Altherr
Wit: Abraham Strickler, William Marye and William Almond
Dated: 24 June 1809   Proved: 9 June 1815

Will Book H - page 270

ABRAHAM SHERFEY, Shenandoah County. Wife: Anna. Father:
Casper Sherfey in Mariland. My mother: Magdalena Sherfey.
Brother-in-Law: Joseph Gary. My eleven children: John
Sherfey; Joshua Sherfey; Magdalene Sherfey; Solome and
Barbara Sherfey; Abraham Sherfey; Anna Sherfey (only 7
children named). Mentions: younger children shall be put
or hired out by minister or Elders of our Babtis Church.
Mentions: 250 acres to be sold.
Exors: John Kagy and Jacob Garber
Wit: George Weaver, Burnhard Goetz and Martin Goetz
Dated: 28 May 1812   Proved: 12 Oct. 1812

Will Book M - page 246

BENJAMIN SHIREMAN, Shenandoah County. Mentions: Jacob
Stultz - all my estate both real and personal. My father
and mother: Bernhard Shireman and Catharine. My brother:
Peter Shireman.
No Exor. named
Wit: John Rode and George Shrum
Dated: 6 April 1822   Proved: 14 Oct. 1823

Will Book H - page 186

ANTHONY SHOMO, Shenandoah County. Wife: Elizabeth Shomo.
Dau: Polly - now insane. Sons: William (youngest); John
(eldest); Joseph and Daniel.
Exors: Wife, Elizabeth Shomo and son, John Shomo
Wit: Isaac Gore, Henry Fry and Henry Spitzer
Dated: 19 March 1812   Proved: 13 April 1812

Will Book A - page 52

STEPHEN SHOWMAN, County of Dunmore, Colony of Virginia.
Wife: Barbara. Son: Stephen Showman. Dau: Barbara Showman.
Exor: Wife, Barbara Showman.
Wit: _____ (Ger.), Jacob Rinker, Jr. and Henry Surber
Dated: 10 Jan. 1774   Proved: 24 May 1774

Will Book M - page 238

STEPHEN SHOWMAN, Shenandoah County. Wife: Elizabeth.
Children: Elizabeth Showman; Magdalene Showman; Catharine
Showman; Jacob Showman. Sons: George Showman and Stephen
Showman - all my lands and plantation. Children of my
dau. Barbara (late the wife of John Stoneburner).
Exors: Sons, George Showman and Stephen Showman
Wit: George Keller and Absalom Rinker
Dated: 21 March 1823   Proved: 13 Oct. 1823

Will Book T - page 274

JACOB SHRYOCK, Shenandoah County. Wife: Amelia Shryock - my whole estate both real and personal. Daus: Susan H. Riddleberger, her husband Madison Riddleberger; Catharina Berry; Louisia Ann Shryock; Emily L. Guinn; Ann Julia Shryock. Sons: Frederick S. Shryock; Henry S. Shryock.
Exors: Wife, Amelia Shryock and Samuel Ott
Wit: Richard Proctor, Alexander Bowman and Peter Ligget
Dated: 8 May 1833   Proved: 8 Feb. 1836

Will Book E - page 447

JOHN BERNARD SIBERT, Shenandoah County. First born son: Moses - 50 acres. Son: Isaac - 50 acres. Son: Jacob - 50 acres. Dau: Mary - 50 acres. Dau: Elizabeth - 50 acres. Son: Bernhard - 25 acres. Sons: Adam and Peter.
Exors: Sons, Jacob, Adam and Peter
Wit: Jacob Hoak, Jonathan Moore and _____ (Ger.)
Dated: 20 May 1801   Proved: 13 July 1801

Will Book Z - page 42

MARY SIGLER, Shenandoah County. Son: William Zigler.
Dau: Hester Bird.
Exor: Son, William Zigler
Wit: J. S. Pennybacker and Hiram Bowman
Dated: 12 June 1849   Proved: 8 Oct. 1849

Will Book R - page 427

MICHAEL SIGLER, Shenandoah County. Wife: Mary. Son: William - tract of land on which I now live, also, 70 acres of land in addition to first named tract except the part I intend for Hannah Hickle's children (who live in Ohio). Daus: Hetty Bird; Anna Stewart; Hannah Hickle. Grandson: William LaFayette Bird.
Exor: Son, William Sigler
Wit: Aaron Moore and Abram Fravel
Dated: 16 Feb. 1832

CODICIL to Will of MICHAEL SIGLER - Mentions: Som, William to purchase a tract of land in State of Ohio for dau. Hannah Hickle and her children. Mentions: grandson, LaFayette Bird.
Wit: Aaron Moore, Abram Fravel and Sutton I. Harris
Dated: 15 Jan. 1833   Proved: 11 Feb. 1833

Will Book E - page 426

JOHN WILLIAM SIGN, Shenandoah County. Wife: Mary Sign.
Daus: Elizabeth Sign; Catharine; Mary; Anne; Catharine, Jr.
Sons: Henry Sign; Peter Sign; Adam and John.
Exor: Son, Adam Sign
Wit: Philip Williams, William Kennedy and Samuel Clayton
Dated: 4 April 1789   Proved: 13 April 1801

Will Book O - page 425   NUNCUPATIVE WILL

DR. JOHN SIMMS, Shenandoah County, at the house of
John Jones of the County of Culpeper, Virginia. Wife:
Isabella - all my property.
Exor: Edmond Broadus
Wit: Philip Thornton and Matilda I. Jones
Dated: 17 Sept. 1828   Proved: 13 Oct. 1828

Will Book A - page 392

JOHN SIVELY, Shanano County. Mentions: brothers and sisters,
viz: Jacob Sively; Peter Sively; Joseph Sively; George Sively;
Eve Brown; Barbary Sively; Elizabeth Sively; Margaret Sively;
Magdalene Sively; Mary Sively and Betty Sively.
Exor: Reuben Moore
Wit: _____(Ger.) and John Brown
Not dated   Proved: 30 May 1782

Will Book A - page 85

FRANCIS SLAUGHTER, Dunmore County. Wife: Jemima.
Exor: Wife, Jemima Slaughter and Hankerson Read
Wit: Gabriel Jones, Abraham Bird and Philip Slaughter
Dated: 2 Sept. 1774   Proved: 27 Feb. 1776

Will Book G - page 125

ADAM SMITH, Shenandoah County. Wife: Hannah Smith. Son: Adam Smith - the plantation whereon he now liveth. Son: John Smith - the plantation whereon he now liveth. Son: Isaac Smith - the land which I have in the State of Ohio. Son: William Smith - has received his full share. Daus: Elizabeth Huffman; Mary Evensob; Catharine Andrake; Hannah Krouse; Phebe Smith; Nancy Coffman. Granddaughter: Elizabeth Houser.
Exors: Samuel Walton and Moses Walton
Wit: John Lickliter, John Spitler and Mathias Spitler
Dated: 16 June 1807   Proved: 8 Sept. 1807

Will Book P - page 442

ADAM SMITH, Shenandoah County. Dau: Betsy Smith, now Betsy Proctor. Son-in-Law: John Proctor. Mentions: Philip Smith's heirs, viz: Catharine Smith; Michael Smith; Benjamin Smith; John Smith; Polly Smith. Mentions: Samuel Smith, son of A. Smith and Susan Colwell, dau. of Adam Smith and wife of Jerry Colwell. Mentions: John Smith, son of Adam Smith, dec'd. Mentions: widow of Adam Smith, dec'd.
Exor: Son, John Smith
Wit: Martin Stomback, Philip Kibler and John Ligget
Dated: 21 April 1830   Proved: 10 May 1830

Will Book H - page 423

HANNAH SMITH, Shenandoah County, widow of Adam Smith, dec'd. Dau: Phoebe Smith - one dollar. Children of my dau. Elizabeth, who was the wife of Absalom Hoffman, who is now deceased: Hannah Huffman; Isaac Huffman; John Huffman; William Huffman. Children of my dau. Mary Roof which is now dec'd.: Noah Roof and Mary Roof. Mentions: Elizabeth Smith, dau. of my dau. Susanna Smith. Daus: Caty, wife of Jacob Anderick; Hannah, wife of Daniel Krouse; Nancy, wife of John Coffman.
Exor: Son-in-Law, John Coffman
Wit: E. Rinker, Michael Lindamood and Andrew Lindamood
Dated: 8 Dec. 1813   Proved: 7 June 1813 (?)

Will Book C - page 234

HENRY SMITH, Shenandoah County.   Wife: Margaretha.   Dau: Mary Barbara Smith.
Exor: Wife, Margaretha
Wit: George Wisman and Nicholas Wisman
Dated: 10 Sept. 1790   Proved: 30 Dec. 1790

A true translation from the German original - David Jordan

Will Book O - page 465   NUNCUPATIVE WILL

JOHN W. SMITH, Shenandoah County.   Wife: Barbara Smith.
Mentions: infant heirs.
Wit: John Strickler and Daniel Brubaker
Dated: 23 Aug. 1828   Proved: 10 Nov. 1828

Will Book A - page 383

JOSEPH SMITH, Shanando County. Dau: Ann - my negro slaves named Nell and Frank. Dau: Elizabeth - negro slave named Sam. Dau: Susanna - the negro child of Nell and Frank. Dau: Rachel - negro slave named Bill. Daus: Margarett and Sarah. Mentions: Dau. Mary Christina's heirs. Son: James - all lotts and parcels of land in Town of Strawsburg and negro slave named Peter. Granddaughter: Ann Reynolds, youngest child of my dau. Mary Christina. Grandson: Joseph Reynolds, son of Margarett. Brother: Robert Smith - to be guardian over my son until he is of age. Mentions: my plantation on the River Shanando (188 acres) - to be sold.
Exors: Brother, Robert Smith and son, James Smith
Wit: Alexander Machir, Thomas Welsh, Christopher Dosh and John Machir
Dated: 11 May 1781   Proved: 25 April 1782

Will Book U - page 269

REBECCA SMITH, of the town of Strasburg, Shenandoah County.
Niece: Elizabeth Chandler - all my Estate, real and personal.
Mentions: niece's husband and children (not named).
Exor: Levi Crabill
Wit: Joseph S. Spengler and D. Stickley
Dated: 28 May 1836   Proved: 12 March 1838

Will Book M - page 202

ROWLEY SMITH, Shenandoah County. My children: Clarifsa; Jane; Sophia; Elhanan; Narcissa; Sidney Smith; Joseph; Arthur and Marion. My brother: John Smith of Fauquir Co. Children of my son, Dudley Smith (dec'd.).
Exor: Son, Sidney Smith
Wit: Elias Clark, William Fish and Rowley McKay
Dated: 19 May 1823   Proved: 9 June 1823

Will Book P - page 222

SIDNEY SMITH, Shenandoah County. Wife: Elizabeth. My children: (not named).
Exor: Joseph S. Spengler
Wit: Jno. A. Catlett, Thomas Williams and William R. Ashley
Dated: 15 Aug. 1829   Proved: 7 Sept. 1829

Will Book E - page 372

WILLIAM SMITH, Shenandoah County. Wife: Elizabeth Smith - all my black slaves as her own property during her natural life. Mentions: William, son of my brother, David; Maryann Dawbens, dau. of my brother, Samuel. Mentions: Demone Williamson (widow) - the cow she has youse of now. Mentions: Sarah Wyatt, dau. of my brother, Samuel; Alexander Smith, son of my brother, David; William Smith, son of Samuel and Mary Smith; Jonathan Hall.
Exors: Wife, Betty, Andrew Muirheid and Michael Crouse
Wit: George Feather, Thomas Hall, George Riner and Peter Weaver.
Dated: 22 Nov. 1797   Proved: 9 June 1800

Will Book V - page 262

WILLIAM SMITH, Shenandoah County. Wife: (not named). Mentions: tract of land containing 150 acres and another 50 acres - to be sold. Son: William L. Smith - the land I now live on containing 275 acres. Daus: Elizabeth Smith; Margaret Shull; Mary Funkhouser. Son: Mathew H. Smith - 110 acres of land. Son: John L. Smith. Mentions: children of my dau. Eleanor Campbell dec'd.
Exors: Sons, William L. Smith and Mathew H. Smith
Wit: Joseph Wattson and Isaac Boehm
Dated: 6 March 1837   Proved: 10 Aug. 1840

Will Book Z - page 66   NUNCUPATIVE WILL

BARBARA SMOOTZ, Shenandoah County. Next of kin: Philip Smootz; George Smootz; Henry Wilkin and Madalene, his wife; Jonathan Heisey and Sarah, his wife. Mentions: John Smootz - a certain Bond executed to her by Joseph Keller and Japheth Keller, committee of George Feckley.
Wit: Samuel Kern and Abraham Fauber
Dated: 27 Aug. 1849   Proved: 12 Nov. 1849

Will Book Q - page 127

FERDINAND SMUCKER, Shenandoah County. Wife: Rosina Smucker.
Sons: Joseph Smucker; Ferdinand Smucker; John Smucker.
Daus: Mary Ann Smucker; Eliza Smucker; Rosina Smucker; Norma Smucker.
Exors: Brother, Jacob Smucker and son, Joseph Smucker
Wit: Samuel R. Bader and Henry Baserman
Dated: 12 Dec. 1829   Proved: 13 Dec. 1830

Will Book Q - page 76

ABRAHAM SMUTZ (SMOOTZ), SENIOR, Shenandoah County, miller. Mentions: My real Estate being on both sides of Tom's Brook, together with seperate tract of 74 acres - to be sold. Daus: Catharine Smutz; Sarah Smutz; Mary Smutz; Elizabeth, wife of Benjamin Doll; Margaret Smutz; Magdaline Smutz. Sons: David Smutz; Joseph Smutz; Valentine Smutz; Samuel Smutz; Abraham Smutz. Grandchildren: Elizabeth Ruts; Catharine Ruts; Lydia Ruts (children of my dau. Lidia, dec'd., late wife of John Ruts).
Exors: Sons, David Smutz and Valentine Smutz
Wit: Phineas Orndorff and _____(Ger.)
Dated: 22 June 1825   Proved: 12 Oct. 1830

Will Book S - page 493

ABRAHAM SNAPP, Shenandoah County. Wife: Elizabeth - all my personal property.
Exor: Joseph Hyde
Wit: Jacob Snapp and Benjamin Kronk
Dated: 3 March 1835   Proved: 13 April 1835

Will Book D - page 26

JOSEPH SNAPP, County of Frederick, but a freeholder in County of Shenandoah. Wife: Elizabeth. Mentions: Exors. shall build a fit dwelling house for my wife on land which I lately purchased of my brother, Lawrence Snapp. Two children: Elizabeth and Joseph.
Exors: Brother, Philip and brother-in-law, Henry Keller
Wit: Simon Harr, Adam Sherman, Jr. and Jacob Snapp
Dated: 18 March 1791   Proved: 30 June 1791

Will Book A - page 420

LAWRENCE SNAPP, Parish and County of Frederick. Wife: (not named) - 1/3 plantation, negro woman named Hannah, Lott in Town of Woodstock purchased of Will Slaughter. Son: John Snapp - tract of land whereon he now lives I purchased of Richard Campbell. Son: Lawrence Snapp - tract of land containing 413 acres which I obtained a Deed from Proprietors Office. Son: Peter Snapp - tract of land (400 acres) whereon the Mill stands. Son: Philip Snapp - 430 acres whereon my son, Philip now lives. Son: Joseph Snapp - 1/2 tract of land purchased of Samuel Vance containing 200 acres. Son: Abraham Snapp - other half above tract of land. Son: Jacob Snapp - tract containing 548 acres, remainder of tract of 1,791 acres being part whereon dwelling house stands. Dau: Christina, wife of Michael Speagle - 264 acres I purchased of John Magill, Esq. (in City of Philadelphia). Dau: Margarett, wife of Henry Keller - 264 acres. Dau: Susanna Snapp - 413 acres I purchased of William Wadlington.
Exors: Son, John Snapp and son-in-law, Michael Speagle
Wit: John Crookshands, George Keller and _____ (Ger.)
Dated: 5 April 1782   Proved: 27 June 1782

Will Book E - page 446

MARGARETT SNAPP, Shenandoah County, widow of Lawrence Snapp, dec'd. Daus: Margaret, wife of Henry Keller; Susanna, wife of John Harr. Mentions: my children's children: children of Christina and Michael Speigal; children of Peter Snapp; children of Joseph Snapp.
Exors: Son, Philip Snapp, son-in-law, Henry Keller and son-in-law, John Harr
Wit: Isaac Miller and Jacob Funk
Dated: 9 May 1801   Proved: 14 July 1801

Will Book C - page 83

PETER SNAPP, Shenandoah County. Wife: Catharine. Two young children: Margaret and Susanna. Margaret (when she becomes of age) - the Mill and 200 acres which my father, Lawrence Snapp (dec'd.) Willed to me. Susanna - remaining part of my land.
Exors: Brother, Philip Snapp and brother-in-law, Henry Keller
Wit: Simon Harr, John Harr, Martin Bearth and Lawrence Snapp.
Dated: 8 Dec. 1789   Proved: 31 Dec. 1789

Will Book H - page 234

PHILIP SNAPP, Shenandoah County. Wife: Sally. Three grandsons: John Snapp; Joseph Snapp; Jacob Snapp (children of my son, Abraham Snapp, dec'd.) - 200 acres of land to be laid off for them at lower end of my plantation. Dau: Margaret - 200 acres of land I have made Deed to her husband, Henry Browning and herself, also, plantation whereon I now live. Mentions: 37 acres I bought of John Snapp.
Exors: Henry Keller and his son, Lawrence Keller
Wit: Martin Hupp, George Hupp, Lawrence Snapp and Jacob Nehiser
Dated: 18 June 1812   Proved: 13 July 1812

Will Book M - page 20

HENRY SNELL, Shenandoah County. Dau: Katharine, my only child and who is single - all my possessions and land (about 250 acres). Mentions: Brother Jacob Snell's children who are 11 in number all living in Rockingham Co. No Exor. named
Wit: James Modesett, Anahel Slushere and Katharine Snell
Dated: 4 March 1822   Proved: 13 May 1822

Will Book B - page 180

GEORGE SNIDER, Shenandoah County. Wife: Elizabeth Snider. Eldest son: (not named).
No Exor. named
Wit: Jacob Shaver, Philip Summers and Conrad Bornton
Dated: 9 April 1781   Proved: 28 Oct. 1785

Will Book A - page 220

JACOB SNIDER, County of Shanando. Wife: Ann Mary. Sons: Jacob and John (youngest). Dau: Magdelean
Exor: Wife, Ann Mary
Wit: None
Dated: 1 July 1778   Proved: 29 July 1779

Will Book H - page 488

MARTIN SNIDER, Shenandoah County. Wife: Christina - all my land and plantation as long as she bears the name of my widow, also, negro boy by name of Aaron. The child: (not named).
Exor: John Snider
Wit: David Hay and John Hay
Dated: 21 July 1812   Proved: 11 Jan. 1813

Will Book U - page 478

ANN E. SNYDER, town of Mount Jackson, Shenandoah County. Granddaughter: Elizabeth Snyder. Mentions: Barbara Snyder, wife of John B. Snyder - the house and lot in Mount Jackson. Mentions: George M. Snyder, oldest son of John B. Snyder.
Exor: Philip Stover of Narrow Passage
Wit: William Sigler, W. D. Farra, John Stuart and John L. Smith.
Dated: 3 May 1838   Proved: 7 Jan. 1839

Will Book P - page 103

DANIEL SNYDER, SENIOR, Shenandoah County. Wife: Elizabeth Snider. Son: Martin Snyder - tract of land whereon he now lives. Son: Daniel Snyder, Jr. - tract of land whereon he now lives. Youngest son: John Snider - tract of land whereon I now live. Daus: Katharine Kibler; Eve Pence; Elizabeth Kibler.
Exor: John Kibler
Wit: Ambrose C. Borten, David Kaufman and John Kaufman
Dated: 17 Nov. 1812   Proved: 11 May 1829

Will Book Z - page 205

JOHN M. SNYDER, Shenandoah County. My mother: (not named) - my share in the house in which she resides. Brothers and sisters: (not named).
Exor: Philip Stover
Wit: L. Triplett and Ephraim Will
Dated: 11 Feb. 1850   Proved: 8 April 1850

Will Book A - page 124

MARTIN SNYDER, Dunmore County, Province of Virginia. Oldest sons: Martin and Daniel - the plantation to divide amongst them. Youngest son: John. Dau: Anna.
No Exor. named
Wit: _____(Ger.), George Koonce and Michael Wise
Dated: 25 Feb. 1777   Proved: 22 April 1777

Will Book I - page 191

MARTIN SNYDER, Shenandoah County. Mentions: brother, Daniel's son, John Snyder - land on the north side of the Hawksbill being 133 acres. Mentions: Philip Kibler's wife, Katharine. Nephews: Henry Pence and his wife, Eve; Daniel Snyder. Nephew (?): Elizabeth Kibler.
No Exor. named
Wit: John Pence and Rowland Yowell
Dated: 20 Jan. 1815   Proved: 13 March 1815

Will Book R - page 450

PETER SNYDER, Shenandoah County. Wife: Ann Maria - tract of land whereon I now live containing 348 acres. Dau: Ann Wiseman, wife of John Wiseman - tract of land whereon they now live containing 32 acres. Son-in-Law: Absalom Rinker, in trust for my dau. Mary Bowman, wife of Christley Bowman - tract of land whereon they now live containing 130 acres and another tract of 120 acres purchased by me from Christley Bowman. Dau: Elizabeth, wife of Absalom Rinker.
Exors: Sons-in-Law, John Wiseman and Absalom Rinker
Wit: Jos. H. Samuels, Joseph Pittman and Andrew Pittman
Dated: 24 July 1832   Proved: 11 March 1833

Will Book O - page 311

ANDREW SOMMER, Shenandoah County. Wife: Frany Sommer.
Dau: Catherine Leary and her three children, widow of
Jeremiah Leary, dec'd. Her children: Frances Leary;
Sarah Leary and Joseph Leary.
Exor: Jacob Fisher
Wit: Samuel R. Bader, Jacob Jacobs and John Gochenour
Dated: 23 July 1823

CODICIL to Will of ANDREW SOMMER - Mentions: Wife to
have two cows.
Wit: same as above
Dated: 2 Oct. 1824   Proved: 12 May 1828

Will Book B - page 334

GEORGE SOMMER, Shenandoah County. Wife: Mary Margaretha
Sommer. Youngest son: Andrew Sommer - plantation contain-
ing 160 acres. Sons: Johannes Sommer and Michael Sommer (dec'd.).
Mentions: heirs of dec'd. son, Michael Sommer, namely:
John Sommer; Paul Sommer and Andrew Sommer. Daus: Elizabeth
Yeager and Eve Black.
Exors: John Mauk and Philip Wendel
Wit: Alexander Hite, Abraham Hockman and John Hockman
Dated: 19 June 1782   Proved: 26 April 1787

Will Book U - page 78

JACOB SOMMER, of Strasburg, Shenandoah County. Wife:
Catharine - my out lot near Strasburg of 15 acres. Sons:
William and Henry - tract of land lying on the River called
Finley Tract. Son: John - 50 acres. Son: Samuel - plant-
ation lying on the River called the Sibert place. Daus:
Mary Ann; Sarah Jane; Susanna Creamer; Catharine Vincent.
Exors: Son, John Sommer and Daniel Stickley
Wit: Isaac Hurn, P.F. Eberly and Joseph Wattson
Dated: 5 May 1837

CODICIL to Will of JACOB SOMMER - Mentions: my slaves.
Wit: same as above
Dated: 5 May 1837   Proved: 10 July 1837

Will Book P - page 27

JOHN SOMMER, Shenandoah County. Wife: Ann Sommer - two negro girls, Camilla and Leah. Son: Joseph Sommer - tract of land whereon he now lives same I purchased of Alexander Hite. Son: Jacob Sommer - tract of land on which I now live, also, ten acres and negro girl named Barbara. Dau: Margaret Hazel. Dec'd. son, Philip's four children: Eliza; Ann; Harrison and Mary Sommer. Son: Isaac Sommer - tract of land on which he now lives. Son-in-Law: John Stover and Elizabeth his wife - tract of land on the North Fork of the Shenandoah River. Granddaughter: Ann Hazel. Mentions: Catharine Sommer, widow of my dec'd. son, Philip - the house and lot in town of Strasburg.
Exors: Son, Joseph Sommer and son-in-law, John Stover
Wit: Joseph Spengler, Samuel Kerns, Sen. and John Crabill
Dated: 22 March 1828   Proved: 9 March 1829

Will Book R - page 233

MATHIAS SOMMERS, Shenandoah County. Wife: Rachel. Two sons: Jacob Sommers and Samuel Sommers. Mentions: two orphans of my son, George Sommers, dec'd.
Exors: Sons, Jacob Sommers and Samuel Sommers
Wit: John Keffer, Christian Buyner and Simeon Yager
Dated: 29 Aug. 1829   Proved: 7 May 1832

Will Book A - page 388

MICHAEL SOMMERS, County of Shanando. Wife: Anny. Three daus: (not named).
Exors: John Mauk and Christian Copp
Wit: Samuel Mills and Martin Black
Dated: 1 April 1782   Proved: 30 May 1782

Will Book Q - page 96

ABRAHAM SONENFRANK, Shenandoah County. Wife: Maria Sonenfrank. Dau: Maria Nezelrodt - all my land.
Exor: Son-in-Law, Ludwig Nezelrodt
Wit: Peter Sayger, Peter Baker, Jacob Barb and B. Foltz
Dated: 26 May 1815   Proved: 8 Nov. 1830

Translated into the English language by oath of Charles Fisher.

Will Book T - page 334

DOCTOR JOSEPH F. SONNENSTINE, Shenandoah County. Wife: Catharine Sonnenstine. Dau: Musilla, wife of Jacob Snapp. Younger children: (not named).
Exor: Wife, Catharine Sonnenstine
Wit: George Alldoerffer and Samuel R. Bader
Dated: 26 Feb. 1825

CODICIL to Will of DR. JOSEPH F. SONNENSTINE - Mentions: two tracts of land given to my wife, Catharine Sonnenstine.
Wit: Samuel R. Bader and Samuel Baserman
Dated: 22 Oct. 1827   Proved: 13 June 1836

Will Book W - page 110   NUNCUPATIVE WILL

HARRIET SONNER, Shenandoah County. To Wit: This day Jacob Pifer and George Sonner personally appeared before me a Justice of the Peace in and for said Shenandoah County and made oath that Harriet Sonner, dec'd. told them that her desire was that her mother, Susanna Sonner, should have all her estate that was coming to her from her uncle, Jacob Sonner, dec'd. - signed: Joseph Zea.
Dated: 4 Feb. 1842   Proved: 7 March 1842

Will Book V - page 513

JOSEPH SONNER, Shenandoah County. Wife: Susanna - the farm upon which I reside. Three youngest sons: William; Richard; James. Other children: John; George; Harriet; Regina.
Exor: Wright Gatewood
Wit: Jacob Pifer and John B. Davis
Dated: 14 April 1838   Proved: 13 Sept. 1841

Will Book D - page 488

FREDERICK SOXMAN, Shenandoah County. Wife: Elizabeth. Sons: Daniel; Adam; Christian. Dau: Elizabeth, wife of John Speagle.
Exors: Son, Christian and John Speagle
Wit: Joseph Pugh, John Grove and Elizabeth Cook
Dated: 11 Nov. 1795   Proved: 12 Jan. 1796

Will Book O - page 175

DANIEL SOXSMAN, Shenandoah County. Brothers: Adam Soxsman; Christian Soxsman. Sister: Elizabeth Rootz.
Exor: Jacob Haun (of John)
Wit: Michael Effinger and John Haun
Dated: 29 Aug. 1827   Proved: 12 Nov. 1827

Will Book X - page 269

ISAAC SPENCER, Shenandoah County. Wife: Elizabeth Spencer. Son: Edward - all my personal Estate. Sons: William; Isaac; John Henry. Daus: Rofsetta Mourey and Sarah Jane White. Granddaughter: Eliza Jane Spencer.
Exor: Joseph P. Mahaney
Wit: Wattson Perry and Tobias Eshelman
Dated: 13 Sept. 1845   Proved: 13 Oct. 1845

Will Book U - page 267

BARBARA SPENGLER, Shenandoah County. Sister: Catharine Tidewick, wife of Jacob Tidewick of Hardy County. Mentions: children of my brother, Philip Spengler.
Exor: George Maphis
Wit: John Thornberry and Joseph Layman
Dated: 19 Feb. 1838   Proved: 12 March 1838

Will Book K - page 26

MICHAEL SPIEGLE, Shenandoah County. Wife: (not named) - the old plantation that I now live on, purchased of Jonas Little and that part I purchased of Joseph Inabnet, Jacob Inabnet and Jacob Inabnet, Jr. Two youngest sons: Michael Spiegle and William Spiegle - to divide the above mentioned tract when they arrive at age 21 years. Son: Laurence Spiegle tract of land I purchased of Jacob Rambo. Son: Peter Spiegle - the remaining tract of the plantation with the 3 1/2 acres I purchased of Jacob Coffman. Grandson: John Spiegle (son of John Spiegle, dec'd.) Granddaus: Margaret Spiegle and Catharine Spiegle (children of John Spiegle, dec'd.). Daus: Margaret, wife of Jacob Funkhouser; Mary Spiegle; Eve Spiegle; Elizabeth Spiegle; Sarah Spiegle and Susannah Spiegle.
Exors: Sons, Peter Spiegle, Laurence Spiegle and son-in-law, Jacob Funkhouser.
Wit: William H. Dulaney, John Thompson and _____ (Ger.)
Dated: 3 April 1804   Proved: 11 March 1816

Will Book P - page 430

ABRAHAM (ABRAM) SPITLER, SENIOR, Shenandoah County.
Daus: Elizabeth Rosenberger; Anna Rothgeb; Susanna Hite;
Mary Rothgeb; Magdalene Sciles. Three sons: Abram; Isaac
and Daniel. Mentions: children of my son, Joseph Spitler,
dec'd.
Exors: Abram Spitler, Jr. and William R. Almond
Wit: Edw. Almond, Mann Almond and John Haun
Dated: 28 July 1825   Proved: 10 May 1830

Will Book K - page 358

JOHN SPITLER, SENIOR, Shenandoah County. Wife: Catharine.
Two sons: John Spitler and Mathias Spitler - the land and
plantation whereon I now live on Stony Creek. Grandson:
David Spitler. Granddaughter: Catharine Spitler (dau. of
my son, Mathias Spitler). Daus: Anna; Margaret; Elizabeth,
wife of Peter Linkhairy.
Exor: Joshua Voltz, Sen.
Wit: George Coffelt, Martin Voltz and Jacob Rinker
Dated: 7 Oct. 1814   Proved: 8 Dec. 1817

Will Book V - page 115

WILLIAM STEENBERGER, Shenandoah County. Wife: (not named) -
that part of the real Estate whereon we now live, known by
the name of Mount Airy, also slaves. Son: Peter H. Steenberger - upward to two thousand acres lying in Mason County,
Virginia on the banks of Ohio. Dau: Mary, who is married
to James M. H. Beale. Mentions: Heirs of my son, William,
dec'd. Daus: Caroline Blackford; Catharine Schmucker, her
husband, Samuel Schmucker. Son: John B. Steenberger - full
possession of Mount Airy after the death of his mother.
Exor: John B. Steenberger
Wit: John Morgan, George Setzer and Jonathan Shull
Dated: 23 March 1838   Proved: 9 Sept. 1839

Will Book S - page 376

WILLIAM STEENBERGER, JUNIOR, Shenandoah County. Wife:
Elizabeth C. Steenberger. My children: (not named).
Exor: Brother, John B. Steenberger
Wit: Jno. W. Rice, Reuben Miller and John Neff

CODICIL to Will of WILLIAM STEENBERGER, JR. - Mentions:
Exors. to sell part of my estate for the benefit of my estate.
Dated: 24 Dec. 1834   Proved: 12 Jan. 1835

Will Book G - page 463

MARY STEIGLER, Shenandoah County. Sons: John Hup (dec'd); Samuel Hup; Martin. My first husband, Casper Hup (dec'd). Daus: Barbara Moffet; Mary Dundore; Elizabeth Thomas.
Exor: Henry Greenwood
Wit: Henry Greenwood, George Black and George Hupp
Dated: 22 Dec. 1808   Proved: 7 May 1810

Will Book U - page 279

HANNAH STEPHENSON, Shenandoah County. Daus: Isabella Taylor; Hannah Stephenson; Margaret Humpston. Sons: Robert Stephenson; John Stephenson; William Stephenson. Mentions: Nancy Stephenson, dec'd.
Exor: Son, Robert Stephenson
Wit: Joseph Wattson and Henry Artz
Dated: 12 Feb. 1829

CODICIL to Will of HANNAH STEPHENSON - Mentions: Revoke the legacy of my three daus. and now bequeath same to Celia and Milly, two colored women belonging to my son, Robert. Also, change legacy of sons.
Wit: Joseph Wattson and Joseph Switzer
Dated: 13 Jan. 1837   Proved: 12 Feb. 1838

Will Book L - page 148

JAMES STEPHENSON, Shenandoah County. Wife: Hannah Stephenson. Four daus: Isabella Taylor; Hannah Stephenson; Nancy Stephenson; Elizabeth Clayton (dec'd.). Sons: John Stephenson; William Stephenson; James Stephenson; Robert Stephenson. Grandchildren: Eliza Clayton; Lucinda Clayton; Susan Clayton; Polly Clayton; Hannah Clayton; Marinda Clayton; Harriet Clayton; Julia Ann Clayton; Emily Clayton; Nancy Clayton.
Exor: Son, William Stephenson
Wit: Joseph Wattson, Philip Swartz, Jacob Windle and Jonathan Pitman
Dated: 13 Jan. 1816   Proved: 10 Nov. 1819

Will Book M - page 247

NANCY STEPHENSON, of Strasburg, Shenandoah County.
Mentions: Nancy Clayton. My mother: Hannah Stephenson.
Brothers and sisters living: John Stephenson; William
Stephenson; Hannah Stephenson, Jr. and Margaret Stephenson.
Exor: Robert Stephenson
Wit: Philip Bufsard and Leonard Balthis
Dated: 6 June 1823　　　　　　　　Proved: 10 Nov. 1823

Will Book B - page 150

WILLIAM STEPHENSON, Shanando County. Son: James Stephenson -
plantation I now live on. Dau: Mary Newell, wife of Samuel
Newell. Grandsons: William Newell and James Newell. Grand-
daughters: Jean Newell; Marthe and Mary Newell; Marget Newell.
Exor: Son, James Stephenson
Wit: John Willson, Thomas Newell and Robert Jamison
Dated: 1 July 1782　　　　　　　　Proved: 28 April 1785

Will Book E - page 55

BENJAMIN STICKLER, Shenandoah County. Wife: Anny. Sons:
David; Samuel; Abraham. Daus: Elizabeth; Catharine; Regina;
Franey.
Exors: John Stover and Daniel Stover
Wit: Jacob Hoover, Daniel Beam and Philip Spengler
Dated: 11 April 1796　　　　　　　Proved: 13 Dec. 1796

Will Book G - page 59

SABASTIAN STICKLER, Shenandoah County. Wife: Mary. Dau:
Susannah - plantation whereon she now lives adjoining
Michael Hemlin, Ludwig Blefsing, George Weaver and Jonas
Rinehart (314 acres). Mentions: John Getz who bought the
plantation whereon I now live. Granddaughter: Philipna -
who is living with me.
Exors: Lewis Blefsing and Jacob Stiegel
Wit: George Ruth, Elizabeth Ruth and Lawrence Pittman
Dated: 4 April 1805　　　　　　　　Proved: 14 April 1807

Will Book Q - page 283

JAMES STINSON, SENIOR, Shenandoah County. Wife: Mary - negro girl named Rhody. Son: John Stinson - tract of land whereon he now lives (132 acres), another tract containing 216 acres, and another small tract. Son: James Stinson - tract of land containing 252 acres and another tract granted by John Page, Governor of Virginia bearing date 11 June 1803 containing 100 acres, another tract cantaining 310 acres. Grandson: Wiley S. Roy - tract of land granted to me by Linah Mims, Governor of Va. bearing date 26 Nov. 1813, containing 286 acres. Dau: Anna Roy - two tracts of land of 100 acres. Son-in-Law: William Roy. Granddaughter: Polly Day, late Roy - negro girl named Harriot.
Exor: James Stinson, Jr.
Wit: George Bowman, Gibson N. Roy and Robert Lockhart
Dated: 10 Jan. 1825   Proved: 8 Nov. 1830

Wills and Accts. (1809-1863) - page 2

SOLOMON STOCKSDALE, Parish of Beckford, Shenandoah County. Wife: (not named). Dau: Polly. Mentions: friend, David Woolf in State of Maryland. Mentions: Negro boy, Peter.
Exor: Michael Haas
Wit: Thomas C. Hampton, Daniel Madiera, Simeon Yager and Christian Huffman
Dated: 10 May 1809   Proved: 16 May 1809

Will Book M - page 343

DANIEL STOCKSLAGER, town of Strasburg, Shenandoah County. Wife: (not named). Four sons: Jacob; Abraham; Philip and William. Five daus: Margaret; Anna; Esther; Sarah and Catharine. Mentions: my two town lots adjoining John Rufsell and my out lot - to be rented.
Exor: Son, Jacob
Wit: Adam Keister, John Marshall and John Rufsell
Dated: 19 March 1824   Proved: 10 May 1824

Will Book F - page 419

FREDERICK STONEBARGER, Shenandoah County. Son: Luis - all my land lying between Philip Long's and John Newman's. Son-in-Law: Jacob Judy - all my land that lies between John Newman and George Hawn's. Youngest son: Frederick Stonebarger
No Exor. named
Wit: Achery Berry, _____(Ger.) and Henry Alishite
Dated: 27 Dec. 1805   Proved: 10 March 1808

216

Will Book W - page 303

WILLIAM STONER, Shenandoah County. Wife: Margaret. Son: Abraham - the grist-mill and all the woodlands; to support and maintain in a decent and becoming manner my son, John during his natural life. Daus: Mary Ann; Solina; Elizabeth; Catharine - the farm on which I now reside containing 271 acres. Grandson: John Frederick Stoner. Two granddaus: Eliza and Catharine Green, children of my dau. Esther.
Exor: George Hupp
Wit: William Elbon, Samuel Walter and Henry Artz
Dated: 6 March 1843   Proved: 8 May 1843

Will Book F - page 167

DANIEL STOUT, Shenandoah County. Wife: Margaret. My children: (not named). Mentions: the Mill and plantation to be sold.
Exors: Henry Huddle and William Philips
Wit: Jacob Lantz, George Mourer, George Feather and John Hammon.
Dated: 13 Aug. 1803   Proved: 10 Oct. 1803

Wills and Accts. (1809-1863) - page 52

CHRISTIAN STOVER, town of Strasburg, Shenandoah County, son of Peter. Wife: Elizabeth - the tract of land I purchased of Samuel Funk and the tract I purchased of Jacob Funk, also the house and lot whereon I now live. Mentions: Daniel Spengler (son of Anthony Spengler) - the plantation in Frederick County, Va. Mentions: two slaves, Sally and Caty. Mentions: Elizabeth Utz, wife of John Utz - the house and lot I purchased of Jacob Funk (son of Joseph Funk). Mentions: Catharine Spengler, wife of Anthony Spengler. Mentions: brothers and sisters.
Exors: Joseph Spengler and Philip Williams
Wit: William M Bayly, Adam Keister and Joseph Stover
Dated: 21 Oct. 1817

CODICIL to Will of CHRISTIAN STOVER - Mentions: give wife, Elizabeth, 5 acre lot which I purchased of Isaac Funk, exor. of Christian Stover, dec'd. Mentions: Wife's father, Peter Smith, dec'd.
Wit: Will M. Bayly, Samuel Gardner and David Yost
Dated: 9 May 1818   Proved: 25 May 1818

Will Book I - page 186

CHRISTIAN STOVER, JUNIOR, of Strasburg, Shenandoah County. Wife: Susan Stover - house I now live in together with 2 half acre lotts and part of another Lott adjoining Jacob Lambert, also, 5 acres adjoining George Cooper. Also, my black boy, Gerrard. My sister Mary Stover's two children: Jacob and Mary. Son: Nimrode Stover. Daus: Lydia and Fanny Stover.
Exor: Isaac Funkhouser
Wit: George Cooper, Martin Zea and Sam Gardner
Dated: 10 Feb. 1815   Proved: 13 March 1815

Will Book K - page 209

JACOB STOVER, Shenandoah County. Two sons: John and Joseph Stover - jointly all the land that I may possess at my death. Also, my black man, Peter and black woman, Rede and her three male children, Charles, William and Arch. Dau: Frainey (who is an idiot). Dau: Catharine Stover. Dau: Betsy - to have black girl, Nancy. Each of my single daus: (not named). Two sons-in-law: Samuel Burner, Senior and Samuel Burner, Junior.
Exors: David Stickly and son, John Stover
Wit: Samuel Gardner, Jonas Crabill, Joseph Stover and Jacob Bauserman
Dated: 6 Jan. 1816   Proved: 13 Jan. 1817

Will Book L - page 280

JOHN STOVER, Shenandoah County. Wife: Barbara - land whereon I now live containing 673 acres. Also, one third of the estate of my brother, Joseph Stover (dec'd.) which I am entitled, also, four negro boys and two negro girls. Dau: Frainey. Grandchildren: Philip and Marilla, children of my son, Joseph Stover (dec'd.). Dau.-in-Law: Elizabeth Stover, widow of my said son, Joseph. Mentions: Jacob Ott appointed trustee for my said dau. Frainey and guardian of grandchildren, Philip and Marilla. Mentions: one half acre which I have given for a school house (which is built).
Exor: Jacob Ott
Wit: P. Williams, David Stickley and John Stover
Dated: 12 Dec. 1820   Proved: 12 Feb. 1824

Will Book L - page 161

JOSEPH STOVER, Shenandoah County. Brothers: Jacob Stover; John Stover; Christian Stover. Mentions: Jacob Kershwiler (my sister Catharine's son). Sisters: Ann Stickley and Regina Stover.
(PART OF WILL MISSING)
Exors: John Croudson and John Stover
Wit: Samuel Mills, Peter Snapp and Jacob Conrad
Dated: 7 June 1788

13 Dec. 1819 - A writing purporting to be last Will and Testament of Joseph Stover, dec'd. was produced into Court by George Hupp who intermarried with Catharine Spengler, who was a dau. of Regina Spengler, now dec'd., who was a sister of the dec'd. Joseph Stover and having heard some testimony and opposition thereto by Elizabeth Stover, widow and relick of the dec'd., on motion of the said Elizabeth Stover. The Court doth appoint Anthony Spengler to collect and preserve the Estate of said dec'd.

10 Jan. 1820 - This matter being contintued over from the last Court. It is proved by the oath of Philip Williams that the said Will is the handwriting of Samuel Mills, that he believes the signature of said Stover to have been written by himself and that the said Mills appears to have signed his name as a witness being well aquainted with said Mills and Stover and further that the said Mills and Peter Snapp who appears to be another witness are dead. And further proved by oath of Philip Spengler who also testified to the handwriting of Joseph Stover, Samuel Mills and Jacob Conrad. The Law directs Elizabeth Stover, widow of the dec'd. having relinquished her right.

Will Book E - page 308

PETER STOVER, Shenandoah County. Wife: Frainey Stover. Son: Jacob Stover - all that plantation deeded (170 acres). Son: John Stover - plantation on Narrow Passage containing 673 acres. Son: Christian Stover - Lotts #1,2,3,82,83,84, #85 and 98 in town of Strawsburg. Son: Joseph Stover - remainder Lotts (in and out lotts) town of Strasburg. Daus: Elizabeth Spengler (dec'd.); Ann Stickler; Catharine _____; Regina Spengler. Mentions: Peter Stover and Joseph Stover.
Exors: Son, Joseph Stover and Philip Spengler
Wit: Alexander Hite, Thomas Nowell and _____ (Ger.)
Dated: 8 Aug. 1795   Proved: 10 Sept. 1799

Will Book G - page 331

SAMUEL STOVER, Shenandoah County. Wife: Barbara Stover.
Son: Daniel Stover - that part of my land whereon I now
live. Son: Samuel Stover - that part of my plantation
which is to the south of my son, Daniel. Son: David Stover -
my Estate in the County of Culpeper. Son: John Stover -
500 acres of land on the Ohio. Son: Joseph Stover - 500
acres of land on the Ohio. Mentions: Estate to be divided
equally among my seven children.
Exors: Sons, Daniel Stover and Samuel Stover
Wit: Davis Allen, Samuel Lams, John Fristoe, Samuel
Stickler and Isaac Stickler
Dated: 22 March 1805   Proved: 11 Sept. 1809

Will Book M - page 480

MICHAEL STRAUSNIDER, Shenandoah County. Wife: (not named).
Son-in-Law: George Marker - the lands on which I reside.
Daus: Sarhe Lou; Hannah Orndorfe; Rachael Strausnider.
Sons: John Strausnider; Joseph Strausnider; Isaac Strausnider;
Jacob Strausnider; Peter Strausnider; Elijah Strausnider;
Solomon Strausnider; George Strausnider; Benjamin Strausnider;
Adam Strausnider.
Exor: Son-in-law, George Marker
Wit: James Copelin, Benjamin Williams, Sen. and Samuel Shell
Dated: 5 Dec. 1824   Proved: 13 Dec. 1824

Will Book G - page 150

DANIEL STRICKLER, Shenandoah County. Mother: Barbara
Strickler. Sisters: Margaret Jones (husband, Thomas Jones);
Caty Strickler. Brother: Joseph Strickler.
Exor: Brother, Joseph Strickler
Wit: William Hershberger, Abraham Strickler and Leittice
Burner
Dated: 16 Aug. 1807   Proved: 12 Oct. 1807

Will Book K - page 247

ISAAC STRICKLER, Shenandoah County. Wife: Katharine Strickler. My four children: Jacob Strickler; Elizabeth Burner; John Strickler; Nancy Beaver. Mentions: John Beaver, husband of my dau. Nancy and John Burner, husband of my dau. Elizabeth. Mentions: my son Jacob is now in the Army in Canada and said to be dead. Mentions: John Brubaker to be appointed guardian for my wife. Mentions: plantation and slaves - to be sold. Step-dau: Mary Beaver.
Exors: Son, John Strickler and son-in-law, John Beaver
Wit: Daniel Beaver, James Modesitt and William R. Almond
Dated: 2 July 1814   Proved: 18 May 1817

Will Book F - page 327

ISAAC STRICKLER, JUNIOR, Shenandoah County. Brother: Daniel Strickler - to have land left to me by my brother John's last Will and Testament. Brothers and sisters: Daniel; Barbary; Maria; Magdalena; Susanna; Eve.
Exor: Brother, Daniel Strickler
Wit: John Roads, John Peyton and David Grove
Dated: 21 May 1803   Proved: 9 April 1805

Will Book F - page 30

JOHN STRICKLER, Parish of Beckford, County of Shenandoah. My half-brother: Isaac Strickler - part of land which was tevsitet (sic) between him and his brother, Daniel Strickler as tevsitet (sic) and apart by John Roads, Peter Hestant and Samuel Stover, it being part of his father's estate.
Exor: John Broombaugh
Wit: Daniel Strickler and David Beaver
Dated: 18 Jan. 1802   Proved: 13 Sept. 1802

Will Book D - page 453

JOSEPH STRICKLER, Shenandoah County. Wife: Barbara. Sons: Abraham; Daniel; Joseph. Daus: Mary; Dorothe; Elizabeth; Barbara; Ann; Margarett; Catharine. Mentions: Christina Swygera.
Exor: Abraham Strickler
Wit: John Strickler, John Roads and George Koonts
Dated: 23 April 1795   Proved: 8 Sept. 1795

Will Book V - page 448

JOSEPH STRICKLER, Shenandoah County. Wife: Barbara.
Sons: Joseph Strickler; Henry Strickler; Jacob Strickler;
Emanuel Strickler; John. Daus: Barbara and Nancy.
Mentions: land in Spotsylvania - to be sold. Also, slaves
to be sold.
Exor: Son, Emanuel
Wit: Moses Walton, Hezekiah Webster and Lucinda Webster
Dated: 18 April 1841   Proved: 10 May 1841

Will Book G - page 409

MAGDALENE STRICKLER, Shenandoah County. Mentions: my
daughter which is a new born babe (not named). Brother:
Samuel - to bring up said child. Sisters and Brothers:
Barbara; Daniel; Mary; Susannah; Eva.
Exors: John Roads and Abraham Strickler
Wit: Daniel Kaufman, Daniel Strickler and Dorotha Kaufman
Dated: 24 Nov. 1809   Proved: 8 Jan. 1810

Will Book F - page 47

ELIZABETH STRICKLEY, Shenandoah County. Son: Isaac
Strickley. Mentions: Dorothy Strickley, dau. of my
late husband, Jacob Strickley. My four youngest
children: Leah Strickley; Gabrel Strickley; Judath
Strickley; Cathene Strickley.
Exor: Jacob Rinker
Wit: John Colville, Ann Colville and John Peebles
Dated: 16 Aug. 1802   Proved: 11 Oct. 1802

Will Book G - page 232

HERMAN STROMER, Shenandoah County, yeoman. Wife: Mary -
half of my moveable estate. Mentions: Frederick Sower -
other part of my estate. Mentions: Philip Summers.
Mentions: books, writings, eight silver buttons, silver
seale - to be sent home to Germany.
Exors: William S. Marye and Frederick Sower
Wit: Peter Blauser and Thomas Duckwiller
Dated: 24 July 1808   Proved: 12 Sept. 1808

Will Book O - page 151

JOSEPH STROTHER, Shenandoah County. Wife: Amelia. My
Godson: William B. Bryan (who I have adopted). Sister:
Mary Menefee, wife of William Menefee. Niece: Sarah Menefee.
Exor: David Crawford
Wit: George F. Hupp, William Anderson and Robert Turner
Dated: 18 Feb. 1826   Proved: 10 Sept. 1827

Will Book E - page 40

ZACHARIAH SUGART, Shenandoah County. Sons: Michael Sugart;
Zachariah Sugart and Frederick Henry Sugart.
Exors: Sons, Michael Sugart of Shenandoah Co. and Zachariah
Sugart of Rockingham Co.
Wit: Isaac Goare, Jacob Woltz and Jacob Stiegel
Dated: 15 Sept. 1795   Proved: 13 April 1796

Will Book G - page 80

MATHIAS SUMMERS, Shenandoah County. Wife: Mary Barbara -
the house and lott now occupied by George Shrum. My three
children: Mathias; Catharine; Barbara.
Exors: Son, Mathias and son-in-law, Jacob Brown
Wit: James Chipley, Abraham Coffman and Caleb Davis
Dated: 20 Feb. 1807   Proved: 8 June 1807

Will Book O - page 202

PHILIP SUMMERS, Shenandoah County. Son-in-Law: George
Prince - all my land and Estate of every kind, both real
and personal. Sons: Philip Summers (oldest); Michael;
Joshua; Joseph. Daus: Elizabeth Shank; Magdalena Horde;
Eve Avery and Sally Prince. Granddau: Elizabeth Welch.
Grandson: Wesley Brubaker.
Exor: Son-in-Law, George Prince
Wit: Valentine D. Taylor, Daniel Blofser, Jacob Smith
and Frederick Huffman, Jr.
Dated: 17 March 1827   Proved: 7 Jan. 1828

Will Book O - page 518

CATHARINE SUPINGER, Shenandoah County. Son: Jacob.
Mentions: heirs of Jacob, viz: Robert and John. Three
daus: Mary; Catharine and Elizabeth.
Exor: Martin Boehm
Wit: Robert Newell and William Boehm
Dated: 25 Feb. 1825   Proved: 9 Feb. 1829

Will Book H - page 490

CONRAD SUPINGER, Shenandoah County. Wife: Esther Supinger.
Five daus: Christina; Elizabeth Pitman; Peggy; Lydia; Sarah.
Son: Joseph - my plantation whereon I now dwell containing
228 acres. Mentions: my daughters I give and bequeath the
house formerly occupied by my father but now unoccupied.
Exor: Wife, Esther Supinger
Wit: _____(Ger.), John Miller and George Miller
Dated: 5 June 1813   Proved: 13 Dec. 1813

Will Book F - page 253

JOHN SUPINGER, SENIOR, Shenandoah County. Wife: (not named).
My two sons: John and Jacob - I leave the plantation whereon
I live, equally divided. Son: Isaac. My three daus: Polly
Henkins, her husband George Henkins; (two daus. not named).
Exor: George Lind
Wit: Daniel Boehm, Joseph Kackley, William Newell and
John Trout
Dated: 12 Sept. 1804   Proved: 8 Oct. 1804

Will Book A - page 146

HENRY SURBER, Shenandoah County. Wife: Rosina.
Children: (not named).
Exors: Wife, Rosina and brother, Jacob Surber
Dated: 16 March 1778   Proved: 30 April 1778

Will Book K - page 278

JOHN SWARTZ, SENIOR, Shenandoah County. Wife: Susanna
Swartz - full possession of my land and plantation (230
acres) for five years. Son: Philip Swartz - the tract
of land whereon he now lives, the same I purchased of
Jacob Grove containing 100 acres. Son: George Swartz -
that tract of land I purchased of John Alsep. Son:
Jacob Swartz - that tract of land that may be lay'd off
by division of home plantation. Son: John Swartz - tract
of land I purchased of Ulrick Heller, whereon John Heller,
Jun. now lives containing 50 acres. Son: Christian Swartz -
that tract of land herein given to my said wife. Mentions:
all property not herein before devised, given and bequeathed shall be sold at public sale. Daus: Hannah, wife
of Henry Wilkins; Barbara Swartz; Christina Swartz.
Exors: Two sons, Philip Swartz and George Swartz
Wit: John Layman, Samuel R. Bader and George Wisman
Dated: 8 April 1817   Proved: 11 Aug. 1817

Will Book I - page 60

MARTIN SWARTZ, Shenandoah County. Wife: Mary Eve Swartz.
Son: Jacob Swartz - all my plantation and land I now live
on containing 136 acres. Son: John Swartz - all the
plantation I bought of Frederick Mauck containing 100
acres adjoining the plantation I now live on. Son: Peter.
Daus: Elizabeth Swartz; Ragel Swartz; Mary, wife of
George Vogelsong; Catharine, wife of Andrew Coffman;
Catharine (?), wife of Jacob Miller.
Exors: Wife, Mary Eve Swartz and son, John Swartz
Wit: Samuel R. Bader, John Swartz and Abraham Crabill
Dated: 1811   Proved: 9 May 1814

Will Book K - page 27

PETER SWARTZ, SENIOR, Shenandoah County. Wife: Susannah
Swartz - my negro girl, Nancy. Dau: Catharine, wife of
John Kline - tract of land she and her husband now live
on being upper part of land I bought of Paul Summers con-
taining 45 or 50 acres. Son: Peter Swartz - tract of land
and plantation being upper part I bought of Paul and John
Summers, Sen. (of which I sold 60 acres to Christian
Wohlgemuth) - 45-50 acres. Son: George Swartz - plantation
I now live on lying and being on the North River (287 acres).
Dau: Elizabeth, wife of John Hottel - my negro girl, July.
Daus: Barbara, wife of Philip Wendel; Regel (dec'd.), late
wife of Emanuel Wendel; Hannah, wife of Peter Blind. Mentions:
negro boy, Billy, shall not be sold as long as my widow lives.
Exors: Son, George Swartz and former son-in-law, Emanuel Wendel
Wit: George Copp, John Crebill and Samuel R. Bader
Dated: 7 Aug. 1814   Proved: 11 March 1816

Will Book B - page 260

CHARLES TAYLOR, Shenandoah County. Wife: Barbary Taylor.
Children: Elizabeth; John; Mary; Susannah; Henry; Joseph;
Charles; Ann; Rebecca and William Taylor.
Exors: Tavenor Beale, Daniel Strickley, Elinor Dobkin and Thomas Edgill
Wit: Daniel Strickley, Elinor Dobkin and Thomas Edgill
Dated: 19 Sept. 1785   Proved: 24 Nov. 1785

Will Book Y - page 210

ELIZABETH TAYLOR, Shenandoah County, relick of Joseph
Taylor, dec'd. Mentions: Henry Artz - the house and land
on which I now live. Mentions: Anthony Willard. Mentions:
William Smith (a free man of color) - the house in which
he now resides and the Blacksmith shop.
Exor: Andrew Hoffman
Wit: Hamilton Maupin and George Grandstaff
Dated: 3 March 1841   Proved: 13 Dec. 1847

Will Book V - page 470

CATHARINE TEATER, Shenandoah County. Mentions: Jacob
Rodeheffer - all my property.
Exor: Jacob Rodeheffer
Wit: George Shrum and James Rodeheffer
Dated: 14 Dec. 1837   Proved: 7 June 1841

Will Book M - page 125

WILLIAM THOMPSON, Township of West Nottingham, Chester
County, State of Pennsylvania, miller. Wife: Elizabeth
Thompson. Mentions: Jane Reynolds. Son-in-Law: Hugh
Remsey. Dau: Jane Ramsey. Son: Robert Thompson - one
dollar. Son: John Thompson - that plantation which I
purchased of the Nisby's, lying in Shenandoah County,
Virginia. Heirs of my son, William Thompson (dec'd.) -
plantation I purchased of John Janny lying in Chester Co.,
State of Pennsylvania. Dau: Mary Scott - tract of land
lying in New London, Chester Co., Pennsylvania. Dau:
Elizabeth Thompson - all the rest of my property, my Mills
and lands on Octorars Creek.
Exors: Dau., Elizabeth Thompson and William Thompson
Wit: David Clindenmin and David Cooper
Dated: 1 Aug. 1814   Proved: 11 Nov. 1822
                             (Shenandoah Co., Virginia)

Will Book I - page 189

PETER TISINGER, Shenandoah County. Wife: Elizabeth.
Sons: John Tisinger; George Tisinger. Son: Henry Tisinger - that part of my plantation whereon I now live containing 270 acres and another small tract behind Buckhill containing 30 acres. Dau: Magdalene - part of my plantation which I had run-off for my son, George, containing 205 acres.
Daus: Barbara, wife of William Bowman; Caty, wife of David Funkhouser.
Exor: Son, John Tisinger
Wit: S. Walton, Joseph Ozburn and John Ryman
Dated: 13 Feb. 1815   Proved: 13 March 1815

Will Book Y - page 114

SUSANNAH MARGARET TROOK, Shenandoah County, consort of Nicholas Trook, dec'd. Daus: Rebecca, wife of Emanuel Rinehart; Catharine Tysinger. Granddaughter: Susannah Margaret Trook.
Exors: John Stoneburner and William Smith Arthur
Wit: James N. Swann and Richard Lamerson
Dated: 3 June 1847   Proved: 12 July 1847

Will Book M - page 107

NICHOLAS TUSING, Shenandoah County. Wife: (not named). Son: Adam Tusing- the place where I now live. So-in-Law: Henry Tusing - the place which I bought of my brother, Philip Tusing. Mentions: George Kips (my dau.-in-law ?) - a tract of land in Rockingham County. Mentions: Elizabeth and Samuel Price.
Exor: Adam Barblo, Susanna Tusing and Henry Billhymer
Wit: John Tusing, Susanna Tusing and Henry Billhymer
Dated: 9 March 1817   Proved: 10 Feb. 1825

Will Book F - page 374

JOHN VANNORT, Shenandoah County. Sons: William Vannort; Peter Vannort. Grandson: William Vannort (son of Peter Vannort). Daus: Jerima Roberts; Rebecca Emmons; Elizabeth Vannort.
Exors: John Carson and William Carson
Wit: Thomas Smith, John Nicholas and Mary Nicholas
Dated: 5 April 1805   Proved: 7 Oct. 1805

Will Book X - page 362

SOLOMON VEACH, Shenandoah County. Wife: Polly Veach.
Sons: Jacob (youngest); Levi Veach; Isaac Veach. Daus:
Anna Veach; Catharine Veach; Leah Veach; Elizabeth Veach;
Polly Veach; Christina Veach; Harriet Veach. Sons:
Washington Veach; William Veach; Harrison Veach (who left
home under age for which reason I do not make them equal).
Exor: David McInturff
Wit: Henry McInturff, Sen., Henry S. McInturff, Silas
Munch and Frederick McInturff
Dated: 19 Jan. 1846   Proved: 9 March 1846

Will Book B - page 413

ADAM VOLKNER, Shenandoah County. Wife: Anne Volkner.
Sons: John; Henry and Adam Volkner. Daus: Marine Richards,
wife of George Richards; Magdalene Volkner.
Exors: Brother, Henry Volkner, Alexander Hite and Jacob
Stickley
Wit: Philip Aker and Frederick Hite
Dated: 15 Nov. 1787   Proved: 27 Dec. 1787

Will Book S - page 32

JOSHUA VOLTZ, Shenandoah County. Son: Jonathan Voltz -
land and plantation whereon we now reside lying on Stony
Creek, including the Grist Mill and Saw Mill (573 acres).
Condition that he and his heirs shall constantly take care
of and maintain my dau. Dorothy Voltz (who is insane).
Son: Martin - my large German Bible which he shall give
his son, John. Mentions: Four tracts of land to be sold,
viz: 139 acres adjoining Frederick Craig; 317 acres adjoin-
ing Walter Newman; 200 acres west side of Buckhill; other
lying on Stony Creek adjoining land devised to my son,
Jonathan (350 acres). Daus: Rosina, wife of Andrew
Lindamood; Christina, wife of Jacob Lindamood; Magdalene,
wife of Peter Sayger. Son-in-Law: George Miller, wife is
Margaret. Mentions: Barbara Rinker (dau. of Henry Rinker)
now living with my son, Jonathan.
Exor: George Lantz
Wit: W. W. Magruder, John Sibert and P. Williams
Dated: 20 Sept. 1831   Proved: 12 Aug. 1833

Will Book H - page 122

PETER VOLTZ, Shenandoah County. Son: George Voltz - all my plantation and lands whereon I, myself and my said son George now live containing 240 acres which I purchased of Michael Shoemaker. Mentions: children of my dau. Elizabeth Stickley, dec'd. My nine daus: Mary, wife of John Wiltfany; Catharine, wife of Daniel Stout; Margaret, wife of George Dellinger; Magdalene, wife of Emanuel Dellinger; Susannah, wife of Henry Hoshour; Julianah, wife of Peter Hoshour; Eve, wife of Christian Dellinger; Rosinah, wife of Jacob Helsley, Jun.; Barbara, wife of George Anderick. Sons: Joshua Voltz and Joseph Voltz.
Exor: Joshua Voltz
Wit: Jacob Rinker, Absalom Rinker and Godfrey Miller
Dated: 5 June 1807   Proved: 9 Dec. 1811

Will Book E - page 431

ULRICK WAGGONER, Shenandoah County. My children: Elizabeth, wife of Peter Tisinger; Barbara, wife of Henry Renninger; Christina, wife of Henry Rinker. Dau: Betty - 160 acres. Grandson: John Tisinger - 105 acres. Betty's son: Joshua Fultz. Mentions: tract of land (350 acres) and tract of land (475 acres). Mentions: land in Rockingham Co. sold to Richard Hughes, but not yet titled.
Exor: Jacob Rinker
Wit: George Keller, George Rinker and Peter Ritsenhelser
Dated: 10 May 1801   Proved: 8 June 1801

Will Book M - page 397

GEORGE WALL, Shenandoah County. Wife: Abigail. My children: Polly; Edmond; Lucy; Abigail. Mentions: Edmond Northern (who is uncle of my dau. Polly). Mentions: James White of Frederick County; William Collins; Christian John Ceroer. Son-in-Law: Thomas Perry.
Exors: Wife, Abigail Wall and som, Edmond Wall
Wit: Jacob Keamy, Arnold Bonkfield and Nancy Robeson
Dated: 13 May 1824   Proved: 9 Aug. 1824

Will Book N - page 418

HENRY WALTON, Beckford Parish, Shenandoah County. Wife: Catharine. Son: Daniel Walton - all my real Estate containing 362 acres. Son: Martin Walton. Daus: Christina Foltz, late Walton; Magdalene Rofs, late Walton; Catharine Clem, late Walton; Barbara Sibert, late Walton; Elizabeth Clem, late Walton. Mentions: children of my son, Henry Walton.
Exor: Jacob Burner
Wit: George Bowman and Christian Smith
Dated: 3 May 1823   Proved: 12 June 1826

Will Book W - page 347

SAMUEL WALTON, Shenandoah County. Wife: Sarah. Sons: Edward Walton; Charles Walton; Jesse; Reuben. Dau: Allanter O. Miller.
Exors: Sons, Edward Walton and Charles Walton
Wit: Moses Walton, James Gummer and Samuel Zehring
Dated: 21 Feb. 1843   Proved: 7 Aug. 1843

Will Book H - page 210

SAMUEL WAY, Shenandoah County. Wife: Sarah Way. Stepson: Samuel Offner - my house and lott in town of Woodstock and five out lots near town of Woodstock.
Exor: Henry Keller
Wit: David Jordan, George Ott and Calib Davis
Dated: 21 Feb. 1812   Proved: 14 April 1812

Will Book R - page 125

HENRY WEATHERHOLTS, Shenandoah County. Son: Jacob Weatherholts - 180 acres of land. Grandchildren: (children of my son, Jacob Weatherholts) viz: Henry Weatherholts; Jacob Weatherholts; John Weatherholts; Catharine Weatherholts; Dianah Weatherholts; Isaac Weatherholts; Polly Weatherholts. Son: John Weatherholts. Daus: Barbara, wife of Frederick Bish; Magdalena, wife of Daniel Runion; Christena Weatherholts. Mentions: children of my dau. Catharine Williams, dec'd
Exor: Christian Dellinger
Wit: Ephraim Rinker and Jacob Barb
Dated: 13 April 1830   Proved: 9 Jan. 1832

Will Book O - page 116

ADAM WEAVER, Shenandoah County. Son: George Weaver - all my plantation and land whereon I now live. Four daus: Anna, wife of Christian Olmeth; Barbara, wife of Abraham Neff; Mary wife of George Kerh and Catharine Weaver.
Exor: Son, George Weaver
Wit: John Neese and Jacob Rinker
Dated: 28 April 1818   Proved: 11 June 1827

Will Book I - page 180

ELIZABETH WEAVER, Shenandoah County. Step-daughter: Polly Weaver. God-dau: Elizabeth Fetzer (dau. of Joachino Fetzer). Seven step-children: (not named).
Exor: Jacob Knisely
Wit: Michael Feiter, Mary Keffer and Simeon Yager
Dated: 3 Feb. 1815   Proved: 13 Feb. 1815

Will Book I - page 518

GEORGE WEAVER, Shenandoah County. Wife: Mary Weaver. Son: Michael Weaver - my plantation whereon I now live. Son: Christian Weaver - 2 acres of land. Sons: Jacob Weaver; John Weaver; Martin Weaver; George Weaver. Daus: Rosina Myers; Elizabeth, wife of John Kerlinger; Magdalene. Mentions: Mary Hickle (wife of George Hickle).
Exor: Son, Michael Weaver
Wit: Isaac Samuels, John Morgan and Benjamin Hawkins
Dated: 13 Dec. 1815   Proved: 13 Feb. 1816

Will Book U - page 268

MAGDALENE WEAVER, Shenandoah County. Husband: Frederick Weaver - all my land I inherited from my father, John Reaser, dec'd. (18 acres in Shenandoah Co. and 400 acres in State of Tennessee). Mentions: sisters and brothers (not named).
Exor: None
Wit: Thomas McCord, John B. Snyder and John Ruts
Dated: 17 March 1835   Proved: 8 Feb. 1836

Will Book H - page 420

PHILIP WEAVER, Shenandoah County. Wife: Anne. Two sons: George and John Weaver - tract of land whereon I now live. Sons: Frederick Weaver and Conrad Weaver. Daus: Philipena Weaver, Sally, wife of Peter Coffman; Catharine; Polly, wife of Abraham Coffman; Elizabeth, wife of Jacob Miller.
Exor: John Hawn
Wit: John Frantz and Adam Soxman
Dated: 7 Sept. 1812

CODICIL to Will of PHILIP WEAVER - Mentions: I do hereby revoke and disanul the forgoing Will to Sally Coffman, wife of Peter Coffman and do hereby devise the said Sally Coffman one dollar.
Dated: 2 Dec. 1812   Proved: 10 May 1813

Will Book Y - page 344

DANIEL WEBB, Shenandoah County. Wife: Elizabeth. Dau: Mary, wife of John Lentz.
Exor: Edward Walton
Wit: Samuel Walton, Jos. M. Allen and David May
Dated: 25 March 1846   Proved: 11 Sept. 1848

Will Book Y - page 458

HARMON WEBB, SENIOR, Shenandoah County. Sons: David Webb; Reuben Webb; Isaac Webb; John Webb; Noah Webb; Samuel Webb. Mentions: housekeeper, Ann Mumaw. Daus: Sarah Barb and Catharine Webb.
Exor: R. M. Conn
Wit: John Hunsberger, Philip Miller, John Chrisman and R. M. Conn
Dated: 6 Feb. 1849   Proved: 12 March 1849

Will Book N - page 223

JACOB WEEKLEY, Shenandoah County. Children: William; John; Enoch; Elijah; Sally; Susannah; Nancy; Jacob; Joseph; Thomas; Rubin. Mentions: heirs of Isaiah (dec'd) viz: Winifred; Catharine and Elizabeth.
No Exor. named
Wit: Alexander Furnell and Reubin Furnell
Dated: 9 April 1821   Proved: 10 May 1824

Will Book M - page 297

JOHN WEEKS, Shenandoah County.   Wife: Mary Weeks.
Exor: Wife, Mary Weeks
Wit: William Payne and James Allen
Dated: 3 Aug. 1823   Proved: 10 Feb. 1824

Will Book S - page 346

SAMUEL WEEKS, Shenandoah County. Wife: Elizabeth. My children: Theodore; James; William Henry; Margaret Ann.
Exor: Joseph Borden
Wit: John Snarr and Benjamin Kronck
Dated: 21 Oct. 1834   Proved: 10 Nov. 1834

Will Book G - page 214

CONRAD WEGMAN, SENIOR, Shenandoah County. Sons: Henry Wegman and John Wegman - my plantation whereon I now dwell, equally divided. Daus: Barbary; Catharine; Anny Mary, wife of Daniel Bowman. Mentions: heirs of my son, Conrad Wegman, Jr. (dec'd.).
Exors: Sons, Henry Wegman and John Wegman
Wit: David Jordan and Mathias Zehring
Dated: 3 May 1804   Proved: 13 June 1808

Will Book S - page 130

CLARA WELSH, Shenandoah County. Mentions: Pricilla Funk, widow of Isaac Funk; George F. Hupp; William McCord; Francis Cary; Charles Hauck; Mary Hauck; Clara Cary, late Clara Hauck. Mentions: Rebecca Funk and Caroline Funk (daus. of Pricilla Funk).
Exor: Charles Hauck
Wit: George Dosh, Jacob Funk, Sen. and Jacob Funk, Jr.
No date   Proved: 9 Dec. 1833

Will Book I - page 184

JOHN WENDEL, SENIOR, Shenandoah County, son of Christopher.
My children: John Wendel; George Wendel; Sarah, wife of
Daniel Hoffman; Catharine, wife of John Windel (son of
Valentine); Elizabeth, wife of Peter Swartz or Black, Jun.;
Mary, wife of Philip Roads; Ragel, wife of Henry Reynolds;
Rebecca, wife of George Wetzel; Christina, wife of John
Baker; Rosina, widow of Paul Wisman (dec'd.). Granddaughter:
Juliana Wisman - being a lame child of my dau. Rosina Wisman.
Son: George Wendel - tract of land and plantation whereon
he and myself now live containing 146 acres. Son: John
Wendel - I gave land lying in Toms Brook.
Exors: Sons, John Windel and George Windel
Wit: Samuel R. Bader, Frances Rees and Daniel Windel
Dated: 27 July 1814   Proved: 13 Feb. 1815

Will Book M - page 296

BALTASER WERNER, Shenandoah County. Mentions: Christian
Neff.
Exor: Christian Neff
Wit: David Neff, Samuel Ryman and Abraham Neff
Dated: 3 Dec. 1823   Proved: 9 Feb. 1824

Will Book A - page 20

WILLIAM WHITE, County of Frederick, Colony of Virginia.
Wife: Nancy (Ann). Sons: James; William; Britain; John;
Benjamin. Daus: Mary and Elizabeth. Mentions: John
Jackman - shall posses the land he now lives on for 5 years.
Exors: Wife, Ann and Joseph Allen
Wit: John Jackman, Will Webb and Richard Jackman
Dated: 18 May 1771   Proved: 24 Nov. 1772

Will Book N - page 440

JACOB WHITMOYER, Shenandoah County. Wife: Barbary.
Children: Christian; Lyddy; Jacob; Joseph; John; Samuel.
Exor: Samuel Newman
Wit: George Mourey, Martin Kagy, David Neff and David Oroack
Dated: 30 May 1826   Proved: 7 Aug. 1826

Will Book K - page 444

VALENTINE WHITMOYER, Shenandoah County. Wife: Elizabeth.
Children: John; Frederick; David; Jacob; Emanuel; Catharina; Elizabeth; Polly; Anna; Hanna.
Exor: Son, Jacob
Wit: Jacob Roudabush and Henry Bushong
Dated: 9 May 1818   Proved: 8 June 1818

Will Book O - page 202

LORENZO WHITTINGHAM, Shenandoah County. My mother: Margaret Whittingham of the County of Farquier, Virginia.
Exor: Thomas Dwyer
Wit: Thomas Blackford, Beverley Smith, James W. Smith, William Leepert and John Batman
Dated: 8 Dec. 1827   Proved: 11 Feb. 1828

Will Book Z - page 109

WILLIAM WICKS, SENIOR, Shenandoah County. Eight children: Amelia Wicks; William Wicks; Sarah Gray; Grafton Wicks; Caroline Powel; Addson Wicks; Louisa Kemp; Henrietta Maria Wilkins.
Exor: Rev. Jacob Sterwalt
Wit: Charles Spitzer, Samuel Henkel, Martin Urner and Solomon D. Henkel
Dated: 8 Jan. 1844

CODICIL to Will of WILLIAM WICKS, SENIOR - Mentions: I do hereby revoke the said legacy given my son, Grafton.
Wit: Samuel G. Henkel, Martin Urner and J. R. Sibert
Dated: 18 Nov. 1845

CODICIL to Will of WILLIAM WICKS, SENIOR - Mentions: Dau. Louisa Kemp to have the house and quarter acre lot in town of New Market.
Wit: same as above
Dated: 19 Jan. 1846   Proved: 7 Jan. 1850

Will Book P - page 252

ELIZABETH WILHOIT, Shenandoah County, widow of the late
Michael Wilhoit of Madison County, Virginia. Son: Adam
Wilhoit. Dau: Frances Finks, wife of Joel Finks.
No Exor. named
Wit: Thomas Brittan, John Sanford and Samson Berry
Dated: 2 April 1822　　　　　Proved: 12 Oct. 1829

Will Book V - page 440

KATHARINE WILKIN, Shenandoah County, widow of Godfrey
Wilkin, Senior. Daus: Mary Bachman and Esther Lence.
Son: Philip Wilkin.
Exor: Henry Bachman
Wit: Samuel Borden, Jacob Schmucker and Benjamin Kronk,Sen.
Dated: 13 Sept. 1838　　　　Proved: 10 May 1841

Will Book I - page 471

JOHN WILL, Shenandoah County. Wife: Susanna. Son: John
Will - 273 acres of land, the same land and plantation
whereon he now lives. Son: George Will - 280 acres of
land and is the same plantation whereon I now live. Son:
Michael Will. Two daus: Catharine Pitman and Susanna
Pennewitz. Son: Philip Adam Will - remainder of my land
containing 294 acres.
Exor: Peter Overholser
Wit: Jacob Rinker, George Fletcher and _____(Ger.)
Dated: 2 May 1812　　　　　Proved: 9 Oct. 1815

Wills and Accts. (1809-1863) - page 145

JAMES C. WILLIAMS, Shenandoah County. Wife: Catharine.
Mentions: Samuel Pollock, who is bounded to me as an
apprentice. Dau: Sarah Elizabeth.
Exor: Brother, Philip Williams, Jr.
Wit: P. Williams and Philip C. Jones
Dated: 27 Aug. 1829　　　　Proved: 29 Sept. 1829

Will Book Y - page 343

MARTHA WILLIAMS, County of Frederick, State of Virginia.
Dau: Mary C. Simpson. Son: Jared Williams. Grandchildren:
Matilda Launtteroy; Mary S. Hopkins; Martha Parrow and
William S. Parrow; Joseph Pitman. Mentions: Elisha Williams;
Matilda Miller; Louisiana Gatewood; Eleanor A. Pitman;
Gustavas A. Williams.
Exor: Son, Jared Williams
Wit: Simon Carson, Elisha Carson and J. W. Carson
Dated: 16 Dec. 1845   Proved: 11 Sept. 1848

Wills and Accts. (1809-1863) - page 218

PHILIP WILLIAMS, Shenandoah County. Dau: Lucey Hill -
all my slaves. Dau: Ann Jones, wife of Philip C. Jones -
tract of land called Black Oak Ridge (75 acres). Son:
Philip Williams, Jr. Dau: Mary Susannah Magruder - the
home and lot I purchased of Henry H. Gray. Son: Samuel
C. Williams - the house and lot whereon he now lives
which I purchased of Green B. Samuel. Daus: Sarah Tryman
and Elenor Boyd. Mentions: granddaughter, Sarah Elizabeth,
dau. of my son, James C. Williams (dec'd.).
Exor: Son, Samuel C. Williams
Wit: None
Dated: 28 Nov. 1839   Proved: 6 Apr. 1846

Joseph H. Samuels and Joel Pennybacker testified the said
Will is wholly in the handwriting of Philip Williams.

Will Book G - page 410

BERNARD WILLY, Shenandoah County, Minister of the Gospel.
Wife: Christina. Children: Mary; Elizabeth; Henry;
Magdalene; Margaret.
Exors: Jacob Gochenour and wife, Christina
Wit: Daniel Hisey, Martin Hupp and Simeon Yager
Dated: 5 June 1809   Proved: 8 Jan. 1810

Will Book I - page 95

PHILIP WINDEL, SENIOR, Shenandoah County. Wife: Elizabeth Windel. Daus: Barbara, wife of John Zentmeyer; Rebecca Wendel. Sons: Christian Windel and Daniel Windel - my Blacksmith tools. Son: Philip Windel - a piece of land. Son: Emanuel Windel - a piece of land. Three sons: David Windel, Christian Windel and Daniel Windel - my land and plantation I now live on situated and lying on both sides of Toms Brook adjoining land of my brother, John Windel and Abrahma Smootz and others.
Exor: Son, Emanuel Windel
Wit: Samuel R. Bader, Frances Reese and _____(Ger.)
Dated: 18 Dec. 1813   Proved: 8 Aug. 1814

Will Book D - page 178

AUGUSTINE WINDLE, Shenandoah County. Eldest son: Jacob Windle - my large German Bible. Youngest son: John - the plantation whereon I now live containing 150 acres. Other children: Augustine; Mary, wife of Augustine Borden; Elizabeth, wife of John Bushong; Sarah, wife of Jacob Groves.
Exors: Son, Jacob Windle and son-in-law, Augustine Borden
Wit: Peter Windle, _____(Ger.) and John Windle

CODICIL to Will of AUGUSTINE WINDLE - Mentions: Give my true and faithfull slave Negro Harry his freedom.
Wit: Samuel Mills, John Cline and George Ganz
Dated: 27 Sept. 1792   Proved: 25 Oct. 1792

Will Book O - page 314

AUGUSTINE WINDLE, County of Harrison, State of Indiana. Wife: Barbara Windel - all my land in Indiana. My children: (not named). Mentions: my property in County of Shenandoah, Virginia - to be sold.
Exor: Henry Keller
Wit: Gillan Harris and Abraham Rhode
Dated: 30 Dec. 1825   Proved: State of Indiana
                                    25 Feb. 1826
                                    State of Virginia
                                    13 May 1828

Will Book D - page 97

CHRISTOPHER WINDLE, SENIOR, Shenandoah County. Wife: Catharine. Sons: Philip Windle and John Windle - my plantation containing 110 acres, together with the Mill. Sons: Christopher Windle, Jr. and Daniel Windle. Daus: Mary Snapp, wife of John Snapp; Elizabeth Hoffman, wife of John Hoffman; Catharine Conrad, wife of John Conrad. Grandsons: Christopher Conrad and John Conrad. Mentions: 120 acres of land now in dispute with Grantees of Joist Hite.
Exors: Sons, Philip and John Windle
Wit: Alexander Hite, Henry Horsafluke and Henry Hotzenbeller
Dated: 27 Feb. 1791   Proved: 29 Dec. 1791

Will Book F - page 348

JACOB WINDLE, Shenandoah County. Wife: Elizabeth Barbara Windle. Son: Jacob - the plantation whereon I now live when he arrives at age 21 years. Daus: Sarah Keckley; Mary; Elizabeth; Barbara. Mentions: Brother, Augustine Windle appointed Guardian to my children.
Exors: Wife, Elizabeth B. Windle and son-in-law, Joseph Keckley
Wit: George Lind, James Stephenson and John Stickley
Dated: 12 June 1805   Proved: 9 Sept. 1805

Will Book D - page 250

VALENTINE WINDLE, Parish of Beckford, County of Dunmore, Colony of Virginia. Son: Peter Windle - my Psalm Book and 100 acres of land whereon I now dwell. Son: John Windle - 100 acres. Five daus: Barbara and Mary Windle (three daus. not named).
Exors: Augustine Windle and John Philip Windle
Wit: Samuel Mills, John Windle and _____(Ger.)
Dated: 29 Dec. 1791   Proved: 25 Oct. 1792

Will Book X - page 49

JOHN WINE, Shenandoah County. Wife: Elizabeth Wine.
Son: John Wine (youngest son) - all my land I now posses
which is 211 acres. Other children: Rebecca (my oldest
dau.), wife of John Bowman; Michael (my oldest son);
Susanne; Catharine (youngest dau.), wife of John Neff, Jr.
Exor: Son, Jacob Wine.
Wit: George Moore and Adam Miller
Dated: 20 March 1835   Proved: 13 Jan. 1845

Will Book M - page 105

MICHAEL WINE, Shenandoah County. Wife: Susannah. Son:
Michael Wine - all the plantation whereon I now live.
Son: Christian Wine - all the plantation which I bought
of Adam Zirkle. Other children: George; John; Daniel;
Elizabeth Wine; Barbara; Catharine; Susannah; Magedlien.
Exors: Sons, Michael and John Wine
Wit: George Mourey and Isaac Stover
Dated: 11 June 1821   Proved: 14 Feb. 1823

Will Book U - page 353

GEORGE WISMAN, Shenandoah County. Two sons: George Wisman
and Jacob Wisman - tract of land containing 62 1/2 acres.
Son: Jacob Wisman (above) - the plantation whereon I now
live (122 acres). Daus: Magdalene, wife of Lawrence
Spiegel; Catharine, wife of Philip Borden; Christina
Wisman; Elizabeth, wife of Adam Soxman; Rebecca, wife of
Joseph Layman. Mentions: heir of my dau. Rosina Hahn -
Jacob Hahn. Granddaughters: Lydia Long and Dorothy Ann
Long. Sons: John Wisman and Philip Wisman. Mentions: two
daus. of Christina Wisman.
Exor: Sons, George Wisman and Jacob Wisman
Wit: Simeon Yager, Joseph Wisman and Jonathan Fravel, Jr.
Dated: 13 April 1833   Proved: 13 Aug. 1838

Will Book Z - page 344

JOSEPH WISMAN, Shenandoah County. Wife: Elizabeth.
My children: (not named).
Exor: Brother, Philip Wisman
Wit: Daniel Hottel and John Maphis
Dated: 27 April 1850   Proved: 9 Dec. 1850

Will Book Z - page 112

NICHOLAS WISMAN, Shenandoah County. Wife: Barbara Wisman. Son: Joseph Wisman - tract of land and plantation I and he now live on containing 118 acres, also, 23 acres of my Black Ridge tract. Son: Adam Wisman - remainder of my land. Son: Philip Wisman. Daus: Catharine, wife of Henry Cline; Christina, wife of Samuel Bear; Magdalene, wife of George Fetzer; Barbara, wife of Henry Gochenour; Susanna, wife of Daniel Rhode.
Exors: Son, Adam Wisman and son-in-law, George Fetzer
Wit: Samuel R. Bader, John Roth and George Maphis
Dated: 10 Sept. 1825   Proved: 11 March 1850

Will Book A - page 160

PHILIP WISMAN, County of Dunmore, Colony of Virginia. Wife: Catharine Wisman. Sons: John Wisman; George Wisman; Nicholas Wisman. Dau: Magdalene Wisman. Mentions: oldest dau. Mary's children, namely: Adam Darting and Catharine Darting. Son-in-Law: Thomas Wisman.
Exors: Wife, Catharine Wisman, George Mavis and Godfrey Wilkin
Wit: Henry Watsell, John Kingree and Nicholas Watsell
Dated: 3 Jan. 1778   Proved: 28 May 1778

Will Book E - page 330

GEORGE ADAM WOCKER (WALKER), Shenandoah County. Brother: Henry Wocker - my plantation whereon I now dwell, Willed to me from my father, John Wocker (dec'd.). Sisters: Eve, wife of Jacob Sheetz and Barbara, wife of John Clem. My mother: Margareth Walker. Mentions: children of my step-brother, Elias (dec'd.).
Exor: Brother, Henry Wocker
Wit: Charles Smith, John Hebner, Sen. and Peter Tisinger
Dated: 14 Aug. 1799   Proved: 10 Dec. 1799

Will Book Q - page 125

HENRY WOCKER, Shenandoah County. Wife: Elizabeth Wocker. Son: Henry Wocker - the land and plantation whereon I now live. Daus: Elizabeth, wife of Christian Mumaw; Susanna; Anne, wife of John Sheetz. Sons: Peter and Philip. Mentions: children of my son, John Wocker and children of my dau. Rebecca, alias Catharine, wife of William Bufsy.
Exor: Absalom Rinker
Wit: Robert Turner, P. Williams and Samuel Pollock
Dated: 1 June 1830   Proved: 13 Dec. 1830

Will Book E - page 232

JOHN WOCKER, Shenandoah County. Wife: Margaret. Son: George Adam Wocker - plantation whereon I now live (200 acres). Son: Henry Wocker. Daus: Margaret, widow of Ulry Nease (dec'd.); Mary, wife of Michael Neas; Eve, wife of Jacob Sheetz; Barbara, wife of John Clem. Mentions: Heir of my dau. Catharine- John Kirchoff, who married said Catharine and received her share. Dau: Elizabeth - one dollar account of her disobedience to her mother and me.
Exors: Wife, Margaret and son-in-law, Jacob Sheetz
Wit: Jacob Stiegle, Adam Nees and John Beck
Dated: 20 March 1796   Proved: 12 March 1799

Will Book E - page 325

JACOB WOLF, Shenandoah County. Wife: Catharine. Sons: John Jacob Wolf (dec'd.) and Augustine Wolf (dec'd.). Daus: Ann Clara, widow of George Caufeld (dec'd.); Susannah, wife of William Kelp; Margretha (dec'd.) who was wife of Christian Funkhouser (dec'd.). Mentions: George Jacob Woolf.
Exors: Daus., Ann Clara, widow of George Caufeld, Susannah, widow of William Kelp and my dau.'s son, John Adam Caufeld.
Wit: George Fravel, David Jordan and _____ (Ger.)
Dated: 20 April 1795   Proved: 10 Dec. 1799

Will Book F - page 79

CHRISTIAN WOLGEMUTH, Shenandoah County, miller. Wife: Rosina. Daus: Elizabeth; Catharine; Mary. Son: Jacob.
Exors: Frederick Fox (State of Maryland) and Abraham Bideler of Shenandoah County
Wit: Jacob Bushong, Frederick Bozerman and _____ (Ger.)
Dated: 2 Feb. 1803   Proved: 7 March 1803

Will Book P - page 107

BENJAMIN WOOD, Shenandoah County. Wife: Elizabeth P. Wood.
Children: David Wood; Benjamin H. Wood; William F. Wood;
Nancy Jones, wife of Wharton Jones; Sarahan Wood; Edward
Whitfield Wood; Mary Mahala Wood. Mentions: children of
my son, Harrison Wood, viz: Emily Elizabeth Wood; Thompson
Wood and Benjamin Franklin Wood.
Exors: Wharton Jones and Benjamin H. Wood
Wit: John Koontz and Christian Horn
Dated: 5 Nov. 1828 Proved: 12 May 1829

Will Book P - page 102

DINAH WOOD, Shenandoah County. Seven daus: Milly Nichols;
Eleanor Nichols; Nancy Nichols; Polly Moore; Elizabeth
Ashford; Sarah Wood; Lydia Allen. Sons: William Sandy
and Vincent Sandy.
Exor: Joseph Allen
Wit: James R. Robertson, John Presgraves and Benjamin Sedwick
Dated: 11 Dec. 1828 Proved: 11 May 1829

Will Book L - page 350

JOHN WOOD, Shenandoah County. Wife: Rachael. Children:
Abigail; Polly; John; Nehemiah; Moses; William; Asa; Abin;
Jefse; Sally; Nancy; Elizabeth; Rachael. Mentions: Dau.
Polly's son, Jefse. Dau. Polly's husband, William Moody.
No Exor. named
Wit: John Payne, Benjamin Wood and Joshua Wood
Dated: 21 May 1821 Proved: 13 Aug. 1821

Will Book K - page 162

NEHEMIAH WOOD, Shenandoah County. Wife: Dinah. Children:
John Wood; Benjamin Wood; Jefse Wood; Nehemiah Wood; Joshua
Wood; Lettecus Atwood; Margaret Wood (widow of my dec'd. son
William Wood). Grandchildren: Sally Young and John Young
(children of my dec'd. dau., Nancy Young).
Exors: Sons, John Wood and Benjamin Wood
Wit: James R. Robertson, William Hancock and Elizabeth
Hancock
Dated: 6 April 1816 Proved: 7 Oct. 1816

Will Book B - page 421

PHILADELPHIA WOODMAN, of Marsanuta, County of Shanadow, Colony of Virginia. Mentions: Mary Bellows; Mary Coffman; Martin Coffman, Sen. and Martin Coffman, Jun. Mentions: One half of my Estate to Martin Coffman's Church for relief of the Poor and one half to John Koonz's Church for relief of Poor. Mentions: Ann Bongerman - my big Bible; Amelia Boon - my white silk handkerchief. Mentions: Martin Coffman's two daus., Mary and Motlen.
Exors: David Coffman and Martin Coffman
Wit: John Coffman and Ann Bongerman
Dated: 31 Dec. 1787   Proved: 31 Jan. 1788

Will Book B - page 313

DAVID WOOLMAN, Rowan County, State of North Carolina. Wife: (not named) - my worldly belongings in Carolina. Dau: Susannah, my first born. Dau: Elizabeth - my worldly Estate in the State of Virginia. Mentions: friend, Joseph Strickler - gray horse with my saddle that I rode thereon. No Exor. named
Wit: William Bolton, Abraham Strickler and Adam Baker
No date   Proved: 22 Feb. 1787

Will Book K - page 179

JOHN WRAWLINGS (RAWLINGS), Shenandoah County. Wife: Sarah Wrawlings.
Exor: Wife, Sarah Wrawlings
Wit: George Oakely and Abraham Brown
Dated: 5 April 1815   Proved: 9 Dec. 1816

Will Book Q - page 286

WILLIAM WRIGHT, SENIOR, Shenandoah County. Wife: Mary - all my personal and real estate as long as she lives. Mentions: three grandchildren (not named).
Exor: Andrew Bushong
Wit: Henry Bushong, Samuel Hawkins and Rhesa Hawkins
Dated: 6 May 1829   Proved: 7 Sept. 1829

Will Book M - page 162

JOSEPH YEAGER, Shenandoah County. Wife: Barbara. My three children: Jacob Yeager; Mary, wife of Jacob Good; Joseph Yeager.
Exors: Son, Jacob Yeager and son-in-law, Jacob Good
Wit: P. Williams, Jacob Ott and Philip Miller
Dated: 8 March 1823   Proved: 8 April 1823

Will Book L - page 218

EDWIN YOUNG, Parish of Beckford, Shenandoah County. Wife: Frankey Young - two negroes, to wit: Esquier and Winney. Son: John - tract of land I bought of Enoch Job. Son: Edwin Young - tract of land I bought of Abraham Hollingsworth in Job's bottom, also, 70 acres in the steep hollow. Son: William Young - tract of land I bought of John Heastant where I now live containing 472 acres. Other children: Luthia Young; Betty Johnstone; Frankey; Nancy; Daniel Young. Mentions: Exors. to sell tract of land on the Blue Ridge in Mariland Gap, also, small tract I bought of James M. Foley.
Exors: Brother, Sinett Young, William Williams and son-in-law, John Burner.
Wit: L. Mackintosh, John Wendell and Edwin Young 3rd.
Dated: 9 Dec. 1792   Proved: 9 April 1793

Will Book W - page 176

ANN ZEA, Shenandoah County. Grandson: Joseph Dosh. Granddaughter: Elizabeth, wife of Franklin Hamner, formerly Elizabeth Dosh. Children: Joseph Zea; Philip Zea. Mentions: children of Mary Dosh and children of Margaret Stover.
Exor: Son, Joseph Zea
Wit: John W. Farra, Jacob Kern and Jacob Buck
Dated: 29 Dec. 1841   Proved: 8 Aug. 1842

Will Book U - page 421

MARTIN ZEA, Shenandoah County. Wife: Ann. Son: Joseph
Zea - the house and lot in Strasburg. Son: Philip Zea -
the house and lot in which I live. Mentions: children
of my deceased daus. Mary Dosh and Margaret Stover (their
fathers, George Dosh and Joseph Stover).
Exors: Sons, Joseph Zea and Philip Zea
Wit: Robert Turner, Jno. G. Schmitt and P. Williams, Jr.
Dated: 19 Sept. 1834

CODICIL to Will of MARTIN ZEA - Mentions: I have sold the
interest of my wife in some land near Strasburg to Joseph
Stover.
Wit: John H. Lee and Reuben A. Bird
Dated: 7 Jan. 1837   Proved: 12 Nov. 1838

Will Book K - page 253

MATHIAS ZEHRING, Shenandoah County. Wife: Rebeckah.
Son: John Zehring - tract of land adjoining Christian
Baver, also, place adjoining Benjamin Allen. Son: Mathias-
plantation whereon I now dwell. Mentions: other lands
equally divided between above two sons. Dau: Magdalene,
wife of Michael Ott - house and lot in town of Woodstock.
Step-dau: Rebecca Miller - that house and lot in town of
Woodstock adjoining Philip Miller and Jacob Knisley.
Exors: Son, John Zehring, Jacob Ott, John Roads and
David Jordan
Wit: Jacob Good, Michael Haas and Michael Feater
Dated: 14 June 1806

CODICIL to Will of MATHIAS ZEHRING - Mentions: Personal
estate be equally divided between my said three children
and my step-dau. Rebecca Miller.
Wit: Abram Lambert and P. Williams
Dated: 5 May 1817   Proved: 9 June 1817

Will Book Z - page 1

SAMUEL ZEHRING, Shenandoah County. Brothers: Mathias
Zehring; Joseph Zehring; John Zehring. Sister: Sarah
Lutz. Niece: Mary H., dau. of Andrew Funkhouser.
Exor: Mathias Zehring
Wit: Jacob Lutz, Harrison Foltz and Andrew Funkhouser
Dated: 6 June 1849   Proved: 15 Aug. 1849

Will Book G - page 185

ANNA ZELL, widow of Nicholas Zell, late of Earl Township in County of Lancaster and State of Pennsylvania but now of the County of Shenandoah, Virginia. Sons: John ; Jacob and Nicholas. Daus: Barbara, wife of Henry Rohrer; Anna; Frany; Mary, wife of Thomas Gollagher; Elizabeth, wife of John Kerlin.
Exors: Son-in-Law, Beanhard Getz and Jacob Stiegel
Wit: David Kerlin, Jacob Kerlin and David Getz
Dated: 8 Jan. 1806 Proved: 12 April 1808

Will Book W - page 494

MAGDALINA ZIMMERMAN, Shenandoah County, widow of Peter Zimmerman, dec'd. Son: Philip - the house where I live. Son: Jacob. Granddaughter: Magdalina.
Exor: Son, Philip
Wit: John Smutz, Michael Wine and _____ (Ger.)
Dated: 9 Nov. 1832 Proved: 8 July 1844

Will Book I - page 492

PETER ZIMMERMAN, Shenandoah County. Wife: Magdalene. Step- son: Philip Dingledine (son of my wife) - all my lands and plantation whereon I now live.
Exors: John Kagey and Philip Dingledine
Wit: Christian Neff and Abraham Neff
Dated: 28 July 1814 Proved: 11 Dec. 1815

Will Book L - page 49

ELIZABETH ZIRCKEL, Shenandoah County, wife of Andrew Zirckel (former wife of Christian Ruff, dec'd.). My six daus: Esther; Elizabeth; Mary; Regina; Christina; Susannah. Dau. Elizabrth's husband, Nicholas Nagel; dau. Christina's husband, David Nagel. Mentions: money which William Richards owes to Christian Ruff's heirs.
Exor: Son-in-Law, John Runion of Rockingham County
Wit: John Zirckel and John Huffman
Dated: 1 June 1806 Proved: 9 March 1819

Will Book H - page 117

MICHAEL ZIRCKEL, Shenandoah County. Wife: Catharine. Son: George - part of my plantation. Son: Lewis Zirckel - part of my plantation adjoining Conrad Pence's land. Son: Jonathan - old tract on the timber ridge. Mentions: land joining lands to old John Glick's (211 acres) - to be sold. Mentions: Son, John's dau., Lydia. Other children: (not named).
Exor: Son, Lewis
Wit: John Bowman, Andrew Zirckel, Jun. and John Zirckel
Dated: 20 June 1811 Proved: 11 Nov. 1811

Will Book K - page 95

ANDREW ZIRKLE, Shenandoah County. Wife: Elizabeth. Son: Andrew - two tracts of land whereon he now lives. Sons: Adam; John (dec'd.); Samuel; Abraham; Philip. Daus: Elizabeth and Eave. Mentions: children of my son, Michael (dec'd.), viz: Samuel, Abraham and Philip.
Exor: Philip Hupp
Wit: George Mourey, John Brennes and D. Strickler
Dated: 7 Jan. 1815 Proved: 10 June 1816

Will Book P - page 311

ELIZABETH ZIRKLE, Shenandoah County, widdow and relick of
George Adam Zirkle, dec'd. Son: John Zirkle - one dollar.
Son: Benjamin Zirkle - one dollar only. Son: George Zirkle -
one dollar. Dau: Rosannah Meek - one dollar. Other children:
Elizabeth Kipps; Catharine McCarty; Christener Rup; Mary
Olinger; Eve Hinkle; Susannah Howdeshall - all to share in
all my Estate. Mentions: Hugh Meeks.
Exor: Samuel Newman
Wit: Michael Nees and _____(Ger.)
Dated: 29 Aug. 1821   Proved: 11 Jan. 1830

Will Book E - page 379

GEORGE ADAM ZIRKLE, Shenandoah County. Wife: Elizabeth.
Son: John - 225 acres. Son: George - 275 acres. Son:
Benjamin - 200 acres. Daus: Christina; Eve; Mary; Susannah;
Rosannah; Elizabeth; Catharine.
Exors: Son, John and Jacob Kips
Wit: George Olinger, Francis Scibert and Isaac Gore
Dated: 19 Aug. 1800   Proved: 8 Sept. 1800

Will Book U - page 11

JOHN ZIRKLE, Shenandoah County. Wife: Rofsanna. Mentions:
Erasmus Zirkle (son of my dec'd. son, Jacob Zirkle) - the
Mill and 35 acres. Mentions: Amanda Zirkle (dau. of my
dec'd. son, Jacob). Son: George Zirkle - remainder of the
above land on which the said son, George now resides (150
acres). Dau: Elizabeth, wife of Michael Nefs - 70 acres
of land. Son: Philip - remainder of old tract (80 acres).
Son: Cornelius. Son: Paul - the Sawmill, including Hemp
Mill, small house, Shop and 5 acres.
Exors: Son, Philip Zirkle and Michael Neese
Wit: Henry Kips, Benjamin Zirkle and John G. Zirkle
Dated: 3 March 1837   Proved: 8 May 1837

INDEX

ABBOTT, John Westley	195	ALLEN, Jackson	2,?
William	55,59	James	3,67,162,23?
ABELL, Ezekiel	1	James Monroe	?
Jane	1	John	3,17(
Jeremiah	1	John J.	?
John	1	John James	?
John, Sen.	1	Joseph	2,3,91,10?
Joseph	1		234,24?
ACHER, Catharine	1	Jos. M.	23?
George	1	Lydia	2,3,24?
Henry	1	Mary	2,?
Jacob	1	Moses	4?
Michael	1	Nancy	?
AILSHIRE, Daniel	17	Ralph	?
Lufsa	17	Rebecca	?
AKER, Philip	228	Reuben	1,2,9(
ALBERT, Nicholas	66	Reuben, Jun.	?
Philip	183	Reuben, Sen.	?
Rebecca	183	Rhesa	3,90,91
ALBRIGHT, John	132,145		92,15(
ALISHITE, Henry	216	Robert	3,?
ALLDENFER, Frederick	78	Robert M.	
ALLDOERFFER, Geo.	211	Sarah	2,3,9
ALLEN, Aaron	1,3	Thomas	1,3,4
Abegail (Abagail)	4,151		146,15
Agnes	3	Thomas, Jun.	
Algernon S.	4	Thomas G.	
Anna	3	Thomas M.	
Barbara	2	Wesley	
Benjamin	3,246	William	3,4,137,14
Betty	1,2	William T.	
Cislia	2	ALLENSWORTH, Eliza	3
David	4	Harrison	3
David H.	4	James	3
Davis	1,2,12,220	Philip	3
Deborah	2	ALLESHIRE, Jonas	3
Elizabeth	1	ALLISON, Henry	3
Eunice	3	ALMOND, Edward	96,190
Frances	153		21
George	1	Mann	21
George W.	2	Marm	19
Hannah	3	Maun	9
Homer	2	William	35,92,134
Isaiah	143		135,19
Isreal	1,2,154	William R.	190,213
			22

ALSEP, John 85,225
  Joseph 85
ALSHITE, Christian 29,52,
  96,104,140
ALTDOERFFER, Christina 5
  Frederick 5
  George 5
  John 5
ALTER, Jacob 175
  John 175
ALTHERR, John 197
  Mary 197
ALTORFFER, Frederick 111
AMMON, Ernest 5
  Margaretha 5
ANDERICK, Barbara 229
  Caty 201
  Elizabeth 5
  Frederick 5
  George 229
  Jacob 201
  John 5
  Joseph 5
  Sarah 5
ANDERSON, Alexander 37,49
  Catharine 5,6
  Elizabeth 5,6,54
  Isabella 37
  James 6
  John 6,31
  Maria 6
  Margarett 5,6
  Mary 5
  Samuel 6
  Washington 6
  William 223
ANDRAKE, Catharine 201
ANDRICK, Anna 6
  Elizabeth 6
  Frederick 6
  George 6,94
  Jacob 6
  Joseph 6,93,183
ANDY, Elizabeth 82
  William 82
ANSPACK, Eve 7
  Sarah 7
ANSPAUCK, Sally 128
ARRINGTON, Amy 28

ARTERBURN, Peter 7
  Sarah 7
ARTHUR, James A. 54
  Joseph 64
  Wm. Smith 227
ARTZ, Benjamin 7
  Christian 7
  Christina 7
  Elizabeth 7
  Henry 7,149,177,
  214,217,226
  Jacob 7,8
  John 7,8,87
  Mary 7,8
  Rebecca 7
  Sarah 129
ASHBY, Will R. 179
ASHFORD, Elizabeth 243
ASHLEY, William R. 203
ASHMEAD, Joseph 176
ATTDOERFFER, Catharine 86
  John 86
ATWOOD, Betsy 185
  Edwin 8
  Elizabeth 8
  James 8
  Jane 8
  John 8
  Lettecus 243
  Nancy 8
  Susanna 8
  Thompson 8
  William 8
AULD, C. 136
AUMILLER, Eave C. 8
  George 8
  Henry 8
  Mary 8
AVERY, Eve 223
BACHMAN, Abraham 9
  Ann 9
  Catharine 8
  Christian 9
  Daniel 9
  David 9
  Henry 8,236
  Jacob 9
  John 9
  Mary 9,236

BACKER, Anthony	9	BAKER, Rudolph	104
Barbara	9	Samuel	10,73
Jacob	9	Sibilla	94
John	9	Thomas	20
Joseph	9	William	10,25,56,
Margarite	9		75,89,108
Philip	9	BALTHAS, Leonard	79
Philip Peter	9	BALTHIS, George	10
Philip Peter, Sen.	9	John	10
Resina	9	Leonard	10,104,215
BACKMAN, John	159	Leonard, Sen.	10
BADER, Samuel R.	5,8,15,	Valentine	10
	20,63,66,72,	William	10
	75,80,83,86,	BALTHIZ, William	43
	87,101,103,	BARB, Adam	10,11,196
	111,112,114,	Anna	10,190
	149,156,182,	Catharine	11
	191,192,194,	David	10
	204,209,211,	Gideon	11
	225,234,238,	Henry	10,11,82,95
	241	Jacob	10,190,
BAILEY, William	172		210,230
BAINDER, John	133	Jacob, Jr.	190
BAIR, M. S.	11	Magdalene	10
BAKER, Adam	244	Peter	174
Christian	74	Polly	97
Christina	20,234	Ruth	11
Cronomer	100	Sarah	232
Daniel	25,156	William	11,97
Dorothy	10	BARBLO, Adam	227
Eliza	73	BARCLAY, Benjamin	1
Elizabeth	10	BARDEU, Nicholas	112
Esther	177	BARE, Ann	100
George	9	Barbara	58,80
Heironimus	9,53,172	Christina	11
Henry	9,10,177	Elizabeth	147
Isaac	10	John	147
Jacob	96,190	Joseph	11
John	234	Michael	58
Joseph	10,94	Naason	11
Lewis	10	Philip	80
Mary Gertrout	9	Rebecca	11
P.	49	Samuel	5,11,127,165
Peter	10,210	BARKETT, Joseph	158
Peter, Jun.	190	BARNELL, James	170
Peter, Sen.	74	BARNES, Charles	58
Philip	10	John	58

BARNES, Joseph	58	BAUSERMAN, Jacob	12,101, 218
BARNETT, Catharine	11	Rebecca	101
Elizabeth	164	Reuben	12,69
Michael	11	Sarah	101
William	11	William	12
BARNS, Charles	88	William, Jr.	101
Joseph	143	William, Sen.	12
BARRET, Isaac	15	BAUZERMAN, Catharine	13
Mary	15	Frederick	13
BARRINGTON, Andrew	12	Michael	13
Ann	12	William	81
Martha	12,25	BAVER, Christian	246
Mary	12	BAYLEY, Will M.	23,57
Peggy	12	William	87
William	12	BAYLY, Isabella	140
BARTON, David	95	Polly	27
Joseph	109	Thomas P.	179
Lydia	109	Will M.	43,101,177,217
Richard	95	BEAKHIM, Isaac	100
BARUKER, Adam	12	BEALE, Betty	110
Joseph	12	James M. H.	213
BASERMAN, Henry	149,194, 204	Mary	213
Samuel	211	Travnor	3,31,110,226
BASLER, Michael	82	BEALER, Ulrick	112
BASSARD, Philip	149	BEAM, Daniel	215
BASYE, John	115	Mary	28
BATHIS, John	134	BEAR, Christina	241
BATMAN, John	235	Samuel	241
BATTHIZ, John	145	BEARD, Jacob	177
BATTICE, Jacob	12	Mary	177
John	12	BEARDBACK, Adam	183
Margaret	12	BEARSH, Catharine	13
Regina	12	George	13
William	12	Lewis	13
BAUCKMAN, Jacob	54	BEARTH, Martin	206
Mary	54	BEAS, Isaac	25
BAUGHMAN, Catharine	160	BEATTY, John E.	18
Henry	126	BEAVER, Daniel	85,92, 143,221
Jacob	126,160	David	39,127,221
BAUHMAN, George	131	John	221
BAUMAN, John	11	Mary	221
Samuel	76	Nancy	221
BAUSERMAN, Abraham	12	BEAVERS, Mary	194
Henry	12	BEAZLEY, Charles	13
Isaac	12		

BEAZLEY, Isaac	13	BERGMAN, Andrew	73,174
Mariam	13	BERNHERD, George	14
Mark	13	BERRY, Achory	109,216
Rebecca	13	Ann	113
Sarah	13	Catharina	199
BECHTEL, Marty	192	Samson	236
BECK, John	14,242	BERTZ, John	181
Rosina	14	BETTS, Anna	121
BECKER, Adam	14	BEYDLER, Abraham	15,16, 75,149
John	14	Abraham, Jr.	16
Maria	14	Barbara	15,121
Peter	14	Dorothy	16
BECKTEL, Barbara	14	Isaac	101,121
Catharine	14	Jacob	15
Dorotha	14	Rebecca	16
Elizabeth	14	Susanna	15
Eve	14	Ulrick	15
Henry	14	BEYER, Adam	16
John	14	Jacob	16
John P.	176	John	16
Magdalene	14	Leonhard	16
Mary	14	Lifs	16
Tobias	14	Magdalena	16
BEELER, William	27	Moly	16
BEIDLEMAN, Daniel	157	Peggy	16
John	108	BIDELER, Abraham	242
BELLAS, George	77	BIDLERMAN, Catharine	183
BELLOWS, Mary	244	Daniel	183
BENDER see PAINTER		BILLER, Catharine	16
BENDER, Adam	15	Christian	16
Christina	15,132	George	16
David	15	George, Jr.	16
George	15,129	Rebecca	16
Isaac	15	BILLHYMER, Henry	227
Jacob	15	BINGHAM, Henry	77
John	15,66	BIRD see BYRD	
John, Sen.	132	BIRD, Abraham	17,91,161, 163,200
Mary	58	Catharine	17
Mathias	15	Elizabeth	17
Peter	15	George	17,134, 153,194
Philip	15,66		
Regina	15		
Samuel	15,58	Hannah	17
BENTZ, John	124	Hester	199
BERGER, Simon	52	Hetty	199
BERGFIELD, Caroline	176		

BIRD, John	33		BLEU, Mary	98
Lydia	17		BLIND, Abraham	18
Magdalene	17		Catharine	18
Margaret	17		David	18
Mark	17,47,147,		Elizabeth	18
	174,182		Hannah	18,225
Mary	17,33		Isaac	18
Mounce	56,186		Jacob	18
Peter	27,29		Mary	74
Rachel	17		Mary Ann	18
Rebecca	91		Michael	18,74
Reuben	134		Peter	18,225
Reuben A.	17,246		Soloman	18
Wm. LaFayette	199		Sophia	18
BISH, Barbara	230		William	18
Frederick	230		BLINT, Marget	172
Tevel	162		BLOSSER, Barbara	184
BIXLER, Anna	17,93		Daniel	41,223
John	17		Jacob	40
Michael	17,93		BLY, Adam	20,195
Nancy	17		Elizabeth	19
Peter	17		Esther	122
BLACK see SWARTZ			George	19
BLACK, Eve	209		Isaac	122
George	90,214		Jacob	19
Martin	210		John	19,122,134
Peter, Jr.	234		Jonathan	18
BLACKFORD, Benjamin	13,79		Joseph	122
Caroline	213		Mary	20
Thomas	17,41,235		Mary Magdelon	19
BLACKWOOD, James	113		Philip	18,19
John	83,141		Susanna	89
BLAUSER, Peter	222		William	89
BLAZER, Ann	81		BLYE, John	134
BLESSING, Abraham	17,18		BODELL, Adam	19
Barbara	17		David	19
Catharine	17		George	19
Christian	17		George, Sen.	19
Christina	17		Jonas	19
Elizabeth	17,18		Malinda	19
Henry	17		Mary	19
Jacob	17		Michael	19
John	17,18		William	19
Lewis	17,18,215		BOEHM, Abraham, Jr.	158
Ludwig	215		Anna	75
Magdalene	17		Barbara	19
Mary	18		Benjamin	75
Michael	99		Catharine	19

BOEHM, Daniel	19,224	BORDEN, Ananias	92
David	75	Augustine	20,238
Dorothy	19	Catharine	240
Elizabeth	19	George	11
Franey	19	Hannah	20
Heustant	19	Joseph	20,233
Isaac	203	Mary	238
Jacob	19,193	Philip	73,240
John	5,75	Philip, Sen.	155,156
Levina	42	Reincard	20
Magdalene	19	Samuel	155,236
Martin	73,160,224	Sophia	86
Mary	19	Ulrick	155
Rachael	75	BORGER, Ann Mary	20
Regenia	19	George	20
Regina	19	Henry	20
Reuben	19	Michael	20
Samuel	18,19	BORNTON, Conrad	206
William	224	BORT, John	194
BOHM, Charles	176	BORTEN, Ambrose C.	96,207
BOIT, Andrew	169	BOSSERMAN, Frederick	20,
Salome	169		63,86
BOLSON, William	174	Henry	20
BOLTON, William	244	Judith	20
BOND, Edward	2	Samuel	20
George	69	Sarah	20
John	3	BOUGHMAN, Barbary	21
Lydia	1	Henry	21
Mary	60	Henry, Sen.	21
Rachael	69	Jacob	21
Susanna	3	John	21
BONGERMAN, Ann	244	Mary	130
BONKFIELD, Arnold	229	BOWER, Ann	21
BOOKER, John Philip	20	Catharine	189
Mary	37	Christena	21
Nancy	20	Christian	21
Sally	20	Clarisey	21
William	20	Elizabeth	21
BOON, Amelia	243	George	21,135,169
Pearces	99	Henry	21
BOOTEN, Ambrose C.	165	Henry, Jr.	21
Elizabeth	70	Jacob	158
BOOTON, Abrose C.	42,135	Lawrence	2:
BORAKER, Barbara	76	Magdalen	2:
Michael	76	Margaret	13!

BOWER, Nicholas	189	BOYD, Caroline	24
Philip	61	Elenor	237
Henry, Jr.	11	Frances	24
BOWMAN, Abraham	23	Henry Prater	24
Adam	22	James Wilson	24
Alexander	199	John	24
Ann	23	John F.	24
Anna	106	Rachael Amanda	24
Anna Marie	22	Stephen Decatur	24
Anny Mary	233	Virginia	24
Barbara	104,227	William	24
Benjamin	22,47,189	BOYER, Elizabeth	24
Benjamin, Sen.	8	George K.	24
Catharine	23	Henry	114
Christina	107	Jacob	24
Christley	208	Mary	114
Daniel	22,233	Peter	24,195
David	22,23,107	William	24
Elizabeth	22,77,102	BOYERS, Henry	114
Eve	22	Rebecca	25
George	12,22,23,	BOZERMAN, Frederick	242
	44,121,126,	BRANAMAN, Daniel	56
	146,216,230	BRANHAM, Betty	12
Geo. Adam	22	R.	171
Henry	22	Reubin	189
Hiram	199	William	12
Isaac	23,77,151,186	BRANNAMAN, Abraham	39
Jacob	23,68,106,107	Abraham, Sen.	144
John	22,23, 106,129	Daniel	25,186
	178,240,248	Mary	25
Joseph	15,23,46	BRANNER, Michael	128
Leah	106	BREEDLOFE, Barbara	193
Lydia	23	George	193
Magdalene	189	Isaac	193
Mary	22,23,129,208	John	193
Peter	22,46	Martin	193
Philip	23	BREEDLOVE, Barbara	197
Rebecca	22,23,68,240	Eve	197
Robert	23,24,37	George	197
Samuel	23,24	John	197
Sarah	24	Martin	197
Stephen	78,102	BREEKBILL, Jacob	10
Susan	24,37	BRENNER, John	158
Susannah	12,23	BRENNES, John	248
Washington	23	BRENT, Robert	69
William	227	BRENTZ, Philip	175

BRIGHT, Michael	191	BROWNING, Henry	26,206
BRIGHTLAW, Catharina	38	Henry R.	18
George	38	Jane	26
BRILL, Polly	42	John Henry	26
BRINKER, Barbara	91	Margaret	206
Conrad	3	BROWNLOW, Isaac	26
George	23,119,139	BROY, Esabella	13
Mary	3	BRUBAKER, Abraham	26,110, 163
William	91		
BRITTAN, Thomas	41,236	Abraham, Sen.	26
BROADBACK, Adam	25	Anna Maria	26
Anna Y.	25	Barbara	26
Barbary	25	Catharina	26
Jacob	25	Christina	26
John	25	Daniel	5,175,202
Philip	25	Elizabeth	26,182
BROADUS, Edmond	200	Emanuel	182
William F.	26,113	John	26,144,221
BROBECK, John	25,71	Peter	26,144
Joseph	25	Susana	26
Margaret	25	Wesley	223
Mary	25	BRUMBACH, Jacob	85
BROCK, Abraham	26	BRUMBACK, Daniel	21
Barbara	26	BRUNNER, John	115
Catharine	26	BRYAN, William B.	223
Christina	26	BUCHER, Magdalen	172
George	26	BUCK, Charles	27,77,84
Henry	26	J. N.	179
Jacob	26	Jacob	245
Juliana	26	John	27,32,77, 177,179
Lea	26		
Magdalena	26	Mary	179
Mary	26	Miriam	179
Michael	26	Peter	179
Rudolph	26	Sally	32
Sarah	26	Samuel	27
Susannah	26	Thomas	27,77,145
BROOMBAUGH, John	221	Thomas, Jr.	37,179
BROWN, Abraham	244	Thomas, Sen.	37
Amos	172	Thomas F.	179
Eve	200	William	27
Henry	166	BULER, Catharine	27
Jacob	223	John	27
John	148,163,166,200	William	27
Joseph	58	BULLETT, Mary	150

BUMD, F. W.	176
BURGER, Eliaabeth	40
Michael	40
BURKHEAD, Barbara	27
Elizabeth	27
George	27
Mary Eva	27
Simon	27
BURNER, Abraham	28
Adam	121
Anny	28
Barbara	31
Barbary	28
Catharine	28,85
Christiner	28
Daniel	49
Elizabeth	221
Esther	28
Franky	28
Henry	48,83
Isaac	28
Jacob	28,31,187,230
Jacob, Jr.	28
James	121
John	28,221,245
Jonas	7
Joseph	28
Katharine	28
Leithia	28
Leittice	220
Mary Ann	121
Michael	28,78
Noah	119
Polly	121
Sally	7
Samuel	28
Samuel, Jr.	218
Samuel, Sen.	218
Sarah	28
BUSH, Philip	123
BUSHONG, Andrew	67,92,244
David	114
Elizabeth	62,238
Henry	235,244
Jacob	65,193,242
John	12,123,238
Magdalene	12
Peter	62,128
BUSHWELL, John	143
BUSSARD, Philip	215
BUSSERMAN, Ann	109
BUSSEY, Cornelius	88
Eve	88
BUSSY, Catharine	241
Rebecca	241
William	241
BUSWELL, Anna	29
George	29,96,184
John	29
Jonathan	29
BUYNER, Christian	210
BYER, Nancy	114
BYRD see BIRD	
BYRD, Abraham	30
Andrew	29,152
Catharine	152
Catherian	29
Clara	29
Derick	30
Henry	29
Jacob	29
John	29,194
Mounce	16,29,30,42,116
Peter	194
Polly	30
Rachel	16
Rebecca	91,189
Ruth	189
Sally	30
Solina	29
William	29,30,124
William, Jr.	188
William, Sen.	30
CABEY, Andrew	60
CAGY, John	9
CAHORN, William	154
CALDREIDER, Anna Mary	193
CALFEE, Benjamin	30
Bettey	30
Charles	30,183
Henry	30,183
James	30
John	30,183
Sarah	30,183
William	30,151,183
CALLENDER, Ann	52

CALLENDER, Michael	52
CALLY, Jane	91
CALVERT, Catharine A.	188
John S.	188
Mary Frances	188
CAMEL, Abraham	137
Betsy	88
Eve	137
CAMPBELL, Agnes	30
Alexander	30
Andrew	30
Catharine	30
Charles	30
David	108
Eleanor	203
Elizabeth	30
Ellick	30
Janet	30
John	30,145
John Hamilton	30
Lettice	30
Letty	30
Margaret	30
Rebecca	31
Rebekah	31
Richard	31,205
Samuel	30
CAPP, Anna Eliz.	8
Andrew	31
Elizabeth	31
Eve	31
George	31
Jacob	31
John	31
Mary	31
Mary Eliz.	31
Michael	31
CAREASON, Mary	51
CARLEMS, Lydia	108
CARNAGEY, Jos.	31
CARNAGIE, Andrew	31
James	31
CARNAGY, James	138
CARRIER, Solomon	31
CARRYER, Henry	157
Richard	113
CARSON, Elisha	237
J. W.	237
John	227
Simon	4,237
William	4,180,227
CARTER, Catharine	174
Elizabeth	174
John A.	174
Susan	174
William A.	174
CARVER, Martin	47
CARY, Clara	233
Francis	233
CASE, Mary Ann	180
CATHEY, William	105
CATLETT, Catharine	32,77
Charles	32,77,120
Jno. A.	203
Letty	27
Susannah	32
CAUFELD, Ann Clara	242
George	242
John Adam	242
CAUFFELD, George	117
CAUFFMAN, Adaulph	32
Adolph, Jr.	32,33
Andrew	32,33
Andrew, Sen.	33
Christina	33
Daniel	32
Elizabeth	32
George	32,33
George, Jr.	33
George, Sen.	33
Jacob	32,188
John	32,33
Rebecca	33
Rosannah	32,33
CAUFMAN, Augustine	33
Leonard	107
Margaret	107
Mary Catharine	33
CAULDWELL, David	34
Elizabeth	34
John	34
Mark	34,189

CAULDWELL, Mary C.	34
Sally	34
CAVEL, John	89
CEROER, Christian J.	229
CHADDUCK, Eli	13
CHANDLER, Elizabeth	202
CHIPLEY, James	223
CHRACK, Peter	73
CHRISMAN, John	232
T. C.	179
CIBLER, Catharine	53
William	53
CIRCUS, John	34
CLAIG, Elizabeth	34
Thomas, Sen.	34
CLARK, Elias	203
CLAYTON, Amila	35
Eliza	35,214
Elizabeth	214
Emily	214
Hannah	35,214
Harriet	35,214
Julia Ann	214
Julian	35
Lucinda	34,35,214
Marinda	35,214
Nancy	34,35,214,215
Nimrod	43
Polly	35,214
Samuel	200
Susan	214
Susannah	35
William	35
CLEINDENDST, David	35
Polly	35
CLEM, Barbara	241,242
Benjamin	166
Catharine	230
Daniel	35
David	126
Elizabeth	35,44,230
Henry	35
Jacob	35
John	35,241,242
Joseph	35
Julia	35
CLEM, Michael	35,192
Phibo	166
Polly	44
Rebecca	35
CLEVINGER, Asa	36
Joseph	36
Mary	36
CLICK, Christian	47
Elizabeth	47
John	9,83
John, Jr.	47,76,126
John, Sen.	126
CLINDENMIN, David	226
CLINDENST, Isaac	106
Lidia	106
CLINE, Catharine	125,241
Henry	193,241
Jacob	34
John	117,125,238
CLINEDINST, John	25
CLIPPLE, Michael	148
Michael, Sen.	36
CLIZER, Barbara	36
David	36
John	36
Martin	36
Mathias	36
CLOCK, Dorothy	51
CLOUD, Daniel	20,37
Elizabeth	37
Hanah	37
Henry	37,151
Isaac	37
James	37
Letice	37
M.	4
Margaret	37
Mary	37
Mordecai	4,24,37
Nancy	37
Sally	37
W. M.	75
William	37
Winefret	37
CLOWER, Catharine	37
Frances	37

CLOWER, George	37	COFFMAN, David	17,29,39,
George B.	37		83,244
Henry	37	Elizabeth	29,33
Jacob B.	37	Isaac	39
John	37	Jacob	15,39,135,212
John G.	37	John	33,38,39,61,
Joseph H.	37		93,99,167,
Polly	97		188,201,244
Samuel	97,123	Joseph	38,39
COCHENOUR, Abraham	38	Magdalene	39
John	137	Maria	39
COCKEROUR, Abraham	155	Martin	39,85,96,97
COCKLEY, Mary	70	Martin, Jun.	244
COFFEHEL, Henry	187	Martin, Sen.	244
John	187	Mary	9,39,167,
COFFELD, Adam	122		188,244
Catharine	88	Mathias	33
Clara	122	Michael	39
Elizabeth	88	Michael, Sen.	39
George	122	Motlen	244
Jacob	157	Nancy	39,201
Peter	88	Peter	39,232
COFFELT, Augustine	38	Polly	232
Catharine	38	Rebecca	173
Daniel	38	Reuben	188
Elias	38	Rosanah	39
Elizabeth	38,65,95	S.	125
George	38,48,61,	Sally	232
	65,180,213	Samuel	38,39,124,170
Gertrout	95	Susanna	82
Henry	38	Wendle	110
Jacob	38,48,95,106,	William	70
	118,129,180	COFMAN, Andrew	110
John	129	Augustine	110
Mary Barbara	38	Barbara	110
Peter	110,157	Catharine	110
COFFMAN see KAUFFMAN		Catharine Eliz.	110
COFFMAN, Abraham	223,232	Daniel	110
Adam	33,110	Elizabeth	110
Andrew	38,39,70,225	Henry	110
Anna	39	John	110
Augustine	118	Wendel	110
Barbara	39	COIL, Peter	168
Benjamin	11,39	COILE, Abraham	40
Catharine	38,39,225	Betty	40
Caty	93	Catharine	40
Christina	39	Dorothy	40

COILE, Elizabeth	52	COMER, Sally		41
Henry	40	Samuel		41
Jacob	40	Sarah		40
John	40,52,145,172	Susannah		41
Peter	40	CONN, Catharina		193
Rosina	40	James		41
Samuel	99	James, Jr.		41
Susannah	40,145	John		21,72
COLLINS, William	229	Mary		41
COLVEL, Rebecca	101	R. M.		15,189,232
COLVILLE, Agnes	40	Raphael	1,36,41,90,167	
Ann	222	Raphael, Jr.		41
James	40,140	Ruth		41
John	40,140,149, 160,222	CONNER, James		42,64
		John		42
Mary	140	Rosanna		42
Samuel	40	Samuel		42
Vastine	140	Severn		42
COLWELL, Jerry	201	William		42
Susan	201	Zadock		42
COMBS, Job	81,162	CONNERY, John		164
Nancy	89	CONNOR, James		169
Sarah	179	CONRAD, Catharine		239
COMER, Adam	40	Christopher		239
Anna	41	Henry		127
Augustine	41	Jacob		219
Barbara	41	John		239
Catharine	41	COOK, Barbary		42
Christian	70	Elizabeth		211
Christopher	41	Jacob	10,42,43,188	
Daniel	40,41	John	42,71,76, 124,188	
Elizabeth	41			
Frederick	5,40	John, Sen.		42
Henry	40	Mary		42
Isaac	41	COOKE, Jacob		65
Jacob	41	COOL, Conrad		128
John	40,41	COOLEY, John		28
John, Sen.	40	COONS, Abigail		42
Jonas	40,41	Barbara		19
Julian	41	Geo. Washington		42
Magdalin	41	Isaac		42
Martin	40	Michael		42
Mary	41	Nancy		42
Mary Ann	40	Philip		19
Michael	41	William R.		42
Michael, Sen.	41	COONTZ, George		178
Philip	5,40,41	COOPER, Barbara		87

COOPER, Betsy	12	COVERSTONE, Catharine	44
David	226	Daniel	44
Elizabeth	43,113	Elizabeth	44
Elizabeth C.	43	Jacob	31,44
George	10,43,53,57,	COVNER, Frederick	47
	138,142,162,218	CRABEL, Abraham	100
George, Sen.	87	CRABELL, David	13
Henry	43	CRABILL, Abraham	45,46,
Isaac	43		75,121,225
Jacob	142	Abraham, Jr.	116
Jeremiah	12	Barbara	45
John	43,140	Benjamin	46
Joseph	43	Catharine	121
Mary	43	Christian	45,46
Mary Eliz.	43	David	46,103,121
Mary Magdalene	43	David, Sen.	45,116
Patsy	87	Elizabeth	45
Rebecca	43,87	Jacob	65
Samuel	43	Jacob, Sen.	80
William S.	43	John	45,46,210
COP, Peter	1	Jonas	45,46,218
COPELAND, Ann	99	Jonas S.	46
COPELIN, James	220	Levi	45,46,202
COPENHAFER, George	10,44	Lewis	46
Jacob	44	Madalene	46
Regina	10	Mary	46,121
Susanna	44	Obed	45,46
COPP, Andrew	44	Rachael	45,46
Ann	53	William	45
Anna Susanna	86	CRABLE, Abraham	123
Barbara	194	Jonas	36
Christian	111,210	CRAGE, Elizabeth	171
Elizabeth	53,111	John	171
Eve	53	Mary	171
George	44,86,120,225	Peter	171
Jacob	44,53	CRAIG, Frederick	228
John	26,44,194	George	168
Reuben	53	Peter	21
Samuel	44	Rebecca	168
Susan	53	CRAIK, Peter	21
Susannah	44	CRAWFORD, David	5,47,77,
William	44		142,188
CORBIN, Thomas	121	Elizabeth	77
CORDELL, John	123	James	145,147
COUNTZ, Abalon	9	William	47
Philip	9	William A.	105

CRAYBILL, David	15
Catherine	80
Elizabeth	15
John	80
CREABILL, Christian	86
Elizabeth	86
Jacob	86
CREAMER, Susanna	209
CREBILL, John	225
CRISSER, Elizabeth	47
CROCKSHAN, John	107
Margaret	107
CROFS, Rachael	173
CRON, Tane	51
Targus	51
CRONS, Tergas	1
CROOKSHANDS, John	205
CROUDSON, John	138,219
CROUS, Michael	63
CROUSDON, Jno.	147
CROUSDORF, Elizabeth	86
Philip	86
CROUSE, Catharine	47
Daniel	47
Jacob	47
Michael	47,184,203
Michael, Sen.	47
CROW, Betsy	134
William	134
CROWES, Michael, Sen.	74
CRUM, Ann	47
John	47
William	30
CRUMB, John	190
CULLERS, Daniel	144
Henry	44,121,144
John	48
Mary	48
CULLY, Betsey Ann	91
Hannah	91
CUNNINGHAM, Hannah	48
James	85,191,197
John	48
Jonathan	48
Ruth	48
Thomas	106
William	48,164
CURREY, John	188
Lidia	188
CURRIN, Edward	84
CURRY, Jane	122
CYFORD, Adam	195
DACKER, David	116
DAKE, Barbara	48
Catharine	48,88
Elizabeth	48
Eve	48
John	48,88
John, Sen.	48
DAKER, Adam	66
DANNER, Samuel	195
DANNOR, Isaac	67
DARING, Henry	101,130
DARST, Daniel	144
DARTING, Adam	48,49,241
Barbra	49
Catharine	241
Caty	49
Hannah	49
John P.	48,49
Mary	49,241
Petter	49
Philip	49
Philip G.	48,49
DAVID, Betsy	180
Catharine	180
Henry	49
Jacob	49
Magdalena	49
Maglina	49
Margareta	49
Mary	49
Michael	49
Susanna	49
William	49,129
DAVIS, Amelia	24
Caleb (Calib)	223,230
John B.	211
Robert	24
Thomas	190
DAWBENS, Maryann	203
DAY, Agnes	3
John	3
Nancy	3

DAY, Polly	216	DENNIS, William	166
DEACOT, George	107	DENNISON, Elizabeth	150
DEDERICK, John	60	Robert M.	150
DEDEWICK, Becky	49	DENTON, Abraham	51
Jacob	49	Abraham, Sen.	51
Rachael	49	Benjamin	51
Sarah	49	Christina	51
Stephen	49	George	51
DEDIMAN, George	136	Isaac	51
DEDKISON, Elizabeth	105	Jacob	51
DEEL, Adam	21	John	51
Elizabeth	21	Margaret	51
DEER, Mathias	114	Martha	51
DEETHEWECK, Stephen	172	Mary	51
DELINGER, Elizabeth	49	Phebe	51
George	135	Secvilla	51
Henry	49	DERK, Catharine	52
DELLINGER, Absalom	51	George	52
Anna	68	Jacob	52
Barbara	102	John	52
Benjamin	50	Mary Eliz.	52
Catharine	50	Simon	52
Christian	6,50,229,230	Tobino	52
Christly	53	DETERICK, Philip	82
Dorothy	50,106	DEW, George	52
Elizabeth	50,51	DICKEMAN, Thomas	60
Emanuel	50,229	DICKER, Adam	52
Eve	229	David	52
Frederick	50,51,67,68	Jacob	52
George	14,27,40,50,	John	52
	76,95,102,	DICKINSON, John C.	174
	127,229	DILLER, Levi	137
Henry	50,51	Peter	137
Jacob	33	DILLY, John	132
John	50,51,68,171	DINGES, Catharine	33
Joshua	51	Rachel	33
Magdalene	50,229	DINGLEDINE, John	81
Margaret	50,51,68,229	Philip	247
Margareta	50	DIPBOY, Abraham	168
Martin	51,106	Anna	168
Rebecca	50,51	DISERT, James	61
Rosina	50	DOBBIN, Griffeth	172
Sally	171	Rubin	186
Sybilla	50	DOBKIN, Elinor	226
DEMPSEY, Thomas	148	DODSON, Charles	52
DENISON, Edward	150	Dorcas	53
Mary	150	Elizabeth	52

DODSON, Jacob	53	DOUGHERTY, Mary	54
John	52	William	54
Joseph	53	DOUGLAS, Kathern	19
Martha	53	DOULD, Margaret	160
Mary	53	DOWNEY, D.	49,113
Peter	52,53	Darby	54
Ruth	53	Eleazer	54,113
Thomas	88	John	54
William	53	Lythia	54
DOLL see DULL		William	54,113
DOLL, Benjamin	204	DOYLE, Alexander	161,196
Elizabeth	53,204	DRUCK, George	54
Frederick	53	Henry	54,117
Jacob	18	John	54
Nicholas	53	Nicholas	54,117
Rebecca	18	Philip	54
DONNELSON, Elizabeth	127	Susanna	54
DONNER, Jacob	157	DRUMMOND, Henry	98
DOSH, Ann	87	DUCKWILLER, Thomas	222
Barbara	53	DULANEY, Charles	55
Catharine	53	Elizabeth P.	55
Christopher	9,53, 57,202	Elkanah	55
		Fortunatus F.	55
Christopher, Sen.	53	Peggy	55
Elizabeth	53,245	William	55
George	53,87,104,144, 177,233,246	William H.	55,212
		DULL see DOLL	
Henry	87	DULL, Abraham	55
John	53,57,87	Elizabeth	188
John H.C.	87	Frederick	101
Joseph	245	George	1
Magdalene	53	John Nicholas	31
Margaret	9,53	Nicholas	148
Maria Ann	87	Peter	188
Mary	53,245,246	Philip	55
Mary Catharine	87	DUNAVAN, Isaac	75
Regina	53	Katharine	75
Samuel H.	87	DUNBAR, John	151
Thomas W.L.	87	DUNDOR, John	54
William	53,87	DUNDORE, Mary	214
DOUGHERTY, Abraham	54	DUNHAM, Lewis	10
Elijah	54	DUNIVAN, Elizabeth	55
Gervao	54	Isaac	55
John	54	Mary Ann	55
Lewis	45	Thomas	55

DUNNIVAN, Isaac	121	EGAN, Rachael	58
DURST, Abraham	56	ELBERN, William	184
Abram	56	ELBON, William	217
Benjamin	58	ELIOTT, Jane	113
Isaac	56	ELSHEID, Mary Eliz.	86
Joseph	56	ELZEE, Thomas	177
Mary	56	ELZEY, William	45
Paul	56	EMETT, Lewis	70
Samuel	56	EMMONS, Rebecca	227
DURTING, Adam	99	EMSWILLER, Catharine	15,59
DUSKINS, Sarah	54	George	59
DUST, Abraham	110	Henry	59
Paul	66	Jacob	15,59
DUVALL, Sarah	41	John	15,59,133
DWYER, Thomas	235	Philip	59
DYSERT, Abraham A.	56	ERISMAN, Elizabeth	59
Catharine	56	Jacob	59
Cornelius	121	ERVINE, F. Milton	43
Elizabeth	121	ERWIN, Barbara	60
James	56	Christina	60
Mary	56	Elizabeth	60
EBERLY, Catharine	45,57	Eve	60
Christina	57	George	60
Daniel	9,45,56,57,101	John	60
Elizabeth	56,57	John E.	61
George	56,57,87	Joseph	60
Isaac	56	Magdaline	60
Jacob	45,46,56,57	Philip	60
Jeremiah	9,45,57	ESHELMAN, Adam	60,72
John Jacob	57	Anna	60
Joseph	56	Barbara	60
Mary	56	Elizabeth	60
Mary Eliz.	57	Katharine	60
P.F.	209	Magdalene	60
Philip	101	Peter	60,104
Sarah	56	Rebecca	60
Susan	56,101	Samuel	60
EDGILL, Thomas	226	Sarah	60
EDMONDS, Elias	58	Tobias	60,72,212
Sarah	58	ESTEP, Rosanah	183
EFFINGER, Barbara	58	William	183
John	55,127,176	EUMAN, Christian	76
John I.,Sen.	58	EVANS, Aaron	93
Michael	58,184,212	Betsy	60
Peter	58	Cloeve	60
Samuel	58	David	60
William	58	Elijah	60

EVANS, Eliza	97		FANSLER, Barbara	61
Hezekiah	60		Frederick	61,106
James	60		Margaret	61
Jeremiah	60		Peter	61
Jesse	60		FARRA, J. W.	184
John	127		Jacob	186
Jonathan	100		John	102
Joseph	17,36,39, 41,93,173		John W.	144,245
			Polly	102
Margot	60		W. D.	143,207
Margretha	127		Washington	123
Mary	60		Whiting D.	154
Mary Ann	60		FARTICK, Andrew	62
Samuel	60		Jacob	62
Susanna	60		Nicholas	62
William	60		FASMER, Mathew	144
EVENSOB, Mary	201		FATELY, David	53
EVEY, Christnah	59		FAUBER, Abraham	62,204
John	59		Christian	62
EWING, John	33,169		Elizabeth	62
Margaret	33		Jacob	62
EYSTER, William	104		John	62
FADELEY, Elizabeth	33		Joseph	62
Hannah	38		Peter	62
FADELY, Augustine	61		FAUNTEROY, Eliza B.	23
David	33,61		Joseph M.	23
Elizabeth	61		FAUNTTEROY, Matilda	237
Eli	61		FAWSETT, Joseph	175
Hetty	61		FEAGEL, Susanny	100
Isaac	51		FEATER, Michael	246
Jackson	61		FEATHER, George	38,108, 118,157,161, 170,185,203,217
Kenas	61			
Leah	51			
Lorenzo	61		FEATLY, Jonathan	157
Marelean	33		FECKLEY, Anna	63
Mary Ann	61		George, Jr.	63
Wm. Henry	61		George, Sen.	63
FADLEY, David	118		FEDLE, David	118
Elizabeth	118		FEDLEY, Elizabeth	133
Jonathan	118		Michael	133
Lewis	121		FEDTZER, Andrew	176
Mary	118		FEITER, Michael	231
FAIRFAX, Thomas Lord	83, 181		FELLER, Jacob G.	75
			Johnannes	78

FELLER, Samuel G.	108	FINKS, Frances	236
William G.	108	Joel	236
Ulrich	78	FINLEY, James, Sen.	64
FELLSMIRE, Abraham	63	Samuel C.	18
Catharina	63	FINLY, Henry	114
Elizabeth	63	FINTER, Andrew	88
John	63	Margaret	88
Modelena	63	FISH, Richard	24
Susannah	63	William	203
FELMOYERS, John	52,63	FISHER, Adam	64
FELTZ, George, Jr.	21	Ann	80
FELZER, Jackman	127	Anna	64,65
FERGERSON, Robert	24	Anna Maria	65
FERGUSON, Mary E.	97	Barbara	15,64
FERNLER, Mary Barbara	21	Charles	58,77,109,
Peter	21		115,210
FERNSLER, Barbara	88	Christina	64
Didrick	63	David	64
Elisa Margaret	63	Elias	55
Frederick	63,88	George	15,34,64,80
Henry	63	George, Sen.	64
Peter	63	Jacob	64,65,80,209
William	63	Jacob, Sen.	65
FERNTZLER, William	106	John	64
FESELL, John	63	Martin	64
Sabastian	63	Mary	80
FETZER, Catharine	64	Rebecca	80
David	64	Rachael	64
Eliza	64	Samuel	64
Elizabeth	71,231	Sarah	64
Frederick	71	William	64
George	53,64,241	FITCH, Polly	134
James	55	William	134
Joachino	231	FITZER, Mary	65
John	64	Reuben	65
Joseph	78	FLEMINGS, John	165
Lydia	64	FLETCHER, George	236
Magdalene	64,241	John	58
Mary	64	Rebecca	58
Mary Ann	64	FLORA, Susannah	22
Samuel	64,65,67	FOBY, John	136
Susannah	64	John, Jr.	136
William	64	FOGELSONG, Catharine	65
FEW, Samuel	127	Jacob	65
FILSMOYER, Michael	138	FOLAND, Henry	59
FILSMOYERS, George	174	John	59

FOLAND, Mary	59
FOLEY, James M.	245
S.	28
Selby	187
FOLK, Sarah	98
FOLTZ see FULTZ, VOLTZ	
FOLTZ, B.	210
Bolthis	65
Catharine	66
Christina	66,230
Daniel	65,66
Elizabeth	66,132
Fred.	66
George	65
Harrison	246
Isaac	94
Jacob	137
John	2,65,66,68, 69,168,169,170,190
John Martin	66
Jonas	53
Joseph	65
Joshua	69,94,121
Magdaline	59,66
Margarett	66,170
Martin	59,155
Mary	168,169
Maryann	66
Peter	66,76
Reuben	137
Rosianna	66
FORD, Dabny	40
FORRER, Christian	41,118
Henry	41
Samuel	41,118,134
FORSTER, Barbara	66
Catharine	66
Elizabeth	66
George	66
John	66
FOSTER, Robert H.	58
FOUSH, Catherina	66
FOUST, Jacob	66
Ludwig	66
Margrate	66
Philip	66
FOUT, Adam	11
Peggy	11
FOVER, Christian	59,187
Samuel	59
FOX, Frederick	109,242
Peter	96
FRANK, Catharine S.	139
FRANTZ, John	232
FRANZ, Henry	132
FRAVEL, Aaron	38
Abraham	77,184
Abram	199
Alice	67
Anna	67
Benjamin	115,146
Eli	67
Elizabeth	67,146
Elsy	67
George	67,131,176,242
Henry	51,71,101,120
Henry, Jr.	101
Henry, 4th	67
Jacob	51,67,134, 141,170
James	24
James G.	165,182
Jonathan	50,51,67,240
Joseph	64,67
Mary	67,167
Milly	134
Polly	51
Rebecca	67
Samuel	67,167
William	67
FRAVELE, Benjamin	68
George	68
Henry	68
Henry, Sen.	68
Jacob	68
Jonathan	68
Joseph	68
Mary	68
FRAVILL, Henry	48
FRAVELL, George	123
FREE, Cornelius	4
FREES, Eave	96

FRENCH, Elizabeth	42	FRYE, Joseph, Sen.	69
FRICK, William	176	Leah	69
FRISTOE, James	13	Magdalena	69
John	220	Mary	69
FRUASE, Elizabeth	96	Michael	69
FRY, Catharine	133	Phelpina	69
Caty	132	Philbena	168
Christina	68,133,193	Philip	69
Dianna	68	Rebecca	70
Edward M.	142	Samuel	60,69
Elizabeth	14,142	Sarah	70
Frainey	14	Will	70
Frederick	193	William	9,69
George	68	FULTZ see FOLTZ,VOLTZ	
Hanson	68	FULTZ, Daniel	70
Henry	47,68,133,198	Elizabeth	104,133
Jacob	47,133,193	Frederick	70
John	14,68,133	John	70,87,173
Leah	56	Joseph	53
Lidia	14	Joshua	229
Lydia	68	Joshua, Jr.	93,108,133
Magdelene	132,170	Martin	70
Mary	132,133	FUNK, Abraham	71
Michael	132	Adam	71,107
Moses	68	Barbara	71
Peter	14	Barbary	71
Philbena	68	Caroline	233
Philip	51,56	Catharine	71,173
Rebecca	68	Caty	71
Samuel	142	Dorothy	71
William	68,132	Elizabeth Ann	91
FRYE, Abraham	70	Elizabeth	71
Absalom	69	Flora	71
Ann	70	Harvey	71
Anna	69	Henry	71
Benjamin	69,70	Isaac	71,121,173,
Catharine	70		217,233
Christina	69	Jacob	47,71,111,151,
Elijah	69		195,205,217
Elizabeth	9,60,70	Jacob, Jr.	233
George	69	Jacob, Sen.	233
Henry	69,133,168	John	71
Jacob	69,70	Joseph	91,217
John	69,70,168	Judith	71
John A.	70,84	Magdalene	71
Joseph	69,70	Mary	71

FUNK, Noah	71	FUNKHOUSER, Louisa A.	154
Obed	71	Magdalene	71
Pricilla	233	Margaret	75,212
Rebecca	121,233	Margretha	242
Samuel	91,217	Maria	72
FUNKHOUSER, Abraham	25,	Martha	75
	69,71,72,73,	Martin	72
	74,171,196	Mary	71,73,74,141,203
Absalom	72	Mary H.	246
Andrew	73,150,246	Mary Harriet	150
Ann	71,101	Milton	75
Anna	73	Noah	101
Anthony	60,72,194	Peggy	73
Barbara	16,71,72,73,	Philip	141
	74,130,177,180	Polly	168
Barbary	73	Rebecca	168
Betty	169	Rachael	72
Catharine	72,171	Regina	71
Caty	227	Samuel	18,71,154
Christian	72,74,141,	Sarah	75,194
	168,242	Solomon	72
Christina	74,180	Susannah	74
Daniel	71,72,73,74	William	75,168
David	18,71,72,73,74,	William D.	73
	75,154,180,227	FURNELL, Alexander	232
Dorotha (Dorothy)	74,	Reubin	232
	75,111	GABLE, Abraham	75
Eliza	75	Daniel	75
Elizabeth	18,19,73,	Elizabeth	75
	74,154	Henry	75
Eva	141	Peter	75
Flora	18	Polly	75
Franey	74	Rachael	75
George	73,74,138,	Sarah	75
	171,177,180	GABRIEL, Margaret	160
Henry	75	GAINES, Aaron	159
Isaac	38,73,75,168,218	Benjamin	159
Jacob	14,16,26,71,	Cornelius	197
	73,74,75,88,90,	Magdalena	159
	111,171,196,212	GANDER, Anne	76
Jacob, Sen.	74	George	40,76,194
Joel	73	Henry	76
John	72,74,75	John	76
John, Sen.	71	Mary	139
Katharina	75	GANDY, Nancy M.	154
Levi	72,173	GANZ, George	238

273

GARBER, Abraham	76	GEIB, John		117
Anna	76	GENLING, Andrew		93
Barbara	76	GEORGE, John		8
Catharine	76	Thomas		153
Daniel	76,149	GERBER, Jacob		126
Elizabeth	76	Martin		181
Jacob	76,149,150,	GETS, Barbara		125
	152,184,197	GETZ, Bernard		3,247
John	76	David		247
John, Sen.	76	John		215
Joseph	76	Moses		163
Magdalene	76	GEYER, Abraham		78
Martin	76,125,184	Andrew		78
Rebecca	76	Catharine		78
Samuel	76	David		78
GARDNER, Samuel	34,87,	Elizabeth		78
	100,217,218	George		78
GARRETT, Christina	75	Gertrout		78
GARY, Joseph	197	Henry		78
GATEWOOD, Chaney	76	Jacob		78
Charles	76	John		78,131
J.	60	Madalene		78
John	32,77	GIBBONS, Isaac		77
Louisiana	237	GIBLER, Elizabeth		78
Philip	23,32,77	John		42,78,123
Susanna	77	Joseph		78
W.	43	Magdalena		78
Wright	76,211	Magdalin		42
GAUTZER, George	52	Maria		78
GAW, Barbara	77,181	Philip		78,98
Jacob R.	77,105	Sally		78
John	22,77,147,	Susanna		78
	184,192	William		78
Joseph	77	GILHAM, William		173
Polly	147	GILL, Harrison		92
Rebecca	77	John		176
Robert	22,68,77,95,	Sarah		92
	98,99,181	GILLOCK, Hannah		79
Robert, Jr.	77	John		79
GEEDING, Henry	86	GISTERT, Christopher		79
Maria	86	Eva Rosina		79
GEFFELER, Barbara	78	Rosina		79
Catharina	78	GLEISER, Mathias		124
Christian	78	GLENN, George D.		79
Eva	78	John		79
Joseph	78	GLICK, John		181,248
Magdalena	78	GOAR, Ann		79
Ulrich	78	Catharine		79

GOAR, Eleanor	79	GODFREY, John	40
Henry	79	GOETZ, Bernard	169,197
Isaac	79	Christina	88
John	79	David	171
Lydia Eliz.	79	Magdalene	171
Margaret	79	Maria	171
Robert	79	Martin	197
Sarrah	79	Philip	88
GOARE, Isaac	223	GOLLADAY, Ann	81
GOCHENOUR, Abraham	80,81, 86,100,116,159	Christina	81
Anna	81	Daniel	48,81
Barbara	81,241	David	46,55,81
Catharine	80,116, 141,159	Elizabeth	81
		Jacob	12,81,195
Christian	81	Jacob, Sen.	81
Christina	80,86	John	81
Daniel	80,81	Joseph	81
Eliza	81	Magdaline	81
Elizabeth	80,81,191	Mary	12,81
Emanuel	80	Rebecca	81
Franey	194	Susannah	81
Henry	64,80,81,126, 191,241	GOLLAGHER, Mary	247
		Thomas	247
Jacob	80,81,83,133, 141,237	GOLLEDAY, Rebecca	104
		GOOD, Abraham	82,83,95,167
Jacob, Sen.	66,80	Barbara	83
James Harvey	116	Benjamin	83
John	80,81,191, 194,209	Elizabeth	82,83,168
		Esther	83
John, Sen.	81	Frances	82
John Henry	116	Jacob	82,83,89,123, 125,152,184, 245,246
Jonathan	81,194		
Joseph	38,80,81,83, 117,159		
		John	44,69,82
Katharine	194	Mary	62,82,83,245
Levy	81	Molly	69
Magdalene	80	Peter	159
Mary	80,81	Philip	168
Rachael	81	Samuel	62,82,113
Sally	141	Susanna	83
Samuel	80,116	William	11,82,83,95,126
Sarah	81	GOODING, Jean	113
Shem	80	William	113
William	55	GOODNIGHT, Christian	11
		Susanna	11

GOODRICK, Rebecca	186	GREEN, Catharine	217
GORDEN, Jane	83	Eliza	217
William	83	Esther	217
GORDON, Alexander	152	GREENWOOD, H. F.	55
Charles	28	Henry	214
GORE, Eliza	97	GREIGSBY, Benjamin	144
David	60	GRIFFEN, Daniel	1
Isaac	198,249	GRIFFITH, Cahtarine	84
GORY, Samuel	107	Daniel	84
GOUR, Catharine	63	David	84
GRABIL, Abraham	83	Elanor	84
Anna	159	Elizabeth	84
Barbara	83	Ester	84
Christian	83	John, Sen.	84
Christina	83	Mary	13,84
Daniel	83	Nancy	84
Franecy	83	Rachael	84
George	159	Sally	84
Henry	83	Samuel	84
Jacob	83	William	84
Mary	83	GRIFFY, David	156
GRABILL, Anna	83	William	156
Ephraim	24	GRIKENBERGER, Tekla	104
Jacob	83	GRIM, Philip	43
John	83	GRIMES, Benjamin	84
Margaret	83	Betty	84
GRAFF, Barbary	34	Minca	84
GRANDEL, Godfrey	12	Nancy	84
GRANDSTAF, George	177	Rose	84
Polly	177	Samuel	84
GRANDSTAFF, Barbara	84	GROCK, Henry	56
Catharine	56	GROVE, Ann	172
Elizabeth	129	Catharine	98
George	28,70,78,84, 86,173,226	Christian	97,187
		Daniel	85
George, Sen.	84	David	221
John	78	Frainey	85
Philip	78,84,86,100	Hannah	133
GRANT, Daniel	52	Jacob	122,147,225
GRAY, Henry H.	237	John	211
James M.	97	Joseph	85
Minerva M.	97	Mark	28
Sarah	235	Mary	34,192
GREABILL, Christian	104	Susannah	85
David	104	GROVES, Anne	85

GROVES, Barbary	85	HAISEY, David	87
Catey	85	Elizabeth	87
Christian	85	Frederick	87
David	85	Henry	87
Elizabeth	38	John	87
Ester	85	Joseph	87
Jacob	138,238	Rosannah	70,87
John	85	HALL, Bernard	153
Machdelene	85	John	58,88
Mary Eliz.	85	Jonathan	48,203
Samuel	85	Mary	48
Sarah	238	Rebekah	37
Susanna	85	Thomas	72,203
GRUBB, William	106	HALLER see HOLLAR,HOLLER	
GRUBBS, Cokey	185	HALLER, Barbara	88,118
GRUBS, George	85	Elizabeth	173
GUINN, Emily L.	199	Henry	88
GUMMER, James	230	John	118
GUTH, Jacob	90	Magdalena	48
GUYGER, Jacob	85	Peter	48,66,88
Mary	85	HALLEY, John	58
GYER, John	98	Nancy	58
GYGER, Catharine	161	HALLY, Benjamin	137
John	161	HALTIMAN, Caty	11
HAAS, Catharina	86	Chinley	88
Christina	86	Daniel	11,88
Elizabeth	105	Elizabeth	88
Jacob	86	Esther	88
John	52,83,86,100	Jacob	11,88
John, Sen.	86	John	88
Mary	173	Rachael	11
Michael	7,216,246	Stufle	88
Philip	86,173,187	HAMBLETON, Henry	69
HAASTENT, John	28	HAMILTON, John	56
HACKNEY, Daniel	4	HAMMAN, Jacob	63
HAHN, George	86	Jacob, Jr.	63
Henry	86	John	60
Henry Christopher	87	Peter	10
Jacob	62,86,114,240	HAMMON, Aaron	98
John	86	Anna	111
John, Sen.	36,44	Barbara	89
Maria Catharine	86	Elias	89
Maria Magdalene	87	Flora	89
Rosina	240	George	160,168
HAIRES, Betty	1	Jacob	111
HAISEY, Christian	70,87	John	63,70,89,217
Daniel	87	Lawrence	89

HAMMON, Lidia	168	HARRIS, Sutton I.	143, 150,199
Molly	70	William	28,35,79
Rebecca	89	HARRISON, George	31
Sarah	89	HARROW, David	90
Thomas	194	Henry	90
HAMNER, Elizabeth	245	John	90,129
Franklin	245	Mary	90
HAMPTON, Thomas C.	216	Sarah	28
HANBACK, Mary	109	HASLIP, Sarah	97
HANCOCK, Elizabeth	243	HAUCK, Charles	233
John	114	Clara	233
William	243	Mary	233
HANNEGAN, Michael	89	HAUN, Christina	109
Peggy	89	Jacob	109,212
HARDEIN, Jacob	14	John	64,109,212,213
HARDING, George	4,89	HAUS, Catharine	123
Henry	4,89	John	123
Henry, Jr.	89	HAWKINS, Aaron	1,91,92
Henry, Sen.	89	Anna	91
John	4	Benjamin	2,231
Nicholas	89	Christenah	183
Willmoth	89	Christina	92
HARETT, Sarah	145	Edith Catharine	91
HARMAN, Benjamin	81,92, 101,141	Elizabeth	91
		Eliz. Mary	91
HARMON, Susan	169	James	91,92,151
HARNS, Maria Ann	90	Joseph	91,161
Sutton I.	90	Rebecca	91
HARPINE, Abraham	90,128, 153,158	Rhesa A.	91,244
		Samuel 1,91,161,188,244	
Catharine	90	Sarah	91,92
Elizabeth	90	Sarah Ann	91
Jonathan	131,133, 149,152	HAWLEY, John	7
		Nancy	7
Magdalene	90	HAWN, Christopher	71
Margaret	90	George	216
Mary	90	Henry	53,57
Philip	90,152,153,158	Jacob	92
Susanna	90,133	John	232
HARR, John	205,206	Leah	108
Simon	57,111,148, 205,206	Sarah	108
		HAY, Alexander	92,134
Susanna	205	Barbara	92
HARRIS, Gillan	238	David	92,207
Oliver	42		

HAY, Elizabeth	92
John	92,207
Mary	92
Peter	92
Reuben	92
Susannah	92
HAYMAN, Michael	112
HAYNES, John	127
John F.	43
HAZEL, Ann	210
Margaret	210
HEASTAND, Barbara	93
Henry	93
Peter	93
Peter, Sen.	93
HEASTANT, Jacob	28
John	245
Peter	28,187
HEATWALD, Barbara	59
Christian	59
HEBNER, John, Sen.	241
HEESTANT, Barbara	93
Daniel	93
Henry	93
Jacob	93
Magdalene	93
Peter	93
HEFS see HESS	
HEFS, Anna	183
John Martin	183
Mary	183
Mary Eliz.	183
Samuel	183
William	183
HEFSLER, Ulry	78
HEGAS, Henry	93
HEINKLE, Benjamin	115
HEISE, Anna Maria	86
John	86
HEISEY, Jonathan	204
Sarah	204
HEISHELL, Adam	3
HELLER, Jeremiah	98
John, Jr.	225
Moritz	174
Ulrick	225

HELMICK, John	22
Nicholas	179
HELMS, William	84
HELSEL, Charles	14
HELSLE, Jacob	181
HELSLEY, Christian	94
Daniel	93
Elizabeth	93
Geo. Jacob	93,94
Henry	93,94
Jacob	93,94
Jacob, Jr.	229
Joseph	94
Mary	94
Nicholas	5,93,94
Peter	5,94,180
Philip	5,93,94
Rebecca	93,94
Rosina	93,94,229
Sebilla	93
HELSLY, Geo. Jacob	14
HELSY, John	84
Magdalene	84
HELZEL, Catharine	106
Charles	117
Peter	106
HEMLIN, Michael	215
HEMP, Casper	65
HENDERSON, Margaret	150
William	150
HENDREN, Nancy	37
HENKEL, Helen A. M.	94
Rebecca	94
Samuel	235
Samuel G.	94,167
Silon H.	94
Siram P.	94
Solomon	94
Solomon D.	94,235
Solon P. C.	94
HENKINS, George	224
Polly	224
HENLINE, John	95
Michael	95,185
HENRY, Elizabeth	95
Mary	95

HENRY, Sarah	95	HICKLE, Anna	169
Steward	95	C.	159,171
Susanna	95	Catharine	98
William	95	Christopher	38,98,169
HENSON, William	54	Devault	98
HENTON, George	169	Elizabeth	98,99
Thomas	115	George	98,231
HEP, Mary	184	Hannah	199
HEPNER, Anna	95	Henry	98
Barbara	8	Jacob	98
George	8,95	John	98
John	95	Mary	231
HERBAUGH, Hennah	95	Samuel	98
Isaac	95	Sarah	98
Peter	95	Stephen	72,98
HERGELROLE, Henry	195	HICKMAN, Benjamin	147
HERSHBERGER, Abraham	96	Cossandra	147
Anna	96,97	John	105,137
Barbara	96	Rebecca	7,128
Christian	29,96	Thomas	7,137
Daniel	96	HIGGINS, Henry	93
David	96,97	HILBERT, Bernard	99
Elizabeth	96	George	99
Emanuel	97	Margaret	99
Henry	96,110	Michael	99
Isaac	96,97,115,151	HILL, John N.	143,182
Jacob	9,97,100,162	Lucey	237
John	96,97	Mary	6
Joseph	97	HIMER, Matlener	28
Maria	96	HINER, Herbert	140
Mary	96	HINES, Emanuel	5
Molly	96	HINGER, J. E.	55
Samuel	96,97	HINKINS, George	173
Susanna	96	Jacob	173
William	220	Rachael	173
HESLOP, Sarah	97	HINKLE, Christopher	153
HESS, Abraham	97,126	Eve	249
John	97	HINTON, Ann	99
Margaret	97	George	99
Mary	97	Hannah	99
Peter	97	Thomas	99
HESTANT, Peter	221	HISCOCK, Peris	108
HETER, Christina	98	HISER, Anna Maria	99
John	98	Catharina	99
HETZELE, Henry	61	Elizabeth	99

HISER, Eve	99
Henry	99,134
Jacob	100
Susanna	100
HISEY, Daniel	237
Frederick	93
John	170
HISY, Abram	100
Catharina	100
Christina	100
Elizabeth	100
Jacob	100
John	100
Jonathan	100
Joseph	100
Mary	100
Maryann	100
HITE, Abraham	100
Alexander	9,19,36,47,49 53,57,100,102, 120,123,138,147, 162,172,183,195, 209,210,219, 228,239
Andrew	100
Ann	100
Catharine	162
Daniel	100
Daniel, Sen.	100
David	100
Elizabeth	100
Frederick	100,101,228
Isaac	145
Jacob	36,100,101
Joist	239
Joseph	100
Margaret	100
Mary	101
W.	183
HOAK, Adam	35
Jacob	199
HOAN, George	25
HOCKMAN, Abraham	12,46,47, 101,102,103, 171,209
HOCKMAN, Anna	101,104
Anna Maria	102
Barbara	47,101,103
Barbary	107
Benjamin	24,101,107
Catharine	15,47,101, 102,103
Christena	102,103
Christian	45,101, 102,103
Christina	146
Elizabeth	12,47,101, 102,103,171
Franny	156
George	45,102,103,104
Henry	8,12,15,71, 75,101,102, 103,149,179,193
Henry, Jr.	5
Isaac	102
Jacob	7,96,102,103
John	26,96,102,103, 104,124,209
Joseph	7,67,102
Katherine	12,103
Lidia	47
Magdalene	103
Mary	103,141
Noel	141
Obed	190
Peter	62,82,102, 103,104,116,178
Rebecca	47,178
Reuben	12
Rudolph	101
Samuel	102
Sarah (Sara)	47,101,102
Ulrick	15
HOFFMAN see HUFFMAN	
HOFFMAN, A.	97
Absalom	201
Andrew	35,52,71, 104,186,226
Anna	184
Anne	104

HOFFMAN, Barbara	104	HOLLER, Leah		48
Catharine	16	Mary		106
Christian	10,81,104	Peter		106,110
Christina	81	Polly		106
Daniel	104,234	William		106
David	104	HOLLINGSWORTH, Abraham		245
Elizabeth	201,239	HOLMES, Edmond		8
Frederick	15	James		76
George	3,104	John		8
Henry	104	Sarah		79
Isaac	46	William		76
Jeremiah	104	HOLTZMAN, Frederick		79
John	16,105,239	HOLVAH, Catharine		107
Lewis	104	Conrad		107
Mary	10,77,104,105	George		107
Mathias	104	John		107
Nimrod	16	HOMER, Margaret		151
Peter	53,56,105	Sarah		151
Philip	44	HOMMON, Barbara		107
Robert M. G.	105	Catharine		107
Sarah	234	Elizabeth		107
HOLEMAN, Andrew	105	Eve		107
Daniel	105	George		107
Jacob	21,56,105	John		107
Jacob H.	105	Judith		107
Margaret	105	Maria		107
Mary Ann	105	Susannah		107
Rachael	105	Thomas		107
HOLKER, Adam	63,90	HOOP, Casper		163
Mary	90	John		107
HOLLAR, Catharine	94	Paulser		56
Henry, Jr.	94	Peter		107
Jacob	61	Susannah		107
HOLLER, Abraham	106	HOOVER, Ann		196
Alexander	106	Balzer		107,112
Augustine	48,106	Catharine		107,186
Barbary	33	Christina		10
Catharine	106	Elizabeth		68
David	106	Jacob		107,215
Elias	106	John		10,68,101,107
Elizabeth	106	Margarett		107
Henry	106	Reuben		186
Henry, Sen.	106	William		107
Isaac	106	HOPEWELL, Joseph		146,151
Jacob	106	Samuel		4,34
John	106	HOPEWOOD, Magdalin		100
Joseph	106	HOPKINS, Mary S.		237

HORDE, Magdalena	223	HOTTLE, Daniel	31,130	
HORN, Benjamin	78	George	95	
Christian	243	Jacob, Jr.	31	
Elizabeth	78	Lewis	26	
HORSAFLUKE, Henry	239	Mildred	26	
HOSHOUR, Catharine	25	HOTZENBELLER, Henry	239	
Elizabeth	108	HOUBURT, Cataron	109	
George	108	Catharine	109	
Harriet	25	John	109	
Henry	108,229	Nicholas	109	
Henry, Sen.	108	Peter	109	
Jacob	108	HOUCK, Catharine	101	
John	108	HOUDESHELL, Barbara	109	
Joseph	108	George	109	
Julianah	229	John	109	
Lidia	108	Laurence	109	
Peter	25,108,110,229	Michael	109	
Philip	108	HOUSDON, Benjamin	109	
Rebecca	25	Edmon	109	
Samuel	25,108,129	James	109	
Susannah	229	Nancy	109	
HOSLER, George	166	Polly	109	
Rebecka	166	HOUSE, George	86	
HOTSINPILLER, Eliz.	107	Isaac	86	
Jacob	107	Jacob	86	
HOTTEL, Andrew	112	John	86	
Anna	108	Jonathan	86	
Barbara	53	Polly	86	
Catharine	112	Rebecca	86	
Christina	32,33	HOUSEMAN, George, Jr.	143	
Daniel	109,112,115, 141,240	HOUSER, Ann	110	
Dorotha	112	Elizabeth	110,201	
Elizabeth	225	Henry	110	
George	10,33,108, 112,135	Jacob	110	
Henry	14,112,118	Joseph	117	
Jacob	82,108,112	Leah	65	
Jacob, Jr.	80	Magdalene	110	
John	112,225	Martin	110	
Joseph	53	Mary	110	
Kitty	108	Peter	65	
Mary	112	HOUSERMAN, George, Jr.	143	
Mary Magdalena	115	HOUSHOUR, Henry	110	
Rebecca	108,112	Joseph	110	
Rosina	109	Julias	110	
Samuel	108	Peter	110	
William	108,112	HOUTS, Christopher	107	
		Susanna	107	
		HOUTZ, Catharine Eliz.	110	
		Wendel	110	

HOWBERT, Elizabeth	80	HUDSON, Nancy	112
George	80	Richard	38,112,148
Jacob	134	Sarah	112
Margaret	134	Thomas	94,160
HOWDESHALL, Susannah	249	HUFFMAN see HOFFMAN	
HOWEY, Joseph	172	HUFFMAN, Andrew	186
HOY, Catharina	110	Christian	216
Elizabeth	162	Elizabeth	201
Hannah	114	Frederick	159
John	30,110,114,155	Frederick, Jr.	223
Zahariah	162	Hannah	201
HUBER, Solome	76	Isaac	201
HUDDEL, Charles	112	John	31,201,248
Elizabeth	112	Mary	93
Jacob	112	Philip	54,138
John	112	William	201
HUDDELL, Henry	112	HUFMAN, Joromya	137
HUDDLE, Ann	111	Magdalene	137
Barbara	111	Philip	123
Charles	111	HUGES, Richard	229
Conrad	111	HULL, Catharine	193
Daniel	15,99,111,130	Peter	193
David	111	HULVA, Alexander	113
Elizabeth	111,112	Caty Ann	113
Eve	99	Helenah	113
George	15,111,112,120	HULVEY, John	184
Gideon	111	HUMES, Ann	113
Henry	111,112,217	Thomas	113
Jacob	111,148	HUMPSTON, Margaret	214
Jacob, Jr.	20	HUMSTON, Nathaniel	70,72
Jacob, Sen.	112	HUNNEHOUSER, John	174
John	111,112	HUNSBERGER, John	232
Joseph	111	HUNSTON, Edward	113
Magdalene	111	Edward, Sen.	113
Margaret	111	John	113
Mary	15,111	Lucy	113
Mary Eliz.	111	Mary W.	113
Samuel	12	Matilda	113
Solomon	111	Nathaniel Q.	113
Susannah	111	Thomas	113
HUDSON, Barbara	112	HUP, Abraham	167
Benjamin	68,99,112	Balzer	9
Dorothy	94,112	Casper	214
Elizabeth	112	Elizabeth	92
Esther	122	Frances	92
Jacob	112	John	214
		Samuel	214

HUPP, Benjamin	162
Catharine	159
Emanuel	159
G. A.	174
George	46,56,206,214
	217,219
George F.	13,160,223,233
Lydia	162
M.	66
Martin	13,80,114,119,
	206,237
Mary	125,159
Philip	248
Samuel	125,159
HURBAUGH, Ruth	42
HURBOUGH, Isaac	75,135
Peter	19,134
Polly	135
HURN, Isaac	87,105,209
Mary Ann	87
Sarah	101
HURST, John	114
Judith	114
William	114
HUTCHINSON, George	112
HUTCHISON, John	142
Mary	112
HUVER, David	173
Rebecca	173
HYDE, Joseph	204
HYSE, Christian	66
INABNET, Jacob	212
Jacob, Jr.	212
Joseph	212
IRELAND, Isabella	160
IRWIN, Alfred	77
Joseph	6,11,35,50,
	64,67,103,
	147,181
Thomas A.	34
JACKMAN, John	234
Richard	234
JACOB, Anne T.	114
Catharine	114
Daniel	114
Frantz	114
JACOB, Jacob	114
Julianna	114
Magdelene	114
Susannah	114
JACOBS, Catharine	58,114
David	114
Dilly	114
Jacob	58,114,209
John	114
Julias	114
JAMES, Mary	54
Joseph	117
JAMESON, Robert	70
JAMISON, Robert	215
JANNY, John	226
JAY, Joseph	17
JEFFRIES, Emanuel	97
JENKINS, Ann	114
Elizabeth	114
Jane	114
Jean	114
Josiah	114
Margaret	114
Samuel	114
Sarah	114
Thomas	114
JENNINGS, Joshua	96
William	4,71,151
William, Jr.	4
JOB, Enoch	245
Jamina	164
JOBB, Elizabeth	156
JOHNSON, John	64,71
Susannah	64
JOHNSTON, James	131
Samuel	35
Thomas	4
JOHNSTONE, Betty	245
JONES, Abraham	152
Ann	97,237
Elizabeth	115
Evan	99,107
Gabriel	200
George	41
John	132,152,200
Margaret	220

JONES, Mary Ann	165	KACKLEY, Joseph	224
Matilda I.	200	KAGEY, Abraham	38,80,
Nancy	243		117,159
Philip	87	Anna	117
Philip C.	236,237	Barbara	116
Thomas	96,220	Catharine	116,159
Whorton	13,243	Christian	116,159
William	115	Daniel	116
JORDAN, Barbara	68	David	117,150
Benjamin	115	Elizabeth	116,117
Catharine	115	Henry	25,116,117
Charles	115	Isaac	116
David	14,16,50,52,78,	Jacob	25,45,99
	86,96,115,122,	Jacob R.	116
	123,127,131,145,	John	117,247
	149,157,175,178,	John, Sen.	34
	202,230,233,	John R.	117
	242,246	Martin	116
David, Jr.	186	Mary	45,116
David, Sen.	115	Peter	117
E. R.	1	Samuel	116
Elizabeth	115	KAGY, Abraham	117,158,159
Eve Margaretha	115	Ann	117
Henry	80	Barbara	117
John	68,114,115,156	Christian	117,184
Lewis	115	Elizabeth	117
Margareth	115	Eve	184
Rebecca	80	Henry	56,117,184
Reuben	17	Henry, Sen.	117
Sarah	186	Isaac	117,159
Theodiocus	115	Jacob	117,184
JORDINE, Jeremiah	115	John	47,117,126,
Rosey	115		181,197
Theodiocus	115	Martin	117,234
JOSEPH, Jackson	3	Rudolph	117,159
JUDD, Ann	76	KANN, John	73
Barbara	93	KAUFFELD, Clara	117
Franey	76	George	117
John	76	Jacob	117
Michael	28	John Adam	117
Peirson (Person)	93,130	Margaret	117
JUDY, Abraham	116	KAUFFMAN, Ann	47
Jacob	172,216	Andrew	88
Katharina	116	Barbara	118

KAUFFMAN, Benjamin	47	KEENER, David	120
Christoph	88	Elizabeth	119
Daniel	118	Ulrick	185
David	39,42	KEFFER, John	25,37,210
John B.	42	Mary	231
Martin	96	Nicholas	119,193
Mary	47	Polly	119
KAUFMAN, Adam	118	KEFFERRY, Jeremiah	146
Anna	139	KEIL, Philip	20
Augustine	118	Rachael	20
Barbara	118,139	William	149
Daniel	222	KEISTER, Adam	57,119, 216,217
David	118,207		
Dorotha	222	Catharine	119
Elizabeth	118	KELLAR, Abram	120
Fidiny	118	Elizabeth	120
Frances	139	John	120
Jacob	118	Jose	120
John	118,160,207	Joseph	120
Katharine	118	Rachael	120
Martin	118,139	William	120
Mary	118	KELLER, Abraham	108,142
Mary Catharine	118	Ann	120
Mathias	118	Barbara	120,121
Nancy	118	Barbary	120
Samuel	118	Catharine	121
Susannah	118	Elizabeth	120,192
KEAGY, Anna	119	Frainey	63
Barbara	119	George	53,63,72,108, 111,120,121, 122,146,195, 198,205,229
Christley	119		
David	119		
Eve	119		
Henry	119	Hannah	121
Jacob	119	Henry	74,101,111, 120,205,206, 230,238
John	119		
Magdalene	119		
Mary	119	Isaac	120
Peter	119	Jacob	111,120,121, 122,195
Rudolph	119		
KEAMY, Jacob	229	Jacob, Jr.	181
KEARN, Jane	91	Jepheth	204
KECKLEY, Joseph	239	John	6,121
Sarah	239	Joseph	122,204
KEEBLER, Lewis	191	Lawrence	174,192
Magdalene	191	Leah	122
KEENAN, Levi	26,143	Magdalene	120,181

KELLER, Margarett	205
Mary	120
Rachel	121
Samuel	121
Susanna	121,176
Susannah	121
William	4
KELLY, Charles	96
Mary	96
KELP, Adam	86
Catharine	123
John Adam	123
John Adam, Jr.	123
Jonathan	86,123
Susanna	122,123,242
William	71,122,123,242
KEMP, John N.	41
Louisa	235
KENDAL, James	164
KENDRICK, Abraham	123
Barbary	123
Benjamin	123
Catharine	123
Christopher	123
Mary	123
Jacob	123
KENNEDY, Mary	123
William	200
KENNDY, Hugh	36
KERCHEVAL, Samuel	23
KERFORD, William	84
KERH, George	231
Mary	231
KERLIN, David	181,247
Elizabeth	247
Jaocb	247
John	247
William	113
KERLINGER, Elizabeth	231
John	231
KERN, Henry	83,182
Jacob	245
John	121
Samuel	204
Samuel, Sen.	57
Sarah	121

KERNS, Henry	101
Henry, Sen.	70
Mary	12
Rebecca	101
Samuel	45
Samuel, Sen.	210
Susannah	45
KERSHWILER, Catharine	219
Jacob	219
KESTERSON, Elizabeth	163
KEVLER, Eave	96
KEVRANS, Henry	131
KEYSER, George	96
Hestor	96
KIBLER, Agata	124
Allen	16
Catharina	124
Christian	124
Elizabeth	207,208
John	124,165,207
Katharine	207,208
Lewis	124
Magdalene	124
Martin	13
Mary Magdelene	124
Philip	124,201,208
Wendle	124
William	124
KIBLINGER, Adam	124
Anna Mary	124
Catharin	124
Daniel	124
Elizabeth	124
Eve	124
Jacob	124
John	124
Susana	124
KILE, Caster	53
Henry	53
KINGAREE, Daniel	124
KINGERY, Abraham	124
Anna	124
Caty	124
Daniel	124
Elizabeth	124
Henry	124

KINGERY, John	124
Mary	124
Rebecca	124
Solomon	124
KINGREE, John	241
Solomon	152
KIPPS, Elizabeth	19,125, 249
Eve	124
George	125
Henry	125
Jacob	125
Moses	125
KIPS, George	227
Henry	249
Jacob	125,249
John	125
KIRCHOFF, Catharine	242
John	242
KIRLIN, David	61,125
Elizabeth	125
Jacob	125
John	125
Samuel	125
William	61,125
KISER, Jacob	137
KLANAHAN, Jacob	31
KLEM, Michael	60
KLICK see CLICK,GLICK	
KLICK, Ann	126
Barbara	126
Catharine	126
Elizabeth	126
John, Jr.	126
John, Sen.	126
Mary	126
KLINE, Catharine	225
John	131,225
KLIPPEL, Philip	36
KNEISLEY, Barbara	126
Chapman	126
George	126
Jacob	126
Jacob, Jun.	126
John	126
Susannah	126
KNISELY, Jacob	231
KNISFLY, Anthony A.	16
John	16
KNISLEY, Barbara	132
Jacob	246
John	132
KNISLY, Catharina	127
David	127
George	127
Henry	127
Jacob	127,178
John	127
Magdalene	127
KNOP, John	127
Mary	127
KNOPP, Mary	127
KNUPP, Jacob	131
KOCH, Henry	5
KOFFELT, Peter	106
KOHENOUR, Elizabeth	64
John	64
KONTZ, Michael	189
KOONCE, George	208
KOONTS, George	221
KOONTZ, Anna	128
Barbara	128
Catharine	128
Christina	128
Elizabeth	1~3,177
Eveline	128
George	128,136,177
Henry	128
John	128,243
Lydia	128
Mary	128
Michael	128
Michael, Sen.	128
Polly	128
Samuel	128
Sarah	128
Susan	128
William J.	128
KOUNTZ, John	143
KOONZ, John	244
KOWENSTEIN, Jacob	157
KRECH, John	93

KRIBS, William	56	LANTZ, Abraham		59
KRONCK, Benjamin	233	Andrew		129
Jonathan	121	Christina		141
KRONK, Benjamin	12,62, 204,236	Elizabeth		15
		Eve		59
Magdelene	194	George	48,106,129, 141,157,228	
Mary	70			
William	70,194	Jacob	15,47,51,56, 59,61,66,106, 129,157,168,217	
KROUCE, George	60			
Joseph	60			
KROUSE, Daniel	201	Jacob, Sen.		23
Hannah	201	John		51,129
KUHL, Catharine	128	Margaretha		129
Conrad	128	LAPOPP, Rebecca		87
Ernest	128	LAUCK, W. C.		139
John	128	LAW, John K.		176
KUNS, Michael	76	LAWRANCE, William		42
KUNTZ, George	139	LAWRENCE, Edward		20
KURAN, Eli	114	Lewis		185
KURTER, Catherine	100	LAYMAN, Ann		130
LAID, D.	40	Benjamin		130
LAMBERT, Abraham	22,54, 129,176	Catharine		130
		Christena		130
Abraham, Jr.	85	Isaac		130
Abram	7,246	John		130,225
Barbara	9	Joseph	24,130,212,240	
Catharine	45	Rebecca		240
David	129	Roseanah		130
Elizabeth	45,129	Sarah		130
Eve	128	Susannah		130
Henry	129	LEAR, Conrad		193
Isaac	45,129	LEARY, Catherine		209
Jacob	9,218	Frances		209
Joseph	45	Jeremiah		209
Mary	129	Joseph		209
Mary Catharine	45	Sarah		209
Sarah	54,129	LEAVELL, Edward		130
William	45,129	Mary Ann		130
LAMERSON, Richard	227	LEEPER, William		79
LAMPTON, Joshua	164	LEE, Catharine		160
LAMS, Samuel	220	John H.		246
LANDIS, Benjamin	125	Rachael		130
Elizabeth	125	Richard		130
LANGDON, Jonathan	110	LEEPER, William P.		64
LANSBERRY, John	83	LEEPERT, William		235

LEETH, George	130	LIND, George	19,40,53,
James	130		138,224,239
Leah	131	LINDAIMUTH, Christina	168
Lydia	130	George	168
Nancy	130	Mary	168
LEGGETT, John	78	Michael	168
Philip	188	LINDAMOOD, Andrew	68,132,
LEHEW, John	37		201,228
Moses	13	Catharine	132
Spencer	37	Christena	132,228
LENARD, Catherine	131	Elijah	132
Henry	131	Eliza	189
John	131	George	68,132,168
Michael	131	Henry	47,68
LENCE, Esther	236	Isaac	69
LENTZ see LANTZ		Jacob	132,138,228
LENTZ, Anna Catherina	131	Joseph	132
Anna Maria	131	Magdalene	132
Catharina	131	Mary	132
Elizabeth	131	Michael	132,201
George	20,131	Philip	68
Geo. Adam	131	Rebecca	69,132
Henry	131	Regina	132
Jacob	131	Rosina	228
John	232	LINDAMUDE, Andrew	133
Katharine	20	Christena	133
Mary	131,232	Christopher	133
Philip	131	Frainey	133
LESHER, John	15,106	George	133,138
LEWIS, Cafsandra	176	Louise	65
Thomas	105,107,115	Mary	168
LICHLITER, Adam	132	Michael	133
Catharine	132	Philip	65,168
Conrad	126,132,182	LINDAMUTH, Geo. Henry	47
Daniel	132	LINDEMOOD, Geo. Henry	20
David	132	Michael	20
Henry	126,132	LINEBERGER, Peter	178
Jacob	132,157	LINEWEAVER, Catharine	133
John	132	Christena	133
LICKLITER, Adam	8,121	Elizabeth	133
Catharine	121	Jacob	133,189
Conrad	8	John	133
John	201	Margaret	133
LIGGET, Catharine	78,147	Mary	133
John	201	Philip	133
Peter	78,199	Sarah	133

LINK, Catharine	134
John	73
Mary	73
LINKHAIRY, Elizabeth	213
Peter	213
LIONBARGER, Peter	28
LIONBERGER, Ann	134
Daniel	134
David	134
John	134
John, Jr.	134
Peter	66,109,190
Reuben	134
Susannah	134
LIONBURGER, Peter	85
LITTLE, Jonas	212
Joseph	39
Mary	51
LOCK, Dycia	134
John	134
LOCKHART, John	42,142
Robert	216
LOCKMILLER, Barbra	134
Catharina	134,135
George	134
Jacob	95,135
John	134,135
Leah	42
Martha	42
Mary	19
Solina	135
William	135
LOINBERGER, Abraham	135
Barbara	135
David	135
Jacob	135
John	135
John, Sen.	135
Joseph	135
Leah	135
Magdalene	135
Mary	135
Peter	135
Rebecca	135
Samuel	135
Susannah	135

LOKAY, James	30
LOMAS, Catharine	10
George	10
LONAS, Adam	135
Barbara	94
George	94,135
Henry	94,135
John	14
Leonard	174
Livila	94
Magdalene	14
Rosina	135
LONG, Abner	71
Adam	136
Dorothy Ann	240
Elizabeth	135
Frankey	136
George	157
Henry	106,157
Isaac	136
Jacob	135
James	136
John	135
Jonas	136
Lewis	136
Lydia	240
Mary	19,136,157
Nathan	136
Philip	136,216
Philip, Sen.	136
Reubin	136
Susannah	135
LONGAIRE, Isaac	104
LONGEARE, John	58
LONGNECKER, Ulrick	47
LOUDER, John	98
Philip	98
LOUDERBACK, Abraham	136,137
Barbara	136
Barbary	137
Christina	136
Daniel	136,137
David	136,137
Elizabeth	136,137
Eve	136

LOUDERBACK, John	136
Joseph	104,136,137
Magdalene	137
Mathias	136,137
Philip	137
Rubin	137
Sarah	136,137
Susanna	136
LOVE, Daniel	137
Elizabeth	137
Polly	137
Sarah	137
Tabitha	137
LOVELL, Charles	54
LUCAS, Jacob	182
LUDWICK, Joseph	129
LUDWIG, Jacob	152
Joseph	59
LUTHER, Christian	123
Christina	123
Diller	137
Elizabeth	137
John	137
Louisa	137
LUTS, John	170
LUTZ, Abraham	168
Catharine	168
Caty	138
George	138
Jacob	68,138,150, 168,246
John	11,138
Jonas	138
Joseph	138
Lydia	11
Margaret	138
Marie	87
Mary	138
Michael	138
Modleen	138
Sarah	246
Susannah	63,138
MACANTUR, Casper	138
Christopher	138
Daniel	138
David	138
MACANTUR, Frederick	138
John	138
John, Sen.	138
Margaret	138
Mary	138
Rozeanah	138
MACHIR, Alexander	31,44, 138,202
Angus	138
Betsy	138
Elizabeth	139
Harriet	139
Henry	138
James	138
John	10,138,195,202
John, Jr.	31,142
Joseph S.	139
Magdalena	138
Margaret	138
Philip	139
Philip A.	139
Sarah	138
Scota	138
MACK, George	98
MACKINTOSH, L.	245
MADIERA, Daniel	216
MAFIUS, Barbara	139
Catharine	139
David	139
Elizabeth	139
George	139
George, Jr.	154
Jacob	139
John	139
Joseph	139
Magdalene	154
Samuel	139
MAGART, Christian	139
Isaac	139
Mary	139
MAGERT, Bence	139
Daniel	139
David	139
Elizabeth	139
Henry	139
Jacob	139

MAGERT, John	139	MARKENTURFH, David	162
Margaret	139	MARKER, Amos	140
Rudolph	139	George	220
MAGGERT, Benjamin	140	Hannah	140
Jacob	140	John	192
John	96	Sarah	192
Susana	140	MARKS, James	141
MAGGOT, Christian	118	Jane	141
MAGILL, John	205	John	141
MAGRUDER, Mary S.	237	Mary	141
W. W.	25,37,47,119, 141,228	Thomas	141
		MARSH, Catharine	142
Dr. William	5	Edward	142
William W.	24	MARSHALL, Henry	13,129
MAHANEY, Elisha	140	John	104,216
Isabella	140	Julia	129
Joseph P.	140,212	MARTIN, Anna Maria	123
Lewis	140	John	123
Rachel	140	Thomas C.	4
Stephen	140	Thomas G.	89
Stephen M.	140	William	122,185
Washington	117	MARTY, Laurence	103
MAHONEY, Hannah	140	MARYE, Duana	169
Isaac P.	140	James T.	84
Isabella	140	Mary	169
Stephen	147	William	41,59,118, 135,197
Thomas L.	140		
MALLORY, Lucy	113	William S.	84,169, 197,222
MALONEY, John	19		
MANUEL, William	17	MATHANY, Daniel	54
MAPHIAS, Joseph	178	Joseph	3
Maria	178	MATHES, Abraham	142
MAPHIES, Samuel	139	Benjamin	142
MAPHIS, Adam	141	Betty	142
Anna	141	Henry	142
Catharine	15,141	Isaac	142
Elizabeth	15	James, Jr.	145
George	24,141,174, 212,241	James, Sen.	142,145
		Rebeckah	142
George, Sen.	141	Rachel	142
Hannah	141	Sally	142
Jacob	141	William	142
John	24,141,240	MATHEW, James, Sen.	89
John M.	24	MATHEWS, Alexander	142
Philip	141	Benjamin	142
Samuel	141	George	142
William	141	Gressel	142

MATHEWS, James	142
Jeremiah	142
John	142
MATTHEWS, Abraham	120
Benjamin	120
Elizabeth	120
Isaac	120
James, Sen.	172
Rebeckah	120
Sarah	120
William	120
MAUCK, Abraham	143
Anna	143
Barbara	143
Catharine	142,143
Christina	64
Daniel	118,143
David	143
Elizabeth	143,155
Frederick	225
George	155
Jacob	143
John	64,139
Joseph	143
Maria	143
Rebecka	143
Robert	143
MAUK, Daniel	143
Henry	139
Jacob	143
John	46,209,210
Joseph	143
Rebecka	143
Robert	143
Rosina	10
MAUPIN, Hamilton	226
MAURER, Charles C.	55
John	129,173
MAVIS, Adam	191
Ann Apple	48
George	11,185,241
Mary	191
MAVIUS, George	193
MAY, David	232
MAYBERRY, Nancy	189
MAYER, William	136

MC ALLISTER, Lucy	143
Robert	143
MC CANN, James	154
MC CARTH, Dianah	144
Elizabeth	144
Hannah	144
James	144
Jonas	144
Margaret	144
Mary	144
Sarah	144
MC CARTY, Catharine	249
MC CAULEY, Patrick	150
Sarah	150
MC CLANAHAN, Rebecca	146
MC CLELLAN, John	150
MC CLUNE, Elizabeth	54
MC CORD, Catharine	102
Isaac	50
Mary	50
Sarah	144
Thomas	102,115,186,231
William	26,144,233
MC DANIEL, Jonathan	99, 167
MC DOWELL, Andrew	150
Rebecca	150
MC ENTOR, Frederick	138
John	138
MC GAHEY, Elizabeth	6
MC GOWAN, Jane	144
John	144
Pheobe	144
MC ILREE, Mary	54
MC INTUF, David, Sen.	126
MC INTURF, David	44,157, 162
Frederick	192
George	31,44
MC INTURFF, David	144,228
David, Jr.	180
David, Sen.	180
Frederick	228
Henry	180,228
Henry, Sen.	228
MC KAY, Abraham	164

MC KAY, Andrew	145	MILEY, Joseph	146
George	120,145	Martin	83,146
Isaac	164	Mary	146
James	145	MILLER, Abraham	13,149, 153
Jeremiah	48,130,131,145	Abraham, Sen.	146
Lidia	145	Adam	148,240
Mary	145	Adolph	101
Nancy	145	Allanter O.	230
Robert	89,131,145	Ann	153
Rowley	203	Ann H.	179
William	31,130,145	Anna	63,149,191
Zachariah	4	Anthony	150
MC KEAN, Jno., Jr.	150	Barbara	73,147,148, 149,177
MC KENNEY, John	111	Benjamin	3,30,170
MC KENNY, Mary	177	Bettsy	150
MC MANNUS, Patrick	77	Catharine	3,13,88, 146,147,149, 151,225
MC MICHAEL, Hannah	154		
MC MOLLIN, Cathia	117		
MC QUAY, Samuel	132	Caty	150
MC WAY, Andrew	132	Christian	58,78,147
Samuel	132	Christian, Sen.	77,147
MEEK, Rosannah	249	Christina	87,146
MEEKS, Hugh	249	Clara	30
MEILEY, David	154	Daniel	76
MEILY, John	122	David	149
Joseph	102	Dorothea	148
Martin, Sen.	154	Edward	148
Rebecca	102	Elizabeth	34,88,147, 148,150, 151,232
MELCHER, Wendel	14		
MENEFEE, Mary	223		
Sarah	223	Eve	114,147
William	223	Felde	114
MENG, Victoria	97	Frederick	147
MERCER, Elizabeth	145	George	13,57,106,146, 149,224,228
MESINS, John	11		
METZ, John	66	George, Jr.	109
MEYER, Barbara	145	George, Sen.	147
Henry	145	Godfrey	73,94,148,229
John	145	Henry	147,148,149
Michael	145	Ira	3
MEYERS, Martin	167	Isaac	4,37,146, 151,205
MIDDLETON, Elizabeth	127		
John	127	Isreal	3
MILEY, Daniel	146	Jacob	4,10,83,84,90, 101,120,146,148, 149,156,225,232
Elizabeth	43,83		
Isaac	43		
John	146		

MILLER, Jacob W.	147
James	145,146,151
John	4,65,88,147, 148,149,150, 160,191,224
Jonathan	60,65
Joseph	78,146,148,149
Julia Ann	79
Lewis	148,177
Lydia (Lidia)	13,168
Magdalene	149,177
Margaret	228
Maria	13
Maria Catharine	86
Mark	63,148,149
Martin	149
Mary	3,97,150, 172,174
Matilda	237
Nancy	147,149
Peter	84,87,88,100,120
Peter, Jr.	86
Peter, Sen.	86
Philip	73,123,147, 148,149,178, 232,245,246
Polly	2
Rebecca	148,150, 151,246
Rebekah	34
Reuben	36,134,147, 153,213
Richard	3
Robert	129,150
Rosana	13
Salome	147,149
Samuel	129,149,150
Samuel C.	147
Sarah	3,20,149, 150,151
Sereptia	149
Susan	78
Susana	148,149
Susannah	54,82
Thomas	144,168,169
Thomas J.	184
MILLER, Tomy	71
Ulrick	146
William	20,34,146, 151,174
MILLS, Samuel	11,99,105, 112,124,151, 152,210,219 238,239
W. James	151
MIMS, Linah	216
MINCEER, Elizabeth	169
Jacob	169
MINICK, Mathias	62
Nanna	62
MITCHELL, Susannah	31
MOATZ, Henry	197
Jacob	197
Michael	197
MOCK, George	94
MODESETT, James	206
MODESITT, James	221
MOFFET, Barbara	214
MOFFETT, Aaron	92
Anderson	115
Daniel	162
Mary	92,162
Thomas	92
MOHLER, Samuel	15,181
MOILY, Martin	50
MOODEY, Bryant	151
John	151
Moses	151
William	151
MOODY, Moun	58
Polly	243
William	243
MOORE, Aaron	92,151,199
Abraham	152
Anne	153
Catharine	153
Charles	91,151,152
Charles S.	152
David	152
Elijah	152
Elizabeth	152,153
Eliz. Mary	152

MOORE, George	62,152, 153,240	MORT, Mary	99
Hannah	153	MOUL, Jacob	85
Helena	152	MOURER, Ann Mary	155
Jacob	152	Barbary	155
James	182	Charles	102
John	29,153	George	155,185,217
Jonathan	85,152,199	Jacob	155
Joseph	3,153	John	100,155
Lydia	152,153,154	John, Jr.	155
Martha	51	John, Sen.	155
Mary	152	Lennerd	155
Morgan	152	Leonhart	155
Phebe	152	Mary	155
Polly	243	Mickel	155
Polly Ann	152	Philip	155
Reuben	2,3,37,62,82, 152,153,200	Rebecca	155
		Valentine	155
		Vollentin	155
Reubin	153	William	135
Samuel	91,92,151	MOUREY, Elizabeth	173
Sarah	152,153	Frederick	72
Sarah Çatharine	152	George	29,125,131,156, 158,171,188,194, 234,240,248
Solomon	153		
Strother	152		
Thomas	153	John	72
Thomas, Sen.	153	John S.	173
William	3,151	Rossetta	212
MORE, Charles	154	MOURY, George	29
David	154	MOUSER, Henry	93,155
Jonathan	154	Mary	155,156
Lydia	154	MOYER, Abraham	170
Polly	154	Ann Mary	88
MOREHEAD, Sarah	113	Christian	26,90
Susanna	113	George	88,157
MORELAND, William	13,43, 44,113	Jacob	148
		John	156
MORGAN, Amanda M.	154	Martin	156
Ann	154	Polly	69
Elizabeth	114,154	Susannah	170
John	98,153,154, 213,231	MOYERS, Barbara	156
		Christian	156
Jonas	154	Christian, Sen.	156
Maureen	154	Frederick	157
MORLEY, Christena	154	George	157
Jacob	166	Henry	157
Martin, Sen.	154	Isaac	156

MOYERS, Jacob	157	NAGEL, Christina	248
John	157	David	248
Maryann	157	Elizabeth	248
Michael	156	Nicholas	248
MUCK, Mary	100	NAGLE, Peter	124
Rosina	57	NAIL, Elizabeth	40
MUIRHEID, Andrew	203	NAISWANDER, Jacob	70
MUMAW, Christian	241	Margaret	70
Elizabeth	241	NALE, Susannah	96
Jacob	112	NEAS, Adam	26,158
MUNCH, Betsy	157	Dolly	158
Caty	157	Elizabeth	158
David	14	John	158
George	157	Mary	242
John	157	Michael	26,158,242
Magdalena	157	NEASE, Elizabeth	168
Mary	157	George	160
Peter	114	John	26,168
Philip	157	Margaret	242
Rosina	14	Ulrick	135
Silas	228	Ulry	242
MUNDELL, John	41	NEES, Adam	242
MUNSON, George C.	150	George	63
MURPHEY, James	89	Jacob	158
MURPHY, Dycia	134	Joseph	158
James	161	Mary	158
Magdalena	161	Michael	158,249
William	110	NEESE, John	231
MUSSELMAN, John	85,97	Michael	249
MYER, Frederick	157	NEFF, Abraham	8,83,158,
John	157		159,231,234,247
Mary	157	Abraham, Jr.	158
MYERS, Catharine	158	Abram	160
Christian	158	Adam	160
Isaac	135,158	Anna	159,160
John Isaac	158	Barbara	159,231
Jonas	158	Catharine	126,158,240
Mary	128	Christian	158,159,
Peter	158		234,247
Polly	158	Christian, Sen.	159
Rebecca	158	Christley	160
Rosina	231	Daniel	159
Samuel	128,158	David	8,159,234
MYRES, Mary	7	Elizabeth	159,160
Samuel	7	Frances	117,126

NEFF, Francis	74,158, 159,160	NEWLAND, Andrew	161
		Anne	161
Henry	81,159	Deborah	92
Jacob	76,110,117, 144,158,159, 160,163,191	Elizabeth	161
		Isaac	161,181
		John	161
Jacob, Sen.	159	Margaret	161
John	39,158,158, 160,213	Mary	181
		Polly	161
John, Jr.	158,240	Rebecca	161
John, Sen.	158	S. F.	116
John Henry	158,159,160	Susannah	161
Joseph	116,159	NEWLEN, Daniel	161
Mary	159	Elizabeth	161
Michael	38,80,81, 116,159	John	161
		Joseph	161
Samuel	159	Mary	161
NEFS, Aaron	125	William	161
Elizabeth	160,249	NEWMAN, Ann	161,162
George	160	Barbara	140
Jacob	160	Catharine	162
Michael	125,160, 166,249	Francis M.	161
		George	161
Samuel	160	John	116,152,161, 162,185,216
NEHISER, Jacob	206		
NEHR, John	181	John P.	161
NELSON, Henry, Jr.	58	Jonathan	162
NEUHAM, Wesley	152	Joseph M.	161
NEWELL, David N.	160	Mary	161
Elizabeth	160	Phebe Ann	161
James	215	Polly	152
Jane	160	Samuel	161,162,234,249
Jean	215	Sarah Ann	161
John	160	Thomas	140
Margaret	160	Walter	30,162,228
Marget	215	Walter N.	161
Marthe	215	NEZELRODT, Ludwig	210
Mary	215	Maria	210
Nancy B.	160	NIBERGER, Christina	142
Rebecca	160	Jacob	142
Robert	160,224	NICE, John A.	82
Samuel	160,215	NICELY, John	102
Sarah C.	160	NICHOLAS, Abigale	162
Thomas	9,19,40,160,215	Abraham	186
William	160,215,224	Daniel	162
William L.	160	Henry	38

NICHOLAS, Jamime	162	OAKELY, George		244
John	162,227	OAKLEY, George		154
Magdalena	38	OBERHOLDSER, Barbara		163
Mary	227	Eaff		163
Moley	162	Peter		163
Nancy	162	Samuel		163
Rhoda	118	OBERHOLSER, Anna		8
Richard	162	Peter		8
Thomas	162	ODELL, Abigal		164
NICHOLLS, Simon	113	Abraham	130,164
NICHOLS, Eleanor	243	Andrew		164
John	121	Ann		164
Milly	243	Benjamin		164
Nancy	243	Calop		127
NICKELS, Harrison	146	Elijah	51,164
NICKOLES, Elizabeth	35	Elizabeth		164
NIE, Margaret	162	Isaac	127,164
Ulrick	162	James		164
NIEBERGER, Ann Mary	162	Jeremiah		164
Christian	162	John	164,178
Christian, Sen.	162	Jonathan		164
Christopher	162	Leah		164
Elizabeth	162	Samuel	131,164
Jacob	162	Sary		164
John	162	Silvanes		164
Magdeline	162	Stephen	28,164
Margaret	162	OFENBACKER, Christina	165
NIGHT, William	84	Eve		165
NIGLSWONGER, Christian	19	Frederick		165
NISELY, Anthony	148,163	Jacob		165
Barbara	163	John		165
Jacob	163	Peter		165
John	163	Rachel		165
NISWANDER, Jacob	83	Rosanna		165
NOEL, Catharine Ann	163	O'FERRELL, Dennis	165
Elizabeth	163	OFFENBACKER, Barbara	165
Jacob	14,21,60,68,	Christina		165
	69,112,132,135,	Eva		165
	163,181,187	Frederick		165
Jacob, Jr.	60	Jacob		165
Samuel	163,187	John		165
William	163	Peter		165
NORTH, John	56	Rosina		165
NORTHERN, Edmond	229	OFFENBOCKER, Barbary	165
NOWELL, Thomas	219	Jacob		165
NULEN, Daniel	163	John		165
Rebeckah	163	Magdalena		165
NUNN, John	84	OFFNER, Samuel		230

OHAVER, Isaac	182	OSWALD, Caroline	167
Magdalene	182	Samuel	167
OLDENBROUCK, Daniel	166	OTT, Elizabeth	37
Eleonoraw	166	George	37,230
Hannah	166	Henry	93,148
Jacob	166	Jacob	43,80,121,218,
Lewisee	166		245,246
OLDHARE, Ann Mary	193	Jacob, Jr.	5,6
John	193	Jno.	28,93
OLDHER, Frederick	130	Magdalene	246
OLINGER, Adam	116,166	Mary	6
Catharine	166	Michael	28,246
David	166	Samuel	78,199
Elizabeth	166	William	6,43,47,105,127
Eve	166	OVERALL, Hannah	130
George	249	Isaac	76,120
Isaac	166	John	120
Mary	249	OVERHOLSER, Adam	167
Philip	166	Anna	167
Polly	166	Benjamin	167
Rebecca	166	Christian	167
Sarah	166	Jacob	167
William	166	John	167
OLLINGER, Adam	106	Mary	167
Elizabeth	106	Moses	167
Jacob	191	Peter	167,236
OLMETH, Anna	231	Samuel	99,167
Christian	231	Susanna	167
OMARTE, Christian	188	OVERHOLTZER, Peter	40
George	188	OWEINGS, William	114
Jacob	188	OZBURN, Joseph	168,187,227
ONEAL, John	2,79	Rosena	168
O'NEIL, Charles	192	Sarah	3
O'NIEL, Anna	167	PAGE, John	216
ORNDORF, Jonathan	69	PAINTER see BENDER	
Priscilla	69	PAINTER, Abraham	168
ORNDORFE, Hannah	220	Abram	169
ORNDORFF, Christina	169	Adam	167,168
Ellen	20	Anna	168
Jacob	64	Catharine	59,186
Philip	169	Christina	64,167
Philip, Jr.	95	Conrad	47
Phineas	10,18,20,53,	Cornelius	141
	82,133,155,204	Elizabeth	168
OROACK, David	234	George	129,133,168,
			169,177,180

PAINTER, George W.	169	PEER, Catharine	75
Isaac	168,169	David	169
Jacob	163,167	Henry	174
James	186	Jacob	141,182
John	67,129,133, 167,168	John	169
		Jonathan	169
John, Jr.	167	Joseph	169
John, Sen.	168	Samuel	169
Joseph	167	PEERY, Wattson	27
Lucinda	167	PENCE, Betsy	169
Magdalene	167	Catharine	169
Mary	133,168,169, 177,180	Conrad	169,248
		Daniel	96
Mathias	15,168,179	David	170,172
Nancy	136	Emanuel	96
Peter	106	Eve	172,207,208
Philbina Catharin	168	Frederick	96
Philip	15,20,59,66, 133,168	George	143,170,194
		Henry	208
Rachael	133	Isaac	121
Rosina	20	Jacob	96,165,170,172
Sarah	54	John	29,169,170, 172,208
Samuel	119,186		
William	168	Joseph	170
PANGLE, Rhoda	190	Lewis	13,96
William	190	Lydia	169
PARKELY, Jacob	11	Margaret	170
Mary	11	Mary Catharine	170
PARKINS, Isaac	140	Morgan	170
Mary	140	Nicholas	170
Nathan	140	Peter	170
PARKS, George	165	Philip	26,169
James	169	Reuben	121
Julia	169	Susanna	169
PARROW, Martha	237	William	170
William S.	237	PENEWIT, John	153
PAUL, Jonathan	18	PENKINE, Bennett	195
PAYNE, John	243	PENNEWIT, George	50
W. W.	154	PENNEWITZ, Susanna	236
William	77,128,233	PENNYBACKER, Benjamin	170
PAYTON, Elizabeth	65	Charlot	170
PEAL, Berman	162	Daniel	34
Catharine	162	Derick	170
PEAR, Phillip	19	Elizabeth	154
PEEBLES, John	222	George	30,34,170, 188,189

PENNYBACKER, George M.	29	PETERSON, Charles	13
Isaac	170	Mary	13
J. S.	199	Sarah	13
Joel	25,30,116,125, 170,171,237	Sarah Ann	13
		PEYTON, John	221
Margaret P.	171	PFEIFFER, Anna Mary	172
Mark	170	Augustine	172
Nancy	170	Godlove	172
Nathan	170	PFIFER, Barbara	172
Rebecca	170	David	172
Samuel	170,171	Henry	172
Sarah	170	Henry, Sen.	172
PENNYPACKER, D.	29	PFIFFER, Elizabeth	190
PENNYWIT, Anna	171	Joseph	190
Jacob	171	Levi	190
John	171	Rebecca	190
Margaret	171	PHAU, Eliza	98
Rosina	171	Sarah	98
Samuel	171	PHILIPS, Christina	32,70
PENNYWITZ, Ana	171	John	32,70,173
Elizabeth	171	William	32,33,70,84, 87,106,155, 173,196,217
Jacob	171		
John	171		
Margaret	171	PIDILER, Abraham	101
Rosina	171	PIERCE, George	4
Samuel	171	PIFER, Jacob	211
PENTZ, Geo. Philip	171	PILGRAM, Theodore	176
Jacob	171	PINGLEY, David	173
John	29,171	Elizabeth	173
Mary	171	Harriet	173
Philip	171	James A.	173
PERAL, Phebe	54	Jeremiah	173
PERRY, Elizabeth	172	John	173
James	172	John Wm.	173
Margarite	172	Joseph	173
Mary	172	Mary	173
Nancy	172	Samuel	173
Samuel	172	PIPER, Barbara	173
Thomas	141,229	David	173
Wattson	212	David, Jr.	75
William	172	Henry	57
PETERS, Catharain	172	Joseph	75,173
Christina	63	PIRKEY, John	139
Peter	48	PISELER, Sarah	173
Ulrick	172	PITMAN, Abraham	45,46,108

PITMAN, Andrew	174
Catharine	2,3,236
David	45,46
Eleanor A.	237
Elizabeth	224
Emanuel	45,46,174
Erasmus	2,3
Esther	174
Jonathan	45,46,57,214
Joseph	174,237
Lawrence	174
Nicholas	102
Philip	170,174
Susannah	45,46
PITTMAN, Andrew	208
Emanuel	192
Jonathan	46,122
Joseph	208
Lawrence	215
Philip	9
PLUMLY, Phebe	51
POKE, Adam	72,174
Elizabeth	174
John	10
POPE, John	19
POLLOCK, Alexander	3
Samuel	236,241
POTTER, Lyman	108
POWEL, Caroline	235
PRESGRAVES, John	243
PRICE, Ann	175
Edward	174,175
Elizabeth	179,227
John	175
John, Sen.	175
Nancy	174
Peter	190
Samson	175
Samuel	227
Sarah	175
Thomas	174,175
William	175
Zackeriah	174,175

PRINCE, Catharin	175
Elizabeth	175
George	175,223
Godlip	175
Henry	175
Magdalene	175
Maria	175
Philip	175
Sally	223
Susanna	175
PRINTZ, Barbara	175
PROBSTING, Antoinetta	176
Christian	176
Eleanor	176
Frederick	176
Julia	176
P. A.	176
Theodore C.	176
PROCTER, Hannah	155
PROCTOR, Betsy	201
John	201
Richard	199
PRYCE, Augustus J.	144
PUGH, Joseph	79,110, 176,211
RADER, Michael	136
Ruth	99
RAMBO, Jacob	79,212
RAMEY, Aaron	37
Valentine	197
William	37
RAMSEY, Hugh	226
Jane	226
RAMY, John	10
Rebecca	10
RANTZ, Susanna	176
RAPEHOLTZ, Jacob	48
RAU, John H.	37
RAWLINGS, John	244
READ, Hankerson	200
REAGAN, Charles	1
Elizabeth	10
Jacob	10,43

REAGAN, John	176	RHINEHART, William	169
Mary	176	William R.	168,177
Susanna	176	RHODE, Abraham	238
REASER, John	231	Daniel	231
RECTOR, Anna	159	John	65
Conaway	159	Susanna	241
REDDENOUR, Adam	48	RHODES, Anna	178
REDER, Eliz. Martha	160	Daniel	178
REDMOND, Nancy	13	Isaac	178
REED, Abraham	144	John	178
Elizabeth	98	John, Jr.	178
Mitchel	54	John, Sen.	93
REEDY, Abraham	62	Joseph	55,178
Augustine	177,189	Levi	178
Jacob	62,106	Maria	178
John	62,177	Mary Ann	177
Magdalene	62	Michael	178
Rachael	106	Susana	178
REEFER, Eve	167	RICABOHER, Adam	178
REES, Frances	234	Barbara	178
REESE, Catharine	104	Henry	178
Esther	177	John	178
Frances	238	Magdaline	178
Isaac	177	Marget	178
Joseph	177	Peter	178
REMY, Elijah	177	RICARD, Henry	64
John	137,177	RICE, Jno.	81,153
Thomas	177	Jno. W.	161,213
RENNER, Henry	64	RICHARD, Elizabeth	13
RENNINGER, Barbara	229	RICHARDS, Catharine	40
Henry	229	Charles	178
RENO, William	51	Elijah	75,135
REUBEN, John	3	Elizabeth	178
REYNOLDS, Ann	202	George	228
Elizabeth	34	Henry	69,70
Henry	234	Isaac	141
Jane	226	Marine	228
Joseph	202	Regina	141
Margarett	202	William	248
Mary Christina	202	RICHARDSON, Catharine	179
Regel	234	Isabella	179
William	4,34,146	John C.	177,179
RHINEHART, Andrew	177	Marcus C.	179
Barbara	168,169	Marquis	179
Jonas	177	Rebecca	176
Mary	178	Samuel	32,37,84,100,179

RICHARDSON, Samuel B.	179
William	84,119,176,179
William H.	179
RICKARD, Jacob	156
John	101
Maria	101
Mary	156
RICKENBERGER, Abraham	179
Anny	179
Elizabeth	179
Jacob	179
John	179
Peter	179
Philip	179
RICKETTS, Anthony	180
Elijah	180
Jarrid	180
John	180
Margaret	180
RIDDLE, George	15
RIDDLEBERGER, Madison	199
Susan H.	199
RIDENOUR, Adam	177
David	180
Henry	101,180
John	180
Jonas	180
Magdalene	180
RIDER, Jacob	73
William	20
RIFFEY, Andrew	180
Ann	180
Ann Mary	118
Henry	118
Mary	33,180
RINEHART, Adam	180
Andrew	180
Barbary	181
Catharine	181
Elizabeth	59,181
Emanuel	227
George	180
James	74
John	59,180,181
Jonas	95,171,180,215
Ludwick, Sen.	181
Ludwig	76,181

RINEHART, Magdalene	180,181
Michael	180
Rebecca	227
Rosina	180
William	67
RINER, George	203
RINKER, A.	65,93,98,106,129,168,171,181
Abraham	5
Absalom	45,54,106,108,110,118,121,181,183,198,208,229,241
Anna	181
Barbara	181,228
Barbary	96
Catharine	181
Christina	229
Dorothy	93
Dorothea	181
E.	201
Eleanora	181
Elizabeth	181,208
Eliz. Ann	181
Ephraim	133,153,181,230
Erasmus	99,181
Fenton T.	182
George	21,32,33,52,110,179,181,187,229
Henry	21,52,93,98,181,228,229
Henry St. John	182
Isaac	181
Isreal	121
J. P.	23
Jacob	14,15,21,40,60,68,73,74,76,77,83,86,88,94,95,97,98,99,107,110,126,133,135,149,157,167,169,171,180,181,213,222,229,231,236
Jacob, Jr.	6,38,40,50,52,53,66,111,127,148,175,182,184,187,198

RINKER, Jacob, Sen.	6,50, 63,98,133, 181,187
Jacob G.	98,182
John	67,181
Joseph	181
Lemuel H.	98
Levi	98,99,128,150, 159,168,171
Magdalene	32,33
Margaret Jane	98
Mary Catharine	181
Philip	181
Samuel	67,99
William	181
RITSENHELSER, Peter	229
RITENOUR, Catharine	24
ROACH, Malow	195
ROAD, Philip	147
ROADCAP, Abraham	100
George	76
Peter	139
ROADS, David	156
Eve	189
John	26,39,85,93, 96,124,143,187, 189,192,197, 221,246
Joseph	45,134
Mary	45,234
Michael	101
Noah	45
Philip	234
Susanna	173
Valentine	72
ROBERTS, Jerima	227
ROBERTSON, Betsey	182
Charles	182
Edward	182
Gary	182
James R.	243
John	182
Joseph	85
Katy	182
Lucy	123
Maximillian	58
Polly	182
William	182
ROBESON, Nancy	229
RODE, George	195
John	198
Susannah	195
RODEFFER, David	11,37
RODEHEFFER, George	182
Jacob	141,182,226
James	226
John	182
Mary	182
Phebe	13
Philip	149,182,188
Rebecca	149
Samuel	191
Samuel, Sen.	182
RODES, Absalom	183
Barbary	183
Christina	183
Elizabeth	183
John	183
Lucy (Susy)	38
Margaret	183
Susannah	183
Vallentine	183
RODHAVER, Adam	64
ROFS, Magdalene	230
ROGER, John	145
ROGERS, James	183
ROHRER, Anna	183
Barbara	247
Daniel	183
Elizabeth	183
Henry	183,247
Jacob	183
Urshula	183
ROLAND, Henry	137
ROOF, Anna	183,184
Barbara	184
Christianny	184
Elizabeth	183,184
Fanny	183,184
Jacob	184
John	184
Martin	25,183,184
Mary	201
Noah	201
Samuel	183,184

ROOP, George	184	ROTHGEB, Daniel		116
Henry	184	David		139
Jacob	184	David, Jr.		100
John	184	Mary		139
Margarett	184	ROUDABUSH, Jacob		235
Martin	184	ROUGEL, Daniel		108
Michael	184	Mary		108
ROOTS, Mary	53	ROUSH, Barbara		63
Michael	53	Jacob		52
ROOTZ, Elizabeth	212	John		115
John	13	ROW, Barbary		195
RORER, Elizabeth	70,184	David		195
Henry	70,184	Elizabeth		195
RORH, Michael	85	Henry		195
ROSEBROUGH, Betsy	42	ROY, Anna		216
ROSENBARGER, Henry	27	Elijah		185
Rudy	27	Gibson		76,216
ROSENBERGER, Abraham	62	James		185
Anthony	9	Jean		185
Henry	89	John		185
ROTECAP, Abraham	184	Polly		216
Anna	184	Rachael		120
Barbara	184	Wiley S.		216
Christian	184	William		185,216
David	184	RUBEY, Catharine		168
Elizabeth	184	Jacob		168
Ester	184	RUBFREIT, Elizabeth		21
George	184	John		21
George, Sen.	184	RUBLE, John		48
Isaac	184	Sarah		48
Jacob	184	RUBY, Barbary		185
John	184	Catharine		182,185
Joseph	184	Elizabeth		185
Mary	184	Henry		182,185
Michael	184	Jack		91
Reuben	184	Jacob	3,61,129,185
Samuel	184	John		185
ROTH, David	20	Magdalena		185
Elizabeth	20	Philip		121
John	15,101,103,241	RUDDELL, Archibald	185,186
Joseph	124	Catharine		186
Michael	15,66,80	Elizabeth		185
ROTHEHEFFER, Anthony	185	George		185,186
Catherine	185	Isaac		185
David	185	James	16,22,126,
John	185			185,186
Samuel	185	John		186

309

RUDDELL, John, Sen.	186	RUPERT, Adam	187
Mary	185,186	Christian	187
Rebecca	186	Daniel	187
RUDDLE, George	186	Elizabeth	187
Isaac	186	Gideon	187
James	186	John	187
John	186	Margaret	187
Susan	186	Mary	187
Susan Ann	186	Moses	187
RUDOLPH, Adam	75	Peter	187
RUFF, Anna	183	Solomon P.	94
Christian	248	RUSH, Barbary	183
Esther	248	Wellington	92
Jacob	184	RUSSELL, Deborah	4
Mary	248	E. E.	184
Regina	248	John	127,216
Susannah	248	Moses	69
RUFFNER, Abraham	187	Robert	4
Ann	28	Robert S.	146
Anna	187	Thomas	4
Barbara	187	William S.	17
Benjamin	187	RUST, Abraham	38
Catharine	187	Annamaria	38
Elizabeth	93,187	Elizabeth	38
Emanuel	187	Mathias	38
Joseph	187	RUTH, Abraham	63
Joshua	187	Elizabeth	215
Manuel	187	George	215
Margaret	162	RUTS, Catharine	204
Martin	162,187	Elizabeth	204
Mary	187	John	204,231
Michael	187	Lydia	204
Peter	187	RYAN, Anthony	117
Peter, Sen.	187	Catharine	184
Reginia	187	Edward	187
Reuben	187	Eleanor	187
Susanna	187	Solomon	175
RUFNER, Benj.	28	Thomas	53,187
Elizabeth	28	RYE, George	6,64,65
Emanuel	85	RYMAN, Elizabeth	108
RUNION, Daniel	230	John	227
John	248	Joseph	108,133,181
Magdalena	230	Samuel	234
RUNTY, John	177	RYNHART, Rosina	63
RUP, Christener	249		

SAGER, Abraham	149,188		SAUM, Frederick	189
Absalom	190		Jacob	189
Ann	188		John	133,189
Chrisla	188		Mary Ann	189
Christian	188		Nicholas	130,189
Delila	188		SAUR, Balsar	190
Ely	188		Barbara	190
Esther	188		Frederick	190
Gabriel	42,182,188,191		SAYGER, Adam	10
Jacob	149,188		Anna (Anne)	10,97,190
John	55,188		Conrad	190
Mary	149,182,188		Magdalene	228
Rosina	191		Peter	190,210,228
Samuel	149,188		Philip	11,97
Sarah	188		SAYLORS, William	89
Susannah	188		SCANLAND, Benjamin	190
SAIRFAS, Jacob	158		Fielding	190
SALVAGE, Catharine	188		SCANTLING, James	7
SAMPLES, Alice	99		Mary	7
SAMUEL, Green B.	82,237		SCARBAUGH, Michael	119
SAMUELS, Abraham	189		SCHICKENDANTZ, Christina -	
Elizabeth	188			190
G. B.	30,147		Philip Henry	190
Green	188,189		SCHIRTZER, Philip	49
Isaac	2,188,189,231		SCHMIDT, Dr. John G.	97
John	189		SCHMITT, John G.	62,67,82,
Joseph	77,91,92,151,189			92,130,246
Joseph H.	2,30,208,237		SCHMOOTZ, Mathias, Sen.	191
Mary	188,189		SCHMUCKER, Anna	16
Rutha	188		Catharine	213
Sarah	189		Ferdinand	65
Stark	91		George	77
SANDERS, Thomas	64		Jacob	236
SANDSBURY, Thomas	113		Joseph	16
SANDY, Vincent	243		Rebecca	54
William	243		Samuel	54,213
SANFORD, John	236		SCHMUTZ, Abraham	81,191
SANLAW, Anna	189		Anna	191
Emanuel	189		Barbara	191
SAP, Abraham	156		Elizabeth	191
SAUCK, Emily	6		Jacob	191
SAUM, Adam	189		John	191
Anna Mary	189		Mathias	191
Christian	156,189		SCHOOLY, Sisly	1
Daniel	189		SCHROFFE, Charles M.	183
Eve	189			

SCIBERT, Abraham	192	SETZER, George	213
Francis	249	John	160
George	192	SEVESQUE, John	1
Henry	192	SEXTON, Charles	20
John	192	SHACKELFORD, William	55
Mary	192	SHAEFFER, Catharine	193
Moses	192	Christopher	193
SCOTT, Mary	226	Daniel	193
SCRWIND, Ann Mary	21	Henry	193
Peter	21	Henry B.	193
SEAGER, Abraham	191	Margaretha	193
Catharine	191	Paul	193
Christian	191	SHAFER, George, Sen.	156
Conrad	191	SHAMBOUGH, Daniel	73
Gabriel	191	SHANK, Corlena	193
Mary	191	Elizabeth	223
Samuel	191	John	193
SECRIST, Mary	136	Martin	193
Michael	136	SHARP, George	185
SEDWICK, Benjamin	243	SHARRER, John	47
SEEVY, Eva	106	SHAVER, Catharine	101
John	106	Cornelius	101
SEGER, Adam	174	Daniel	193
SEHUE, Ann	154	Elijah	49
SEIBER, Andrew	66	Elizabeth	109
SEIPLE, Catharine	191	Eve	194
Conrad	191	George	16,27,107,
Elizabeth	191		116,194
Frederick	191	George, Sen.	194
Hannah	191	Henry	194
SEIVER, Bernhard	192	Jacob	194,206
Isaac	192	John	11
Jacob	71,74,192	Jonas	194
James	108	Margaret	11
Jarida	192	Mary	16
John	192	Otilla	194
Lawrence	192	Philip	121,194
Moses	192	Polly	121
Palser	175	Solomon	194
William	75,108,192	SHEARER, Daniel	1
SEIVERT, Adam	114	SHEARMAN, Adam	195
Elizabeth	114	Adam, Jr.	100
SELLER, John	127	Adam, Sen.	195
SENSONEY, P.	4	Bevey	195
SENSONY, Mary A.	75	Catharina	195

SHEARMAN, Jacob	24,195	SHENK, Ann	96
John	195	Caroline	197
Margaret	24	George	197
Polly	195	Isaac	96
Sally	195	Jacob	190
Susannah	195	John	96,175,197
SHEETS, George	13	Martin	197
Jacob	13	SHERFEY, Abraham	197
SHEETZ, Anne	241	Anna	197
Betsy	196	Barbara	197
Catharine	173,196	Casper	197
Christiana	195	Ester	82
Daniel	195,196	John	197
Eve	196,241,242	Joshua	197
George	196	Magdalena	197
Henry	195,196	Solome	197
Henry, Sen.	195	SHERFIG, Abraham	83
Jacob	70,196,241,242	Benjamin	89
John	195,196,241	SHERMAN, Adam, Jr.	205
Joseph	196	SHIPE, Daniel	132
Leah	196	John	121,132
Margaret	196	Sarah	121
Mathias	196	SHIPLEY, James	184
Peter	196	SHIREMAN, Adam, Jr.	120
Philip	196	Barney	70
Polly	196	Benjamin	198
Sophia	196	Bernhard	198
SHEFFER, Abraham	196	Catharine	70,198
Catharine	196,197	Elizabeth	75,130
Elizabeth	196	Mary	120
Henry	196	Peter	198
James	196	SHIRLEY, Zachariah	116
Joseph	196	SHIRMAN, Adam	162
Magdalena	196	SHOE, Augustine	151
Michael	197	Jesse	78
Solomon	196	SHOEMAKER, Anna	108
SHELL, Samuel	42,220	Eve	88
SHELTON, Catharine	197	George	38
Isaac	197	Henry	108
John	13,197	Jacob	108
John, Sen.	197	John	61,88
Joseph	197	Margarete	108
Moses	164	Michael	108,229
Samuel	197	SHOMO, Anthony	198
William	197	Daniel	152,198

SHOMO, Elizabeth	198
John	99,125,198
Joseph	198
Polly	198
William	19,152,198
SHOWMAN, Barbara	198
Catharine	198
Elizabeth	198
George	198
Jacob	198
Magdalene	198
Stephen	94,198
SHROFFE, Barbara	147
George	147
SHRUM, Frederick	39
George	6,11,21,32,33, 38,39,42,70,81, 87,98,130,141, 173,183,188,191, 195,196,198, 223,226
SHRYOCK, Amelia	199
Ann Julia	199
Frederick	199
Henry S.	199
Jacob	199
Louisia Ann	199
SHULER, Michael	165
SHULL, John	56
Jonathan	213
Margaret	203
Maria	56
SHUTTERS, Rachael	169
Solomon	169
SIBERT, Adam	199
Barbara	230
Bernhard	199
Betsy	22
Catharine	132
Elizabeth	199
Francis	125
George	31
Henry	35,132
Isaac	199
J. R.	235
SIBERT, Jacob	199
John	141,228
John B.	199
Joseph R.	167
Lorenzo	142
Mary	22,199
Moses	199
Peter	199
SIGDNOR, Richard M.	23
SIGLER, Mary	199
Mary E.	154
Michael	63,199
William	171,199,207
SIGN, Adam	200
Ann Mary	124
Anne	200
Catharine	200
Catharine, Jr.	200
Elizabeth	200
Henry	200
John	200
John Wm.	124,200
Mary	200
Peter	200
SIMMS, Isabella	200
Dr. John	200
SIMPSON, Mary C.	237
SIMUND, Henry	79
SINE, Adam	109
George	21
Mary	21,183
Peter	106,122
Susanna	122
SINK, Cutlip	107
Philip	181
SITTLER, Isaac	123
SIVELY, Barbary	200
Betty	200
Elizabeth	200
George	200
Jacob	200
John	200
Joseph	200
Magdalene	200
Margaret	200

SIVELY, Mary	200
Peter	200
SIVER, Henry	33
SIX, Barbara	5
Barbary	6
Catharine	72
Eliza Ann	6
Elizabeth	6,72
Isaac	5,72
John	72
Mary	6
Peter	6
Philip	5
Sally	6
Sarah	6
SKEEN, Phebe	152
Reuben	152
SLAUGHTER, Francis	200
Jemima	200
Philip	200
Will	205
SLUSHERE, Anahel	206
SMELLING, Thomas	51
SMITH, A.	201
Adam	201
Alexander	203
Ann	202
Arthur	203
Barbara	132,133,202
Benjamin	177,201
Betsy	201
Beverley	235
Catharine	77,201
Charles	20,129,241
Christian	230
Clarissa	203
Conrad	15
Daniel	22
David	203
Dudley	203
Elhanan	203
Elizabeth	51,201, 202,203
George	53
Hannah	201
SMITH, Henry	202
Isaac	1,201
Jacob	71,182,223
James W.	235
Jane	203
John (Jno.)	1,4,8,36, 60,71,111,133, 164,190,201, 203
John C.	176
John L.	203,207
John W.	202
Joseph	47,90,202,203
Judith	114
Magdelena	102,132,133
Margaretha	202
Marion	203
Mary	1,203
Mary Barbara	202
Mathew H.	203
Michael	201
Narcissa	203
Nathan	88
Peter	102
Phebe	201
Philip	201
Polly	201
Rachel	202
Rebecca	202
Robert	202
Rowley	203
Samuel	49,111,133, 201,203
Sarah	202
Sidney	203
Solomon	111,132
Sophia	203
Susanna	201,202
Thomas	177,227
William	201,203,226
William L.	203
Willmoth	89
SMOOT, D.	165
SMOOTZ, Abraham	64,81,141, 191,238

SMOOTZ, Abraham, Jr.	204
Barbara	63,204
George	204
John	204
Mathias	63,191
Mathias, Sen.	191
Philip	204
Regina	191
SMUCHER, J. Peter	29
Eliza	204
Ferdinand	204
Jacob	204
John	204
Joseph	204
Mary Ann	204
Norma	204
Rosina	204
SMUTZ, Abraham	204
Abraham, Sen.	204
Abram	188
Barbara	188
Catharine	204
David	204
John	247
Joseph	204
Magdaline	204
Margaret	204
Mary	204
Mathis	124,188
Mathias, Sen.	131
Samuel	204
Sarah	204
Valentine	204
SNAP, John	111
SNAPP, Abraham	204,205,206
Adam	25
Catharine	102,206
Elizabeth	120,204,205
George	19
Jacob	106,204,205,206,211
John	70,205,206,239
Joseph	120,205,206
Lawrence	172,205,206
Margaret	205,206
SNAPP, Mary	239
Musilla	211
Peter	205,206,219
Philip	1,102,192,205,206
Sally	206
Susanna	205,206
SNARR, Henry	49
John	233
SNEIDER, Mary	110
SNELL, Henry	206
Jacob	206
Katharine	206
SNIDER, Ann Mary	207
Christina	207
Elizabeth	206
George	206
Jacob	207
John	57,207
Magdelean	207
Martin	207
Peter	15
SNYDER, Ann E.	207
Ann Maria	208
Anna	208
Barbara	207
Daniel	208
Daniel, Jr.	207
Daniel, Sen.	207
Elizabeth	207
George M.	207
John	22,178,208
John B.	207,231
John M.	208
Josh	90
Martin	207,208
Peter	170,208
SNYDOR, William	72
SOLOMON, Aaron	160
SOMANSTINE, Catharine	12
SOMER, Bolser	17
Philip	175,192
SOMMER, Andrew	209
Ann	210
Catharine	209,210

SOMMER, Eliza	210
Frany	209
George	209
Harrison	210
Henry	209
Isaac	210
Jacob	46,209,210
Johannes	209
John	209,210
Joseph	210
Mary	210
Mary Ann	209
Mary Margaretha	209
Michael	209
Paul	209
Philip	210
Samuel	209
Sarah Jane	209
William	209
SOMMERS, Anny	210
George	210
Jacob	210
Mathias	210
Michael	210
Rachel	210
Samuel	210
SOMMERTON, Catharine	20
Joseph	20
SONAFRANK, Abraham	88
SONENFRANK, Abraham	210
Maria	210
SONNAR, Philip	147
SONNENSTINE, Catharine	211
Dr. Joseph F.	211
SONNER, Harriet	211
George	211
Jacob	100,211
James	211
John	211
Joseph	211
Philip	52
Regina	211
Richard	211
Susanna	211
William	211
SOURWINE, Christian	82
Mary	82
SOWER, Frederick	194,222
SOXMAN, Adam	211,232,240
Christian	211
Daniel	211
Elizabeth	211,240
Frederick	211
SOXSMAN, Adam	212
Christian	212
Daniel	212
SPANGLER, Anthony	151
Catharine	151
Elizabeth	151
Joseph S.	139,151
Margaret	151
Philip	151
Regina	151
Solomon	134
SPEAGLE, Christina	205
Elizabeth	211
John	211
Michael	205
SPEIGAL, Christina	205
Michael	205
SPENCER, Edward	212
Eliza Jane	212
Elizabeth	212
Isaac	212
John Henry	212
Joseph	135
William	212
SPENGLAR, Elizabeth	172
SPENGLER, Anthony	35,45, 46,57,217,219
Barbara	212
Catharine	217,219
Cyrus	119
Daniel	217
Elizabeth	219
John	46
Joseph	35,46,57,87, 210,217
Joseph S.	202,203
Philip	10,135,177, 212,215,219

SPENGLER, Philip, Jr.	35	STEGLE, Jacob	191
Regina	219	STEIGEL, J.	126
SPERRY, Joseph	112	STEIGLER, Mary	214
SPIEGEL, Lawrence	240	STENSON, James	142
Magdalene	240	STEPHENSON, Hannah	214,215
SPEIGER, Anna	104	James	9,40,214, 215,239
SPIEGLE, Catharine	212	John	214,215
Elizabeth	212	Margaret	215
Eve	212	Nancy	214,215
John	212	Robert	214,215
Laurence	212	Samuel C.	43
Margaret	212	William	43,214,215
Mary	212	STERRETT, James	54,109
Michael	212	STERWALT, Rev. Jacob	235
Peter	212	STEWART, Anna	199
Sarah	109,212	Nathaniel	28
Susannah	212	STICKLER, Abraham	26,215
William	109,212	Ann	219
SPIGLE, Mary	44	Anny	215
Michael	44,148	Benjamin	215
William	44	Catharine	215
SPITLER, Abraham	97	David	215
Abraham, Jr.	100,116,212	Elizabeth	215
Abraham, Sen.	213	Franey	215
Abram	213	Isaac	220
Anna	213	Jacob	52
Catharine	213	Joshua	88
Daniel	213	Mary	215
David	213	Regina	215
Isaac	100,213	Sabastian	215
John	201,213	Samuel	215,220
John, Sen.	213	Susanna	215
Joseph	213	STICKLEY, Ann	219
Margaret	213	D.	46,71,202
Mathias	201,213	Daniel	71,144,209
Susanna	29	David	35,100,173,218
SPITTLER, Abraham	52	Elizabeth	122,229
Abraham, Jr.	52	Gabriel	121
SPITZER, Charles	19, 167,235	Jacob	228
Henry	152,198	John	122,239
STANBACK, George	197	Peter	73
STEEL, Catharine	184	Rebeah	121
STEENBERGER, Elizabeth	213	Samuel	68,69
John B.	213	Tobias	168
Peter H.	213	STICKLY, Catharine	172
William	1,2,152,170,213	Philip	46
William, Jr.	213		

STIEGEL, I.	191
J.	154
Jacob	9,12,89,158, 215,223,247
STIEGLE, Jacob	26,27, 128,242
STIGELER, John	17
Sebation	17
STICLER, David	14
George	14
STINSON, James, Sen.	216
James, Jr.	185,216
John	216
Mary	216
STOCKSDALE, Polly	216
Solomon	216
STOCKSLAGER, Abraham	216
Anna	216
Catharine	216
Daniel	177,216
Esther	216
Jacob	177,216
Margaret	216
Philip	216
Sarah	216
William	216
STOLL, Polly	38
STOMBACK, George	193
Martin	201
STONEBARGER, Frederick	165,216
Luis	216
STONEBURNER, Barbara	198
Christina	98
John	198,227
STONER, Abraham	26,184,217
Catharine	217
Daniel	135
Elizabeth	217
John	217
John Frederick	217
Margaret	217
Mary Ann	217
Sarah	135
Solina	217
William	72,75,217
STOUT, Catharine	229
Daniel	17,229
Margaret	217
STOVER, Abraham	74,75, 155,156
Alexander	85
Barbara	191,218,220
Barbary	28
Betsy	218
Catharine	64,170,218
Christian	191,217,219
Christian, Jr.	218
Christley	43
Daniel	85,215,220
David	80,156,220
Elizabeth	210,217, 218,219
Ester	80
Fanny	218
Frainey	218,219
Frederick	170
Isaac	240
Jacob	47,187,218,219
John	80,104,145,210, 215,218,219,220
Joseph	43,218,219, 220,246
Lydia	218
Magdalene	80
Margaret	245,246
Marilla	218
Mary	85,218
Mathias	64
Michael	191
Nimrode	218
Peter	217,219
Philip	22,186,207, 208,218
Rebecca	170
Regina	219
Samuel	26,220,221
Sarah	24
Susan	218
Susan Ann	186
STRAUSNIDER, Adam	220
Benjamin	220

STRAUSNIDER, Elijah	220	STRICKLER, Mary	221,222
George	220	Nancy	222
Isaac	220	Rebecca	45
Jacob	220	Samuel	26,110,159,
John	220		184,222
Joseph	220	Susannah	221,222
Michael	220	STRICKLEY, Barbara	18
Peter	220	Cathene	222
Rachael	220	Daniel	226
Sarhe Lou	220	Dorothy	222
Solomon	220	Elizabeth	222
STRICKEL, Jacob	109	Gabrel	222
STRICKLER, A.	178	Isaac	222
Abraham	39,101,118,	Jacob	222
	159,184,197,	Judath	222
	220,221,222,244	Leah	222
Abram	76	STROHT, Jacob	137
Ann	221	STROMER, Herman	222
Barbara	29,220,221,222	Mary	222
Barbary	221	STROTHER, Amelia	223
Benjamin	47,187	Joseph	223
Betsy	141	STROTHERMAN, Stephen	11,
Catharine	35,221		190
Caty	220	STROUT, John	121
D.	248	STUART, John	207
Daniel	45,93,141,	STULTZ, Jacob	198
	220,221,222	SUGART, Frederick H.	223
David	30,35,139	Michael	223
Dorothe	221	Zachariah	223
Eliza	76	SUMMER, Barbara	156
Elizabeth	221	Philip	124,172,194
Emanuel	222	SUMMERS, Barbara	190,223
Eve (Eva)	221,222	Catharine	223
Henry	76,139,222	John	225
Isaac	26,144,221	Joseph	223
Isaac, Jr.	221	Joshua	12,223
Jacob	100,221,222	Mary Barbara	223
John	17,76,136,	Mathias	223
	202,221,222	Michael	223
Joseph	35,143,162,	Paul	225
	220,221,222,244	Philip	206,222,223
Katharine	221	SUPINGER, Barbare	36
Magdalene	221,222	Catharine	224
Margaret	221	Caty	71
Maria	221	Christina	36,224

SUPINGER, Conrad	224
Mrs. E.	18
Elizabeth	36,224
Esther	224
Isaac	224
Jacob	36,46,224
John	19,122,224
John, Sen.	224
Joseph	190,224
Lydia	224
Mary	71,224
Michael	36
Peggy	224
Peter	36
Robert	224
Sarah	190,224
Ulrick	146
SUPTON, Bathisheba	1
SURBER, Catharine	88
Henry	118,198,224
Jacob	88,148,157,224
Mary Catharine	118
Rosina	224
SWAN, Catharine	176
SWANN, James N.	227
SWARTZ see BLACK	
SWARTZ, Barbara	225
Christian	225
Christina	225
Dorothy	90
Elizabeth	112,225,234
George	18,90,176,225
Jacob	225
John	20,69,225
John, Sen.	225
Joseph	20,139
Lydia	69
Martin	225
Mary Eve	225
Peter	112
Peter, Jr.	234
Peter, Sen.	225
Philip	27,191,214,225
Regel	225
Samuel	69
Sarah	139
Susannah	225
SWAYNE, John	18,42
SWAYNIE, Elizabeth	169
John	169
SWEETZER, Henry	9
SWILER, Jacob	166
SWINDLER, John	96
SWITZER, Anna	72
Joseph	72,214
SWYGERA, Christina	221
TALBERT, Mary	24
TARKLESON, George	128
TATE, Andrew	176
David	176
TAYLOR, Ann	226
Barbary	226
Bradford	7
Charles	56,226
Elizabeth	226
Henry	226
Isabella	214
Jacob	144
John	39,226
Joseph	191,226
Mary	226
Rebecca	226
Susannah	226
Valentine D.	223
William	226
TAZWELL, Littleton	108
TEATER, Catharine	226
TEMPLETON, Jany	3
John	3
TERRCE, Polly	130
TETT, Catharine	190
THOMAS, Elizabeth	214
Isaac	152
John	116,152
Rachel	160
Rebecca	154
THOMPSON, Elizabeth	58,226
John	127,212,226
Mary Jane	92
Robert	226
Wesley	92
William	128,226
THORNBERRY, John	65,178,212

THORNBURGH, Margaret	150
THORNTON, John	136
Philip	200
TIBBS, Algernon	97
Duskin	30
TIDLER, Samuel	161
TILLER, Samuel	167
TIPTON, John	20
TISINGER, Catharine	54
Elizabeth	227
George	227
Henry	54,227
John	227,229
Magdalene	227
Peter	227,229,241
Samuel	23
William	98
TOMLINSON, Edward	11
TOMPKINS, George	77
TOWNSEND, Joseph	183
Robert	183
Ruth	183
TRIPLETT, John	113
L.	99,208
William H.	180
TROOK, Nicholas	227
Susannah Margaret	227
TROOKE, Philip	167
Rebecca	167
TROUT, Elizabeth	7,128
Henry	7,128
Isaac	7,77,97,128,129
John	224
Lewis	168
Mary	7,128
Philip	7,128
Rebecca	7,128
TRUCK, Nicholas	54,109
TRUMBA, Susannah	97
TRYMAN, Sarah	237
TULLIS, Jonah	18
TURNER, Robert	45,67,154, 155,186,189, 223,241,246
TUSING, Adam	227
Henry	227
Nicholas	227
Philip	227
Susanna	227
TUSINGER, Michael	59
Peter	107
Susanna	59
TUSSING, Daniel	73
TUTT, Henry	17,134
TUTWEILER, Leonard	56
TYLER, David	144
William	131,164
TYREE, William	174
TYSINGER, Catharine	227
ULLANDER, Jacob	155
URNER, Martin	235
UROE, William	4
UTINGER, John	156
UTZ, Elizabeth	217
John	217
VANCE, James	40
John	40
Joseph C.	30
Mary	40
Sam	123
Samuel	205
William	40
VANNORT, Elizabeth	227
John	227
Peter	227
William	227
VARNA, John	190
VARNER, Barbara	97
David	97
John	139
VEACH, Anna	228
Catharine	228
Christina	228
Elizabeth	228
Harriet	228
Harrison	228
Isaac	228
Jaocb	228

VEACH, Jesse	157
Joseph	146
Leah	228
Levi	228
Polly	228
Solomon	228
Washington	228
William	228
VINCENT, Catharine	209
VOGELSONG, George	225
Mary	225
VOLKNER, Adam	228
Anne	228
Henry	228
John	228
Magdalene	228
VOLTZ see FOLTZ, FULTZ	
VOLTZ, Dorothy	228
George	229
John	228
Jonathan	228
Joseph	229
Joshua	228,229
Joshua, Sen.	213
Martin	213,228
Peter	229
VORSTER, J.	176
WADINGTON, William	205
WAGGONER, Betty	229
Elizabeth	229
Ulrick	229
WAGGONNER, Christenah	62
Jacob	62
WAKEMAN, Henry	22,102
John	22,102
WALKER see WOCKER	
WALKER, Geo. Adam	241
John	197
Margareth	241
WALL, Abigail	229
Edmond	229
George	229
John	4
Lucy	229
Polly	229

WALTER, Samuel	217
WALTERS, Daniel	99
WALTHER, Henry	157
WALTON, Barbara	230
Catharine	30,230
Charles	230
Christina	230
Daniel	230
Deborah	1
Edward	30,190,230,232
Elizabeth	230
Henry	230
Jesse	230
John	3
Joseph	60,75
Martin	230
Magdalene	230
Mary	82
Moses	3,25,50,59,73, 119,125,152,161, 183,201,222,230
Reuben	25,50,119, 125,183,230
S.	227
Samuel	3,107,201, 230,232
Sarah	230
WAMBLER, Catharine	135
Jonas	135
WANDER, Elizabeth	153
WARD, Sehanah	154
WAREN, Michael	99
WASFIELD, Rachael	38
WATKINS, Archable	113
Enoch	113
William	83
WATSELL, Henry	241
Nicholas	241
WATSON, Joseph	69,72
Josiah	69
WATTEN, Cabin Lev	91
WATTSON, Joseph	16,18,24, 57,71,73,95, 122,140,160,173, 190,203,209,214

WAY, Samuel	230
Sarah	230
WEAKS, Richard	161
Susanna	161
WEATHERHOLTS, Catharine	230
Christina	230
Dianah	230
Henry	230
Isaac	230
Jacob	230
John	230
Polly	230
WEAVER, Adam	231
Anne	232
Catharine	231
Christian	157,231
Conrad	232
David	18,74
Doradey	157
Dougherty	157
Elizabeth	74,157,231
Frederick	231,232
George	11,82,83,157, 167,197,215, 231,232
George, Sen.	17
Jacob	231
John	157,231,232
Magdalene	231
Martin	231
Mary	157,231
Michael	2
Peter	203
Philip	232
Philipena	232
Polly	231
Rachael	18
WEBB, Catharine	232
Daniel	181,232
David	232
Elizabeth	232
Harmon, Sen.	232
Isaac	232
John	232
Noah	232
Reuben	232
Samuel	232
William (Will)	48,107, 163,234
WEBSTER, Elizabeth	150
Hezekiah	222
John S.	150
Lucinda	222
WEEKLEY, Catharine	232
Elijah	232
Elizabeth	232
Enoch	137,232
Isaiah	232
Jacob	232
John	232
Joseph	232
Nancy	232
Rubin	232
Sally	232
Susannah	232
Thomas	232
William	232
Winifred	232
WEEKS, Elizabeth	233
Grafton	188
James	233
John	233
Margaret Ann	233
Mary	233
Samuel	112,233
Theodore	233
William Henry	233
WEGMAN, Barbary	233
Catharine	233
Conrad, Sen.	233
Conrad, Jr.	233
Henry	233
John	233
WELCH, Elizabeth	223
WELLS, Samuel	79
WELSH, Clara	138,233
Thomas	138,202
WENCH, Andrew	167
WENDEL, Barbara	225

WENDEL, Benjamin	10
Catharine	10
Christopher	234
Emanuel	225
George	234
John	234
John, Sen.	234
Philip	209,225
Rebecca	238
Regel	225
WENDELL, John	245
WENDLE, Augustine	120
Daniel	22
WERDENBERGER, Eliz.	63
WERICK, Andrew	169
WERNER, Baltaser	234
WERTERBERGER, Adam	63
WEST, Sally	150
WESTENBERGER, George	78
WETHERTON, John	142
WETSEL, Christina	33
WETZEL, Charles	118
Christina	118
David	110
George	130,171,234
James	110
John	118
Leah	110
Rebecca	234
WETZELL, Jackson	23
WETZLE, John	106
WEVER, S.	176
WHISLER, William	158
WHITE, Ann	234
Benjamin	234
Britain	234
Elizabeth	234
George	88
James	229,234
John	64,234
Mary	234
Nancy	234
Rebecca	64
Sarah Jane	212
Thomas	54
Westly	115
William	234
WHITEHEAD, Peggy	88
WHITING, John	135
WHITMOYER, Anna	235
Barbary	234
Catharina	235
Christian	234
Christina	57
David	235
Elizabeth	235
Emanuel	235
Frederick	235
Hanna	235
Jacob	234,235
John	234,235
Joseph	234
Lyddy	234
Polly	235
Samuel	234
Valentine	235
WHITMYER, Jacob	159
WHITSON, Catharine	58
James	131
John	88
Joseph	131
Margaret	131
Rachael	58,88
Ruth	58,88,143
WHITTINGHAM, Lorenzo	235
Margaret	235
WHYSON, Joseph	69
WICKS, Addson	235
Amelia	235
Grafton	235
William	235
William, Sen.	235
WILEY, Martin	189
WILHOIT, Adam	236
Elizabeth	236
Michael	236
WILKIN, Anna	68
Barbara	68
Catharine	130
George	68
Godfrey	130,236,241
Henry	68,112,204
Jacob	191
Katharine	236

WILKIN, Madalene	204
Mathias	68,120
Philip	121,236
WILKINS, Hannah	225
Henrietta M.	235
Henry	83,225
WILL, Catharine	29
Ephraim	208
George	29,134,196,236
John	236
Michael	236
Philip A.	236
Susanna	236
William	29
WILLARD, Anthony	226
WILLIAMS, Benjamin	95
Benjamin, Sen.	75,220
Catharine	38,230,236
Catharine M.	161
Elisha	237
Eve	85
Gustavas A.	237
J.	90
James	189
James C.	51,147,236,237
Jared	237
John	46,130,166
Martha	237
Nancy	133
P.	45,51,54,58,59, 67,78,80,97,103, 109,121,147,177, 189,218,228,236, 241,245,246
P.,Jr.	43,78,147, 165,181,246
P., Sen.	97
Philip	32,85,192, 200,219,237
Philip, Jr.	97,142,182, 236,237
Philip, Sen.	142
Samuel	44,45,64,70,126
Samuel C.	186,237
Sarah Eliz.	236,237
Thomas	203
William C.	4,138,245
WILLIAMSON, Demone	203
Jacob	125
Philip D.	4
Rebecca	4
WILLIS, Nancy	42
WILLS, Lewis	158
WILLSON, Anne	160
John	215
WILLY, Bernard	237
Christina	237
Elizabeth	237
Henry	237
Magdalene	237
Margaret	237
Mary	237
WILSON, Ann	186
Barbara	173
Brigit	30
Dennis	92
Elizabeth	173
Jane	150
John	30
Mary	173
WILT, Peggy	75
WILTFANY, John	229
Mary	229
WIMER, Mary	40
WINDEL, Barbara	238
Catharine	234
Christian	238
Daniel	234,238
David	238
Elizabeth	238
Emanuel	238
George	234
John	234,238
Philip	238
Philip, Sen.	238
Valentine	234
WINDER, Henry	196
WINDERS, Clem	17
Molly	17
WINDLE, Augustine	238,239
Barbara	239
Catharine	239
Christopher, Jr.	239
Christopher, Sen.	239

WINDLE, Daniel	239
David	65
Elizabeth	42,239
Eliz. Barbara	239
Jacob	122,147,214, 238,239
John	58,238,239
John P.	239
Lucy	58
Mary	99,239
Peter	238,239
Philip	46,65,120,239
Samuel	2,3,64
Valentine	239
WINE, Barbara	240
Catharine	240
Christian	240
Daniel	240
Elizabeth	240
George	240
Jacob	240
John	76,135,152,240
Magedlien	240
Michael	76,83,149, 150,240,247
Michael, Jr.	156
Michael, Sen.	156
Susannah	240
Susanne	240
WINEGARDNER, Adam	47
Herbert	74
Susannah	47
WINFIELD, Richard	161,188
WINTERHOLDER, Jacob	146
Rachel	146
WINTORF, David	54
Frederick	54
WISCARVER, John	36
WISE, Adam	172
Barbara	172
Catharine	172
John	172
Michael	190,208
Samuel	190

WISEMAN, Abraham	18
Ann	208
Elizabeth	192
John	208
Mary	18
Sarah	18
William	18
WISMAN, Adam	241
Barbara	241
Catharine	146,241
Christina	97,123,240
Dociam	123
Elizabeth	240
George	123,141,202, 225,240,241
George, Jr.	42,123
Isaac	16
Jacob	240
John	97,240,241
Joseph	139,240,241
Juliana	234
Lydia	123
Magdalene	241
Nicholas	78,202,241
Paul	234
Philip	146,240,241
Rosina	234
Sarah	16
Samuel	146
Thomas	241
WOCKER see WALKER	
WOCKER, Elizabeth	11,241, 242
George Adam	241,242
Henry	11,241,242
John	241,242
Margaret	242
Peter	241
Philip	241
Susanna	241
WOHLGEMOTH, Christian	109
WOHLGEMUTH, Christian	225
WOLANDE, Jacob	162
WOLF, Adam	97

WOLF, Augustine	242
Catharine	97,242
Jacob	242
John Jacob	242
WOLFE, Henry	133
Lawrence	48
WOLFENBERGER, Peter	31
WOLFINBURG, Peter	79
WOLGEMUTH, Catharine	242
Christian	242
Elizabeth	242
Jacob	242
Mary	242
Rosina	242
WOLTZ, Jacob	223
WOOD, Abigail	243
Abin	243
Asa	243
Benjamin	96,243
Benjamin F.	243
Benjamin H.	243
David	243
Dinah	243
Edward W.	243
Elizabeth	243
Elizabeth P.	243
Emily Eliz.	243
Harrison	243
Jesse	96,243
John	127,151,243
Joshua	243
Magdalene	127
Margaret	243
Mary M.	243
Moses	243
Nancy	243
Nehemiah	243
Polly	243
Rachael	151,243
Sally	243
Sarah	243
Sarahan	243
Thompson	243
William	243
William F.	243
WOODFORD, Frederick -	130,163
WOODMAN, Philadelphia -	244
WOODS, Catharine	79
Charles	79
WOODWARD, William	24
WOOLEN, John	162
WOOLF, David	216
Geo. Jacob	242
WOOLMAN, David	244
Elizabeth	244
Mary	176
Susannah	244
WOOLMORE, Godfreth	176
WRAWLINGS, John	244
Sarah	244
WRIGHT, Isaac	41,187
Mary	244
William, Sen.	244
WROE, William	58
WUNDER, Charles	153
Henry	115
WYATT, John	163,172
Sarah	203
WYNAT, Catharina	170
John	170
YAGER, Elizabeth	7,54,128
Enoch G.	7,85
Jacob	82
Mary	128
Rebecca	7,128
Sarah	7,128
Simeon	7,28,54,68,85,102,123,128,129,131,139,172,210,216,231,237,240
YANKEY, Michael	152
YEAGER, Barbara	245
Elizabeth	209
Jacob	245
Joseph	148,245
Simeon	189

YOST, David 95,105,177,217
  Jacob 79,138
YOUNG, Daniel 245
  Dorcas (Darcus) 92,151
  Edisin 28
  Edwin 56,89,110,187,245
  Edwin 3rd 245
  Frankey 245
  George 17
  John 243,245
  Joseph 89,99
  Luthia 245
  Nancy 243,245
  Sally 243
  Sinett 245
  William 245
YOUST, Samuel 159
YOWELL, Rowland 208
ZANE, Isaac 100
ZEA, Anna (Ann) 177,245,246
  Joseph 57,87,139,
    211,245,246
  Martin 35,177,218,246
  Philip 245,246
ZEHRING, John 102,103,246
  Joseph 246
  Magdalene 103
  Mathias 85,123,233,246
  Rebeckah 246
  Samuel 150,230,246
ZELL, Anna 247
  Frany 247
  Jacob 247
  John 247
  Nicholas 247
ZENTMEYER, Barbara 238
  John 238
ZERFAS, John 171
  Molly 171
ZERKEL, Adam 21
  Catharine 21
ZEVEHER, Margaret 21
  Nathaniel 21
ZIEGLER, George 84
ZIGLER, William 199
ZIMMERMAN, George 181

ZIMMERMAN, Jacob 247
  Magdalina 247
  Peter 64,126,247
  Philip 247
ZINK, Lawrence 14
ZIRCKEL, Andrew 248
  Andrew, Jun. 248
  Catharine 248
  Elizabeth 248
  George 248
  John 248
  Jonathan 248
  Lewis 248
  Lydia 248
  Michael 248
ZIRCKLE, Geo. Adam 144
  Jacob 95
ZIRKEL, Hannah 94
  Lewis 94
ZIRKLE, Abraham 248
  Adam 240,248
  Amanda 249
  Andrew 248
  Benjamin 249
  Catharine 249
  Christina 249
  Cornelius 249
  Eave 248
  Elizabeth 248,249
  Erasmus 249
  Eve 249
  George 191,249
  Geo. Adam 249
  Jacob 249
  John 125,184,248,249
  John D. 188
  John G. 166,249
  Lewis 169
  Mary 249
  Michael 197,248
  Paul 249
  Philip 166,248,249
  Rosannah 249
  Samuel 248
  Susannah 249

Other Heritage Books by Amelia C. Gilreath:

Frederick County, Virginia Deed Book Series
Volume 1, Deed Books 1, 2, 3, 4: 1743-1758
Volume 2, Deed Books 5, 6, 7, 8: 1757-1763
Volume 3, Deed Books 9, 10, 11: 1763-1767
Volume 4, Deed Books 12, 13, 14: 1767-1771
Volume 5, Deed Books 15 and 16: 1771-1775
Volume 6, Deed Books 17 and 18: 1775-1780
plus Early Troop Records: 1755-1761
Volume 7, Deed Books 19 and 20: 1780-1785
Volume 8, Deed Book 21: 1785-1789
Volume 9, Deed Books 22 and 23: 1789-1793
Volume 10, Deed Books 24A and 24B: 1793-1796
Volume 11, Deed Books 25 and 26: 1796-1800

Page County, Virginia Will Books A, B, C and Deed Book A, 1831-1848

Shenandoah County, Virginia Abstracts of Wills, 1772-1850

Shenandoah County, Virginia Deed Book Series
Volume 1, Deed Books A, B, C, D: 1772-1784
Volume 2, Deed Books E, F, G, H: 1784-1792
Volume 3, Deed Books I, K, L: 1792-1799
Volume 4, Combination Minute Book: 1774-1780
and Deed Books M and N: 1784-1792
Volume 5, Deed Books O, P, Q: 1804-1809
Volume 6, Deed Books R, S, T: 1809-1813
Volume 7, Deed Books U and V: 1813-1815
Volume 8, Deed Books W and X: 1815-1817
Volume 9, Deed Books Y and Z: 1817-1820

www.ingramcontent.com/pod-product-compliance
Lightning Source LLC
Chambersburg PA
CBHW071315150426
43191CB00007B/626